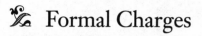 # Formal Charges

Formal Charges

 The Shaping of Poetry
in British Romanticism

Susan J. Wolfson

Stanford University Press, Stanford, California 1997

Stanford University Press
Stanford, California
© 1997 by the Board of Trustees of the
Leland Stanford Junior University
Printed in the United States of America

CIP data are at the end of the book

Stanford University Press publications are
distributed exclusively by Stanford University Press
within the United States, Canada, Mexico, and
Central America; they are distributed exclusively
by Cambridge University Press throughout
the rest of the world.

To Ron, for all forms of love

Acknowledgments

A book this long in formation accumulates many debts and depths of thanks. Friends who have been extraordinarily generous with their attention know the extent of my gratitude and the inadequacy of this statement. I have been especially fortunate in the friendship of Peter Manning, Garrett Stewart, William Keach, and Bill Galperin. Each read (sometimes, more than once) large portions (in some cases, all) of this study with rigorous care; their sympathetic intelligence with and critical scrutiny of my discussions have been valuable, vital, and sustaining. William Keach warmly encouraged my care for poetic form and my effort to engage current trends in criticism. Bill Galperin was an acute reader of the formal shape of the book as well as its theoretical commitments. Garrett Stewart offered enthusiasm and a high degree of articulation about local readings as well as critical polemic. The years have deepened my respect for Peter Manning—first my teacher, then my friend, professional colleague, and always an inspiring intellectual model; this book will never reflect the full measure of his sharp critical care for its development, from my initial murmurings to the final draft.

At different phases of my work, I was grateful for encouragement from Tom Edwards, George Levine, Barry Qualls, Bill Dowling, Derek Attridge, Jack Stillinger, David Perkins, Don Bialostosky, Marshall Brown, Mike Macovski, Jerry Christensen, Alan Richardson, and John Paul Riquelme; and for collegiality that accommodated friendly critical opposition, Jerry McGann and Marjorie Levinson. Donald Reiman generously answered questions about Shelley's manuscripts. Adela Pinch gave the almost final draft the benefit of her sympathetic and helpful attention. Specific chapters and phases of argument reflect the generous conversation, careful reading, and alert advice of Terry Kelley, Stuart Sperry, Jim Chandler, Kurt Heinzelman, Christopher Ricks, Christine Gallant, Linda Dowling, John Beer, and my much-missed dear friend, Keith Thomas.

With love and deepest gratitude of all, I dedicate this book to Ron Levao. Even though my reliance on Ron's care and support are habitual, long standing, and well known, this familiarity does not render my latest acknowledgment "pro forma." Ron's generously sustained reading of my work in all its phases, his keen sense of argumentative structure, his unerring critical judgment, and his general encouragement did more than clarify and improve my work; whatever may be valuable or articulate in these pages bears the gift of his sharp intelligence, his sympathetic and scrupulous review, and his loving attention.

In addition to friends and colleagues, I have been fortunate in gifts of time. I began to shape this book towards the end of a sabbatical funded by the American Council of Learned Societies and Rutgers University; a subsequent fellowship from the National Endowment for the Humanities, as well as sabbaticals from Rutgers and Princeton University, sustained its development and completion. It is a pleasure to thank these institutions, and, more particularly, colleagues who were instrumental in securing practical support: Barry Qualls and Richard McCormick at Rutgers; Elaine Showalter and Bob Gunning at Princeton. I also wish to thank Princeton for considerable assistance in meeting the cost for the several plates in this book.

In the course of developing this book, I had opportunities to test my interests in preliminary publications. My present chapters amplify, refine, revise, and in some instances substantially reconceive these initial essays, but these first forms were valuable occasions for me to present my concerns and hear their reception, and I thank my editors and their publications for timely encouragement. Chapter 4, whose original muse was Gene Ruoff's special session at the 1981 MLA Convention, develops an essay from *PMLA* 99 (1984); Chapter 6 draws on essays published in *Keats-Shelley Journal* 34 (1985) and *Review* 14 (1992); Chapter 3 revises and expands an essay written for *Coleridge's Theory of Imagination Today*, edited by Christine Gallant (AMS, 1989); Chapter 5 evolved from an essay in *Studies in Romanticism* 27 (1989); parts of Chapters 2 and 7 appear in somewhat different form in a polemic I wrote for *Aesthetics and Ideology*, edited by George Levine (Rutgers University Press, 1994); part of Chapter 1 was adapted for *Questioning Romanticism*, edited by John Beer (Johns Hopkins University Press, 1995); a version of Chapter 2 appears in *"Speak Silence": Critical Approaches to Blake's "Poetical Sketches,"* edited by Mark Greenberg (Wayne State University Press, 1996).

S.J.W.

✍ Contents

✥ Figures

✁ Abbreviations

The following abbreviations are used throughout the text and notes. Full bibliographical information can be found in the Works Cited.

BL	Coleridge, *Biographia Literaria*, ed. Engell and Bate
BLJ	Byron, *Letters and Journals*, ed. Marchand
BPP	Blake, *Complete Poetry and Prose*, ed. Erdman
KC	*The Keats Circle*, ed. Rollins
KL	Keats, *Letters*, ed. Rollins
LB	Wordsworth, *Lyrical Ballads*, ed. Butler and Green
Letters EY	Wordsworth, *Letters, Early Years*, ed. de Selincourt and Shaver
Letters LY	Wordsworth, *Letters, Later Years*, ed. de Selincourt and Hill
Letters MY	Wordsworth, *Letters, Middle Years*, ed. de Selincourt, Moorman, and Hill
PSL	P. B. Shelley, *Letters*, ed. Jones
SPP	Shelley, *Poetry and Prose*, ed. Reiman and Powers

Formal Charges

Chapter 1

✥ Formal Intelligence

Formalism, Romanticism, and Formalist Criticism

Reading Formalisms and Poetic Forms

Why care about poetic form and its intricacies, other than in nostalgia for a bygone era of criticism?

My purpose in *Formal Charges* is to refresh this interest for criticism today by focusing "an historically informed formalist criticism" on Romantic aesthetics[1]—in no small part because its canonical texts have been cited for a formalism that is naively idealistic, or worse, complicit with reactionary ideologies. I mean to give a different picture by showing how, in theory and practice, Romanticism addressed, debated, tested, and contested fundamental questions about what is at stake in poetic formings of language, and to suggest the importance of these conflicted inquiries to literary criticism today. Along the way, I want to make a case for the pleasures, intellectual and aesthetic, of attending to the complex charges of form in poetic writing.

My method is an intensive reading of poetic events within a context of questions about poetic form and formalist criticism. I offer this method as theory in action, with two related claims: that reading this way in itself constitutes a theoretical commitment, and that such care is needed to review and refine the management of (or inattention to) textual evidence in some currently prevailing polemics. In his Preface to *Lyrical Ballads*, Wordsworth suggests that "if Poetry be a subject on which much time has not been bestowed," any "judgment" of what it says and how it says it "may be erroneous, and . . . in many cases it necessarily will be so" (759). The "time" of which he speaks is not just "a long continued intercourse with the best models of composition" (ibid.); it is also the time one spends with any one poem. Reading is enlivened by this investment, and its attention to particularities refines judgment. Thus Derek Attridge introduces *Peculiar Language* by questioning the "a priori judgment that renders the reading of literature . . . as a single, homogeneous

activity," and against this "narrowness" he offers his own "interpretative en-
counters" with texts in order "to exemplify some of the complexities of the
activity of reading" (7). Similarly responding to some recent and problematically influential statements about Romantic poetics, Peter Manning offers his
tellingly titled *Reading Romantics: Texts and Contexts*. Manning welcomes New
Historicism but regrets a tendency in its arguments to suppress "the ambiguities of poetic language" and "the slipperiness of its terms" (306–7), which he
sees as one of the perils of "restricting the meanings of the poetic text to the
generalized ideological matrix to which it is declared to belong" (300). No way
of reading is uninflected or neutral in interest, of course, but critical judgment
suffers when complexities are suppressed or not even recognized. My particular concern is with the frequency with which social and political critiques
deem any interest in the local plays of poetic form irrelevant or ideologically
tainted as an old New Critical aesthetic fetish—a judgment often accompanied by limited, even reductive, accounts of how poetic texts perform.

Formal Charges addresses this concern with a contextualized formalist
criticism that remaps New Criticism (especially its claims of literary autonomy and its paradigms of unity and coherence) but frankly retains its commitment to close reading and its care for poetic form. Although attention to
poetic form has fallen from its prestige in the 1940s and 1950s and is often
derided as a myopic and insular criticism, I have been struck by how tenacious
the subject has proven, even for those who meant to move "beyond." Thus
Geoffrey Hartman famously advertised his goal in 1970; yet, five years on-
ward, he found himself "more rather than less impressed . . . by how hard it is
to advance 'beyond formalism' in the understanding of literature" (*Fate* vii)—
and, for many after him, in extra-literary analyses as well. This tenacity is
charged by divergences and contradictions in the very definition of "form"
and the applications of "formalism"—themselves significant legacies of Romanticism's own sophisticated debates about poetic form and its relation to
other cultural forms, even to social and political performance.[2] A renewed appreciation of such problems has been prepared by Garrett Stewart's "formalist
. . . return to textual theory" as a way of "registering the *forms* of cultural
dissemination in both the literary instance and its alternative discursive
modes" (*Reading Voices* 16, his italics) and by Manning's polemical effort, sensitive to American New Criticism's protocols as well as its general antipathy
to Romanticism, "to join formalism with wider concerns" in the study of
Romantic writing, reconnecting it to "the motives from which it springs and
the social relations within which it exists" (*Reading Romantics* 3).

These critics, and I count myself among them, contest such skeptical
analyses as Terry Eagleton's influential "Ideology and Literary Form," which
sees literary form as shaped and limited by the social forms of its historical

moment and typically in the business, consciously or not, of recasting "historical contradictions into ideologically resolvable form" (114).[3] In this analysis, literary form can register the pressure of historical conflicts and contradictions only when it ruptures or collapses. I will be reviewing this equation of literary process with the achievement or failure of "resolvable form" (and the disparaging echo of "organic form"), as well as the sense of Eagleton and others that perceptions of rupture are only in the critic's agency and not ascribable to poetic agency. For now, I want to propose that any criticism interested in the relation of literary form to ideology needs a more refined reading. This particularly matters with poetry, which advertises its definition by form in its stanzas, verses, rhymes, meters, and at the very least, in the radical shaping of the line.

This definition is why I have focused this book on poetic practices. I am concerned not only with poetic form per se and the various ways its differential from prose has been defined, defended, and doubted, but also with events of particular forms (those stanzas, verses, meters, rhymes, and the line), their traditions, and the issues at stake in their Romantic performances. Prose, too, involves form, but the modalities—macro-structures of plot or argument, medial structuring in paragraphs, local syntaxes and verbal patterns—do not confer the kind of discursive identity inscribed by poetic forms.[4] Poetry is precisely, and inescapably, defined by its formed language and its formal commitments. Its forms, as Attridge remarks, resist incorporation "into the kind of interpretation we habitually give to linguistic utterances"; they are not transparent, but invite "apprehension as a formal entity, quite apart from its semantic import" (*Rhythms* 311, 307). I will go further in this study, showing how in the most critical turns of Romantic and post-Romantic poetics, formal elements do not exist "apart" from but play a part in the semantic order, especially when issues of form—poetic and otherwise—are at stake. On such occasions, choices of form and the way it is managed often signify as much as, and as part of, words themselves.

The decisive emergence of American formalist criticism in our century, about 50 years ago, revived this central issue in Romantic aesthetics, namely that the writing and reading of poetry not only could not avoid, but compelled, a recognition of its forms. This concern proves a surprisingly common ground in the diversity of mid-twentieth-century critical theory. Against a then-dominant emphasis on content (manifest or repressed), polemicists such as R. S. Crane argued that nothing in a poem "is matter or content merely, in relation to which something else is form. . . . Everything is formed, and hence rendered poetic" (153). This play of form is why W. K. Wimsatt described poetry as "more than usually verbal": it is "hyperverbal" in the way its "local texture" of form is "supercharged with significance" (*Verbal Icon* 231). At the historical moment of these polemics, Wimsatt was promoting a view of the poem as "an iconic solidity" with "a fullness of actually presented meaning" (ibid.), and Crane was seeking a neo-Aristotelian analytic to identify the determining "principles of structure" in "particular configurations" (184). We need not subscribe to their agenda, however, in order to appreciate their attention to how (as a European contemporary, Jan Mukařovský, put it) poetry makes the linguistic sign "the center of attention" and manipulates its forms as "an indirect semantic factor."[5] A sense both of this work and its ability to situate poetic language meta-formally is what prompted Wimsatt to argue that it "is something like a definition of poetry to say that whereas rhetoric— in the sense of mere persuasion or sophistic—is a kind of discourse the power of which diminishes in proportion as the artifice of it is understood or seen through—poetry . . . is a kind of discourse the power of which—or the satisfaction which we derive from it—is actually increased by an increase in our understanding of the artifice" ("What to Say" 240–41). Any view of poetic artifice that perceives only its power to occlude and mystify misses the canniness of Wimsatt's remarks: the capacity of poetry to strengthen critical understanding by engaging attention with its constructedness, making a reading of its forms fundamental to any reception of or quarrel with its power.

The formal investments of poetry are one reason that criticism has had such difficulty getting "beyond" formalism. Hartman diagnosed his own addiction as an inability to discover a "method to distinguish clearly what is formal and what is not" (*Fate* vii). René Wellek and Austin Warren addressed this problem in *Theory of Literature*, an earlier and for a while very influential polemic for the "intrinsic study of literature." Their call for a study of the "work of art" as "a whole system of signs, or structure of signs, serving a specific aesthetic purpose" was set against their dissatisfaction with "the old dichotomy" between "form as the factor aesthetically active and a content aesthetically indifferent"; they wanted a way to "distinguish between words in themselves, aesthetically indifferent," and the means by which words become "aesthetically effective" (140–41). The method they proposed was predicted by (though not attributed to) a Romantic theorist, Coleridge: it was a cutting across and replacement of the dichotomy of form and content with a theory of form as "that which aesthetically organizes its 'matter'" (241).

This idea of aesthetic agency was valuable in focusing on poetry as a discourse defined, if not necessarily privileged, by its formal actions. At the same time, however, the tactic of aesthetic designation and the presumption of its historical neutrality set forth the terms in which modern formalism, along with the Romantic texts it cited for theoretical precedence, would be discredited. The story of both Romanticism and formalist criticism that I develop in my chapters requires a preliminary view of their interinvolved careers, for better or worse, in critical tradition. Read against these careers, the complications that I study in local poetic sites will emerge more sharply.

Formalisms, Anti-Formalisms

Designating an aesthetic agency, the rationale of mid-twentieth-century formalist criticism, had double force. While classical dichotomizings of form and content were rejected and, within the domain of poetry, undermined, the modern effects were at once integrative and isolationist. The undermining did link form, both as a technique and as a troping of tradition and convention, to semantic work. Yet the desire to protect formalist criticism from contextual claims also suppressed attention—with no small sacrifice—to the way that formal choices and actions, in addition to drawing on literary traditions, were enmeshed in networks of social and historical conditions.

To assess the effect of this twentieth-century formalist criticism on the study of Romanticism and its formalisms, we need to review the general scene onto which it emerged. Modern formalist criticism was itself a revaluation, for the first powerful reviews of Romanticism, a century before, had read in it an anti-formalism symptomatic of intellectual or even moral failure. Hazlitt registered the first charge in his review of *The Excursion* (1814): exhibiting "all the internal power, without the external form of poetry," Wordsworth exposes "the want of an imagination teeming with various forms." Hazlitt may even be punning on a compensation for this want of forms when he goes on to remark that Wordsworth has a way of making "the most insignificant things . . . formidable" (*Works* 4: 120). Writing near mid-century, Charles Kingsley took a wider measure of the symptoms, seeing this want not so much as a problem of mental inventory as of mental character: "a poetry of doubt, even a sceptical poetry, in its true sense, can never possess clear and sound form, even organic form at all. How can you put into form that thought which is by its very nature formless?" (460). His patent reference was to Coleridge's (German-into-English) elevation of "organic form" over the "mechanical regularity" of "a pre-determined form" and his grounding of this aesthetic in nature rather than culture: the processes of organic form are "innate," taking shape as "it developes itself from within. . . . Such is the Life, such the form" (*Lectures* 1: 495). I shall have more to say about the way this aesthetic became a synecdoche for Romanticism; for now, I am concerned with the critical revelation of the first part of Kingsley's charge: how an interpretation of formal practices as the sign of sensibility recast attention to form as something other than subordinate device. Form had meaning.

For serious Victorians, the meaning was default. Arnold implies this in opposing Romantic expression, with its "source in a great movement of feel-

ing," to the poetry of "high seriousness," identifiable in "the noble and profound application of ideas to life . . . under the conditions immutably fixed by
the laws of poetic beauty and poetic truth."[6] The language of laws evokes a
formalism not just of technique but of intellectual judgment and social consequence, and the least of Wordsworth's accomplishments is his "formal philosophy." The "accident . . . of inspiration, is of peculiar importance. . . . It
might seem that Nature not only gave him the matter for his poem, but wrote
his poem for him. He has no style"; "Nature herself seems . . . to take the pen
out of his hand, and to write for him with her own bare, sheer, penetrating
power" (Preface, *Poems of Wordsworth* xix, xxii, xxiv). Mere philosophy in the
neoclassical mode was not the antidote, however, as Arnold's famous judgment on Dryden and Pope makes clear: "Though they may write in verse,
though they may in a certain sense be masters of the art of versification, [they]
are not classics of our poetry, they are classics of our prose" ("Study" 181).
Even so, he was not prepared to work the issue from the other side: to define
an aesthetic domain releasing literature both from the social obligation of applying its ideas to life and from the didactic function of limiting those ideas to
"profound, permanent, fruitful, philosophical truth" ("Function" 266). This
would be the task of A. C. Bradley's inaugural Oxford Lecture on Poetry, "Poetry for Poetry's Sake."

In a pivotal rethinking of poetic function, and with critical attention to
poetry as a verbal form, Bradley disputed the traditional "antithesis of substance and form" favored by the "extreme formalist" (13), and argued that
their identity is "the essence of poetry" (15). Resisting both "the heresy of the
separable substance" (17) that deemed form "negligible" to sense, and "the
formalist heresy" (24) that subsumed content into sensuous effect, he insisted
that "if substance and form mean anything *in* the poem, then each is involved
in the other" (16). Thus, however possible it is to "decompose" poetic experience "and abstract for comparatively separate consideration [the] formal element," in actual reading, he contended, one can never "apprehend this value
by itself"; poetic form is always "a significant form" (19). Bradley's claim for
form as "significant" moved the discussion past the terms of power and relapse
wielded by Kingsley and Arnold, anticipating Cleanth Brooks's radical New
Critical insistence that "form and content cannot be separated" ("form is
meaning") and Roman Jakobson's claim that "poeticalness is not a supplemen-
tation of discourse with rhetorical adornment but a total re-evaluation of the
discourse and of all its components," with the consequence that "in poetry
any verbal element is converted into a figure." In retrospect of these developments, Bradley's terms can be seen to be verging on a semantics of form.[7]

Russian Formalism (with which Jakobson was involved) took this leap,
with a radically material emphasis on technique. Its most extreme positions in
effect signed on to the "formalist heresy" rejected by Bradley, and in this com-

mitment absolutely retracted the Arnoldian value of "application" in assessments of literary power. Not only does form *not* (sub)serve content, the Formalist claim went, but content is just a motivation for, or an effect of, form. The "technique of art," stated a leading theorist, Viktor Shklovsky, "is to make objects 'unfamiliar,' to make forms difficult, to increase the difficulty and length of perception" as "an aesthetic end in itself. . . . *Art is a way of experiencing the artfulness of an object; the object is not important*" ("Art as Technique" 12, his italics).[8] In this lexicon, the work of formal "devices" is to "defamiliarize" and "estrange" ordinary economies of language, denaturalizing their power and, by extension, the power of ordinary structures of reference and modes of perception. The consequences for understanding poetry were severe: if defamiliarization is "found almost everywhere form is found" (18), it is inherent in "poetic speech," a "*formed speech*" in which language is "*difficult . . . attenuated, tortuous*" (22–23). This "stubborn attachment to the intrinsically literary," remarks Fredric Jameson, became the basis of a distinctly "literary" criticism (*Prison-House* 43).

A familiar corollary in later critiques of formalism is that the distinctly literary is also distinctly *not* anything else; it was a criticism in patent retreat from social reference, inflection, or application. Yet such critiques miss how, under the cover of the seemingly isolated literary figure, Russian Formalism theorized literary effect in terms with a potential beyond literary criticism, especially the display of constructedness and the obstruction of transparent apprehension. There were political applications as well for seeing how, in Shklovsky's description, convention "coated" perception "with the glass armor of the familiar" (*Mayakovsky* 68). By "violating the form, [a writer] forces us to attend to it," Shklovsky proposed; defamiliarizing "lays bare the technique" (in his famous phrase), exposing the devices naturalized by customary perception ("Sterne's *Tristram Shandy*" 30). In this analysis of the "play of form upon form," Tony Bennett remarks, "one set of devices [chisels] the ground from beneath another, usually canonical or revered set of devices and, in doing so, wrestles 'reality' away from the terms of seeing they propose, thereby making it the focus of a renewed interest and attentiveness" (55–56).[9] Wrestling over the literary representation of the real could easily be extended to the ideology of the socially "real." And to Shklovsky, any writer producing "this awareness of the form" of the familiar "through its violation" counted in the Soviet world of 1921, "formalistically" at least, as an "extreme revolutionary" ("*Tristram*" 30–31, 27). This Formalism persists in the oppositional aesthetics of subsequent "left formalism."[10]

American formalist criticism emerged in the 1940s for the most part independently from the Russian movement, but it too had a sense of revolutionizing literary study with attention to form as the constitutive element of literary language. This focus may seem insular now, but it was radical in light of then-prevailing modes of analysis, as John Crowe Ransom's prophetically titled *The New Criticism* makes clear. In 1913, Sidney Lee had described literary scholarship as a study of "the external circumstances—political, social, economic—in which literature is produced."[11] By the 1940s, Ransom was feeling that literary study per se had been lost to contextualism, which he summed as "critical theory": "Most critical writing is done in the light of 'critical theory,' which unfortunately is something less than aesthetics" (3). While he did not consider how "aesthetics" might bear a theoretically (and ideologically) cast light, he was alert to what might be lost without aesthetic attention. When the New Criticism of the 1940s devoted itself to the "intrinsic study of literature" (the urging of Wellek and Warren), it also took contextualism—in particular, historicism—as its heuristic antithesis.

For their part, Wellek and Warren went to work defining various "fallacies" of interpretation, ones inclined to "causal" explanation from "extrinsic" reference (authorial intention, biography, historical and social contexts, popular and critical reception, or textual genetics). Brooks's approach to reading in *The Well Wrought Urn*, a primer of New Criticism published in 1947, openly resisted the sway of "historical backgrounds" and "literary history" as the determinants of literary study. In an academic atmosphere that had made reading literature in relation to "its historical context" seem "the only kind of reading possible," Brooks proposed "to see what residuum, if any, is left after we have referred the poem to its cultural matrix" (x) and to assume "that there is such a thing as poetry, difficult as it may be to define," against the view of literature as "synonymous with 'anything written in words'" (216–17). In this criticism's assertion of its "newness," a prevailing contextualism was reformed into a view of the text as discrete artifact, with its own dynamics of "formal structure and rhetorical organization" (218).

We can see why reactions against New Criticism (and the Romantic poetics of "organic form" that seemed complicit) routinely charge it with being both anti-historical and fixated on "mere" technique.[12] Yet the critiques, which are quick to identify the (repressed) historical context within which American New Criticism itself came into power, usually elide the dialectic *with* historicism that is marked, for instance, by Brooks's interest in the residuum "left *after* we have referred a poem to its historical context" (x, my italics).[13] Brooks was not rejecting contextual reference; he was testing whether there is anything in literary—more specifically, poetic—organizations of language that could not be restricted to this information. There is an important difference, of course, between his idea of history as objective "background" and theories of history and literature as mutually implicated in cultural poetics (or, in some analyses, of history as the suppressed referent of literary process). But it is important to recognize that Brooks did not say that studying poetry refused history and culture, only that the former required different kinds and sequences of attention.[14]

It was not formalism per se that discredited New Critics; it was the strategic displacement of context to make "the study of the work of art the centre of their interest" (Wellek and Warren 140) and the regard of form as the product of a historically disinterested, internally coherent aesthetics. This procedure is what focused Jerome McGann's influential but restrictive description of the function of poetic form: "unlike non-aesthetic utterance," poetry offers social evaluations "to the reader *under the sign of completion*" (his italics). While formalists take this sign "as their object of study," he says, we need to see both the "experience of finality and completion" and the "trans-historical" claim as the product of a specific discourse of "historical totality": "integral form is the sign of this seeming knowledge—and it persuades its reader that such a totality is not just a poetic illusion, but a truth" ("Keats" 21–22). Following the Marxist analysis of aesthetic form as one of the ideological forms of social consciousness, McGann deemed poetic forms worth attention only as part of a determining "ideological formation." [15] Formal analysis is a "specialized" approach that will matter only insofar as it can, indeed "must," find its "*raison d'être* in the socio-historical ground" (*Romantic Ideology* 3, his italics). The critical task is to show how "social forms" shape "forms of thought," "forms of consciousness," and "forms (or 'structures') of feeling"—and to reveal the relation of these forms to an "ideological form" (ibid. 12–14). The project, as Catherine Gallagher describes this version of Marxist literary criticism, is to undo the "false resolution" of aesthetic form, exposing "the original contradiction and the formal signs of its irresolvability" (39).

This critique of literary form as part of an ideological totality was typically conducted at the expense of closer reading for how such form might produce local lines of resistance; literary form, at best, was seen as unwittingly betraying the contradictions of its intention to resolve. But another contemporaneous movement against (if not beyond) New Critical formalism did read closely in order to "reveal the existence of hidden articulations and fragmentations within assumedly monadic totalities," in Paul de Man's words (*Allegories* 249)—including the totalizing intentions of critical texts. Where New Criticism rejected a determinate reference to the "intention of the author" (Wimsatt and Beardsley 3), de Man redeployed intention, applying it to New Critics themselves. That "poetic language, unlike ordinary language, possesses . . . 'form'" struck him as a "prefigurative structure" for formalist criticism. The difference, he proposed, is merely temporal, the poetry constituting the "foreknowledge" of the critic and so orienting, by a "dialectical interplay," the "intent at totality of the interpretative process." The peculiar strength of American formalist criticism for de Man was the way, even as it promoted a formalism of totalized understandings, it effected a "disclosure of distinctive structures of literary language (such as ambiguity and irony)" that contradicted its "notion of the integrity of literary form." This disclosure was a kind of prefigurative structure, in turn, for de Man's theoretical interests. He saw the internal evolution of New Criticism as a self-deconstructing one, but pre-vented, by the collusion of its theory of the intentional fallacy with a blindness to its own critical intentionality, from integrating its subversive insights "within a truly coherent theory of literary form" ("Form and Intent" 31–32).[16]

De Man's challenge to the New Critical "theory of signifying form" (which sees language as containing, reflecting, or referring to experience) with a theory of "constituting form" ("Dead End" 232) would eventually lead him to suggest the usefulness of an evolved formalism for social and ideological analyses.[17] But it was not in rapport with de Man that Marxist and New His-toricist critiques were describing the ideologically motivated "constructing functions" of literary form. Although Eagleton, like de Man, was interested in events of incoherence, inconsistency, and self-contradiction in literary form, the investment was different. For him, these events showed how the "ideo-logical struggles" displaced by the "naturalising, moralising, and mythifying devices" of form could also invade form. "Marginalised yet . . . querulously present," these struggles either compel "organic closures [to] betray their con-structing functions" or they rupture literary structure with "self-contradictory forms," "fissures and hiatuses." The literary project of "formal displacements" and "formal discontinuities" is thus inscribed with "formal dissonances" that are necessarily part of the work's "historical meaning" ("Ideology and Liter-ary Form" 124–25; 128–29).

For both de Man and Eagleton, formalism is still regarded as the suspect inheritance of a Romantic ideology of "organic form."[18] Ruptures were taken to be signs of contradictions that it was the business of criticism, operating against poetic cover-ups, to discover and expose. What is missing from the story thus told is any sense of how Romantic formalism itself is involved in this kind of critical project. While it is true that Romanticism is the historical moment when organicist theory received forceful and elaborate articulation, "organic form" is not the whole story of formalism, either in Romanticism or in the full text of New Criticism. The centrality of "organic" form in recent critiques reflects only the partiality with which the official rhetoric of New Criticism appropriated Romanticism—and, not coincidentally, the (still) se-ductive sway of Romanticism's own most idealizing formulations.

The Fortunes of Formalism and the Fate of Romanticism

About Romanticism, twentieth-century formalist criticism is nothing if not ambivalent.

On the one hand, Romanticism seemed antithetical—by force of its resis-tance to, or at least reform of, inherited forms; its reference to historical events; and even internally, its reference to intention and biography demanded by its poetics of expressiveness. "It is not so much a historical statement as a definition to say that the intentional fallacy is a romantic one," remark Wimsatt and Beardsley (6). And it was to Romanticism—not as an aesthetic ideology but as a cultural event—that Wellek and Warren attributed the pervasive contextualism that had taken hold of literary study in their day: "Modern literary history arose in close connexion with the Romantic movement, which could subvert the critical system of Neo-Classicism only with the relativist argument that different times required different standards. Thus the emphasis shifted from the literature to its historical background" (139). And thus the New Criticism took as its antithesis a leagued Romanticism and historicism—with the convenience, as Jameson observes, of repudiating the radical tradition of Romanticism and returning for its models to Metaphysical and Cavalier poetry (*Prison-House* 46). On the other hand, New Criticism kept returning to Romanticism's theoretical writing, especially Coleridge's. The crucial attraction was an idea of literary or, more particularly, poetic language distinguishable from ordinary language by its internally coherent "organic form," a principle by which opposites could achieve unity through a specific aesthetic agency.[19]

This split view of Romanticism—as an inimical contextualism and as a progenitor of theoretical formalism—patterned the way its poetry got discussed, discounted, or evaded altogether for the sake of (and sometimes as a condition of) other critical agenda. Tuned primarily to a theoretical affiliation with Romanticism, New Critical reading of the poetry was sporadic, anomalous, or reformist in effect. New Criticism liked a few well-formed poems displaying tension, irony, and paradox—poems (neither long nor fragmentary) that accorded with their admired canon of similarly well wrought Renaissance, metaphysical, Victorian, and modern lyrics. Brooks's statement that in the best Romantic poems "form *is* meaning" ("Artistry" 251, his emphasis) found its best demonstrations in a sifting of songs, sonnets, and odes, and within these genres, primarily early Blake, early Wordsworth, and Keats. The broad consequence for Romantic studies is recollected by one student of those days, Jonathan Culler: "Those of us who had been nurtured on the New Criticism and thought Donne and the moderns the supreme examples of poetic achievement were inclined to find Romantic poetry the aberration. . . . The Romantics, we had heard, thought poetry a spontaneous overflow of feeling rather than a verbal construct, an expression of personality rather than an impersonal and comprehensively ironic form" ("Mirror" 149). It took a return to literary history via M. H. Abrams's *The Mirror and the Lamp* to show Culler and his generation that "a whole series of contemporary critical concepts" (that is, New Criticism) "had in fact been formulated by Coleridge and other Romantic critics" (150); and it took yet another turn, with de Man and against Abrams, to reveal "a self-deconstructive movement" within Romantic theory of the terms privileged by New Criticism (152).

The initial lack of attention to the Romantic poetics of form in any terms other than "organic form" was exacerbated by subsequent resistances to formalism altogether and a sweeping critique of organic ideology. Eagleton denounced "Culler's structuralism" as "largely compatible with New Criticism. It served chiefly to lend that anemic formalism a new lease of life" ("Idealism" 53). Poetic forms became features to be seen through, read beyond, around, or against. This is not to say that there were not several very fine and still valuable late– or post–New Critical studies of form in particular poets; but these were local forays, tactfully assimilating attention to form to other frames of analysis (biography, literary history, genre, philosophy) rather than asserting its value in the face of its emerging detractors.[20] The polemical studies, by contrast, assaulted formalism and were determined to reorganize the reading of Romanticism in defiance of it. This "challenge to formalist dogma," notes Christopher Norris, "went along with a revived interest" in "the ethos of Romanticism" (*Deconstruction* 116)—the very contextualism that earlier formalist critics wanted to set aside.

The new contexts were various—cultural myth, phenomenology, intertextuality, rhetorical theory, historicism—but each marked its resistance to formalism by shifting the discourse of form away from device and technique. Northrop Frye's reading of Romantic poetry did recognize literature as "an autonomous verbal structure" (*Anatomy* 74) but submerged specifics of form, along with all "discursive verbal structures," into the domain of "informing" myths (352–53). Its project, in Hartman's apt description, was to translate poetic form into a "mediated form called allegory" and in turn to subsume the "allegorical forms" into "archetypes" (*Criticism in the Wilderness* 89–90). Hartman's own philosophically tuned reading of Romantic poetry was not particularly formalist: avoiding "minute stylistic or structural analysis" (*Wordsworth's Poetry* xxi), he focused on the "structures of consciousness" (xvii) reflected in verbal figures, literary modes (epitaph and inscription), and "rhetorical form[s]" such as surmise (11). Psychoanalytic studies of Romantic writers appearing at the same time as Hartman's and Frye's usually elided literary form, except as a signifier of deep truths which, while not exactly imageless, were felt to have little to do with specific formal choices, beyond the choice of imaginative literature itself as a form of displaced expression.[21] Even the most text-based of such criticism, Harold Bloom's reading of ratios of influence, revision, and tropological displacement in Romantic poetry, just glanced at form to note how the subjectivity of the prized "lyric form" courted the shadow of "the precursor" (*Anxiety* 11). So baleful was Bloom's view of the "impasse of Formalist criticism" (12) that to colleagues such as Hartman his seemed an "anti-formalistic theory" (*Fate* 52)—a stance Bloom flaunted in the opening essay for *Deconstruction and Criticism*, "The Breaking of Form": conceding his "own lack of interest in most aspects of what is called 'form in poetry,'" he proposed that "poetic meaning" gleams in "the breaking apart of form" (1–2). About the only formalism to survive this breakup, remarked Frank Lentricchia, was Bloom's own, his "desire to totalize literary history" (350).

And about the only large-scale accounts of poetic forms in these decades saw them as agents of occlusion. De Man read Romanticism the way that he read American formalism—as a rhetoric that displaced, or at least remained strategically blind to, the knowledge that poetic language is always "constitutive . . . unable to give a foundation to what it posits except as an intent of consciousness" ("Intentional" 6). Deconstructive readers inverted New Critical designs. De-privileging the unity vested "in the 'achieved' or 'coherent' form of a literary work," they worked "to see *through* literary form to the way language or symbolic process makes or breaks meaning" (Hartman, "Wild, Fierce Yale" 190). These readings concentrated on subversive tropes and intertextuality, and tended not to see how form, too, might be involved in this critical activity. So, too, Marxist and New Historicist critiques cast Romanticism as an "aesthetic ideology" intent to proffer its poetic forms as autonomous unities, signifying knowledge authorized by nature rather than determined by history and culture. "Organic form" (and the taint of its New Critical renewal) was the summary sign for Romanticism, its formalist poetics, and its dominant critical tradition. It was "*The* Romantic Ideology" in the broadcast of McGann's influential study by the same title.

As with deconstruction, the critic's charge was to expose the complicity of poetic form with this ideology. In "the privilege accorded by the Romantics to the 'creative imagination,'" Eagleton told readers of *Literary Theory*, his terms at once echoing McGann's and parodying Coleridge's,

the literary work itself comes to be seen as a mysterious organic unity, in contrast to the fragmented individualism of the capitalist marketplace: it is "spontaneous" rather than rationally calculated, creative rather than mechanical. . . . At the centre of aesthetic theory at the turn of the eighteenth century is the semi-mystical doctrine of the symbol. For Romanticism, indeed, the symbol becomes the panacea for all problems. Within it, a whole set of conflicts which were felt to be insoluble in ordinary life . . . could be magically resolved. (19–20, 21)

Eagleton is concerned primarily with the imprint of such doctrine on the post-Romantic novel, whose forms of displacement he sees complicit with an emerging of "organicist" social theory: both discourses evoke the "supposedly spontaneous unity of natural life-forms" in order to "denote symmetrically integrated systems characterised by the harmonious interdependence of their component elements" ("Ideology and Literary Form" 103–4). What is problematic for Romanticism itself in this critique is the equation of poetic form with harmony, symmetry, and unity, and so a categorical insulation from the conflicts discovered and contemplated by historicist theory (and its own use of "organic" formulations).[22]

Even so, this view spread to Romantic studies. If Hartman once found fault with the reluctance of formalistic criticism to "demystify" the "disinterested-ness of form in 'To Autumn'" by "discovering behind its decorum a hidden interest" (*Fate* 125), readers such as McGann, David Simpson, and Marjorie Levinson were offering urgent divestments (though not in the economy that Hartman sought), pointedly casting the lexicon of formalism into a syntax of ideological analysis. Simpson reviews Coleridge's theory of organic form as "a discursive response to the material basis of cultural and political life in early nineteenth-century England: wars, civil rights trials, food riots, radical and reform movements."[23] Applying this analysis to canonical Romantic poetry (and without Simpson's interest in questionings and ironies), McGann and Levinson "demystify" the textual processes to expose "an ideological forma-tion," arguing that the literary form masks "the contradictions inherent in contemporary social structures and the relations they support" (*Romantic Ide-ology* 134).[24] The critical terms they use are emphatically reform(al)ist. What is inherent is not a shaping principle of poetic form, but a "determinate" social form whose contradictions are occluded by the text's "manifest theme and *achieved* form" (Levinson, *Wordsworth's* 1, my italics). Thus seeing the poem as "formally a sort of allegory by absence" of what is outside or social (9), the New Historicist is dedicated to reversing the older formalism, working instead to "set . . . form *against* content, process *against* product" (10)—against, that is, the social exterior.

Helpful as these procedures are in historicizing Romantic poetics, McGann and Levinson also tend to limit accounts of poetic form to the organic, the unified, the achieved, the stable. Whatever is factitious, contradictory, and unstable is credited to the world "outside" the poem, or is readable in its form only as the rupture of organicist desire. These critiques seem to require *Tintern Abbey* or Book 1 of *The Excursion* to be paradigms of harmony, even though to many other readers these texts seem deeply divided, incoherent, themselves in the business of critique.[25] A cogent historicist criticism needs a better account of how the designs of unity in these and many other canonical Romantic poems reflect on rather than conceal their constructedness (not only aesthetic, but social and ideological); of how sometimes the textual forms of reconciliation are visibly factitious (not magical); and of how even the theo-retical idealizing of inherent organic form (as so unlikely a critic as Abrams has noticed) contends with the values of will and voluntary purpose (*Mirror* 173). Donald Wesling is not alone in viewing the idealizing discourse as "a calculated overstatement of a literal impossibility," a "hyperbole" deployed as a "rationale for innovation in the patterning of poetic language" (*Chances* 2).

This hyperbole may be "the primary myth of post-Romantic poetics" (2), but it is far less consolidated in Romantic practice, whose debates alternately indulged and critically tested it. Some poems do turn from social conflict, or use their forms to exile and displace disruptive knowledge; but other poems, far from concealing the problematic of form, provoke it anew, as a condition of their very composition.[26]

This contentious and internally divided poetics is also a Romantic legacy. It even fissures the well-wrought urns of New Criticism—and in these events helps explain the uncanny return of formalist reading, in different guises, to those who meant to move beyond.

The Turns and Counterturns of Forms

In *The Well Wrought Urn*, one of the texts credited with bearing the mystified formalist ideology of Romanticism into modern critical thought, Brooks means to draw on Coleridge's famous definition (in the *Biographia*) of imagination as an agent of unity and reconciliation: "poetic structure," Brooks says, is "a structure of meanings, evaluations, and interpretations; and the principle of unity which informs it seems to be one of balancing and harmonizing connotations, attitudes, and meanings" (195). The principle that "unites the like with the unlike" (195) is no magical sleight, however; it confronts and strains under "pressure" and "stresses" (198, 203), with the achieved poem representing "an equilibrium of forces, not a formula" (207). Aware, moreover, of having to insure this equilibrium against disintegration into a metaphysically ironic consciousness of contradiction, Brooks elevates certain cognitive and conceptual figures into structural principles: "wit" announces "the multiplicity of possible attitudes to be taken toward a given situation," while "irony" and "paradox" operate as its expressive "devices" (257). Thus, if irony reports a "recognition of incongruities" (209), it enters poetry as "a device for definition of attitudes by qualification" (257), and when "the poet has no one term" (9), "conflict" is "resolved . . . paradoxically" (13). "The logic of Brooks's argumentation," Timothy Bahti remarks, is to set these structures of cognition over the elusive text: "harmony is achieved and hierarchy established by subordinating the text to its interpretation—because ambiguity as a textual feature is made to enter into paradox as its meaningful articulation" (212–13).

Some antagonists of New Criticism (such as Paul Bové)[27] stress the coherence of Brooks's logic to expose its covert investments, but even more moderate skeptics are caught by his peculiar coercions, evasions, and instabilities. "Opposites can never be said to be resolved or reconciled merely because they have been got into the same poem," protested one of Brooks's contemporar-

ies, Ransom (95), arguing that in some forms of irony "the oppositions produce an indecisive effect" (96), and that "ambiguity, even though it is itself an
effect of logical opposition, may also enforce attention to diffuseness, or pure
heterogeneity of meaning" (103). In some turns of *The Well Wrought Urn*
Brooks himself shows a sensitivity to these challenges and to the leap required
to negotiate them into resolution. In the midst of reasoning that "if the poet,
then, must perforce dramatize the oneness of the experience, even though
paying tribute to its diversity, then his use of paradox and ambiguity is seen as
necessary" (213), the reins of *perforce* and *necessary* and his question-begging
if so heavily qualify (almost torture) the sentence that the critic seems drawn
into the tension-ridden processes he describes in the poetry.

Diversity tilts toward an intuition of a de Manian rhetoric of temporality
when Brooks describes "the essential structure of a poem" as a dynamic "pattern of resolutions and balances and harmonization, developed through a temporal scheme" (203): this is an "action" (204) that in poetry is typically "disruptive" of ordinary semantic coherence (9). Brooks insists there is "no final
contradiction," and that "in dilating on the difficulties of the poet's task," he
does not want to leave the impression of necessary defeat, but his argument
keeps rocking back and forth, worrying the issue: "The poet must work by
analogies, but the metaphors do not lie in the same plane or fit neatly edge to
edge. There is a continual tilting of the planes; necessary overlappings, dis-
crepancies, contradictions" (9–10); in some Romantic odes "the thrusts and
pressures exerted by the various symbols" are "played, one against the other,"
sometimes "perversely," showing language changing "under the pressure of
context," "warped into new meanings"; words in poetry bear no discrete
meaning, but are "a potential of meaning, a nexus or cluster of meanings,"
so that even when they form a statement, this is "warped and bent . . . de-
flected away from a positive, straightforward formulation" (210–11). If the
dominant and subordinate clauses in some of these alertly tortured sentences
were inverted, Brooks's poetics of unity would release a deconstructive difference, and his sense of irony and ambiguity as devices of paradox would shift
into deconstruction's reading of irony and contradiction as a rhetoric of
indeterminacy.[28]

Almost counterintuitively, Brooks's words slip into warps and bends. Citing Coleridge's description of the imagination as a "power" which "reveals
itself in the balance or reconcilement of opposite or discordant qualities," he
reports that among these are *"saneness* with difference" (18, my italics)—an
erratum (or, given its persistence in every edition, a misreading?) yielding the
spectral suggestion that in "difference" looms the *in*sanity of semantic heterogeneity—of everything that resists and subverts the organization of poetic
form. This minor slip looks like a return of the repressed, a concession of the
motives impelling the well-wrought criticism. Another slippery piece of lan-

guage is the iconic title itself, *The Well Wrought Urn*. Its source is Donne's *Canonization*, whose poet boasts to his lover that

> if unfit for tombs and hearse
> Our legend be, it will be fit for verse;
> And if no piece of chronicle we prove,
> We'll build in sonnets pretty rooms;
> As well a well wrought urn becomes
> The greatest ashes, as half-acre tombs . . .

Noting the pun of "pretty rooms," Brooks takes these stanzas as the event they predict (17–21). But the pun is not so precisely containable, for there is another poetic punning—of *verse* as and at the "turn" of the poet's line—a visual pun that releases "well wrought *turn*" as a subversive lexical flux within "well wrought urn." This punning—visual, auditory, and semantic all at once—sets the lover's prediction into elaborate accidents of reading that work against well-wrought containments of meaning in poetic form.[29] A similar (and, I think, allusive) punning lexical slide occurs in Keats's protest to his Urn's "shape . . . / Of marble men and maidens overwrought." As the poet complains, "Thou, silent form, dost tease us out of thought," "dost tease" evokes a homophone for the affect thus frustrated, "dost ease."[30] As Keats makes clear and as we shall see elsewhere in Romantic poetry, such "formal permutations" of words "beyond manifest content," by force of "phonemic contingencies" (in Garrett Stewart's words [4]), often coincide with situations in which larger signs of form—its investment by generic, ideological, and even social convention—are in question.

These subverbal semantics are not what Brooks heard or had in mind in writing about the urns of Donne, Gray, and Keats, or in titling *The Well Wrought Urn*. Even so, the way such slippages invade the language of (and in his case about) poetic form with a faint fissuring of everything well wrought evokes his caution that "whatever statement we may seize upon as incorporating the 'meaning' of the poem, immediately the imagery and rhythm seem to set up tensions within it, warping and twisting it, qualifying and revising it" (197). That this punning disruption by form is produced by the very phrase epitomizing his poetics of unity, ringing and wringing a lexical alternative out of the graphic text, dramatizes the subversive potential in the projects of form. If Brooks never addresses this effect in the way that deconstruction would, he registers the cues.

This latency, to some, implicates deconstruction in the critical ideology it would oppose: both are "text-centered," refusing the reference of language to anything other than (the logic, or illogic of) its structure. Thus McGann sees a common address to literary works as "self-enclosed verbal constructs, or looped intertextual fields of autonomous signifiers and signifieds" in which "the question of referentiality" is a problematic absence, and he advocates a vigorous criticism of all "formalist traditions" (*Historical* 3). Yet reference-oriented New Historicism, Alan Liu argues, has a kind of unacknowledged dependency on notions of form, borrowing "from formalisms early and late, New Critical or deconstructive": not only is New Historicism not "essentially different from formalism," he contends, "it is an ultimate formalism so 'powerful' that it colonizes the very world as its 'text'" ("Power of Formalism" 754–55).[31] Nor did Marxist criticism, Tony Bennett notes, ever really leave formalism behind but, despite its opposition to "Formalism," continues to debate the relation between literary form and the specifics of material history.[32]

To Liu (in some moods) and others, the reluctance or inability of New Historicism to confront its dependency on formalism signifies a conceptual failure.[33] Yet why say "failure"? Formalist criticism, either New Critical or post–New Critical, is not necessarily inimical to the analysis of referentiality desired by the historicist. Resisting the isolationist formalism of early modernism, Georg Lukács once suggested that "the truly social element in literature is the form."[34] Bennett, noting a Formalist theme in Louis Althusser's argument that "the real difference between art and science lies in the *specific form*" of presentation ("Letter on Art" 205, Althusser's italics), remarks that the question "of specifying the features which uniquely distinguish works of literature from other ideological and cultural forms" is still the "matter of prime importance" for Marxist analysis that it was for Russian Formalists (122; 41–42).[35] When Althusser, Pierre Macherey, and Eagleton define "literature" by its unique "capacity to reveal or rupture from within the terms of seeing proposed by the categories of dominant ideologies," their task necessarily "becomes that of understanding the formal processes through which literary texts work upon and transform dominant ideological forms" as well as embody, mystify, and reproduce them (8).

Reading form has remained attractive for the good reason that it sharpens critical attention. In a generation before Liu, this case was made by Roland Barthes, who insisted on the necessary relation of (old) historicism to form. Writing in France in the 1950s, when it was not New Critical formalism but structuralism that was challenging historicism, Barthes sought to reconcile the terms that both polemics, however heuristically, had put asunder: the "literary," identified by its display of form; and "history," thought to engage only fact and idea. Historicizing formalist questions in terms that briefly interested even de Man, he insisted that any "total criticism" had to pursue a "dialectical co-ordination" between "ideology," the historically produced content, and "semiology," the "science of forms [that] studies significations apart from their content ("Myth Today" 111–12)."[36] His famous sentence was "that a little formalism turns one away from History, but that a lot brings one back to it," for formalism is one of its "necessary principles" of analysis. Correspondingly, "the more a system is specifically defined in its forms, the more amenable it is to historical criticism" (ibid.).[37]

As Barthes suggests, attention to form can serve ideological critique. One of the touchstones in the disdain for formalism (e.g., McGann, Levinson) is M. M. Bakhtin's *The Formal Method* (1928), an influential quarrel with the (Russian) Formalist notion that the material of poetic language is an abstraction of its form. The counterclaim was that language operates through "ideological formations" (84) within which "the poet does not select linguistic forms, but rather the evaluations posited in them" (122). This is a worthy corrective to some methodological excesses, yet the dichotomizing of form and matter may be less firm than Bakhtin and others assume. Bennett's view that "in the actual conduct of their criticism, the Formalists were not so apolitical, ahistorical or asociological, so 'formalist,' as the stereotype would have" it (29) is evident in Shklovsky's "Art as Technique." One of this essay's most intriguing features is the contradiction between Shklovsky's overt claim that the object is not important in respect to the artfulness of its presentation and the covert signifying of the texts he uses for demonstration. Most of his examples have a political charge, not only in content but also in Shklovsky's commentary: the passages from Tolstoy—about flogging, private property, a military battle—not only focus on tyranny, unequal privilege, or state apparatus, but treat these subjects in linguistic forms that make them seem strange and unfamiliar. If "art removes objects from the automatism of perception" (13), Shklovsky's cases show its technique being mobilized to expose a routine social form to critical analysis, revealing its arbitrariness, its relativity, its constructedness, and, implicitly, its susceptibility to reform.

Because poetry is an even more conspicuous form than the fiction that interests Shklovsky, it has fuller resources for mobilizing this attention. These effects will be the subject of my chapters and will focus my sense that disparagers of formalist criticism need a better view of what form can accomplish. Too many readers today accept Eagleton's marginalizing, simplifying, or simply dismissive attention to poetic form as a labor of "reductive operations," an exercise "preoccupied simply with analyzing linguistic devices."[38] I want to refute the myopia implied by "reductive" and "preoccupied" and the triviality implied by "simply," by demonstrating how, in the critical perspectives that have evolved after New Criticism, attention to form can articulate issues often felt to be inimical: not only the factitiousness of organic coherence, closed designs, and cognitive totality, but also the construction of forms in relation to subjectivity, cultural ideology, and social circumstance. That Romanticism itself is enmeshed in these issues defines an important genealogy for this project.

Romantic Formalisms

That this genealogy may not be obvious reflects the fact that for a long time the prestige of Romanticism and a sense of its modernity were strongly allied, ideologically and stylistically, with its rhetoric of resistance to form, the declarations often sounding like anti-formalism. German Romanticism celebrated a poetics of "chaos," "the infinite," and "the unformed"; and the infiltration of this energy, if not its extremism, was evident in English texts.[39] Whether cast as a progressive "experiment" and "innovation" or allied with "liberty" and "revolution," the rhetoric troped imposed or inherited forms as tyranny or, at the very least, the strictures of unexamined prestige, custom, or habit. In these lights, "Romanticism" appears as a "watershed": for the first time, a pre-existing and prescriptive inventory of forms "is consciously seen as in contradictory connection with what is regarded as poetic," argues Wesling (*Chances* 3); the poetic is precisely a "breakup of formal rhetoric, the transfiguration of figures" (9).

Wesling is self-consciously overstating these actions and overspecifying their historical site, but he means to attest to the force of Romanticism's self-definition against traditional forms. Wordsworth, revoking Dryden's argument that the discipline of verse form is valuable for "putting bounds to a wilde over-flowing Fancy," asserted that all good poetry is a "spontaneous overflow of powerful feelings" and recoiled from "the bondage of definite form."[40] Hazlitt had no trouble retrospectively linking—indeed, attributing the very "origin" of—the formal practices of "the Lake school of poetry" to the French Revolution. Not only did radical politics parallel Lake aesthetics, but they were seen as complicit. A change in poetry "went hand in hand" with "the change in politics," Hazlitt proposed, the one as "complete, and . . . as startling" as the other: "According to the prevailing notions, all was to be natural and new. Nothing that was established was to be tolerated. . . . Kings and queens were dethroned from their rank and station in legitimate tragedy or epic poetry, as they were decapitated elsewhere; rhyme was looked upon as a relic of the feudal system, and regular metre was abolished along with regular government" ("On the Living Poets," *Works* 5: 161–62). In 1818, this extravagant satire was calculated in part to embarrass the subsequent political retreat of the leading Lakers ("the present poet-laureat [Southey] and the two authors of the Lyrical Ballads" [162]), but Hazlitt's retrospect involves more than this local barb. It registers the degree to which poetic form, in both Revolutionary and Regency England, was a politicized practice—and continues to be so every time new practices challenge traditional, or at least prevailing, forms.[41]

This politicizing of form (as in the seventeenth century) is more crucial to

Romantic poetics than the anti-formalism with which its practices were ret-rospectively tagged. With the clench of rhymes on which he arrays more than a few *Songs of Experience*, Blake means to allegorize the "mind-forg'd mana-cles" of social institutions and their repetition in mental prisons. Oppositional poetics held out a promise of revolution, at least in perception. Thus, Cole-ridge describes Wordsworth's poetry of the 1790s as "awakening the mind's attention from the lethargy of custom" and "the film of familiarity" (*Biogra-phia* 2: 7).[42] With bolder verbs, Shelley argues that poetic creation "purges from our inward sight the film of familiarity" and "strips the veil of familiarity from the world" (*Defence* 505), terms that forecast the critical agency that Rus-sian Formalism a century later would attribute to aesthetic deformations of the familiar.[43] In the Romantic arguments, of course, such actions are valued for dissolving customary formations rather than (as in Russian theory) expos-ing them. To Coleridge, poetry dispels films of familiarity in order to reveal those "wonders of the world before us" which override critical analysis in their capacity "to excite a feeling analogous to the supernatural" (2: 7). And what poetry "lays bare" for Shelley is not the constitutive device but an intuition beyond the capture of form: "the naked and sleeping beauty which is the spirit of its forms" (505).[44]

While these awakenings and unveiling do not overtly define a political agenda, the potential looms in the way the unveiled spiritual scene evokes new senses of power and a higher law. Echoing Isaiah 6: 10 and Jeremiah 5: 21, Coleridge heralds an impending revolution in perception: in "consequence of the film of familiarity and selfish solicitude we have eyes, yet see not, ears that hear not, and hearts that neither feel nor understand" (*Biographia* 2: 7). Shel-ley, already confident of dispelling this film, claims that the poet's unveiling at once renders "the familiar world . . . a chaos" and "creates anew the universe" (505)—powers that promote the poet, at the close of his *Defence*, to legislator, however unacknowledged his temporal effect may be.[45] For both Shelley and Coleridge, there is a sensation of poetry's capacity, by the very sign of its un-familiar forming of language, to put historically contingent knowledge in a different perspective and to interrogate its hold. This is a formalism that can even be utopian about failures of poetic form, for dysfunction signifies a po-tentiality toward which social process might strive.

Yet the deeper truth is that Romanticism's poetic forms take shape within complicated literary and cultural contexts. Across the field of its poetry, tra-ditional forms circulate along with a recognition of the necessity of some kind of form, and the politics of liberation contend not only with the attractions of various traditions but with new exertions of will. Los's famous declaration, "I must Create a System, or be enslav'd by another Mans" (*Jerusalem* plate 10: 20; *Illuminated Blake* 289) is attended by the "fury & strength" with which he insists on his own system: "Obey my voice & never deviate from my will" (plate 10: 29). Idealizing theory is strained by internal contradictions, and the most stridently polemical declarations are shadowed and cross-illuminated by practices that register conflicting attitudes—about claims for distinctive aesthetic agency, about what it means to seek expression in poetic form, and about the systems of value involved in this search. The terms of these debates define and invigorate each other in specific sites of writing, even as they expose the range of attitudes in the age.

At one end persist classical notions of form as distinct from matter—emotional, natural, or historical—as that which precedes it, is discrete from it, shapes it, conveys it. In this aspect, form even can be granted authority from its abstraction and precedence, whether in Platonic terms, as the originary ideal of any specific manifestation (hence the idealizing poetics of symbol), or in Aristotelian terms, as the common property of a category (hence the poetics of generic form), or in the neoclassical legacy of generic principles imitated by literary form. Shelley describes a poem as "the creation of actions according to the unchangeable forms of human nature, as existing in the mind of the creator" (*Defence* 485), echoing Wordsworth, who, amidst the modern advertisements of his Preface to *Lyrical Ballads*, speaks of representing "the passions . . . incorporated with the beautiful and permanent forms of nature" (743–44). Years later, in *The Excursion*, his Wanderer raises the stakes to say that these "Forms / Of nature" embody a "pure principle" (4.1208–13). The Neoplatonic tilt of this natural formalism also draws Coleridge's thinking about aesthetic representation: "The ideal consists in the happy balance of the generic with the individual. The former [I think Coleridge is punning on the function, too] makes the character representative and symbolical . . . The latter gives it its *living* interest. . . . '*Forma formans per formam formatam translucens*' [The forming form shining through the formed form] is the definition and perfection of *ideal* art" (*Biographia* 2: 214–15); "Something there must be to realize the form, something in and by which the *forma informans* reveals itself" ("Principles of Genial Criticism" 238).

Coleridge, Wordsworth, and Shelley try to locate aesthetic work along routes of commerce between abstract principle and specific event, so that metaphysical form, embodied form, and poetic form might have open congress with one another in a capacious mimesis. In the field of Romantic writing, however, impasses are conspicuous and contradictions loom.[46] These are perhaps most acute for Shelley, whom Wordsworth judged "one of the best *artists* of us all . . . in workmanship of style" and "the greatest master of harmonious verse in our modern literature."[47] The poignant contradiction of such mastery is Shelley's repeated drive beyond poetic forms to "the eternal, the infinite, and the one" (483)—the realm his *Defence* designates as the origin of the poet's authority and his art; "in language or in form," poetry can only attempt to arrest and veil the "spirit of its forms" (505). It is, correspondingly, the poet's mind and not its poetry that Shelley idealizes as "the mirror upon which all forms are reflected and in which they compose one form" in the Preface to *Prometheus Unbound* (135). In this rule by an idea of "one form," multiple and changeable forms, poetic and otherwise, may evoke an abundance of temporal reflections. Thus, the poet of *Hymn to Intellectual Beauty* dedicates himself to worship "every form containing" this ideal (81–82), and the poet of *Epipsychidion* proposes an (androcentric) erotic liberalism that refuses a sepulchral temporal confinement to "one object, and one form" (172). Yet these and a host of other poems lament even as they theorize this pluralism, sensing it as the reflex of a fugitive and inaccessible unity. Searching for "one form resembling" the "idol of [his] thought," the poet of *Epipsychidion*, "half bewildered by new forms," is betrayed by the plurality of "mortal forms" (250–68).

The language of form has a double operation in these scenes, at once casting an intellectual ideal and, in its attenuated apprehension and representation, exposing an unstable rationale for poetic formalism. The dilemma is not Shelley's alone. Despite over-credited claims such as Anthony Easthope's that "Romantic theory is founded on precisely [a] misrecognition" of representation (123) that left "poetic discourse . . . unproblematized as aesthetic, formal and natural" (23),[48] Romantic texts are more various than monolithic, and their poetic practices are alert to form as a construction. It is hardly the case, for instance, that canonical texts such as the Preface to *Lyrical Ballads* show how "at a stroke, all the specific forms of enunciation that make poetry poetry are rendered accidental to it" and "dismissed" (123). Wordsworth does define poetry as "the spontaneous overflow of powerful feelings" (*LB* 744), but also pauses more than once over what its deliberate forming in meter signifies. He is, moreover, very aware of the signifying value of form per se in his experimental poetics, and what is at stake in an overt refusal of traditional contracts about poetic form. In a vocabulary keyed to the lexicon, Wordsworth states his terms directly at the start: reflecting on the first edition, he congratulates himself for having "formed no very inaccurate estimate of the probable effect of those poems" (741), going on to say that if it "is supposed, that by the act of writing in verse an Author makes a *formal* engagement that he will gratify certain known habits of association," then the resistant practices that he has undertaken "to *perform*" are bound to seem aberrant (742–43, my italics). Form abides as reform.

While his myth of "rural occupations" as the social site where "the passions" are most fully incorporated "with the beautiful and permanent forms of nature" (743–44) had its own illusions, Wordsworth's commitment to it entailed decisions about form that he knew would be provocative. "The clue to his *poetical* theory, in some of its questionable details, may be found in his

political principles; these had been democratical," recalls Christopher Wordsworth (1: 127). Charles James Fox, though a Whig radical, regretted seeing
the measure that conveyed the lofty meditations of *Tintern Abbey* also used for
the humble tales of *Michael* and *The Brothers*: "I am no great friend to blank
verse for subjects which are to be treated of with simplicity," he confessed to
Wordsworth (ibid. 1: 172). This affront was calculated: Wordsworth originally
cast *Michael* as a ballad, a "low" form, then decided to democratize his blank
verse. This is a move that reverses Eagleton's and Easthope's polarities: far
from obscuring the artifice of form, Wordsworth motivates his commitments
to confront and reform certain codes in the institution of literature, and to
challenge, thereby, implied class claims and associations.

At the same time, these polemics are beset by contradictions, especially
about the rationale for meter. The one habit of association that Wordsworth
does preserve is his commitment to "metrical language" as an "exponent or
symbol" of the poetic contract (*LB* 742). Not only do these habitual forms
throughout the volume contradict the Preface's polemically modern insistence
on the spontaneous and organic origination of poetry, but in 1800, there was
a further political embarrassment in this metrical standard's seeming collabo-
ration with any number of conservative eighteenth-century theorists. A contrary essay published in 1796 in the liberal *Monthly Magazine* asked in its title,
"*Is Verse essential to Poetry?*" and stayed to answer, "Whatever is the natural
and proper expression of any conception or feeling in metre or rhyme, is its
natural and proper expression in prose" (455).[49]

The question is politically infused: it is only the elitism of some poets, this
essay contends, that effects the "exclusive appropriation of the term *poetry*, to
verse." With "arrogant assumption," this "ambitious race" of writers, "not
satisfied with holding the almost undisputed possession of the first division in
the ranks of literary merit, have . . . conjured up a wall of separation between
themselves and other writers. Fancying the inhabitants of this consecrated inclosure a privileged order, they have been accustomed to look down, with a
kind of senatorial haughtiness, upon the prose-men, who inhabit the common
of letters, as a vulgar, plebeian herd." In these class politics, the "monopoly"
of verse over the domain of poetry in the "republic of letters" is as "arbitrary"
as any of the linguistic signs "used to express the description of objects," and
metrical composition is the ally of a dubiously "consecrated inclosure" (453).
The essay proceeds to undermine the "solid foundation" of meter both as sign
and agent of poetry's "privileged order." The strategy is to expose the self-
subverting irony of the terms of privilege by converting class distinction into
generic constriction, revealing esteemed "inclosure" as imprisonment: there
is no aesthetic basis for "confining the productions of the muses within the
enclosure of measured lines" (453), "the narrow inclosure of metre" (455).

The analogy to class politics is scarcely casual, for in the 1790s the privileged orders, alarmed by the Revolution abroad and its reverberations at home, were retrenching and shoring up their vulnerable privileges. The word *inclosure* is particularly charged, for this decade was also witnessing an acceleration in the enclosure of open fields and common lands, acts of definition and discrimination that at once served the interests of landowners and produced wide-scale misery in the dispossessed "plebeian herd."[50]

In addressing the aesthetic difference obtruded by metrical composition, Romantic poets enter key debates—about the origin of poetic form and the status of poetic language, as well as about the agency of poetic form in examining other cultural forms. Questions about the significance and function of meter press on just about every poet with an inclination to theorize.[51] Wordsworth's 1802 Preface asserts that there "neither is, nor can be, any essential difference between the language of prose and metrical composition" (*LB* 749). Yet all the poems have a metrical line, and even in 1800 Wordsworth argued the case, contending that "the perception of similitude in dissimilitude" produced by this formalism is essential to poetic, or for that matter, any kind of pleasure. This "principle" not only generates "the sexual appetite, and all the passions connected with it," but on it also "depend our taste and our moral feelings" (756). In a long addendum in the 1802 Preface, he even theorizes meter in terms that risk contradicting his idealization of rural life, describing its dissimilitude as part of the poetic "distinction" that "will entirely separate the composition from the vulgarity and meanness of ordinary life" (750).

Coleridge (despite valuing "organic" over "mechanical form") is never apologetic or defensive about metrical difference and distinction, frankly advertising his commitment to the difference inscribed by its formation: "I write in metre, because I am about to use a language different from that of prose" (*Biographia* 2: 69). Although he emphatically disdained the criterion of "superficial *form*" by which any construction in rhyme and meter may be called poetry (2: 11–12), he insisted that poetry required engagement with some rule of form:

Imagine not I am about to oppose Genius to Rules—No!—the Comparative value of these Rules is the very cause to be tried.—The Spirit of Poetry like all other living Powers, must of necessity circumscribe itself by Rules, were it only to unite Power with Beauty. It must embody in order to reveal itself. . . . This is no discovery of Criticism—it is a necessity of the human mind—& all nations have felt & obeyed it, in the invention of metre, & measured Sounds, as the vehicle ⟨& Involucrum⟩ of Poetry. (*Lectures* 1: 494)[52]

Perfectly Coleridgean is the formalist antipathy of one of the self-described "last romantics" to free verse as, paradoxically, an inhibition of self-expression:

"Because I need a passionate syntax for passionate subject-matter," writes Yeats, "I compel myself to accept those traditional metres that have developed with the language" (522). With similar caution, Arthur Symons's retrospect on the Romantic movement argued that the "laxer" form of prose, "not, indeed, bound by formal laws at all," effects a release from "limits" that is as much a "danger" as a "privilege" (4–5). A respect for restraint and balance persists in the "New Formalism" of the 1980s, whose practitioners value traditional forms as a kind of antidote to the immediacy of self and culture and thus a "mediation between public feeling and private expression."[53] In the decade of *The Well Wrought Urn*, such sense possessed Allen Tate, who insisted (in his pointedly titled *Reason in Madness*) that "the formal qualities of a poem are the focus of a specifically critical judgment because they partake of an objectivity that the subject matter, abstracted from the form, wholly lacks" (110).[54]

These cautionary turns to form are not so much anti- as late-Romantic. Shelley's *Defence*, for all its aspiration to the spirit over the material of form, turns out to include a defense of meter, too. Meaning to set aside the "vulgar error" of distinguishing "between poets and prose writers" and to consider only "the distinction between measured and unmeasured language" (484), he had to concede that most poets, at least, have chosen to express the harmonies of imagination in "arrangements of language, and especially metrical language" (483). And Keats, despite his belief that "if Poetry comes not as naturally as the Leaves to a tree it had better not come at all" (*KL* 1: 238–39), appeals to the cultural standard of poetry as measured verse when he begins his rhymed and artfully stanzaic "Lines on Seeing a Lock of Milton's Hair" by hailing Milton as the "Chief of organic Numbers"—the epithet insisting on measure, whatever the organic justification.[55] Byron's formalism not only signed on to the metrical contract but flaunted a fondness for the additional form of rhyme: "Good workmen never quarrel with their tools," he declares (*Don Juan* 1.201), implying that failure to rhyme is not only a default of craft but a contamination of genre.[56] These commitments echo in Frost's famous declaration to Brooks and Robert Penn Warren: "I'd as soon write free verse as play tennis with the net down. I want something there—the other thing—something to hold and something for me to put a strain on; and I'd be lost in the air with just cutting loose" ("Craft" 203). Punning with "put a strain on," Frost makes poetic performance a definition against "something there—the other thing." "Let chaos storm! / Let cloud shapes swarm! / I wait for form," is the cry of his Pertinax, tenaciously submitting *storm* and *swarm* to the already articulated "form" of rhymed iambics.[57]

In the Romantic precursors, such senses of poetic form as material and constructed can operate in complicated and unstable alignment with—or put a strain on—theories of informing principle (and there is a classical basis for this instability as well).[58] A revealing crux is blank verse. Milton famously troped it as liberty from bondage, and Dryden offered several views, variously disagreeing (it is still "fetter'd" and "constrain'd" by numbers), worrying about the implication (it is too allied to impulses "Wild and Lawless"), finding it "nearest Nature" in its imitation of "ordinary conversation," or de-poeticizing it (it is "more properly, *Prose Mesurée*").[59] Some recent critiques, focusing on the discourse that opposes blank verse to "Art and Order" and allies it with "Nature," discern an ideological practice that conceals the status of the form as production and thus conspires (as in the ideology of "organic form") with mystified interests. This is Easthope's line. Yet in blank-verse practice after Milton, the issue was precisely its artifice. Dryden stresses the art as much as the illusion, calling it "Poetick Prose," "measur'd Prose," and both Wordsworth and Byron thought it "the most difficult," not the most natural, form to write—"infinitely the most difficult," said Wordsworth.[60] Eighteenth-century theories of elocution frequently insisted that it had to be recited so as to distinguish its formal art from prose.[61] In this line, too, Wordsworth argued that "as long as verse shall have the marked termination that rhyme gives it, and as long as blank verse shall be printed in lines, it will be Physically impossible to pronounce the last words or syllables of the lines" without giving them "an intonation of one kind or an other, or to follow them with a pause, not called out for by the passion of the subject, but by the passion of the metre merely" (*Letters EY* 434).

This sense of formal agency appears in such famous claims as Wordsworth's equation of poetry with the "spontaneous overflow of powerful feeling," for it turns out that feeling itself is "formed" by "habits of meditation" (Preface, *LB* 744). Formal agency even manages to figure into one of Romanticism's most innovative, seemingly antiformalist projects: autobiography. Its subjective poetics seem the vital antithesis of fixed form (originary, organic, spontaneous), but Wordsworth, for one, stages the subject in important ways both as constituted and made legible by form—a texture refuting Easthope's claim that Romanticism epitomizes the illusion of the subject appearing "fully present to itself in a signified without a signifier, a represented without means of representation," in language "virtually untrammelled" by "specific forms of enunciation" (123). An early draft of *The Prelude* displays just this canny trammeling, and not merely by force of the reflexiveness of writing as a poet about becoming a poet—the "contradiction and complexity . . . inscribed in the very form of Wordsworth's text" that even Eagleton regards as "a condition of [its] superior value."[62] It does so with what Eagleton calls "a certain curvature in the ideological space in which texts play"—a play that Wordsworth shapes with the word *form* itself.

This word first appears in the verse in the same paragraph in which the autobiographer tries to formulate the import of several immediately previous

recollections of boyhood thefts. Each theft, he reflects, had recoiled in an arrest of the self by a formative discipline:

> The mind of man is fashioned & built up
> Even as a strain of music: I believe
> That there are spirits, which, when they would form
> A favored being, from his very dawn
> Of infancy do open out the clouds
> As at the touch of lightning, seeking him
> With gentle visitation[.] quiet Powers!
> Retired and seldom recognized, yet kind,
> And to the very meanest not unknown;
> With me, though rarely,
> They communed: others too there are who use,
> Yet haply aiming at the selfsame end,
> Severer interventions, ministry
> More palpable, and of their school was I.   (MS V, 3ʳ: 67–80)

Just as palpable is the work of form, signaled by the placement of the word
itself at the turn of the line, and framed by the way the paragraph that ends
with "I" begins with a figure of self as the intentional formation of other powers. The poetic "I" comes into being in form cast as a system that precedes it,
takes possession of it, and defines it. There is no better demonstration of Stuart Curran's claim that poetic form was an "inescapable . . . necessity for Romantic subjectivity, a ground for either commitment or disengagement, but
always a ground for self-mirroring and self-creation" (*Poetic Form* 216). Yet, if
knowing the self involves recognizing the self through form, this is no smooth
or untroubled ground in Wordsworth's text. For one, the analogy to musical
composition is shifty: as a strain in music, the self is composed—fashioned
and built up by formal relations—but since the author of this passage is himself a composer, these spirits and powers of formation, although projected as
external in agency, also imply his present act of autobiographical fashioning.
The powers that form the mind, that is, are staged in a scene of which the
poet's mind is not just a reflector but the formulator.

   This kind of reflexivity animates many sophisticated autobiographies; what
distinguishes Wordsworth's enactment is the way his verse form operates as a
trope for its own formalism: the lines above appear in the manuscript as a
blank-verse sonnet-stanza.[63] Although later versions do not preserve this form,
the textual archeology is telling, for it shows how deeply Wordsworth's autobiographical investigation is tuned to a sense of self as a composition of
forms.[64] The story of Romanticism and poetic forms, as we shall see, is fundamentally involved with these sorts of dialectics and the oscillations into
which they sometimes fall—between projects to manage information through
the service of form and recognitions of the information produced by the agency

of form itself. Not only do these turns implicate and mutually define one another, but in certain critical stages of negotiation they challenge distinction.[65]

Critical Stages

My chapters feature texts that shape poetic form into its own critical statement, by force of experimental agenda or traditions pressed to new extremes. In these actions, I show how formalist poetics and practices can set the grain of aesthetics against dominant ideologies and their contradictions, even as (in the story we hear today) they are shaped by them.

The chapter on Blake shows his earliest, unilluminated volume, *Poetical Sketches* (1780), predicting many of the key issues of Romantic formalist theory and practice, as Blake draws its formal actions into visual, rhetorical, and ultimately political registers of significance. I turn next to some of the theoretical issues of poetic form brought into focus by the career of Coleridge's ambivalent engagement with simile, a rhetorical form with implications for poetic practice. Coleridge, I argue, confronts the patent constructedness of simile in ways that urge him to address the very foundations of poetic form. I then follow the forms of revision that come to possess and virtually define Wordsworth's autobiography, showing how his perpetual revision contends with the poetic text and its poetic "self" as historically disjunctive forms prone to open-ended transformation, and confronts these transformations, in turn, as disclosers of new gaps and uncertainties in the imagined originary moment.

A concern with the self as a decentered textual form also focuses my chapter on Byron, in which I examine how a seemingly perverse but deliberate choice of the heroic couplet—a model of formal decorum—to tell the tale of a heroic outlaw in *The Corsair*, tests the force of dominant forms (social and literary) in the poetics and politics of opposition. Keats wrestles with the issue of self and form at a revelatory moment in his late career—as the writer of personal lyrics to Fanny Brawne. Moving away from (maybe beyond) the formalism of "Great Odes" of 1819—those poems seemingly destined for high New Critical formalism—these later lyrics, caught up in psychological crises and historical contingencies, thwart Keats's dearest charge to poetic form as a means of masculine mastery and poetic self-definition. My final chapter concerns Shelley's effort to invest poetic performance with social agency. Here, I examine the consequences in two seemingly opposite but deeply related modes—the political exhortation of *The Mask of Anarchy* and the intimate addresses to Jane and Edward Williams—to show how Shelley personalizes the social and socializes the personal with reciprocal questions about the service of poetic form to poetic authority. This crisis is an appropriate conclusion for the study as a whole, for Shelley's socially contextualized poetic forms write an agenda for a contextualized formalist criticism.

In order that I may concentrate on distinctive textures of engagement, these discussions are necessarily selective. But I mean them to be productively so, suggesting how other texts can be read to extend and elaborate the argument at hand. Another selection is my focus on the poets who have been "canonical" for most of our century's study of Romanticism. I do not assume this canon uncritically, but I locate this study in it because it is the reference and deep background of modern and post-modern debates about poetic form, and therefore my necessary ground for addressing charges that the forms of canonical Romantic texts matter only in terms of a culturally determined aesthetic ideology.[66] I mean to show how these texts submit cultural information to the pressure of aesthetic practice, and in so doing not only contribute to the cultural text but apply their own critical intelligence.

My argument is that Romanticism's involvement with poetic form, in its contentious theorizing and in divergent practices, participates in central discussions of its historical moment: the relation between "nature" and "art"; the economy of self, culture, and tradition in literary language; the question of form as resource or restraint, as enabling order or coercive design; the sense of literary and, by implication, any authority as structured and informed as well as individually exerted; and the articulation of form, not merely as a product of social evaluations, but as a social evaluation itself, one of the texts in which culture is written. My deepest claim is that language shaped by poetic form is not simply conscriptable as information for other frameworks of analysis; the forms themselves demand a specific kind of critical attention. Whatever our critical interest, aesthetic or sociohistorical or both, our accounts of Romanticism can only benefit from a careful reading of the formal charges.

Chapter 2

🐾 Sketching Verbal Form
Blake's *Poetical Sketches*

*In the Fifth chamber were Unnam'd forms, which
cast the metals into the expanse.
There they were receiv'd by Men who occupied
the sixth chamber, and took the forms of books &
were arranged in libraries.*
—Blake, "A Memorable Fancy," *The Marriage of Heaven and Hell*

*Here alone I in books form'd of me-
-tals
Have written the secrets of wisdom*
—Blake, *The Book of Urizen*

One Central Form Composed of all other Forms being Granted it
does not therefore follow that all other Forms are Deformity. . . . Here
he loses sight of a Central Form. & Gets into Many Central Forms.
—Blake, annotations to Reynolds's *Discourses*

Blake's privileging of writing makes him less interesting to deconstruction because it makes his work less resistant to its strategies. Everything is open to view.
—Paul de Man, in conversation[1]

Lines and Outlines, Forms and Deformity

At first glance, *Poetical Sketches* averts critical attention. Not only does the title mark a provisional, even casual, composition, done in a few strokes, but its Advertisement begs indulgence for "irregularities and defects . . . in almost every page" of this unrevised "production of untutored youth" (ii).[2] It is, moreover, one of Blake's few unengraved, unilluminated volumes. Yet from the performative charge of this debut, and from its shaping by an imagination already engaged with visual art, there emerges a complex formalist poetic, one involving self-fashioning, poetic tradition, and the work of cultural formation.[3] This very range is energized by opposing attitudes toward form: a political impatience with any "bound or outward circumference / of Energy" (*The Marriage of Heaven and Hell*, plate 4), and an artistic respect for form. "Nature has no Outline: / but Imagination has," declares his epigraph for *The*

Ghost of Abel (*BPP* 270)—a poem from the early 1820s dedicated "To LORD BYRON in the Wilderness," and the epitome of Blake's life-long conviction that the "Reality" of "Every Thing . . . Is its Imaginative Form" (*BPP* 663–64).[4] Notions of form, forms, Form, and formation are everywhere limned in Blake's designs and illuminations, and the vocabulary itself claims an important place in his lexicon.[5]

Poetical Sketches is an early stage of Blake's poetics and the politics of "Imaginative Form," as well as a forecast of later Romantic negotiations with formalism. "Under historical conditions of modernity," Donald Wesling argues, "poetry and commentators are alike meshed in a contradictory structure of thought wherein the highest twin values are the corporeality and the transparency of the medium of language. Poetic form under these conditions is transparent yet insistent, at once a scandal and one of the central issues of post-Romantic poetics" (*Chances* 12). That this "modern" condition is one of Romanticism itself is clear in Blake's *Sketches*, whose critical force in the pre-Revolutionary moment of "the Year MDCCLXXXIII"[6] concentrates on these tensed twin values. Blake is producing poetic form as a medium for a poet's voice; at the same time, his "sketches" provoke attention to form itself—its organization on the page and its status as a motivated and malleable construction, not only in the domain of the aesthetic but also in the habitual formations of self, nation, and history. These different practices bear different values. At times, the forms Blake uses to shape his poetic performance suggest the poet's complicity or entanglement in larger cultural practices; at other times, he mobilizes his forms to expose contingency and a potential for reform. *Poetical Sketches* may draw its artistry in lines of resistance to conventional forms; or it may ironize resistance itself as a conventional form of self-display. In all these events as well as in their aggregate, we see that Blake's formalist practices define no static aesthetic. They are actions that call readers to a critical awareness of the work of form, not only in poetic but also in cognitive, social, and historical processes.

This rhetoric of form involves a textuality whose emergence by the middle of the sixteenth century John Hollander has described: the way "the look of the poem on the page had begun to assume a canonical importance, and patterns of versification and typographical arrangement to play a small but definite role in the history of form" (*Vision and Resonance* 268). *Poetical Sketches* is alert to this "look," and Blake's later illuminated texts fully realize it, although here, the actual visual art is so remarkable that the visual rhetoric of their scripts may recede from notice. It is worth reading some of these scripts, however, because the semiotics of their graphic designs are allied to the formalist experiments of *Poetical Sketches*.[7] Blake's page is a "composite art," Vincent De Luca argues, involving not just the interplay of visual and verbal but also the play of verbal *as* visual.[8] At its most extreme pitch, such as the "wall of words" engraved on the plates of *Jerusalem*, the verbal design assaults percep-

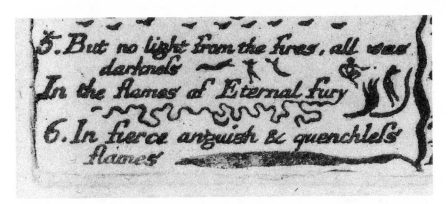

Figure 1. William Blake, detail from *The First Book of Urizen*. Blake's five-line arrangement of these two verses (Chapter III: 5–6), argues the Santa Cruz Study Group, encourages a reading for vertical as well as linear relationships. Copy B, Bentley plate 5, courtesy of The Pierpont Morgan Library, New York, PML 63139.

tion as an agency in "the sublime effect of the poetry itself." In lesser events, too, the effect of mixing pictorial and alphabetic signifiers is to induce "the eye to pictorialize the verbal portion of the plate," diverting attention "from a sequential pursuit of words and lines to a visual contemplation of the whole block of text as a single unit, a panel" (89–90). In both their presence and their form, Blake's scripts are designed with a semantic beyond the semantics of words. This scriptive signifying operates in lines, in discrete words, even in syllables. Thus, the usual editorial practice of "disregarding Blake's original line shape," contends the Santa Cruz Study Group, "does violence to the visual semiotics of Blake's printed page." Their case is a set of lines from *The Book of Urizen*, chapter III, at the bottom left column, plate 5 (see Fig. 1). Noting that letterpress editions (Erdman's in particular) typically straighten these lines to end with *darkness* and *flames*, the Study Group regrets the effacement of the way Blake has arranged the words to read "up and down as well as across," the "vertical relationships imply[ing] a connection between 'no light / darkness,' 'darkness / flames,' and 'fierce / flames'" (306–7).

W. J. T. Mitchell sees this "graphic potential" even in the verging of letters on a "pictorial" value in which "the sensuous surface of calligraphic and typographic forms" suggests "symbolic values." On the title page of *The Marriage of Heaven and Hell*, for instance, the flowing and embellished script of *Marriage* (and, I would add, of the linking *of* and *and*) against the austere Roman capitals of *Heaven* and *Hell* shows Blake "literally embod[ying] in the calligraphic form of 'marriage' the symbolic marriage his 'types' prefigure in the text" ("Visible Language" 83–84). Mitchell has less to say about *Urizen*, feeling that the design of its plates enforces an "increasing separation of tex-

Figure 2. William Blake, detail from *The First Book of Urizen*, Chapter II (mislabeled on this plate). Blake's unorthodox hyphenation of "metals" as "me-/-tals" in verse 6 effects a form of poetic enjambment that semantically isolates the syllable "me." Copy B, Bentley plate 4, courtesy of The Pierpont Morgan Library, New York, PML 63139.

tual and pictorial space" (its crowded two-column format, miming an open book, casts the text as "a strictly verbal, nonpictorial form" [*Composite* 110]). But Robert Essick has discerned an interesting event even in this form. At the bottom of the left-hand column of plate 4 (chap. I), appears a staggered sentence (see Fig. 2).[9] As Blake's etching approached the center margin, Essick surmises, the constraints of his medium "dictated" a necessary hyphenation. Working with the fact that his books "are not just 'formd of me-/-tals'; they are formed *by* the very nature of those metals and the material processes he employed," Blake let his medium "express its own tendencies" with the syllabic form, *me-/-tals*. And by virtue of the fact that "words are composed of a sequence of phonemes and graphemes, any part of which may also be a word," his inscription "generates textual meanings": "An 'accident' resulting from an essential feature of Blake's method of publication has produced a word ('me') with its own associations and contributions to the *Book of Urizen*" (215–16).

The only adjustment I would make to this subtle reading is to propose that the forming of *me-* is no accident at all, but a deliberate choice informed by Blake's sense, so Eliot puts it (writing about Shakespeare), that "verse, whatever else it may or may not be, is itself a system of *punctuation*" in which "the usual marks . . . are differently employed" (letter to *TLS*, his italics). Like enjambment, hyphenation can become a meaningful form. Plate 4 shows that Blake could have put all the letters of *metals* on his next line without leaving a conspicuous blank (his center margin is more erose than regular); or, having embellished other spaces, he could have done so here; or he could have used the customary hyphenation, "met-als" But releasing *me-* from *metals* yields distinct semantic advantages. On the most local level, the phoneme frames the line with a fleeting, but wittily punning, mirror of its preceding sign of self, "I": "Here alone I in books formd of me." Blake's literal forming of *me-* gains further semantic value across *The Book of Urizen* as an ironic limning of Uri-

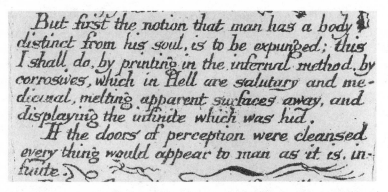

But first the notion that man has a body distinct from his soul, is to be expunged; this I shall do, by printing in the infernal method, by corrosives, which in Hell are salutary and medicinal, melting apparent surfaces away, and displaying the infinite which was hid.
If the doors of perception were cleansed every thing would appear to man as it is, in-finite.

Figure 3. William Blake, detail from *The Marriage of Heaven and Hell*, plate 14. This hyphenation of "me-," orthodox as it is, serves an infernal printing method that displays the "me" hid in the medicinal corrosives of Blake's practices with words. Copy C, courtesy of The Pierpont Morgan Library, New York, PML 17559.

zen's self-involuted knowledge, his tendency to read himself into and in the form of his book. The peculiar phonemic event of *me-* shapes a brief graphic icon of the attitude imaged in the self-concentrated scribe on the title page— "a self-portrait of the artist as a solitary reader and writer of texts, a figure of the textual solipsist" (Mitchell, "Visible" 56).

Blake indulges a similar textual play on plate 14 of *The Marriage of Heaven and Hell* (see Fig. 3). The corrosive action of this verse (again, erased in Erdman's editorial transcription [*BPP* 39]) is its demonstration of "I shall do" in the placement of the phoneme "me-" in a salutary Hell, whose fires melt away habitual lexical surfaces to display the artist's sign for himself in the medicine he prescribes. This is a formalism in which "Every word and / every letter is studied and put into its fit place" (*Jerusalem*, plate 3), in which "a Line or Lineament is not formed by Chance" but is "Itself & Not Intermeasurable with or by any Thing Else" (April 12, 1827; *BPP* 783). In these formations of *me-* from the constraints of a pre-existing material, Blake may seem to anticipate Jacques Derrida's deconstruction of the subject as a function of language ("Différance" 145–46), or even Roland Barthes' claim that it is language only that "acts, 'performs,' and not 'me'" ("Death" 143). Yet the writerly presence of Blake's hyphen, even as it distills its *me-* in a material script, also resists resigning all authority to the text. The idiosyncratic hyphenation shows how forms of writing can impress the self in writing in ways that paradoxically elude deconstruction by language, medium, or sheer textuality. The graphic expression of *me-* becomes a meta-graphic formation of a poet seizing his line to assert new forms against received structures of grammar, syntax, and verbal integrity.

This visual rhetoric is already being exercised in *Poetical Sketches*, where conventions are deformed by poetic self-inscription. Blake confronts his readers with stanza forms that violate their paradigms ("An Imitation of Spencer"); quatrains and ballad stanzas that refuse rhyme or impose dissonant eye rhymes; rhythms and shifting caesurae that strain against or even defy conventional metrical patterns, and lines whose patently unorthodox stops aggravate an indulgence of enjambment that was already controversial in neoclassical aesthetics:

> O thou, who passest thro' our vallies in
> Thy strength . . . ("To Summer")

> Smile on our loves; and, while thou drawest the
> Blue curtains of the sky . . . ("To the Evening Star")

> Rouz'd like a huntsman to the chace; and, with
> Thy buskin'd feet, appear upon our hills . . . ("To Morning")

> When the whirlwind of fury comes from the
> Throne of God . . . ("Prologue . . . King Edward the Fourth")

> "The narrow bud opens her beauties to
> "The sun, and love runs in her thrilling veins;
> "Blossoms hang round the brows of morning, and
> "Flourish down . . . ("To Autumn")

In the same year these sketches were printed, 1783, Dr. Johnson published his complaint about blank verse being "verse only to the eye." Blake's shaping of his line reverses the valuation, as if from Milton's own description of "sense variously drawn out from one Verse into another" he meant to show the visual potential of "sense" and "drawn out." [10] "The Style that Strikes the Eye is the True Style," he retorts to Reynolds (*BPP* 638), and he elaborates a remark of Berkeley to insist that "Forms must be apprehended by the Sense or the Eye of Imagination" (664).

Satirically theorizing a politics of meter, Robert Graves proposes that "metre considered as a set pattern approved by convention will stand for the claims of society," "the variations on metre" for "the claims of the individual," and "conservatism" for "a jealous maintenance of metre in its strictest usage" (24). What was satire on a cliché in 1925 was taken in earnest by Blake in the 1780s. For some readers of his *Sketches*, such as Osbert Burdett, the "faint irregularity" of Blake's metrics, "waving now toward and now away from the normal measure," is "captivating" (14). But opinion is divided. To Crabb Robinson, the "metre is usually so loose and careless as to betray a total ignorance of the art, whereby the larger part of the poems are rendered singularly rough and unattractive" (Bentley 163). Whatever the reaction, it is clear that Blake's poetics, particularly his poetics of the line, challenge habitual contracts about poetic form. This challenge is most radical in the prose sketches at the back of the volume, forms not properly "poetic" at all, but posing a stylistic redefinition.

Yet throughout *Poetical Sketches*, Blake exerts variation against convention, and innovation against prescription, in ways that test the artist's forms against the authority of cultural and social forms. The master-term "Sketch," in this respect, bears into literary practice some of the social and performative aspects of the salon recitations that preceded the poems' circulation in print.[11] To claim authority as poet, Blake interplays tradition and individual talent, creating in the forms of his "sketches" performances that are as skillful with tradition as they are self-consciously "modern." Well ahead of Eliot, he understood the production of "tradition" by the modern moment—or even Michael Riffaterre's paradox: while "the poetic text is interpreted as a departure from a norm" (he is thinking of an "imaginary nonliterary norm," but literary tradition will also suffice), the "norm is in effect deduced or even retroactively fantasized, from the text perceived as departure" (164). A corollary is de Man's deconstruction of "modernity" as itself historical: it is not only "the principle that gives literature duration and historical existence," but it depends on history for its self-definition; indeed, "the more radical the rejection of anything that came before, the greater the dependence on the past" (de Man, "Literary History" 161–62). These involutions play into the performances of *Poetical Sketches*, which use tradition to ironize as well as to legitimate the display of innovation.

Blake's formalist poetics gain semantic value not only in these turns with tradition but also in the way they compel a reader's involvement in the play of forms. This intertextual field of activity—both across literary history and within the volume's field of repetition, echo and parody—is more important than the question of Blake's actual ordering of the sketches.[12] For rather than yielding a stable, unified image of the cryptic sketcher, "W.B.," the volume sketches various interactions. The correlative to this unnamed and unfixed authorial form is the sketcher's production of his reader, the intelligence in which these formal actions are registered and received.

Blank Verse and the Call to the Reader's Eye

Poetical Sketches repeatedly relates its aesthetic forms to issues of power—the power of poetic voice, of natural forces, of imagination, of social and political systems. The season poems at its front are a series of progressive experiments in poetic power that involve their reader in the play of its forms and at the same time encourage such a reader to reflect on the power and limitations of form itself. The reflection is important, because its issues will be replayed, with more darkly critical elaboration, in the social and political situations of later sketches.

In his initial test of poetic power, Blake casts the form of his verse line for apprehension by a reader's eye in a way that turns out to contribute to the authority of the poet's invocation. Here is the opening call of "To Spring," the first poem of this set:

> O thou, with dewy locks, who lookest down
> Thro' the clear windows of the morning; turn
> Thine angel eyes upon our western isle,
> Which in full choir hails thy approach, O Spring! (1–4)

Geoffrey Hartman notes in all the season poems an "intensely vocative" poetics related to a "sense of poetical vocation." Jonathan Culler discerns a more specific self-constitution in apostrophe: "The object is treated as a subject, an *I* which implies a certain type of *you* in its turn. One who successfully invokes nature is one to whom nature might, in its turn, speak. . . . Thus, invocation is a figure of vocation. . . . voice calls in order to be calling, to dramatize its calling, to summon images of its power so as to establish its identity as poetical and prophetic voice." [13]

A reiterated phrase in Culler's account, "in its turn," is a fortuitous key to the production of a reading audience to complement these images of poetic power (*pace* Hollander's claim that invocation, as a sign of "poetry's discourse with itself," excludes "an audience or an active agent which might respond to the imperatives by clearly observable action," *Melodious Guile* 79). With the turn of the line at the poem's first enjambment—"lookest down / Thro' the clear windows"—the reader's eye performs the action that the poet describes in imagination: at *down*, our eyes move down to the next line, the form of Blake's line making the preposition a directive for reading.[14] This readerly rhetoric invests the sketch with a kind of Barthesian "productivity"—a field "where the producer and reader of the text meet" and enter into "the play of signifiers" ("Theory of the Text" 36, 43). In Blake's text, such meetings lead to a potent fulfillment of the invocation at the very next point of enjambment: "turn / Thine . . . eyes." A reader's eyes must turn from one line to the next, an action that releases the poet's apostrophe from the fictive space of invocation into phenomenological agency. The *thou* invoked by the poet's voice is, referentially, the desired Spring, but in the action of his poetic line, it extends to readers, calling on them, in Wordsworth's phrase, to exert "a co-operating *power*" in the production of meaning (*Essay* [1815]; *Prose* 3: 81). If, as Hartman writes, the "very energy of anticipation" in Blake's poetry enables it to "envision what it calls for" ("Blake" 195), Blake's shaping of poetic form plays an important part by involving the reader in this envisioning.

The turn of verse to the next stanza expands the formalist agency of this invocation to evoke a sensation of a response from Spring itself. The new stanza proceeds from the close of the first on the assurance that a

> full choir hails thy approach, O Spring!
> The hills tell each other, and the list'ning
> Vallies hear; all our longing eyes are turned
> Up to thy bright pavillions: issue forth,
> And let thy holy feet visit our clime. (4–8)

The poetics of stanza two deftly draw the object of the call into the climate of the call. As *O Spring!* completes the syntax and closes the form of the first stanza, this terminal position pivots visually and syntactically as a transition into the next stanza's elaboration. Blake enhances this linking with the faint ad hoc rhyme of a split, interstanzaic couplet: *Spring/list'ning*, a chime that resonates semantically as an anticipatory joining of desire and event, of Spring and its expectation. This formal harmony, strengthened by the next line's *longing*, is sustained by a larger design of correspondence that the full syntax of "all our longing eyes are turned / Up to thy bright pavillions" brings into view. In a chiasmus extended across the first two stanzas, Blake mirrors his initial call to a "*thou* . . . who lookest *down*" to "*turn* / Thine angel *eyes up*on" in the image of "*our* longing *eyes . . . turned / Up.*" The second image does not merely describe desire but shapes a reciprocal poetic form to evoke its object. As the reader's eye turns down and back across the enjambment, the line itself turns back and up to the initial invocation, the entire network of events intensified by the cross-lingual Latin punning of its key word, *turn*, on the visual form that marks poetry itself: the turn of the verse line (*versus: turning*).[15]

Line-endings, Christopher Ricks shows in his remarkable reading of Wordsworth, "can be a type or symbol or emblem of what the poet values, as well as the instrument by which his values are expressed" (91), and they often use the blank space of the page as visual punctuation. Such blanks become the expectant vacancy into which Blake's call issues forth in stanza two (7), and in stanza three they pose anticipatory suspenses on the actions invoked by the enjambed syntaxes:

> Come o'er the eastern hills, and let our winds
> Kiss thy perfumed garments; let us taste
> Thy morn and evening breath; scatter thy pearls
> Upon our love-sick land that mourns for thee. (9–12)

"The eye puts a cheat upon the ear, by making us imagine a pause to exist where there is only vacancy to the eye," remarked John Walker in 1781 about the way Milton's enjambments break the coincidence of syntax and verse (*Elements* 2: 212). He means to advocate pronouncing blank verse without pausing at enjambed terminals, but Blake's "verse to the eye" of the reader motivates the visual semiotics of such "vacancy." Walker almost seems to intuit such effect when, in a later tract, he suggests that the customary term for the event at "the end of every line of verse," "the pause of suspension," should be a "visionary pause" (*Rhetorical Grammar* 174)—an apt term for what Blake produces in the next stanza:

> O deck her forth with thy fair fingers; pour
> Thy soft kisses on her bosom; and put
> Thy golden crown upon her languish'd head,
> Whose modest tresses were bound up for thee! (13–16)

These visionary semiotics are abetted by a melodious plot. In the previous stanza, there is a punning remedy for *mourn* in *morn*, and its force carries over as *pour* draws forward the soft chord of *o'er/morn/mourns* (9, 11–12) through *forth* to pause at an expressive enjambment of languorous delay, before the poem subsides in a harmonious metrical flow whose design bears as much on the poetry of "To Spring" as on its call to "Spring." Naming an audience bound up for Spring, Blake also binds his poetical pattern: "golden crown" chimes a distant rhyme with the first line's "lookest down"; the last *For thee!* recalls the initial *O thou* (as well as repeating itself in line 16 and echoing *forth* in 7 and 14); "let our winds / Kiss" mirrors "pour / Thy soft kisses"; the "dewy locks" of the first imagining of Spring are matched to the "modest tresses" of the waiting land. To apprehend these correspondences of reading is to see poetic form itself mobilized into a syntax for what its voice summons.

No wonder that the next poem, "To Summer," begins by repeating this vocative rhetoric and its appeal to correspondent readerly actions:

> O thou, who passest thro' our vallies in
> Thy strength, curb thy fierce steeds, allay the heat
> That flames from their large nostrils! thou, O Summer,
> Oft pitched'st here thy golden tent, and oft
> Beneath our oaks hast slept, while we beheld
> With joy, thy ruddy limbs and flourishing hair. (1–6)

This petition does not call to absence, but to a fiercely rushing presence that it would arrest. When one reader disparaged Blake's blank verse as "prose cut in slices," he registered an important effect.[16] These odd, prosey cuts enlist reading as an agent of arrest, halting the passage of the eye and its pursuit of the syntax: "throw thy / Silk draperies off" (11–12).

This arrest is also scripted by Blake's several repetitions. After the reiterative halting of the opening vocative, a term of temporal recurrence, *oft*, recurs to hold summer's golden tent in the verbal frame of the line:

> thou, O Summer,
> Oft pitched'st here thy golden tent, and oft
> Beneath our oaks hast slept, while we beheld . . . (3-5)

Beneath and *beheld* form a similar linear frame, tightening it with the etymological link of *beheld* to "holding." These tropings of frames anticipate the anaphora that Blake extends across the interstanzaic space to draw lines of sumptuous containment:

> Beneath our oaks hast slept, while we beheld
> With joy, thy ruddy limbs and flourishing hair.
>
> Beneath our thickest shades we oft have heard
> Thy voice, when noon upon his fervid car
> Rode o'er the deep of heaven; beside our springs
> Sit down, and in our mossy vallies, on
> Some bank beside a river clear, throw thy
> Silk draperies off, and rush into the stream:
> Our vallies love the Summer in his pride. (5-13)

At the start of this sequence, "Beneath . . . // Beneath . . . oft" (5-7) not only repeats but forms a chiasmus with "Oft . . . oft / Beneath" (4-5) to contain "Summer." As Blake modulates this prepositional design into a syntax of *beside*, he assists the poetics of delay by binding the line of "Our vallies love the Summer in his *pride*," a surplus of this singular seven-line stanza, to a soft but semantically important rhyme with *beside*.

Emerging from these holding patterns, and beginning with a sustained anaphora drawn from and incorporating this surplus line, the last stanza casts a network of phonic containments:

> Our bards are fam'd who strike the silver wire:
> Our youth are bolder than the southern swains:
> Our maidens fairer in the sprightly dance:
> We lack not songs, nor instruments of joy,
> Nor echoes sweet, nor waters clear as heaven,
> Nor laurel wreaths against the sultry heat. (14-19)

Blake's rhymes go beyond promising this laurel wreath; they shape a phonic version of it: his final *heat* chimes with *sweet*, a chord that echoes in *wreaths*, which in turn joins the chord of *beneath*; *heat*, moreover, rejoins its own *heat* at the end of line 2—drawing in a wreath of verbal attributes to hold the poetry of summer.

In "To Autumn," Blake takes this self-harvesting further by having the poem draw on the words and imagery of "To Summer," even repeating its three-stanza form:

> O Autumn, laden with fruit, and stained
> With the blood of the grape, pass not, but sit
> Beneath my shady roof, there thou may'st rest.
> And tune thy jolly voice to my fresh pipe;
> And all the daughters of the year shall dance!
> Sing now the lusty song of fruits and flowers.   (1–6)

In the next stanzas, the poet seems to propose a script for the song that he petitions:

> "The narrow bud opens her beauties to
> "The sun, and love runs in her thrilling veins;
> "Blossoms hang round the brows of morning, and
> "Flourish down the bright cheek of modest eve,
> "Till clust'ring Summer breaks forth into singing,
> "And feather'd clouds strew flowers round her head.
>
> "The spirits of the air live on the smells
> "Of fruit; and joy, with pinions light, roves round
> "The gardens, or sits singing in the trees."   (7–15)

But what we discover at line 16 is that the song proposed is already realized: "Thus sang the jolly Autumn." By a sleight of verse form, Blake has transformed invocation into event, vocative into response.[17]

*Pro*vocatively, Blake does not close "To Autumn" with Autumn's song, but with its situation in the impending bleakness it must sustain:

> Thus sang the jolly Autumn as he sat,
> Then rose, girded himself, and o'er the bleak
> Hills fled from our sight; but left his golden load.   (16–18)

The adjectival weight produced by the enjambment of "bleak/Hills" aptly anticipates similar effects in the poem this image prefigures, "To Winter":

> The north is thine; there hast thou built thy dark
> Deep-founded habitation.

In a punning grammar, the terminal *dark* first weighs in as a substantive (a metonym for winter) before the next line shows it modifying *habitation*. The effect is to intensify a sense of this season as one in which the contingent and the attributive usurp substance—so much so that the terminal word of the next stanza's first line, "He hears me not, but o'er the yawning *deep* / Rides heavy," tricks reading: "yawning deep" seems a double adjective for some as-yet-undesignated perilous expanse. The shock of the predicate, "Rides heavy," is that the seeming attribute is really the substance, the condition of a winter sublime and of the paralyzing depth of imagination it evokes.

"To Winter" presses the question of unforming and deforming even further by inverting and subverting the rhetoric of the previous three poems. Most obviously, the poet's call is not for advent, stay, and song, but for refrain, restraint, and retraction: "O Winter! bar thine adamantine doors." Robert F. Gleckner carefully shows how this poem echoes and deforms the previous season poems to turn their generative invocations into a "parodic antimyth" (70) wherein poetic power cancels itself, projects its undoing and ruin. "To Winter" thus looms as the shadow text of all invocation, imagining an audience moving without regard for how it is called. But it also counters this force by closing with an image of the cyclical negation of negation: "till heaven smiles, and the monster / Is driv'n yelling to his caves beneath mount Hecla." As a sign by form to sustain this anticipation, Blake visibly sketches "To Winter" in the pattern of "To Spring": a four-quatrain poem (the others have three longer stanzas).

Seasons need no poet for their advents and passings, and Blake's invocations know as much. These are ultimately tropes of audience, petitions answered by a supportive reader. In "To the Evening Star," Blake romances this reading by invoking an ideal of benignly "glimmering eyes" against the threat of more antagonistic glares:

> Thou fair-hair'd angel of the evening,
> Now, while the sun rests on the mountains, light
> Thy bright torch of love; thy radiant crown
> 4   Put on, and smile upon our evening bed!
> Smile on our loves; and, while thou drawest the
> Blue curtains of the sky, scatter thy silver dew
> On every flower that shuts its sweet eyes
> 8   In timely sleep. Let thy west wind sleep on
> The lake; speak si[l]ence with thy glimmering eyes,
> And wash the dust with silver. Soon, full soon,
> Dost thou withdraw; then the wolf rages wide,
> 12   And the lion glares thro' the dun forest:
> The fleeces of our flocks are cover'd with
> Thy sacred dew: protect them with thine influence.

This blank-verse sonnet impressed Alexander Gilchrist as an example of "poetic power and freshness quickening the imperfect, immature *form*" (1: 25, his italics); but the form is more accomplished than he recognizes, for it is "imperfect" in tacit reference, and resistance, to sonnet tradition. Not only does its most impressive enjambment, "let the wind sleep on / The lake" (8–9), occur exactly at the point where traditional sonnet form would close a unit, but its only gesture toward end-rhyme is a repetition of *eyes* (7, 9), as if insisting on "verse to the eye."

These subtle reforms constellate "To the Evening Star" into an experimental poise against the unsettling vulnerabilities of its temporal imagination

("Soon, full soon"). Note how the unusual anaphoric positioning of the very first rhyme, *Thou* . . . / *Now*, uses its formation across the line in tacit resistance to the impending dark close, by evoking the transition of light for which the poet petitions—its sound expanding into *mountains, crown, our, our, thou, flower, thou*, and counterpointed in the interwoven harmonies of *while* . . . *smile* . . . *Smile* . . . *while* . . . *sil*ence, and *sky, thy, eyes, timely*. This extravagant phonotext involves several semantically resonant enjambments. Aptly, the first of these verses for the eye has to do with vision:

> while the sun rests on the mountains, light
> Thy bright torch . . .

The cut not only exploits the blank space after *light* but also suspends grammar to make *light* seem adjectival to *mountains* (as if these looked light rather than heavy and dark) or adverbial to *rest*, as if it meant *lightly*. Our discovery that *light* is part of an imperative predicate is an emergence on the level of syntax that corresponds to the transfer of light for which the poet calls (and seems himself to spark with the quick rhyme of "*light* / Thy *bright*" across the turn). The shifting syntax—first seeming to image sun-lightened mountains, then petitioning evening starlight—evokes the subtle visual shifts of twilight, wherein forms shimmer in different aspects of perception. Indeed, evening is the brief coincidence of both kinds of light: "the theme is evening," writes Hartman, "but Blake's poetical energy has transformed it into an emblem of dawn" ("Discourse" 227).

This patent aesthetic transformation becomes the subject as well as the form of the next phase of invocation to the star:

> Smile on our loves; and, while thou drawest the
> Blue curtains of the sky, scatter thy silver dew
> On every flower that shuts its sweet eyes
> In timely sleep. Let thy west wind sleep on
> The lake; speak si[l]ence with thy glimmering eyes . . . (5–9)

Here Blake's cuts apply a formal, as opposed to grammatical, punctuation to lines whose rhymes, usually terminal in sonnets, are soft internal soundings: *smile/while*; *Blue/dew*; *sleep/sleep* (this last also pulling in *sweet* and *speak*). The linear frame of *Blue* . . . *dew* in the midst of these is especially effective for its momentary stay against the pressure of syntactic, and temporal, flow: the containment by rhyme forms a delicate pause in the progress of evening, and Blake protracts the effect with its alexandrine, a formal surplus to trope the invocation for the expansive scattering.

The deviation of these forms is evident in the editorial supervision they provoked. Eric Partridge admires Blake's "daringly weak verse-endings" (ix), but Dante Gabriel Rossetti thought the poems "marred by frequent imperfections in the metre . . . best to remove" (Gilchrist 2: 1), and accordingly emended lines 5–6 thus:

> Smile on our loves; and whilst thou drawest round
> The curtain of the sky, scatter thy dew . . .

Lost hereby are both the semantically charged alexandrine and the internal rhyme, *smile/While* (about which Blake cared enough to restore by hand from a misprinted *whilst*). Swinburne keeps both this rhyme and *Blue/dew* when he quotes these lines (p. 11); but he, too, meddles, undoing Blake's containment of the line by the *Blue/dew* rhyme, and further regularizing the meter:

> Smile on our loves; and while thou drawest round
> The sky's blue curtain, scatter thy silver dew . . .

Not only does Swinburne follow Rossetti in revising Blake's "the/Blue" cut but, confronting the "incredible chaos" of most of the volume's blank verse, he endorsed efforts such as Rossetti's "in righting [its] deformed limbs and planing off [its] monstrous knots" (p. 11).[18] The refinements efface Blake's formal play, not only against sonnet form but also against a line's necessary containment by grammar. Not the least of the effects of "Let the west wind sleep on / The lake," for instance, is the way the enjambment opens into the page-space beyond the line's end as a visual protraction of the call to the wind to *sleep on*; not just the evening star but the page itself is asked to "speak si[l]ence." When at the turn of the line, the syntax gives *on* a local habitation, this continuation does not so much revoke the dreamy protraction of "sleep on" as it leaves us, in Hollander's sensitive reading, with a "phantom image," a "blurred superposition of the two syntactic alternatives" (*Vision and Resonance* 115).

Hartman is sufficiently captivated by the paradox of "speak si[l]ence" to call it the poem's "strongest, most startling" figure: it "intimates presence, not absence" ("Discourse" 227). This presence, he concedes, is a precarious moment, for the invocative present shifts into "Soon, full soon, / Dost thou withdraw." There is, moreover, an unsettling double force in this action. As an intransitive verb, *withdraw* names the benign star's vanishing; but as a curtailed transitive, it turns this vanishing into a disclosure, a veil withdrawn to reveal a Miltonic counterworld in which "the wolf rages wide, / And the lion glares," and against which the weak dactyl of the poem's very last word, *influence*, sounds only a cautious hope. Blake's repetition of "while thou drawest . . . scatter thy silver dew" in "Dost thou withdraw . . . cover'd with / Thy sacred dew" evokes two economies and shows their relation: one of protected, shepherded flocks aligned with human loves, and the other of lurking predators.

His enfolding of these apprehensions is more forceful for having been anticipated by the slightly unstable, benignly expanded syntaxes shaping the prayer
all along.

The Figurings of Rhyme

Rhyme, Hollander and Wimsatt help us see, is a double force, allying
sound and sense, figure and reference, but also restricting how lines have to
end. In *Poetical Sketches*, this doubleness pits self-assertiveness against external
restraints. A text, argues Richard Poirier, "generates itself . . . only by compliance with or resistance to forms of language already available to it. The impulse to resist, or at least to modify, is necessarily stronger than is the impulse
to comply, but the two factors coexist in a sort of pleasurable agitation" (29).
Blake's rhymes frequently turn the question of compliance or resistance into
heightened alternatives. Sometimes rhyming corresponds to forms of harmony (love, dance, song), but sometimes it figures entrapment by artifice and
enforcement by law. While the song that begins, "Love and harmony combine" plays the signifying of rhymes to fantastic excess (every line a rhyme or
nearly so), other songs problematize rhyme as a suspect aesthetic illusion. And
still others ironize Milton's troping of release from rhyme as "liberty" from
"bondage"—an irony, I shall show later, that plays a critical part in the political subtext of the later blank-verse sketches.

We see a prediction in the lurid ballad "Fair Elenor." It is unrhymed,
but this is hardly liberty, as the flatly declarative sentences of its first stanza
reveal:

> The bell struck one, and shook the silent tower;
> The graves give up their dead: fair Elenor
> Walk'd by the castle gate, and looked in.
> A hollow groan ran thro' the dreary vaults.

Supplanting rhyme is a pattern of deadening terminal repetitions, internal
echoes, and stark homophones splayed out across the verse: *silent-silent*; *pale-
pale-pale*; *sighing-sighs*; *death-death*; *gate-gate*; *wretch-wretch-wretched*; *vaults-
vaults*; *feet-feet*; *arms-arms-arms*; *dreary-ear-fear-fear-fear*; *dead-dead-dead-
head-dead-shed*—the random but persistent return of their tones evoking a
sense of terror from inescapable forces. Within the tale, Elenor is "Amaz'd"
by events over which she has no control; within the verse, she is caught in a
maze of words that resound lethally and relentlessly, but with no predict-
ability. By the last stanza, this verbal accumulation has taken possession of the
poem in a thematically resonant way:

> She sat with dead cold limbs, stiffen'd to stone;
> She took the gory head up in her arms;

> She kiss'd the pale lips; she had no tears to shed;
> She hugg'd it to her breast, and groan'd her last.

Using a sudden shift into anaphora, whose vertical axis of repetition at once alludes to and writes a more constricting version of the rhyme-forms they displace, Blake enforces a kind of paralysis from which there is no recovery.

Troping *with* rhyme, Blake makes his only *Sketch* in couplets, "Blind-Man's Buff," a wicked satire of Dryden's argument that the chief advantage of rhyme over blank verse is that it "Bounds and Circumscribes" an "Imagination" that might run "Wild and Lawless" (*Works* 8: 100–101). Reversing the order-keeping of Dr. Johnson's claim that poetry that does not strike "the ear" but is verse "only to the eye" loses its distinction ("Milton" 192–93), Blind-Man's Buff, a children's game of all ear and no eye, invites actions so sadistic and "lawless"—and often in "cheat" of the rules of the game—that the poet-reporter is impelled into a summary call for new laws:

> Such are the fortunes of the game,
> And those who play should stop the same
> By wholesome laws; such as all those
> Who on the blinded man impose,
> Stand in his stead; as long a-gone
> When men were first a nation grown;
> Lawless they liv'd—till wantonness
> And liberty began t' increase;
> And one may lay in another's way,
> Then laws were made to keep fair play. (61–70)

But if, as a call for the law and order of fair play, these lines are sound enough as social allegory, the symbolic corollary of their form is less certain. In reminding us that victim and tormentor may change positions, this voice of sober distress still speaks in the popular tetrameter measure of children's rhymes. If this writes a parodic criticism of children's less-than-innocent games, it also casts their local mischief, tricks, and blood-letting confusions as a formal mimicry and rehearsal of worldly plays of power.

The first two of the volume's set of eight rhymed "Songs" ("How sweet I roam'd" and "My silks and fine array") address these darker plots of law and power by deploying their rhyme-forms to tell stories of capture by delusive art and showing how, as Hollander puts it, "the instrument of rhyming, and the sort of linkage it enforces, becomes allegorized as bondage" (*Melodious Guile* 184). These sketches bear more than the "demonstrably simple derivativeness and passive relationship to other songs" that Gleckner sees (55); their patterns are too cagey:

> With sweet May dews my wings were wet,
> And Phoebus fir'd my vocal rage;

> He caught me in his silken net,
>   And shut me in his golden cage.

This is stanza three of "How sweet I roam'd," about its singer's capture by the "prince of love." Is it "simply . . . a first account of the movement from Innocence into Experience, with the deceptions of nature as the responsible agent," as Bloom says (*Blake's Apocalypse* 19)? Or does what Alicia Ostriker calls its "ironic smoothness" (39) evoke the agency of art as well? It is not just that a rapacious Phoebus looks like a prince of love in "sunny beams" (3–4); it is Blake's two tight rhymes at the moment of capture, an effect sharpened by the preceding alternation of tight and loose:

> How sweet I roam'd from field to field,
>   And tasted all the summer's pride,
> 'Till I the prince of love beheld,
>   Who in the sunny beams did glide!
>
> He shew'd me lilies for my hair,
>   And blushing roses for my brow;
> He led me through his gardens fair,
>   Where all his golden pleasures grow. (1–8)

In stanza three the rhymes spring out with the seductive traps of silken "net" and golden "cage." A singer "caught" by love sings in verse caught by rhyme, "the icon in which the idea is caught" (Wimsatt, "One Relation" 165). The rhymes of the last stanza reflect and report this plight:

> He loves to sit and hear me sing,
>   Then, laughing, sports and plays with me;
> Then stretches out my golden wing,
>   And mocks my loss of liberty. (13–16)

"I" had agency only in stanza one, about the era before love; by stanza two this self has become an object, *me*, ruled by *He*: "He shew'd me," "He led me." And the pattern is set: "He caught me . . . / And shut me"; "He loves to . . . hear me sing, / . . . sports and plays with me." This rule is not only of grammar but a function of how *me* is claimed by *He* in a sinister bind of rhyme. The only variance from this strong governor is a ruefully asymmetrical chiming of *me* with the *liberty* that has been lost.

The relation of poetic form to self-possession is the critical issue of another lover's lament, "My silks and fine array." To Brooks, the "discipline of form"—not just poetic form but also "ritual performance"—controls emotion and "makes it precise and deft, graceful and yet resonant" ("Current Critical Theory" 5–6). I find the effects less certain than this, seeing Blake's poetics ironizing the control by form. But what is clear is that Blake has made a reading of form the focus of this question. This "Song" begins,

> My silks and fine array,
>   My smiles and languish'd air,
> By love are driv'n away;
>   And mournful lean Despair
> Brings me yew to deck my grave:
> Such end true lovers have. (1–6)

This singer describes two performances, or forms of social display: a past one of "fine array" and "languish'd air" and a present one of self-dramatizing "Despair." Part of what makes Brooks see form as "discipline" is his sense of how the present, despairing "languishment in earnest" (5) takes the form of a "more serious kind of play" (6). Yet his deeper intuition, if not his argument, is his verging on saying that emotion is not so much articulated in this form as produced and agitated by it: as the singer turns despair into a "ritual performance," she "rehearses" its "set steps . . . in anticipation," as if they were "known and recognized gestures" (5). If this is discipline, it is so with a vengeance, a form that subsumes what it invests—and Blake's own play of form projects the subtle emergence of this power.

We see this effect especially in the rhymes with which Blake subverts the lady's own display. As she speaks of how her affected "smiles and languish'd air" are betrayed to genuine mourning, a spectral pun of *you* in "yew to deck my grave" and its chime in "true" ("Such end true lovers have") evoke the core of her lament: there is no *you*, even in apostrophe, only this emblem of grief and its trace of love lost. The faintly personified love in line 3 is part of this trace: as external force, it turns the self-possessive *my*s of 1 and 2 over to the defeat of "my grave." Blake supplements this event with a syntactic pressure that (despite his semicolon at the end of 3) makes line 4—"And mournful lean Despair"—seem conjunctive, as if "Despair" were in league with love's action. Blake repeats this effect in the first line of the next stanza, "His face is fair as heav'n" (7): while *His* turns out to refer to the jilter, its liminal position, initially and aptly, gives it antecedence in *love* and *Despair*. The fatal trajectory of the song is driven as much as by these anarchic poetics as by its singer's ritualizing, and the conclusion is a figure of their involution:

> When I my grave have made,
>   Let winds and tempests beat:
> Then down I'll lie, as cold as clay.
> True love doth pass away! (15–18)

The rhyme pattern interacts with treacherous repetitions: "I my grave have made" answers the poem's first (almost muted) couplet, *grave/have* (5–6), tightening its fated linkage into fatal action, while the singer's earlier self-regard in the fate of "true lovers" (in this same couplet) echoes in, and as, the final alien abstraction of a fugitive "True love."

Blake heightens the issue of whether form controls or cooperates with anarchic powers in "Mad Song." This singer's voice is an alternative to surrender, but not without other ambiguities: if it invests its art as resistance to larger social and psychological impositions, Blake's poetics of form also show how such resistance can be drawn into other forms of compulsion. L. C. Knights takes up one side of this question, arguing that the declarative emergence of "I" in the final stanza—

> After night I do croud,
>   And with night will go;
> I turn my back to the east (19–21)

—exposes this voice of "distressed and distressing consciousness [as] in fact willed. The speaker exults in his desperat[ion]" (388). Yet this reading of *will* is strained by the form of the stanza's actual close: "For light doth seize my brain / With frantic pain" (23–24). A syntax of self gripped by forces (light and pain) that it cannot control and a verse gripped by tight rhymes and meter spell the compulsion in this will, with the peculiar verb *croud* ("murmur dovelike") adding to the sensation of pure instinct. Even the singer's boasting—

> My notes are driven:
> They strike the ear of night,
>   Make weep the eyes of day;
> They make mad the roaring winds . . . (12–15)

—raises the question of whether "Mad Song" refers to his notes or the wind's roar. That the endwords *night* and *winds* refuse rhyme (not even flirting with the consonance of *dawn-scorn*; *vault-fraught*; *heaven-driven*) underscores the contest of natural force and human song. This is impressed at the very start by a flux of aural and visual forms (in which *winds* plays a part) against the pattern of rhyme and meter:

> The wild winds weep,
>   And the night is a-cold;
> Come hither, Sleep,
>   And my griefs infold:
> But lo! the morning peeps
>   Over the eastern steeps . . . (1–6)

The alliterations undo the forms of the very words, letting the sound of *winds weep* blend into *winds sweep*. This sweep of sound soon infolds *peeps* and *steeps*, words with which the singer images the dawn that will presumably relieve the torments of the windy night. The rueful irony played by the sounds is that day will offer no relief, only perpetuation. The note of day, "But lo!" (5), is absorbed into this flux, its sound returning to the end rhymes in the last, night-bound stanza:

> Like a fiend in a cloud
>   With howling woe,
> After night I do croud,
>   And with night will go;
> I turn my back to the east,
> From whence comforts have increas'd;
> For light doth seize my brain
> With frantic pain. (17–24)

The twice-toned *night* chimes chiefly with its repetitions: "the night is a-cold" (2), "the ear of night" (13). It finally gets another chord in an internal rhyme with the *light* in the penultimate line, but this release only tightens what Gleckner nicely terms the "cyclicity of a perverted eternity" (51), a perversion that is also the work of the verse.

The perversion of verse form on the stage of self-fashioning is most fully displayed in *Poetical Sketches* by "An Imitation of Spencer." Dr. Johnson urged poets away from this elaborate and archaic stanza form,[19] but Blake liked the challenge of simultaneous homage and defiance. His apprentice work convinced him that, *pace* the cult of "original genius," imitation and copying were important exercises: "Imitation is Criticism," he refutes Reynolds (*BPP* 643), and it is also an opportunity to show how "To Particularize is the Alone Distinction of Merit" (641). Blake's imitation of Spenser works out this particularizing criticism by violating its model at almost every turn: its stanzas are, variously, eight, nine, or ten lines; none obeys the Spenserian rhyme scheme and only two end in an alexandrine. Such practices make conservatives impatient, but Blake's "perversity" is a strategic performance, for this is the first of the *Sketches* to focus explicitly on tradition and verse convention, using imitation as a critical review.[20]

The second stanza promotes this critical imitation with a parody of the practices of "modern peers": a debased poet, "brutish Pan," and a debased critic, the quantifying Midas, deal only in "tinkling sounds," "Sound without sense," "tinkling rhimes, and elegances terse"—exactly what Milton scorns in the headnote to *Paradise Lost* as "the jingling sound of like endings." Blake's first stanza sketches new arrangements:

> Golden Apollo, that thro' heaven wide
>   Scatter'st the rays of light, and truth's beams!
> In lucent words my darkling verses dight,
>   And wash my earthy mind in thy clear streams,
>   That wisdom may descend in fairy dreams:
> All while the jocund hours in thy train
> Scatter their fancies at thy poet's feet;
>   And when thou yields to night thy wide domain,
> Let rays of truth enlight his sleeping brain. (1–9)

He petitions the god of poetry in verse that subverts even as it honors Spenser's form. The stanza still rhymes: two triple rhymes including two couplets on the Spenserian plan. But the unrhymed endwords are the thematically potent ones. The most wayward of these end-words is *feet*, with a punning on metrics and a syntactic form, "thy poet's feet," that allows a reference to both Apollo and his earthly disciple. *Wide* and *dight* tease at a match, but Blake resists the lock, keeping his first terminal word free and refusing the formal dictation implied by *dight*, a cognate of "dictate" (arrange or compose). The unrhyme of *dight*, itself Spenserian diction,[21] is a patent reform, set exactly where it should (but does not) complete the first rhyme of a Spenserian stanza. The freedom of *wide* from rhyme gets further semantic value from the way it leads into the open space of the page, as if this were part of a composite figure for the "heaven wide," or "wide domain" from which the poet seeks his forms.

Actually, Blake does rhyme *dight*—not by dictation, but with a scattering of internal rhymes by *light* (2) into *night* and the absorption (verbally as well as thematically) of *light* by *enlight* (8–9), as if to imitate Apollo's scattering of light. The rhyme plays beyond this stanza to endow its sketchings of form with a mythopoetic value. When the poet addresses Mercurius as a figure of "airy flight" (21), not only does *flight* continue to scatter the rhyme of *light*, but as it does so, it extends Apollo's "rays of light" (2) into the sound of "rays of flight," an "assist [to] lab'ring sense" (35) performed by the poet's witty agency of imitation.

Politics in Rhyme, Blank Verse, and the Poetics of Prose

Blake's "Imitation" sets contingency against formula and invention against repetition, with past models inflecting but not prescribing present practice. It is an exercise that is primarily aesthetic but, as we have seen, not exclusively so. In the historical pieces of *Poetical Sketches*, Blake turns this formal sketching to broader cultural concerns. "Gwin, King of Norway," *King Edward the Third*, "Prologue, Intended for a Dramatic Piece of King Edward the Fourth," and "Prologue to King John" are not only about conflicts in the eras of these kings; they are also tuned to England in the 1780s, when the empire was suffering erosions of royal power and prestige at home, being weakened abroad by rebellions and then full-scale war with America and drawn into new conflicts with its long-standing enemies, Spain, and especially France.[22]

In "Gwin," Blake works the ballad form into a dialectic, evoking its tradition as cultural language, but also exploiting the recent emergence of the *literary* ballad to direct a critical reading of its poetic forms. The ballad opens as a caution to "Kings" about the consequences of tyranny, epitomized in Gwin, oppressor of the "nations of the North," then moves into its central drama, a peasant uprising led by "Gordred the giant," who slays Gwin in battle. As David Erdman remarks, there is contemporary relevance in the ballad's "intense, even propagandistic abhorrence of war-making kings" (*Prophet* 18). In having Gwin regard the people whom he oppresses as "the nations black" (35), moreover, Blake evokes the scandal of black slavery some years in advance of the formation of the Society for the Abolition of the Slave Trade (1787).

As much as the ballad's content, its poetics of form convey a political warning. A demonstration of how victims of tyranny will turn violent in an economy of power that offers no alternative to the positions of tyrant and victim registers almost immediately in Blake's mirror images and verbal repetitions. The tyrannical "Nobles" who "feed upon the hungry poor" (5–6) cannot escape a return: "furious as wolves" (27), the poor roar like "lions' whelps . . . / Seeking their nightly food" (19–20). Noble arrogance earns its violence and blackness back to itself: "let ten thousand lives / Pay for the tyrant's head" (31–32), shout the poor, now "numerous sons of blood," as they roll "like tempests black" (17–18) to meet Gwin and "his host as black as night" (55). Blake emphasizes the inevitability of this return not only in such repetitions but also by exploiting puns latent in the name *Gordred* (which he may have converted from Chatterton's "Godred Crovan" for such effects).[23] The alarm sounded by Gwin's watchmen, "the nations black, / Like clouds, come rolling o'er!" (35–36) verges on *rolling gore*, a flood led by Gordred and rhymed aptly in this stanza with its mighty provocation, "Gwin, the son of Nore" (34). This latency soon erupts as "fields of gore" (46), and echoes in the report that "Earth smokes with blood, and groans, and shakes, / To drink her childrens' gore" (73–74). Allied with blood, moreover, *Gordred* releases not only *gore*, but *Gore-dread* and its nearly redundant cause, *gored red*—the second word distilled in the image of the battle's "red fev'rous night" (84).

In this phonic and semantic field impends the *gore*-rhyme *war*, as word and event. And once it sounds (62), the reproduction of violence emerges as the dominant political trope: "The armies stand, like balances / Held in th' Almighty's hand" (66). Blake takes a Miltonic and Homeric image of divine, even cosmic, supervision and converts it to a simile for political inevitability.[24] That "th' Almighty" figures in his ballad only in a simile (and with a pun on military "might") depletes any moral theology. Indeed, the poem's unsimilized theology is a nonpartisan "god of war . . . drunk with blood" (93), the war-gore that unites the sons of Gordred and of Nore in forces that act with the indifferent violence of nature:

> And now the raging armies rush'd,
>   Like warring mighty seas;
> The Heav'ns are shook with roaring war,
>   The dust ascends the skies! (69–72)

As sound and action, *warring* subtends "roaring war" with a cognitive punning that exploits the phonic resonance and from stanza to stanza keeps alliance with *gore*:

> Earth smokes with blood, and groans, and shakes,
>   To drink her childrens' gore,
> A sea of blood; nor can the eye
>   See to the trembling shore! (73–76)

In a *sea* where, punningly, the eye can *see* only blood, distinction of factions is overwhelmed in the common chaos of destruction:

> And on the verge of this wild sea
>   Famine and death doth cry;
> The cries of women and of babes.
>   Over the field doth fly. (77–80)

> Now death is sick, and riven men
>   Labour and toil for life;
> Steed rolls on steed, and shield on shield,
>   Sunk in this sea of strife! (89–92)

"By the time Gordred cleaves Gwin's skull," remarks Gleckner, "the social and political 'meaning' of that victory has paled to insignificance—even irrelevance. . . . Visionary history inheres in the 'vale of death' and in the 'river Dorman' as the loco-descriptive symbols of the universal battle's 'sea of blood'" (119).[25]

This history is also conveyed by the drama of Blake's similes. In advance of the image of the two armies, "like balances / Held in th' Almighty's hand" (65–66), Blake uses simile to suggest a common fate. In the figures of Gordred's "sons of blood" advancing "Like rushing mighty floods" and "Like clouds, come rolling o'er" (24, 36), and of Gwin's troops, which "Like clouds around him roll'd" (60), the same vehicle serves, reinforced by the same stanzaic position of a last line. Over the course of the ballad and battle, Blake moves this parallelism into a semantic figure. First, and again with the force of syntactic repetition, he encompasses both armies not even with the same, but with one common, simile, intensified by a redoubling of tenor and vehicle: "And now the raging armies rush'd, / Like warring mighty seas" (69–70). Tenors and vehicles merge: the armies rush and rage like seas, which themselves are imaged at war. This involution then yields to stark equivalence: the battlefield is not just "like" a sea which is itself a battlefield; sea and battlefield merge: "A sea of blood," a "wild sea," a "sea of strife" (75, 77, 92). This transformation is completed as the metaphor is finally, and literally, overwhelmed by its vehicle, "sea," which emerges in the ballad's final stanza as a universal force, obliterating distinction between tenor and vehicle and, with this erasure, between the armies themselves:

> The river Dorman roll'd their blood
>   Into the northern sea;

Who mourn'd his sons, and overwhelm'd
The pleasant south country. (113–16)

The "human forces actually become what they formerly were merely like,"
observes De Luca; "they are enveloped in the element and annihilated by it"
(77). This envelopment is more haunting for the way the stanza's weak rhymes
release another chord in which *Dorman, northern, mourn'd* absorb and eerily
reverberate the sounds of *war, gore, Nore,* and *Gordred.* Blake's poetics of
rhyme and related repetitions do not imply the moral or political equivalence
of oppressors and desperate subjects; but they do suggest how extreme political imbalances will press toward equalizing parallels, if only, but massively, in
mutually annihilating violent action.

Repetition, in both formal and political registers, writes the political text
of *King Edward the Third.* Formally, it recalls the blank-verse invocations ("O
thou") that open the volume. In literary tradition, the situation of its scenes—
Crécy before the battle of 1346—recalls the Shakespearean stage of English
wars with France. And history impinges on Blake's moment of writing via
particular linguistic signs that provoke awareness of the same antagonisms in
contemporary British tensions with France. The trajectory of this history, extending from Edward's reign to Blake's day, defines the sketch's political per-
spectivism. Edward the Third generates his line in English history, even as
their Shakespearean characters engender Blake's; and all these royal and dramatic precedents, as Erdman carefully demonstrates, resonate in Blake's historical moment in the conduct of King George the Third.[26]

Blake evokes this history of repetitions in the macro-form of this sketch,
its open-endedness. It consists of six scenes: invocations, conversations, debates, and a "war song," all in the hours before the battle. Stopping short of
the battle and British victory does not, as is usually supposed, render the
sketch a "fragment." Nowhere does Blake term *King Edward* such; nor is there
any typographical sign to denote an unfinished text.[27] Its suspense is a formal
determination, not a symptom of an incomplete venture: although Blake's
readers know that the English prevailed at Crécy, as they would in another
cycle of history at Harfleur and Agincourt under Edward's descendant, Henry
the Fifth, Blake's refusal to evoke these outcomes functions semantically as a
refusal of the nationalistic satisfactions such conclusions might supply. He
draws his reader's attention, instead, into various critical perspectives on
the motivations and self-interests that impel England's history of military
adventurism.

This critical perspective has a counterpart in the other form of this sketch,
its blank verse, a measure deeply saturated in tradition and, more specifically,
Milton. Ever since Dryden and Milton, the form had provoked highly charged
political language, of "liberty" on the positive side or "wantonness" and

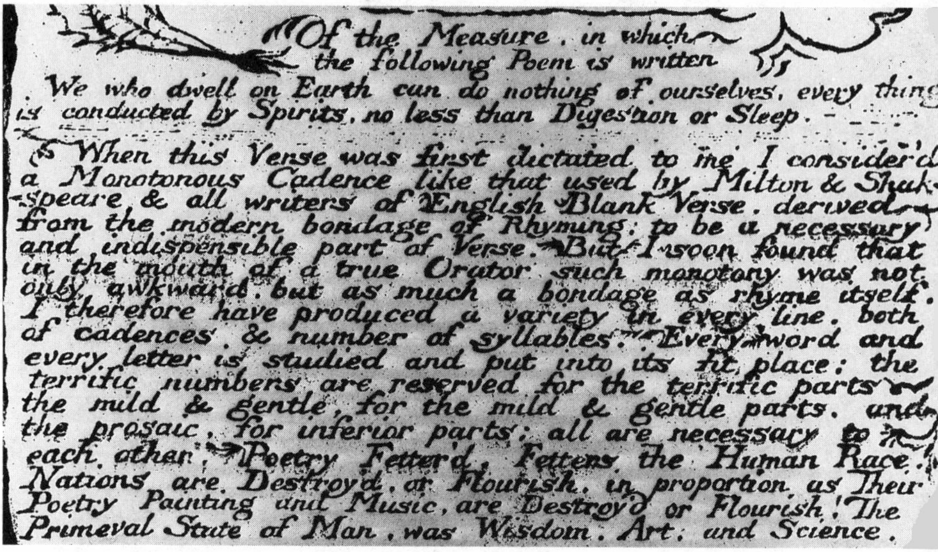

Of the Measure, in which / the following Poem is written

We who dwell on Earth can do nothing of ourselves, every thing is conducted by Spirits, no less than Digestion or Sleep. -

When this Verse was first dictated to me I consider'd a Monotonous Cadence like that used by Milton & Shakespeare, & all writers of English Blank Verse. derived from the modern bondage of Rhyming; to be a necessary and indispensible part of Verse. But I soon found that in the mouth of a true Orator such monotony was not only awkward. but as much a bondage as rhyme itself. I therefore have produced a variety in every line, both of cadences & number of syllables. Every word and every letter is studied and put into its fit place: the terrific numbers are reserved for the terrific parts—the mild & gentle, for the mild & gentle parts, and the prosaic, for inferior parts: all are necessary to each other. Poetry Fetter'd, Fetters the Human Race! Nations are Destroy'd, or Flourish, in proportion as Their Poetry Painting and Music, are Destroy'd or Flourish! The Primeval State of Man, was Wisdom, Art, and Science.

Figure 4. William Blake, detail from "To the Public" at the front of *Jerusalem*: "Of the Measure in which / the following Poem is written." Copy D, plate 3, courtesy of Department of Printing and Graphic Arts, The Houghton Library, Harvard University.

"luxury" on the other—in any event, the opposite of "constraint." That the issue was alive in Blake's day is clear in Kames's summoning of the same discourse: "our verse is extremely cramped by rhyme; and the great advantage of blank verse is, that, being free from the fetters of rhyme, it is at liberty to attend the imagination in its boldest flights" (2: 436).[28] Yet as early as 1804, Blake was raising the stakes. Energized by the revolutions in America and France that were alarming conservatives all over Europe as an apocalypse of wanton lawlessness, he launched a revolutionary poetics in *Milton* that outdid Milton, expressing a heroic contempt for any "tame high finisher" of "paltry Rhymes; or paltry Harmonies" (plate 48A [K41]:9–10). The sneer at "paltry Harmonies" gives no quarter even to blank verse, for it too, as Morris Eaves puts it, is read as one of the "uniform systems of execution owned by the culture, or by poetic tradition" (159); the parodic Miltonic headnote of *Jerusalem*—"of the Measure, in which / the following Poem is written"—calls it bondage, an institutional prescription that can only hinder a "true Orator" (plate 3; see Fig. 4). The declarations are no momentary hyperbole; they are part of the expanding orbit of Blake's casting of innovative poetic style into the semiotics of political vision. The blank-verse poetics of the *Sketches* are Blake's first critical review of Milton's tropes of liberty. The season poems play

a part, applying the form to lyrics and quasi-sonnets and testing its susceptibility to reform.[29] In *King Edward the Third*, Blake plays the other side, em-
ploying the measure to trope its restrictions, a prelude to his declaration of
independence from it in *Jerusalem*.

If in Miltonic legacy, the measure signals "ancient liberty" recovered from
the bondage of inculcated practice, in *King Edward* Blake performs another
turn by leaguing the apparent freedom of the line with a motivated rhetoric, a
recurring imperialist cant of "Liberty." The way the design of the line tropes
the orderings of self-interest that underwrite English claims stirs as the subtle
contradiction in King Edward's opening exhortation to his subjects:

> O thou, to whose fury the nations are
> But as dust!
> .   .   .
> Let Liberty, the charter'd right of Englishmen,
> Won by our fathers in many a glorious field,
> Enerve my soldiers; let Liberty
> Blaze in each countenance, and fire the battle.
> The enemy fight in chains, invisible chains, but heavy;
> Their minds are fetter'd; then how can they be free,
> While, like the mounting flame,
> We spring to battle o'er the floods of death?
> And these fair youths, the flow'r of England,
> Vent'ring their lives in my most righteous cause,
> O sheathe their hearts with triple steel, that they
> May emulate their fathers' virtues,
> And thou, my son, be strong; thou fightest for a crown . . .
>   (1–2; 9–21)

Such rhetoric convinces S. Foster Damon that the sketch, anticipating the war
with France in 1788, is an expression of Blake's youthful, "uncritical patriotism" (228–29). Mark Schorer calls it "an extended defense of war and national interests" (165), and Northrop Frye, "simply 'Rule Britannia' in blank
verse" (*Fearful* 180). Thus, the King goes on to exhort "just revenge for
those / Brave Lords, who fell beneath the bloody axe / At Paris" (43–45) and
proclaims "our right to France" (3.72), while the Bishop, in a business council
at home, describes English merchants as "sovereigns / Of the sea; our right,
that Heaven / Gave to England" (2.78–80). Yet Blake's repeated display of
this rhetoric makes its transparent cant as much an issue as its claims.

As a *poetic* rhetoric, moreover, its form is subtly subversive. Predicting the
cry of *Jerusalem*—"Poetry Fetter'd, Fetters the Human Race!"—Blake motivates the fettered poetry of *King Edward*. Despite its "natural" cadence, the
visible form of the line sets the claims of liberty at odds with the poetics of
liberty and its not-quite-invisible chain of special interests. Edward's manipu-

lative eloquence and pulse-quickening rhythms are thus exposed as a political rhetoric, a coercive design within the language of liberty. With this exposure, Blake implies similar designs in other languages, including those of history and national ideology. And he intensifies this critical regard with a semantics of rhyme in the midst of this blank verse: the chime of *Liberty* / *enemy* / *heavy* / *free* (11–14). Edward's own rhetoric links the middle words to the "fetter'd" minds of France and the first and last to England; but in Blake's verse, one chord joins all. These phonics signify what the sketch exposes at large: British minds, fettered by political and moral self-justification, are less free than they imagine. The chain includes even Edward's blithe description of "Liberty" as "the charter'd right of Englishmen" (9)—a claim that would chime for a reader in the 1780s with emerging critiques of the tyranny veiled in ideologies of "charter'd" rights, including Blake's bitter song, a decade later, on London's "charter'd" streets and "charter'd Thames."[30]

Blake's formalist exposure of chartering forecasts the staging of patent economic self-interest in scene 2. As Edward exhorts his army, his son at home, the Duke of Clarence, celebrates the swirling activity of chartered English business, imagining that from abroad, his father

> sees commerce fly round
> With his white wings, and sees his golden London,
> And her silver Thames, throng'd with shining spires
> And corded ships; her merchants buzzing round
> Like summer bees, and all the golden cities
> In his land, overflowing with honey. (2.9–14)

Frye finds the "most puzzling feature" of the sketch to be "the frankness with which Blake admits that economic ambitions are the cause of the war. Industry, commerce, agriculture, manufacture and trade are the gods directing the conflict"—gods sufficiently "worthy of worship" that "there seems to be no use looking for irony" (180). Erdman finds any irony at best "hidden" (69).[31] But irony presses forth in the next scene when the Prince's minstrel, Sir John Chandos, reacting to his patron's claim of the "spirit of Liberty" within every "genuine Englishman" (3.189–90), observes,

> Teach man to think he's a free agent,
> Give but a slave his liberty, he'll shake
> Off sloth, and build himself a hut, and hedge
> A spot of ground; this he'll defend; 'tis his
> By right of nature. (3.195–99)

The irony of this curriculum is its disparity of form and content: free agency as a subject of instruction; liberty harnessed to the interests of royal power; such interests presented as a "right of nature." Is Sir John speaking in tones of liberal idealism or just political pragmatism? The question becomes more sinister in the rhetoric of the King's rejoinder, "O Liberty, how glorious art thou! / I see thee hov'ring o'er my army . . . / . . . I see thee / Lead them on to battle" (204–7); liberty itself is conscripted to "my" army and a war to secure English commercial hegemony.[32] To underscore the shifty illusions of liberty, Blake bends the formalist poetics of his verse into an insistently critical mirror of the ruling powers. As the Prince announces—

> my blood, like a springtide,
> Does rise so high, to overflow all bounds
> Of moderation; while Reason, in his
> Frail bark, can see no shore or bound for vast
> Ambition (3.234–38)

—Blake's enjambment displays the disease of ambition: if the suspension of *vast* at the end of the line romantically tropes blank space as a visual pun for the unbounded field that the Prince imagines for the enterprises of ambition, the weakness of *bounds* in syntax and sensibility makes an opposite point about this costly intemperance.

An important shift in the poetics of form occurs in scene 4. After sixteen lines, the sketch seemingly sets aside the aesthetics of historical verse drama for prose—specifically, a dialogue between Sir Thomas Dagworth and the Blake-informed voice of "William his Man" in which the mobilization of military enterprise by ambition receives its sharpest commentary. Yet the suggestion of a turn from the rhetoric and aesthetics of illusion to the discourse of frank critique is complicated by the return of the artist in this scene: we hear that the King's minstrel has composed a war-song that has so pleased the Prince (who has an affection for the genre) that he has "made [him] a 'squire"—a reward that inspires him to another song "about all us that are to die, that we may be remembered in Old England" (44–50). Scene 6, the last, is the unmediated script of the minstrel performing this war-song. A composition in blank pentameter stanzas, it displays what has always been the implicit, if unacknowledged, artificiality of the line. With this patent formation of stanzas and song, Blake's sketch concludes by presenting the formalization of war into poetry—and reflexively, implying that national "history" too is an aesthetic formation.

In the aesthetics of desire borne by this war-song, *war* is, significantly, the only rhyme, a sounding intensified by its status within the *Sketches* as a repetition: the opening line, "O sons of Trojan Brutus, cloath'd in war," chiming with "Heated with war" (10) and then "covered with gore" (11), repeats the key rhymes of "Gwin." The repetition is enhanced by a host of other verbal and imagistic repetitions whose cumulative effect is to make the line of Brutus in England seem merely one more warpath. Again we hear of "thunder," of

"Rolling dark clouds," of a "sickly darkness," of the "wrath and fury" of "wild men, / Naked and roaring like lions," of "savage monsters rush[ing] like roaring fire," of "red lightning, borne by furious storms," and a "molten raging sea" (2–31). Even as the song advances a vision of eventual prosperity, its language marks this past violence: the promise that "plenty shall bring forth, / "Cities shall sing, and vales in rich *array* / "Shall laugh, whose fruitful laps bend down with fulness" (46–48) refigures the "firm array" of the Trojan ancestors as they invade Albion (13, 25); the prospect of "Cities" recalls the city in ashes that produced Trojan Brutus; and the summary icon of Liberty, now in the song of Trojan Brutus himself, bears the legacy of violence recorded in the minstrel's opening stanzas:

> "Liberty shall stand upon the cliffs of Albion,
> "Casting her blue eyes over the green ocean;
> "Or, tow'ring, stand upon the roaring waves,
> "Stretching her mighty spear o'er distant lands;
> "While with her eagle wings, she covereth
> "Fair Albion's shore, and all her families." (55–60)

Everything here is a repetition: the roaring waves that Liberty eyes as her domain evoke the "roaring" armies that resisted the invading Trojans (22, 26, 27); and the iconography of the mighty spear, its imperial(ist) thrust, and the eagle, reinscribe the "spears" of the fathers and their spoil of "mighty dead" (34–35), as well as the aggressive "empire"-building that has them roaming "Like eagles for the prey" (42–45). There is a further, and ultimately more potent, range of repetition: in a sketch that opened with the King's manipulative rhetoric of Liberty, the same language is replayed, now fully contextualized in the history of violence that it sustains and perpetuates.

Two contiguous war-songs in *Poetical Sketches* expand this formalist critique by displaying the line in a visionary mode that discloses conceptual and verbal repetition. The first, following *King Edward the Third*, is the sonnet-like "Prologue, intended for a dramatic piece of King Edward the Fourth." Blake's grim joke is that "the Fourth" is not Edward the Third's son (who predeceased his father by a year), but a king born almost a century after Crécy. The thwarted succession is scarcely felt, however, for the term of continuity between the two sketches is a perpetual, incorrigible English thirst for war, reaching not just across generations but across centuries. The "Prologue" gives this language a succinct, ritualistic form, in which repetitions not only echo previous sketches and war-chants, but suggest the frustrating repetitions of history itself:

> O For a voice like thunder, and a tongue
> To drown the throat of war!—When the senses
> Are shaken, and the soul is driven to madness,

Who can stand? When the souls of the oppressed
Fight in the troubled air that rages, who can stand?
6   When the whirlwind of fury comes from the
Throne of God, when the frowns of his countenance
Drive the nations together, who can stand?
When Sin claps his broad wings over the battle,
And sails rejoicing in the flood of Death;
When souls are torn to everlasting fire,
And fiends of Hell rejoice upon the slain,
13   O who can stand? O who hath caused this?
O who can answer at the throne of God?
The Kings and Nobles of the Land have done it!
Hear it not, Heaven, thy Ministers have done it!

The echo of the opening chorus of *Henry V* amplifies the indictment: the allusion to Shakespeare's historical subject, its era located between Blake's two Edwards, again with France as enemy, makes war the inevitable expression of power. The repetitive syntactic and verbal form of "When . . . who can stand?" reaches a stunning modulation in line 13, where the invocation shifts into an interrogation of agency—"O who hath caused this?"—and is answered with a pair of declamations in which "Kings and Nobles" and Heaven's Ministers are indicted together. Blake turns the couplet charge of the final lines in this slightly expanded sonnet into a repetition that exceeds the semantic linkage of a couplet. Erdman wonders about the "inconsistent theology" (*Prophet* 29): the Kings and Nobles who invest themselves as Heaven's Ministers are an affront to the "throne of God," but it is the "throne of God" itself that is the origin and authorizing "drive" of their violence. As in "Gwin," however, the seeming contradiction has a critical point: in a theological register, it indicts God as a creator of violence; in a political register, it indicts earthly tyrants for self-justification as heavenly ministers—and in the self-reflexive irony of the sketch, the charge potentially implicates the poetic agency too, a "madness" of anger and distress that longs for an efficacious thunder of its own.

This poetic agency emerges in "A War Song to Englishmen," whose master trope is also repetition, the reiterated injunction, "Prepare, prepare," which forms and issues a drumbeat for battle. Erdman suspects that this was intended as a second war song from the minstrel and was disjoined from *King Edward* by "typographical mischance" (*BPP* 848; *Prophet* 72); but its placement in the volume, after the short prose sketch "Prologue to King John," produces a more unsettling possibility. Following the "Prologue [for] King Edward the Fourth," "Prologue to King John" wends from tyranny to a concluding prophecy of Albion reborn: "Her sons shall joy as in the morning! Her daughters sing as to the rising year!" Then follows the second "War

Song," with the devastating effect of suggesting that if, as "Prologue to King John" hopes, Albion "may . . . smile again, and stretch her peaceful arms, and raise her golden head, exultingly," in the larger trajectory of her history, her daughters will always be singing her sons off to war.

This unhappy prophecy haunts the three prose-poetry sketches at the back of the volume. All turn to a sometimes specified, sometimes emblematic historical past, and all are cast into a form of writing, prose, a disjunctive heterogeneity that expresses Blake's critical confrontation with the role of poetic form in conveying the pressures of historical awareness in the present moment. These sketches swell the page with words, declining even a shaping by paragraphs. In a field of "poetical" sketches, this contingent textual organization gains effect from the semantic charge of formal difference. The prose line conveys the illusion of an unprescribed outpouring of voice, a force of visionary information uncontainable by poetic form.[33] Blake's refusal, not just of poetic form but of standard prose form, is made to seem the expressive necessity of a primary, unmediated voice of prophesy and political emergency, the ultimate "organic" form. That he should produce this contradiction—extending his elaborate performances of poetic form into their own effacement— may constitute the most radically experimental gesture of *Poetical Sketches*.

Chapter 3

✼ The Formings of Simile
Coleridge's "Comparing Power"

Something there must be to realize the form, something in and by
which the *forma informans* reveals itself: and these . . . in the least possible degree obscure the idea, of which they (composed into outline
and surface) are the symbol. An illustrative hint may be taken from a
pure crystal, as compared with an opaque, semi-opaque or clouded
mass, on the one hand, and with a perfectly transparent body, such as
the air, on the other.
—Coleridge, "On the Principles of Genial Criticism," Essay Third

No simile runs on all four legs (*nihil simile est idem*).
—Coleridge, *On the Constitution of the Church and State*

The Beautiful is the perfection, the Sublime the suspension, of the
comparing Power.
—Coleridge, comment on Karl Wilhelm Ferdinand Solger's *Erwin*

To know that the balance does not quite rest,
That the mask is strange, however like.
—Stevens, "The Man with the Blue Guitar"

Yet not too like, yet not so like to be
Too near, too clear, saving a little to endow
Our feigning with the strange unlike, whence springs
The difference. . . .
—Stevens, "To the One of Fictive Music"

Unity Versus "the shape of formal similes"

A critical charge within Romantic formalism is the pressure it can apply to
its privileged aesthetic principles of unity and organicism, their organizing
designs, and cognitive allies. Coleridge's involvement with the forms and
forming of similes shows us how this criticism emerges, characteristically in
Romantic writing, not from a position of superior intelligence but as an effect
discovered and confronted within poetic work itself, revealing inconsistencies
of principles and practice, even contradictions. Only half the story is told by a

statement that would later be treated as exemplary, both for Coleridge and Romanticism. This is his famous complaint to Sotheby about Bowles's "perpetual trick of *moralizing* every thing," his inability "to see or describe any interesting appearance in nature, without connecting it by dim analogies with the moral world"; a "Poet's *Heart & Intellect* should be *combined, intimately* combined & *unified*, with the great appearances in Nature—& not merely held in solution & loose mixture with them, in the shape of formal Similes" (September 20, 1802; *Letters* 2: 864). To Coleridge, similes and their mode of dim analogy expose only a "formal" relation, opposite and inferior to the organic and consubstantial principles of unity that he would gloss via Plotinus at the close of chapter 6 of *Biographia*: "in order to direct the view aright, . . . the beholder should have made himself congenerous and similar to the object beheld. Never could the eye have beheld the sun, had not its own essence been soliform" (1: 114–15).

It is from such statements that Wimsatt's account of "The Structure of Romantic Nature Imagery" draws its paradigm of a poetics "making less use of the central overt statement of similitude which is so important in all rhetoric stemming from Aristotle and the Renaissance" and instead working tenor and vehicle "in a parallel process out of the same material" (107, 109). Here, Wimsatt argues, "the element of tension in disparity is not so important as for metaphysical wit. The interest derives not from our being aware of disparity where likeness is firmly insisted on [i.e., the metaphysical conceit], but in an opposite activity of discerning the design which is latent in the multiform sensuous picture" (110). So powerfully has this process come to stand not just for Coleridge but for Romanticism itself that some readers, such as Herbert Lindenberger, contend that "distinctions between tenor and vehicle, crucial as they are to the understanding of Renaissance and metaphysical verse, are of little avail" to reading the Romantic rhetoric of interaction in which "the literal becomes figurative and then literal again" (*On Wordsworth's "Prelude"* 69).

That Coleridge is the paradigm in this criticism attests to his status in mid-twentieth-century literary theory (and pedagogy) as the author of the "organic" formalism of fusing "ideas" with their expressive "material" (Wimsatt, 115). His very words, usually about the reconciling and harmonizing agency of imagination, were called upon—notably and influentially by Wimsatt, Brooks, Wasserman, and Abrams—to explicate a distinctly "poetic structure."[1] This Coleridgean formalism virtually reinvented Romanticism as an aesthetic theory as well as an expressive sensibility, and its principles played an important part in the institution of literary study. This development was good for Romanticism insofar as it brought more refined and alert attention to the intelligent textures of its poetry, but its liability was to situate Coleridge and organic form as its synecdoches, and thereby targets for demystifying critique—of Coleridge's theory, of Romantic aesthetic ideology, and of any mode of interpretation (especially the New Critical) exploring or surveying this terrain.

These critiques focused on the binary structure that in one way or another elevates symbol over allegory, metaphor over metonymy, and innately "proceeding" ("organic") poetic forms over arbitrarily "superinduced" or conventionally prescribed ("mechanic") ones. One of the most influential essays was de Man's "The Rhetoric of Temporality," which dismantled these hierarchies to show the instability, frequently the transgressiveness, of its distinctions. It was no small matter to the fate of formalist criticism that this deconstruction not only discerned incoherence in Coleridge's symbolist ideology, especially when read against its assumed antithesis, the allegorical, but also worked its case against the Coleridgeanism of Wimsatt's, Wasserman's, and Abrams's readings of Romanticism. Coleridgean and modern critical formalism were simultaneously discredited. This challenge along lines of rhetorical structure paved the way for political demystifications. Responsive to what de Man called Coleridge's evasion of temporality (the timebound, rather than symbolically present, nature of understanding), these subsequent critiques shifted the terms (sometimes against de Man, too) into an analysis of how such "organic" theory at once evades and is informed by another temporal binding, the sociohistorical situation of its discourse. In this view, organicism and its strategies entailed important political and doctrinal correlatives. What de Manian hermeneutics described as a form of "tenacious self-mystification" in Coleridge's poetics of the symbol ("Temporality" 208), a New Historicist critic such as David Simpson exposed as an ideological interest in presenting "as aesthetic discriminations judgments whose purpose and energy" come "from convictions that are in the final analysis political and social." Coleridge's preference for organic over mechanic form, "for a work of art that excludes the representation of artifice," Simpson argued, is "precisely symmetrical with the preference for a political hierarchy within which some must accept as innate or automatic what is for others a contrived or constructed paradigm"; "mechanic form . . . dramatizes the intervention of human agency," while "organic form disguises [it] as a spontaneous evolution" ("Coleridge" 213, 215).

This elision of constructedness undeniably serves some of Coleridge's values, but its unilateralism is overstated. Coleridge's persistent and insistent definition of poetry as metrical art, to cite a contrasting discourse, is unembarrassed about this constructedness, and, as I have argued elsewhere, this patent, as opposed to mystified, aesthetic agency is related to questions of poetic power that are politically sensitive.[2] In this chapter, I focus on another such potent formation, at once intellectual and poetic, whose critical agency is also, and just as fundamentally, its consciousness of its explicit construction:

the simile. Not only as a subject of theoretical inquiry but also in events of writing, Coleridge's poetics of simile contrast, often contest, and sometimes even threaten to supplant his organic formalism. Although he sees Bowles abusing the figure by making it connect to "dim analogies," this may be a self-discipline, given his slightly satirical picture, a few years earlier, of his own fascination with "dim sympathies" of form:

> Only that film, which fluttered on the grate,
> Still flutters there, the sole unquiet thing.
> Methinks, its motion in this hush of nature
> Gives it dim sympathies with me who live,
> Making it a companionable form,
> Whose puny flaps and freaks the idling Spirit
> By its own moods interprets, every where
> Echo or mirror seeking of itself,
> And makes a toy of Thought. ("Frost at Midnight" 15–23)

Here Coleridge is analyzing, or mocking, the production of simile, but under this cover, also proffering the figure's logic and attractions. He recognizes his tendency to Bowlesian figures: "oft at twilight gloom [a] grave I pass, / And sit me down upon its recent grass, / With introverted eye I contemplate / Similitude of soul, perhaps of Fate!" ("Lines on a Friend" [1794] 35–38).

Such toyings of thought contest Coleridge's title as the champion of organic form and organicist ideology as well as his institution as the patron of their critical party. He is more accurately a double agent, invested in the several competing theories of poetic form that descend from Romanticism. Although Lindenberger and Wimsatt are right about the pervasive rhetoric in Coleridge and Romanticism that blurs literal and figurative, tenor and vehicle, we need to study the many events that resist such conflations or aggravate a disparity—and do so not as an exercise of metaphysical wit but as a critical probing into the poetics of unity. Coleridge's similes are a meta-trope of these events, exposing the unity vested in the privileged form of the symbol as an illusory or factitious (however intensely desired) effect of poetic form.

For all his vehemence about Bowles's tricks of simile, Coleridge indulges the figure in a poem written the same year as this complaint—one whose genre, moreover, courts a symbolic mode: *Chamouny The Hour before Sunrise A Hymn*.[3] The circumstance of its composition is related to its entailment by simile. Although Coleridge names his original inspiration as his sensation on "Sca' fell," among "our humble mountains" (so he reports in the letter on Bowles), he says that he felt the need of another less humble referent, less "disproportionate" to "the Ideas & c" called forth. So, "accidentally lighting on a short Note in some swiss Poems, concerning the Vale of Chamouny, & it's Mountain, I transferred myself thither, in the Spirit, & adapted my former feelings to these grander external objects" (*Letters* 2: 864–65). This "Note" was written by Sophie Christiane Friederika Brun as an appendage to her ode, *Chamouny beym Sonneraufgange: Gedichte*. Coleridge does more than transfer English mountains into Swiss, however. His text also appropriates Brun's note and hymn, transferring and translating her language into his own.[4] This is a procedure that surpasses the Bowlesian artifice of connecting feelings to an interesting appearance of nature's "external objects." Coleridge's connection is to another's text, itself a representation. Brun's language, his actual and only half-acknowledged inspiration, substitutes for, or is, the external object.

On some occasions, then, it is clear that Coleridge is willing to forgo the intimate unity of mind and object urged in his criticism of Bowles and to practice his own loose mixtures and shifty transfers. In one sense, his plagiarizing appropriation of Brun is a kind of (inter)textual similizing, and is mirrored in the way the actual similes of his *Hymn* operate as a semantic trope for the attenuated relation of language and referent. Coleridge begins in a present-tense address to Mont Blanc, a "most awful Form" (5) to the "bodily eye" (14), but his second sounding of the word *form* summons the past tense of memory and an iconic invisibility:

> O dread and silent form! I gazed upon thee,
> Till thou, still present to my bodily eye,
> Didst vanish from my thought: entranced in prayer
> I worshipped the INVISIBLE alone. (13–16)

Recalling a "silent form" that seemed nearly to tease its gazer out of thought, Coleridge uses poetic form to pose a tentative relation between "I" and object: line 16 is organized to allow "alone" a reference both to "I" and "the INVISIBLE." But since "INVISIBLE" is a negative that reports the vanishing of the empirical object, the syntax may link only mutual isolations. To evoke a deeper-than-visible relation, Coleridge summons a more tentative rhetoric:

> Yet thou meantime, wast working on my soul,
> E'en like some deep enchanting melody. (17–18)

Filling the gap of visible form and invisible presence with a simile of deeper melodies to the spirit, Coleridge uses *like* both expressively and dramatically: it is a provisional figure that in its rhetoric and its reflexive relation to the hymn's own melody represents the effort of poetic making.

This double agency also appears in *Reflections on having left a Place of Retirement* as Coleridge recollects its mountaintop view:

> It seem'd like Omnipresence! God, methought,
> Had built him there a Temple: the whole World
> Seem'd *imag'd* in its vast circumference. (38–40, his italics)

The rhetoric of *like*, aided by *methought* and *seem'd* (which he revises from a declarative *Was* in the *Monthly Magazine* text [*Poems* 107]), checks the hyperbole and the symbology of the capital letters. The work of simile as this kind of self-aware figure of desire shapes further revisions of the *Hymn*, as Coleridge expands his explication of the mountain's soul-work by simile into an analogously "constructed" rhetoric, analogy:

> Thou, the meanwhile, wast blending with my Thought,
> Yea, with my Life and Life's own secret joy:
> Till the dilating Soul, enrapt, transfused,
> Into the mighty vision passing—there
> As in her natural form, swelled vast to Heaven! (19–23; *Poems* 378)

In this syntactic dilation, *As* conveys subject into object, poetic "vision" into "the mighty vision," the soul's "form" into Mont Blanc's "Form." But the figure of *As* also concedes their difference, and Coleridge's retrospective gloss repeats this double work in describing himself "gazing on the Mountain till as if it had been a Shape emanating from and sensibly representing her own essence, my Soul had become diffused thro' 'the mighty Vision'; and there 'As in her natural Form, swelled vast to Heaven'" (*Letters* 4: 974). The ambiguous syntax of "as if it" is potent partly for the way its extension enacts the unity it proposes: "it" first seems to refer to "the Mountain" (a self-involved Shape to which the poet's gaze is superfluous); but when the poet's soul is clarified as the referent, the effect is less to cancel than to augment the first suggestion. It comes as no surprise, then, to see Coleridge in the same letter go on to say that with a sufficient "stir of the poetic impulse, . . . I would *allegorize* myself, as a Rock with it's summit just raised above the surface of some Bay or Strait in Arctic Sea" (975, his emphasis).

A display of comparing power in the poetics of harmony is delicately calibrated in "Frost at Midnight," where the restraint strengthens the sentiment. Reeve Parker has described this as a poem whose many sets of companionable forms test the possibility of an "adequate symbology in the natural world" (132). Yet, as we have seen, the poem's representation of dim sympathies flirts with simile, and an early manuscript (ca. 1796) shows Coleridge actually using simile in this test, but in ways that qualify even as they elaborate the harmonies famously figured in the conclusion of the published text (which closes with the first three of these lines):

> Or whether the secret ministery of cold
> Shall hang them up in silent icicles,
> Quietly shining to the quiet moon,
> Like those, my babe! which ere tomorrow's warmth
> Have capp'd their sharp keen points with pendulous drops,

Will catch thine eye, and with their novelty
Suspend thy little soul; then make thee shout,
And stretch and flutter from thy mother's arms
As thou wouldst fly for very eagerness. (MS 4°; *Poems* 242–43)

Like works in two different but complementary ways. Extending the quiet harmonies, the simile gives the icicles imaged only in general the feel of an im-
minent presence and then surmises a reflective joy for the babe in the way
their hanging will "catch" his eye and "suspend" his soul. Yet its temporal
indicators—*ere, will, then*—anticipate a flux of form in which these iconic
icicles will become "pendulous drops" and then, inevitably, another form altogether—a fate half sounded as we hear the stressed syllable of "pendulous"
echo in the chronologically prior "suspend."

The *As* that begins the last line plays into this temporal awareness. It is
both a term of simultaneity and an elided *as if*, a summary doubleness that
reverberates within the poem's larger text of connections: the babe who seems
to "flutter" from his mother's arms recalls the film that "flutters" on the fire-
grate of the poem's present moment, and this "companionable form" (15–19)
in turn recalls the "fluttering *stranger*" on a school-house grate (25–26),
which evokes another, earlier memory of church-bells and a fantasy also conveyed by simile, their sounding "Most like articulate sounds of things to
come" (33). As the poetry links these diverse times, its similes display how
habits of comparison shape these links in default of a pervasive symbology.
This is a self-aware rhetoric of temporality.

If Coleridge's simile-making signifies anything, then, it is his contradictory reflections on language in general. As a philosopher and theorist, he often
sounds logocentric, insisting on imagination as a power of harmony and the
agent of its poetic symbolism. Yet Coleridge's poetic processes themselves are
resistant, often devoted to fragments, disjunctions, and revisions. Earl R.
Wasserman thus cautions against taking his theories to define a poetic "process for the transformation of images into symbols" ("Grounds" 30). Even
some of his famous prose hymns to symbol, such as that of *The Statesman's
Manual*, bear critical contradictions. The theory is one thing, the elaboration
another. "True natural philosophy is comprized in the study of the science and
language of *symbols*," Coleridge-the-theorist states, adding, "by a symbol I
mean, not a metaphor or allegory or any other figure of speech or form of
fancy, but an actual and essential part of that, the whole of which it represents"
(79). "Consubstantial with the truths, of which they are the *conductors*" (*Manual*
29), symbols are distinguishable in this respect from the "disjunction of Faculty" in allegory (*Notebooks* 4503)—and in simile, too, for "similitudes . . . are
always *alle*gorical" — "expressing a *different* subject" across "a resemblance"
of figures" (*Aids to Reflection* 206).[5] For Coleridge, these distinctions involve

more than literary figures; in positing ontological stability and epistemological continuity, they bear on entire modes of thought and imagination:

with particular reference to that undivided Reason, neither merely speculative or merely practical, but both in one . . . contra-distinguish[ed] from the Understanding, I seem to myself to behold in the quiet objects, on which I am gazing, more than an arbitrary illustration, more than a mere *simile*, the work of my own Fancy! I feel an awe, as if there were before my eyes the same Power, as that of the REASON—the same Power in a lower dignity, and therefore a symbol established in the truth of things. (*Manual* 72)

Yet the distinctions are as precarious as they are insistent: to set forth this "undivided" mode of apprehension, Coleridge resorts to a language of division and opposition, invoking a quasi- or dilated simile, *as if*, to illustrate. The syntax of hypothesis abets the rhetoric of simile by straining the connection so arranged.[6] In the paragraph just previous, this "awe" required a rhetoric of comparison—it is "a feeling similar to that with which we gaze at a beautiful infant that has fed itself asleep at its mother's bosom, and smiles in its strange dream of obscure yet happy sensations"—and an *as if* to express the melancholy sense of disjunction from this "same tender and genial pleasure": "It seems as if the soul said to herself: from this state has *thou* fallen!" (*Manual* 71).

Extending imagination to hypothetical sensation by modulating *as* into *as if*, the quasi-comparative rhetoric also reports the difference and loss Coleridge also senses in the production of language:

Hard to express that sense of the analogy or likeness of a Thing which enables a Symbol to represent it, so that we think of the Thing itself—& yet knowing that the Thing is not present to us.—Surely, on this universal fact of words & images depends by more or less mediations the *imitation* instead of *copy* which is illustrated in very nature *shakespearianized/* —that Proteus Essence that could assume the very form, but yet known & felt not to be the Thing by that difference of the Substance which made every atom of the Form another thing/ —that likeness not identity— (*Notebooks* 2274).

Such moods pose the issue that Derrida would address with an analysis of writing as a dangerous supplement: if writing "represents and makes an image," he argues, this happens "by the anterior default of a presence. . . . The supplement is *exterior*, outside of the positivity to which it is super-added" (*Grammatology* 145, his italics). Coleridge's alertness to this poetics of addition not only competes with the symbology that theorizes presence and incorporation; it makes this symbology seem a compensatory desire—thus de Man's reading of his elevation of symbol over allegory as a "defensive strategy," a "tenacious self-mystification" of the impossibility of identity or identification ("Temporality" 208).

Yet in this defensiveness, Coleridge's rhetoric may not be as mystified as de Man claims: recall his famous antipathy to "marble-peach" modes of art that, feigning likeness, subvert the value of "Imitation" as "the mesothesis of Likeness and Difference." (Kames, too, dislikes the art of painted marble in which "the idea of resemblance is sunk into identity" [1: 372–73].) "The Difference," Coleridge insists, "is as essential to it as the Likeness, for without the Difference, it would be Copy or Fac-simile" (July 1, 1833; *Table Talk* 1: 408). Wordsworth's formalist poetics are more deeply devoted to this principle than to any other. Even as he argues that there is no "essential difference" between "the language of prose and metrical composition," he defends meter as a pleasure principle deriving from the vital interaction of "similitude in dissimilitude, and dissimilitude in similitude" (1800 Preface; *LB* 749, 756). So when de Man challenges (New Critical) formalism by asking, "can we take [a] continuity between depth and surface, between style and theme, for granted? Is it not rather the most problematic issue with which the theory of poetry will have to deal?" ("Form and Intent" 23), one answer is that the Romantics' poetics of simile, in theory and in practice, had already posed the question. Coleridge not only thought about the problem, but experienced it as a condition of his intellectual pleasures: just after explaining to himself the tendency of a brain that "tho' it perceives the *difference* of things, yet is eternally pursuing the likenessnesses, or rather that which is common," he reverses emphases: "bring me two things that seem the very same, & then I am quick enough to shew the difference, even to hair-splitting" (December 1804; *Notebooks* 2372). Simile, as a structure negotiated by likeness and difference, spells out the contrary impulses of the mind's analytic impulses.

It is from this opposition of impulses that simile, especially in Coleridge's hands, gains its figurative capacity to set the power of language to construct, connect, and refer against its potential exposure of absence, supplement, and difference; and because it does this in one figure, it can explore the interaction of these energies. This local work taps a latency in the classical conception of representation as *verisimile*. Frye describes the discourse of realism as an "extended or implied simile," or "the art of verisimilitude" (*Anatomy* 136). The term is an apt quasi-oxymoron that mediates a potential polarization (into either a naive poetics of presence or a skeptical concession to device) with the "metaphorical ambiguity of 'resemblance to' (reflection) and 'semblance' (illusion) of reality." It is revealing of Coleridge's intellectual tuning to this doubleness that H. R. Jauss (whom I've been quoting) uses "willing suspension of disbelief" to gloss the aesthetic power so enabled (5). Coleridge's theoretical prescience, as well as his alertness to what is ambiguous or unstable in precursive traditions, makes his legacy to literary theory most fundamentally a text of contradictions. He is as much a precursor of deconstructive as of organicist methods of reading.[7]

This double legacy, which neither can nor should be resolved, is continuously negotiated in his poetics of simile, to which I now turn more detailed attention. Theorizing and writing a poetics of simile, Coleridge finds himself addressing the very processes and performances that define poetic form. His investigation has much to show about the theoretical complexity of Romantic poetics, and it requires a willingness to read the contradictions less as ruptures naively courted by evasion than as a critical language for intelligent divisions and contrary pressures of thought.

The Poetics of Disjunction

Coleridge's ambivalence about simile emerges from a traditional condescension to the figure. In *Jerusalem*, Los's revolutionary proclamation—"I must Create a System, or be enslav'd by another Mans"—is attached to a pledge that elevates this poetic and political imperative over lesser cognitive enterprises: "I will not Reason & Compare: my business is to Create" (plate 10: 20–21).[8] Perhaps the only conservative element in this proclamation is its opposition of analytic comparison to the business of real creation, for this is a poetic that descends quite visibly from classical rhetorics. These discussions typically treat simile as a device of secondary elaboration, a figure for embellishment or a sometimes useful device for instruction, persuasion, communication, or other such effect. Aristotle regards simile chiefly this way, and does not trust it, preferring the method of direct, logical correspondence in metaphor to the strenuous comparison sometimes required by the structure of the simile (3.10.2–5).[9] Quintilian, too, approves of simile as a "means of illuminating our descriptions . . . to help our proof." But he cautions that "anything that is selected for the purpose of illuminating something else must itself be clearer than that which it is designed to illustrate" (8.3.72–73). One must also attend to propriety; Quintilian advised that the best way to refute a simile in debate is to "lay stress on [the] extreme dissimilarity" (*dissimilia*) of what is being compared (5.13.24). Coleridge echoes these precepts, defining metaphor as more integrative: "all metaphors are grounded on an apparent likeness of things essentially different" (*Aids to Reflection* 141). In the work of "resemblance," metaphor is always the definitive "trope," Derrida observes in a similar analysis, adding that "the magnetizing effect of similarity" (versus difference) in the organization of metaphor presupposes "a symbolist position" that has strong affinities to Romanticism ("White Mythology" 13).

Derrida's post-modern critique is pointed toward a metaphysical deconstruction, but it is linked to Coleridge's Romanticism in its reading of figures for play as well as purpose. It is a revealing feature even of classical commentary that simile could register against its protocol this way, producing disruptively exotic comparisons that, while a liability in argument, may enhance oratory. Even in forensics, Quintilian is willing to admire the effect of simile in making speech "sublime, rich, attractive or striking, as the case may be. For the more remote the simile is from the subject to which it is applied, the greater will be the impression of novelty and the unexpected which it produces" (8.3.74). Not only does this view revise Aristotle's sense of the rhetorical impediment posed by a tenor too remote from its vehicle, it virtually prophesies one of the most notorious similes in English poetry: "Our two souls . . . // If they be two, they are two so / As stiff twin compasses are two." Donne's wit draws not just on the outrageous disparity of tenor and vehicle but on the reflexive play of the figure itself, its joining of two, in the scene it describes. Such effects were too extreme for Dr. Johnson, but even he concedes, in his own reflexive rhetoric of simile, that if a "simile may be compared to lines converging at a point," it "is more excellent as the lines approach from greater distance."[10] Coleridge said so too in a remarkable accolade to Donne's energetically mechanic form: this is a poetry made in "Wit's forge and fire-blast, meaning's press and screw" ("On Donne's Poetry").

Coleridge's more habitual tendency as critical reader, however, is to see wide breaches of tenor and vehicle as an extravagance of Fancy, the faculty that "brings together images which have no connection natural or moral, but are yoked together by the poet by some accidental coincidence"[11]—an echo of Johnson's famous complaint in "Life of Cowley" about the far-flung combinations of metaphysical wit, and of a piece with his own judgment of Cowley's as "a very *fanciful* mind" (*Biographia* 1: 84). Coleridge thus invests the notion of a "*leading Thought*" to bring "things the most remote and diverse in time, place, and outward circumstance . . . into mental contiguity and succession," and endorses the view that "the more striking" links will be "the less expected" ("Method," *Friend* 1: 455). Yet if this sounds more like the problem itself, Coleridge's poetry shows a figurative interest in the consequence, presenting thought led by figures as much as figures led by thought. For while in theory, Imagination is preferable to Fancy, and symbol to simile and allegory, in practice, Fancy and its forms of comparison prove a resource for representing those very orders of thought that symbol would overcome: the tentative, the provisional, the uncertain, the ambiguous, the illusory. The poet of *Dejection: An Ode*, for example, recalls a time when

> all misfortunes were but as the stuff
> Whence Fancy made me dreams of happiness:
> For hope grew round me, like the twining vine,
> And fruits, and foliage, not my own, seemed mine.
> But now afflictions bow me down to earth. (78–82)

Representing this illusion in the rhetoric of *like* is apt, for the gap between tenor and vehicle is also a gap between the self and its imagined properties.

The false surmise of misfortune as the stuff of anticipated happiness takes the form of analogy; the erroneous reading of hopeful projections as actual property shapes a simile whose vehicle exposes a categorical difference between "mine" and its perfect rhyme with the delusively fruitful "vine"—a wicked turn on the semantic implication of perfect rhyme as a kind of identity by "similitude." [12] Coleridge's verbal fluxions of internal rhyme amplify this delusion: the delusion of what the self calls its "own" is transliterated in the next line into what is recognized "now"—a shift strengthened by the rhyme of "now" with its defining action, "bow," and its assonance with "down," itself a telling retuning of "own."

Simile as a form of representation not only exposes the formalism of representation, then, but activates poetic form as a representational sign itself. Coleridge uses a knowingly delusive simile to open his sonnet "To Asra," written near the time of *Dejection*, 1801:

> Are there two things, of all which men possess,
> That are so like each other and so near,
> As mutual Love seems like to Happiness?

The question predicates its emotional appeal on the redundancy or superfluity of simile, in the collapse of the structure of "like" into an idealized equation, not only of the "two things," "Love" and "Happiness," but of the reciprocity of the two people whose love annihilates the distance of being only "like." At the same time, the emotional pain of this question, which is really no question but a proposal of desire, is that there is no equation for this speaker: "seems like," devastatingly, names the illusion that even a simile cannot fancifully recuperate. The line that completes this quatrain and grammatically launches the sentence that is also the rest of the sonnet—"Dear Asra, woman beyond utterance dear!"—does not merely offer the conventional compliment that her dearness is incommensurate to utterance; it also dramatically sets the extension of desire "beyond utterance" against the nearness that makes Love possessed a simile for happiness.

Coleridge repeatedly uses such gaps between a simile's tenor and vehicle to expose fragile illusion and error. In *Christabel*, Geraldine "sank, belike through pain" at the castle threshold (129), and then, once Christabel has carried her across, she "rose again, / And moved, as she were not in pain" (133–34); asleep, Christabel "seems to smile / As infants" do, or "Like a youthful hermitess" (317–20), while Geraldine "belike hath drunken deep / Of all the blessedness of sleep" (375–76); the next morning Christabel only looks "as one that prayed" (462), while Geraldine vamps Sir Leoline "like a thing, that sought relief" (593). Similes as a rhetoric of uncertainty form the extended trope of *The Rime of the Ancient Mariner*, repeatedly underwriting the process by which a chance event gets read into significance: [13]

> At length did cross an Albatross,
> Thorough the fog it came;
> As if it had been a Christian soul,
> We hailed it in God's name. (63–66)

As if expresses a desire to bring ideas and images, words and things, into relation. At the same time, Coleridge displays the form to expose its fiction, a
willed association of event and information. With a lighter touch, Keats works
this effect in "Ode to Psyche" as the poet tries to press a tableau of two fair
creatures into a productive narrative:

> Their lips touch'd not, but had not bade adieu
> As if disjoined by soft-handed slumber,
> And ready still past kisses to outnumber. (17–19; 1820 text)

This rhetoric darkens when the figurative elaboration for a poet's heartache
offered at the beginning of "Ode to a Nightingale"—"as though of hemlock
I had drunk, / Or emptied some dull opiate to the drains" (2–3)—forebodes
the trajectory of his consciousness toward the romance with death that emerges
in stanza 6: "Now more than ever seems it rich to die."

The critical pressure of such comparisons—on the form itself and on the
forming of relations from accident and coincidence—often makes them into
scenes of the method. This pressure shapes the epistemological crises that plot
The Rime as a whole and often involve the reader in their dilemma. Consider
the strangeness, in substance and in syntax, of this simile:

> Nor dim nor red, like God's own head,
> The glorious Sun uprist:
> Then all averred, I had killed the bird
> That brought the fog and mist. (97–100)

The logic of the simile aligns the sun with God's head, a figure that appears to
signal the justice, or rightness, of the Mariner's action. This alignment proves
notoriously unstable, yielding to its opposite as soon as the climate changes;
but its instability already stirs in the queasy syntax of the sentence, assisted by
the stanza form: in concert, both forms allow the simile, "like God's own
head," to refer, Janus-like, first to something "dim" and "red" and then, at the
turn of the line, to "The glorious Sun." No wonder that this simile caused the
reviewer for the *British Critic* to "shudder; not with poetic feeling, but with
disapprobation" (14: 365). The sense that results, of a world supervised errati-
cally by a Godhead alternately dim and red or suddenly glorious, is hard to
shake, especially in light of ensuing events. The Sun *does* turn dim and red a
few stanzas on—"All in a hot and copper sky, / The bloody Sun, at noon"
(111–12)—and into a vengeful God soon after, when behind the ribbed ship,
"As if through a dungeon-grate he peered / With broad and burning face"

(179–80). In writing the simile, "like God's own head"—a figure that might have signified the intelligent center of an enlightened universe—into the center of a sentence whose syntax and poetic formation unsettles this theocentricity, Coleridge's syntax involves readers in the disorientation overtaking the crew. His temporary revision of the simile to "like an Angel's head" (1800–1805; *LB* 772) doesn't really help, for the Angel in this world could just as likely be one of the outcast rebels. In this interinvolvement of the poem's readers with the readers in the poem, Coleridge motivates the indeterminate grammar of the simile to insinuate a suggestion that theocentricity may be no more than an illusion produced by a more coherent grammatical structuring.

Throughout *The Rime*, versions of *like* and *as if* convey the falling away of certain reference:

> A speck, a mist, a shape, I wist!
> And still it neared and neared:
> As if it dodged a water-sprite,
> It plunged and tacked and veered. (153–56)

The nervous personification tendered by the Mariner's *as* revokes the generous comparisons that join known and unknown things in epic tradition, refracting the poetics of relation into a disorder of hysterical apprehension. In the *Lyrical Ballads* text of 1798, the syntax was "And, an it dodg'd," making it impossible to distinguish a conjectural syntax ("as if") from a temporal conjunction ("a[s] it dodged"). With the falling away of reference to what can be ordered by logical, and even grammatical, certainty, simile courts horrific conflations and involutions. The verging of figural relations on perceptions of a temporal simultaneity virtually defines the spectral horror of this ghost ship and its occupants:

> And straight the Sun was flecked with bars,
> (Heaven's Mother send us grace!)
> As if through a dungeon-grate he peered
> With broad and burning face. (177–80)

> Are those *her* ribs through which the Sun
> Did peer, as through a grate? (185–86)

The comparisons of *As if* and *as* also signal the impending fate: the Mariner is about to become the prisoner of the game played on this ship. The terror of the game-players themselves is conveyed by a complementary rhetoric of simile in which tenors and vehicles become indistinguishable, in which the spectral and the experiential converge. The "Night-mare Life-in-Death" has "skin . . . as white as leprosy" (192–93), a substitution in which the figure infects the property and becomes its condition—with the illusory enhancement in the *Lyrical Ballads* text of usurping the horror of death itself, for she is "far liker Death than he" (1798: 189). The interior psychological forms of this terror are similarly, and similiticly, self-involved: "Fear at my heart, as at a cup, / My life-blood seemed to sip!" the Mariner cries (204–5), and when he reports how "every soul" of the dying crew "passed me by, / Like the whizz of my cross-bow" (222–23), the reference of his *like* gains peculiar power from the way its vehicle repeats, to reverse, the agency of the earlier shooting of the albatross: the crossbow's arrow, formerly an instrument of aggressive differentiation, now haunts and vexes the Mariner in a simile confirming his isolation from all the crew.

Wordsworth dramatizes an extreme aberration in the similes used by another mariner, the speaker of *The Thorn*, to describe his object of fixation:

> It stands erect, and like a stone
> With lichens it is overgrown.
>
> Like rock or stone, it is o'ergrown
> With lichens to the very top. (10–13)

For his auditor, *lichens*, punctuated by *like*, reverberates extravagantly as *likens*—as if in punning condensation of the over-produced "likenings" this obsessive account sets in play. The project of describing likeness is so intense that the term itself becomes a self-concentrated identity: the hill of moss next to the thorn is "like an infant's grave in size / As like as like can be" (52–53). Both Coleridge and Wordsworth use these haunted tale-tellers to betray the explanatory protocol of simile and implicate the figure in contexts in which all explanations seem problematic. *The Rime* effectively concludes with similes that not only obscure their tenors but also signify rhetorically by reversing the classical decorum of clarification. The Mariner's summary figure for himself deploys a simile whose vehicle expands, without clarifying, his opacity of knowledge: "I pass, like night, from land to land" (586). Although he claims that this global errancy has a mission, to "teach" his "tale," the irony is exposed by the final simile: the thwarted Wedding-Guest who is forced into audience "went like one that hath been stunned, / And is of sense forlorn" (622–23). Subverting the charge to simile as an explanatory and clarifying device, *The Rime* also perverts it from its most traditional Homeric function. Homer's similes, Viktor Pöschl remarks, aim "at illumination of visible relations" and typically derive force from a field of established communal knowledge (81). Thus "symbolizing a calm background of known permanence and continual, harmonious existence," adds Thomas A. Vogler, the Homeric simile implies "an accepted spiritual orientation of the collective consciousness," and bears a "shared sense of value" (9).[14]

Among the few things that may be said to be clear in *The Rime* is Coleridge's use of simile to alienate the world of the poem from any such grid of shared, harmonious experience. Instead, we sense how "method" may exercise

itself in "undue preponderance," creating comparisons that show "the pre-
rogative of the mind . . . stretched into despotism," its domain succumbing to
"the grotesque or the fantastical" ("Method," *Friend* 1: 455). That the Mariner's frame of reference is itself grotesque and fantastical wickedly realizes
what Coleridge found lacking in Bowles, for the Mariner's figures, similes
though they be, are also treacherously "combined & *unified*, with the great
appearances in Nature" in demented perception:

> Day after day, day after day,
> We stuck, nor breath nor motion;
> As idle as a painted ship
> Upon a painted ocean. (115–18)

> The water, like a witch's oils,
> Burnt green, and blue and white. (129–30)

Common points of reference become components of uncommon reports: "A
noise like of a hidden brook / In the leafy month of June" is the innocent
vehicle for the sinister sound of sails moving without wind (369–70); ordinary
sensations yield strange tropes: the Mariner recalls how an eerie wind "fanned
my cheek / Like a meadow-gale of spring— / It mingled strangely with my
fears, / Yet it felt like a welcoming" (456–59).

The poem's two epic similes are a dark parody of the ideal of shared experience. One is the strange simile spun by the Hermit who greets the Mariner's ship in the harbor and hails it in terms that evoke the ribbed, sere-sailed
ghost ship:

> see those sails,
> How thin they are and sere!
> I never saw aught like to them,
> Unless perchance it were

> Brown skeletons of leaves that lag
> My forest-brook along;
> When the ivy-tod is heavy with snow,
> And the owlet whoops to the wolf below,
> That eats the she-wolf's young. (529–37)

First at a loss for comparison, the good Hermit recovers remarkably, not only
giving a likely figure for the Mariner's ship but, more impressively, exposing
the configuration of his own ghoulish preoccupations with adversity, misery,
and predation.

In the other epic simile, just prior to this homecoming, the Mariner senses,
falsely it turns out, that the "spell was snapt" (442)—a moment and a figurative structure that impressed Mary Shelley. The illusion is created when, he
recalls,

I look'd far-forth, but little saw
Of what might else be seen.

Like one, that on a lonely road
Doth walk in fear and dread,
And having once turn'd round, walks on
And turns no more his head:
Because he knows, a frightful fiend
Doth close behind him tread. (1798 text, 449–56)

That Coleridge gives the simile its own stanza endows it with a weird independence from the narrative, making the state of mind it conveys seem as
detachable and free-floating as the wandering Mariner himself. The comma
after "knows" (455) heightens the effect, implying a relative assurance not
factually related to what it claims. This aura is the quality that Shelley translates when she has Victor Frankenstein summon these same lines to express
"the load that weighed upon [his] mind" as he walks the streets of Ingolstadt,
seeking "to avoid the wretch whom [he] feared every turning of the street
would present to [his] view." [15] As often as Coleridge invests poetic language
with the work of intelligible relations, he summons simile, as Shelley's allusion
helps us see, to evoke sensations in which the project of relation recoils—in
which the formal charge of simile is to turn round a circle of subjectivity im-
pervious to clarification.

"Satisfying . . . the desire for resemblance"

The anarchic and fundamentally self-reflexive energy in simile limned in
Coleridge's free-floating stanza is also part of the figure's legacy. Pope felt he
had to defend Homer's similes from the charge of being "too exuberant and
full of Circumstances," of exposing an "Inability to confine itself to that single
Circumstance upon which the Comparison is grounded" (*Poems* 7: 13). The
self-generating expansions of Milton's similes were similarly controversial,
provoking complaints about decorum or calling for careful defense.[16] What
the debate exposes is the protocol that traditionally keeps simile in rein,
namely, its reference to a conceptual ideology. This frame is what underwrites
and supports the explanatory and pedagogic claim of simile, and with sufficient tenacity in rhetorical tradition to give acts of comparison an almost architectonic organization in the psychology, epistemology, and metaphysics of
analogy.

However various Coleridge's play with simile, when the comparisons expand to analogy, the stakes are raised: "language is analogous, wherever a
thing, power, or principle in a higher dignity is expressed by the same thing,
power, or principle in a lower but more known form" (*Aids to Reflection* 205).

Hartley, by whom this thinking was influenced, discourses enthusiastically on such relations: figures of analogy tend to "present themselves to us every-where in natural and artificial Things; and whole Groupes of figurative Phrases . . . pass into analogical Reasoning, and become a Guide in the Search after Truth, and an Evidence for it in some degree" (part 1, prop. 82; 1: 293). In this rapid expansion of figure into evidence, Hartley was accelerated by the moral implications: "Properties, Beauties, Perfections, Desires, or Defects and Aversions, which adhere by Association to the Simile, Parable, or Emblem . . . are insensibly, as it were, transferred upon the Things represented. Hence the Passions are moved to Good or to Evil, Speculation is turned to Practice, and either some important Truth felt and realized, or some Error and Vice gilded over and recommended" (ibid.; 1: 297).

Not that Coleridge was untroubled by Hartley's principles; but in poems of such "intricate analogical ingenuity" and so "implicitly informed by . . . analogical gesture" as "This Lime-tree Bower my Prison," the similes are correspondingly charged.[17] Comparative syntax virtually plots this poem's drama of mind. We first hear its speaker in a hyperbolic sulk, lamenting his loss of

> Beauties and feelings, such as would have been
> Most sweet to my remembrance even when age
> Had dimm'd mine eyes to blindness! (3–5)

This querulous simile has an oddly tentative structure: the present account of what is "lost" gets compared to a future frustration of imagination, making this a simile whose vehicle is conceived only as hypothesis. Coleridge brilliantly accommodates this peculiarity by expanding the whole figure into "blindness"—and, by implication, inviting the compensatory acts of imagination that come into play as the visual field recedes. In this prospect of absence, negation, and invisibility, simile emerges as the agent of restoration.

This conversion begins with the next comparison, as the poet envisions his friend Charles "Struck with deep joy," standing "as I have stood, / Silent with swimming sense" (38–39). This turn of sympathy across time and space through the comparison of *as* propels the verse from the original sensation of deprivation into a moment of spiritual participation, whose present tenses and capacious participles suggest a shared experience as well as a projected fantasy. Together, they

> gaze till all doth seem
> Less gross than bodily; and of such hues
> As veil the Almighty Spirit, when yet he makes
> Spirits perceive his presence. (40–43)

This second *as* (42) enhances the poetics of participation by translating the "such as" that had earlier signified absence and isolation ("such as would have been / Most sweet") into a term of "presence" and relation. The repetition not only aligns the poet's gesture of friendly sympathy with how "the Almighty Spirit" relates to human "spirits"; it also raises the syntax of relation to a principle of divinely sanctioned generosity: Hosea reports how the Lord "used similitudes" to speak to the Israelites (12: 10), and Milton describes the "Son" as the "Divine Similitude" of "th' Almighty Father," "Whom else no Creature can behold" (*Paradise Lost* 3.384–87). These divine poetics implicitly inform the renewal that Coleridge's more humble similes elaborate:

> A delight
> Comes sudden on my heart, and I am glad
> As I myself were there! (43–45)

The exclamation gains force by seeming to absorb its subjunctive *as [if]*, which admits absence, into a comparison of present experiences of gladness. Wordsworth's remark that "in lyric poetry the subject and simile should be as much as possible lost in each other" finds no better satisfaction than in Coleridge's subtle transformations of the figure in this poem.[18]

This deft use of simile to convey correspondence and participation is anticipated, ironically enough, by a sonnet that Coleridge wrote in 1794 "To the Rev. W. L. Bowles" himself. Reading Bowles's "kindred lays" bears a "healing solace" (8), one that works

> While shadowy PLEASURE, with mysterious wings,
> Brooded the wavy and tumultuous mind,
>
> Like that great Spirit, who with plastic sweep
> Mov'd on the darkness of the formless Deep!
> (*Morning Chronicle* text, 11–14)

The shaping of this climactic couplet by simile accords with its tenuous tenor, shadowy pleasure—a penumbral version of the similes that illuminate the correspondence of Spirit and human in "This Lime-tree Bower." This effect is deepened by Coleridge's patently allusive reworking of the image with which Milton addresses his "Spirit" of inspiration at the outset of *Paradise Lost*:

> Thou from the first
> Wast present, and with mighty wings outspread
> Dove-like satst brooding on the vast Abyss
> And mad'st it pregnant: What in me is dark
> Illumine (1.19–23)

In a complex set of transformations, Coleridge's winged and brooding "Pleasure" takes the vehicle of Milton's simile, "Dove-like," into its metaphorical figuring, while his own simile, "Like that great Spirit," uses the "Spirit" of Milton's address as its vehicle. The allusive inversion captures the value that

attracts Coleridge to simile, its capacity to convey the shadowy sensations beyond the call of Miltonic illumination. This value informs his extension and
complication of the figure in his second version of the poem (1796), where the
couplet reads: "As the great SPIRIT erst with plastic sweep / Mov'd on the
darkness of the unform'd deep." Anchoring the line with *As* rather than *Like*
adds a temporal shade to the analogical pattern, making the event in the poet's
mind seem not only preceded by, but simultaneously participating in, the work
of this great Spirit.

And yet the Miltonic figure is double-edged. On the one hand, it implies
an epic correspondent for this moment of individual restoration. With *as* signifying both likeness and repetition, even the notation "erst" works less to
distance the two processes than to establish an original power in an efficacious
temporality, wherein what is "unform'd" (the implication is different from the
first text's *formless*) may anticipate later formation. On the other hand, Coleridge's interiority concedes the fugitive gleam of Milton's answerable style,
the historical remoteness of an age of faith in which a poet could offer interpretation as privileged insight and authoritatively produce similes (so Anne
Ferry writes) to "elaborate and sustain the pattern of contrasts between the
world of 'things invisible to mortal sight' and our fallen world" (69).

Some contemporaneous poems such as "On observing a Blossom on the
First of February 1796" relinquish such nostalgia to accept their modernity,
using their similes in ways that suggest that comparison is just an exercise of
thought—or of writing. Addressing a "Flower that must perish!" Coleridge
spins comparisons with the campy ease of a Shakespearean sonneteer: "shall I
liken thee / To some sweet girl . . . / Nipp'd by consumption mid untimely
charms? / Or to Bristowa's bard . . . ? / or . . . / Shall I compare thee to poor
Poland's hope?" (9–16). While his mockery of this activity as "Dim similitudes / Weaving in moral strains" (19–20) echoes the complaint about
Bowles's "dim analogies," the verb of agency, *weaving*, complicates this judgment by summoning and punning the Latin participle, *textus*.[19] The effect is
to cast similitudes, dim and idle though they seem, as figures for any writer's
method. They may even be this poet's restoration, for in this weaving, he says,
he has found relief "From anxious Self, Life's cruel taskmaster!" (21).

The exercise of invention, the interrogative syntax, and the sheer act of
accumulation organized by nothing more crucial than an equalizing *or* are
recreation in a life that holds other tasks: on this occasion, one thought is as
good as another, and patent simile liberates language into play. As Byron proposes in *Don Juan*, "what you will;— / My similes are gathered in a heap, / So
pick and chuse—" (6.68).[20] For Coleridge's poet, the activity of simile-making
turns out, ironically, to fulfill the harmonizing functions of the symbol: "the
warm wooings of this sunny day / Tremble along my frame and harmonize /
The attempered organ" (22–24). The poem ends, appropriately, with a simile

that is about its own processes of reading the perishable flower: "even saddest thoughts / Mix with some sweet sensations, like harsh tunes / Played deftly on a soft-toned instrument" (24–26). Another poem of the same year, which Coleridge titled "A Simile" (*Letters* 1: 18), playfully enlists the figure as the muse itself. Its project is to "find a likeness for [a] friend" (2) and his wife—a kind of Jack Spratt and wife couple. "Ah then, what simile will suit?" he asks (19), and then tests several. "Thus I humm'd and ha'd awhile, / When Madam Memory with a smile / Thus twitch'd my ear" (23–25); the apt simile (which Coleridge's verbal wit suggests is accomplished by the insertion of "I" into memory's "smile") then unfolds—"A little Ape with huge She-Bear / Link'd by hapless chain together" (27–28), a linking that tropes the formation of simile, at least in the history of complaints about the figure.

The self-reflexiveness of these playful similes bears an energy that is different from, even opposite to, the self-reflexiveness that produces anarchy and isolation in *Christabel* and *The Rime*. Allied with artfully gained harmonies, the aesthetic self-consciousness of these figures suggests why simile is so frequently summoned by Romantic writers to describe poetic process. Keats half-similizes when he says that the "Imagination may be compared to Adam's dream" (*KL* 1: 185), and he casts two similes to describe his sensations on reading Chapman's imaginative translation of Homer:

> Then felt I like some watcher of the skies
> When a new planet swims into his ken;
> Or like stout Cortez when with eagle eyes
> He star'd at the Pacific— (*Poems* 1817)

In a self-measuring against Wordsworth, he offers "a simile of human life as far as I now perceive it. . . . Well—I compare human life to a large Mansion of Many Apartments" (*KL* 1: 280). And in a cunning romance fragment, he makes the failure of simile the end of inspiration: "Alexandre the Conqueroure," enrapt by a sleeping beauty, spins a half dozen similes, but when he gazes on the lady's breast he is stumped. At this moment, "a genyus appearyd" announcing: "'an thou canst not descrybe ye ladye's breste, and fynde a simile thereunto, I forbyde thee to proceede yn thy romaunt.' Thys, I kennd fulle welle, far surpassyd my feble powres, and forthwythe I was fayne to droppe my quille" (Cook ed. 333). In a characteristic Keatsian conflation, erotic and poetic success are synonymous, in this case, both measured by a capacity to generate similes.

This affiliation of comparative power with inspiration impresses Shelley as well, for whom "Reason respects the differences, and imagination the similitudes of things" (*Defence* 480), and who generates three telescoping similes for "the mind in creation": it "is as a fading coal which some invisible influence, like an inconstant wind, awakens to transitory brightness: this power arises from within, like the colour of a flower which fades and changes as it is developed" (503–4). By the play of simile, we may read the poet. F. R. Leavis, though he did not like the effect, recognized it as one of those "essential . . . Shelleyan characteristics." His antipathy to "Ode to the West Wind" recalls complaints about the epic simile made by eighteenth-century critics: a "general tendency" in the elaboration of images "to forget the status of the metaphor or simile that introduced them and to assume an autonomy and a right to propagate, so that we lose in confused generations and perspectives the perception or thought that was the ostensible *raison d'être* of imagery" ("Shelley" 193–94). Deeming this a symptom of Shelley's "weak grasp upon the actual," Leavis resists a compellingly intelligent effect; but others such as William Keach show how deeply such rhetoric is involved with Shelley's project of imaging mental operations.

Wordsworth, too, investigates the self-generating energies of imagination in simile: "Imagination! lifting up itself / Before the eye and progress of my Song / Like an unfather'd vapour" (1805 *Prelude* 6.525–27). Not only is the peculiar reference of the simile itself evocative in the "presencing" work of the apostrophe but, genetically, the passage was linked in Wordsworth's composition to another simile, an epic one conveying his dejection at having crossed the Alps without the expected climax.[21] The mind's creative power is its work of resemblance, claims a great heir of Romantic poetics, Stevens: "the mind begets in resemblance as the painter begets in representation," for resemblance "which seems to be related so closely to the imagination is related even more closely to the intelligence, of which perceptions of resemblance are effortless accelerations" ("Three Academic Pieces" 76, 75). The last poem in *Collected Poems*, "Not Ideas About the Thing / But the Thing Itself," dramatizes this acceleration. It opens in a mental theater of resemblance—"At the earliest ending of winter, / In March, a scrawny cry from outside / Seemed like a sound in his mind"—and ends with an ontology at once advanced and restrained by a simile at the end of the mind and line: "It was like / A new knowledge of reality." If, as Stevens insists, poetry is the meta-text of resemblance, "a satisfying of the desire for resemblance" ("Three" 77), simile is its meta-trope.

Read in this context, Coleridge's similes are compelling for the way they expose the rhetorical strains behind the seemingly effortless accelerations that Stevens celebrates. This exposure is the figurative conversation of the "Effusion" (MS. R) later titled "The Eolian Harp." It opens by dallying with some self-mocking, Bowlesian moralizing about nature as a storehouse of "Meet emblems" for Innocence, Love, and Wisdom (4–9). The "artificiality of the construct" impedes the "fusion of tenor and vehicle in a properly symbolic style," remarks Tilottama Rajan about this rhetoric in "The Eolian Harp"; it thwarts "the imaginative realization of a symbolic landscape instinct with the signatures of consciousness" ("Displacing" 471). I want to suggest that this impediment is calculated in order to foreground the process of signature. The initial emblemizing is merely a more formulaic version of what unfolds from "And that simplest Lute" (R: 12). Both the conjunctive *And* and its placement in the same metrical line (12) that concludes the playful emblemizing draw the ensuing similes for the lute into the fictive trajectory of the initial "emblems":

> How by the desultory Breeze caress'd
> (Like some coy Maid half-yielding to her Lover)
> It pours such sweet Upbraidings, as must needs
> Tempt to repeat the wrong. (R: 14–17)

The only difference is the air of spontaneous invention (motivated by a fantasy of erotic seduction) that displaces conventional readings. The acknowledged artificiality (ironically in terms of the trope, ruefully in terms of the hoped-for seduction) launches the extravagant turn to simile. The amorous poet compares the harp's music to

> such as erst
> Round rosy bowers (so Legendaries tell)
> To sleeping Maids came floating witchingly
> By wand'ring West winds stoln from Faery land;
> Where on some magic Hybla MELODIES
> Round many a newborn honey-dropping Flower,
> Footless and wild, like Birds of Paradise,
> Nor pause, nor perch, hovering on untir'd wing. (R: 20–27)

As the play of simile becomes ever more involuted, each vehicle spinning a new tenor, Coleridge checks it with a softly satiric self-consciousness. Expanding only along the axis of fantasy, or even, as the last vehicle suggests, patently prelapsarian idyll, the terms are finally self-reflexive: the motion ascribed to those Birds of Paradise wittily mirrors the simile-maker's own activity—his enthusiastic and nearly untamed leaping from simile to simile. Even as the famous effusion interpolated more than three decades later—"O! the one Life within us and abroad"—solicits symbol, the shift from idle play into this enthusiastic declaration is subversively abrupt. The composition of these lines is more related to simile than to symbol, for far from being organic to the original inspiration, they were added on like a superinduced gloss.[22]

The original text stays loyal to simile, not only in its visual figures but also, as the next verse paragraph reveals, in its rhetorical ones:

> And thus, my Love! as on the midway Slope
> Of yonder Hill I stretch my limbs at noon
> And tranquil muse upon Tranquillity.
> Full many a Thought uncall'd and undetain'd

>   And many idle flitting Phantasies
>   Traverse my indolent and passive Mind
> 34   As wild, as various, as the random Gales
>   That swell or flutter on this subject Lute.
>   And what if All of animated Life
>   Be but as Instruments diversely fram'd
>   That tremble into thought, while thro' them breathes
>   One infinite and intellectual Breeze (R: 28–39)

The *as* of line 28 is a circumstantial marker of the postures that court such "flitting Phantasies." But its verbal repetitions in line 34 link the posture of the thinker with the play of his thoughts, his physical with his metaphysical receptivity. The stretch of *as* across these senses corresponds to the several hoverings in this scene of mental play: the poet is midway on a slope, at midday, making similes ("as wild, as various, as the random Gales") that mediate first between fantasy and nature and then boldly animate nature itself as vehicle for "Thought." In other early versions of this passage, Coleridge began the pivotal "And what if . . . ?" with *Or*, as if to distinguish its surmise about the unifying principle of diverse framings from the "flitting Phantasies" preceding it (*Poems* 102). Yet "Effusion" not only retains *And* and keeps the surmise in the same verse paragraph, but also bears a simile: "And what if All of animated Life / Be but as Instruments diversly fram'd?" Both the verse form of the paragraph and the rhetorical form of the simile keep the speculation affiliated to other idle plays of thought. Working against the Platonic tradition of hypothetical play as a vehicle for truths, "as" resists making special claims for its tenor. As Demetrius remarks in *On Style*, simile is the "less risky expression" (111).[23] If Coleridge's subsequent erasure of *as* accelerates his surmise, his "what if?" still confronts a reproof from his companion (however undecidable the irony), and this is a scene that every text retains.

In these forms, Coleridge is more prone to skepticism about figures than to a poetics of blithe equivalence. He is aware of how analogical reading, traditionally vested as ontologically informed, may weave relations neither predicated on nor legislated by rational, analogical order; they may even be entirely fictive. In the ironic maneuvering and temporality of his similes, there are even apprehensions of what Barthes terms "the demon of analogy": "analogy implies an effect of Nature: it constitutes the 'natural' as a source of truth; and what adds to the curse of analogy is the fact that it is irrepressible: no sooner is a form seen than it *must* resemble something: humanity seems doomed to Analogy" (*Roland Barthes* 44). Hartley himself could worry that "the Mind being once initiated into the Method of discovering Analogies, and expressing them, does by Association persevere in this Method, and even force things into its System by concealing Disparities, magnifying Resemblances, and accommodating Language thereto" (1: 296–97.) As Wordsworth recalls himself "first beginning in my thoughts to mark / That sense of dim similitude which links / Our moral feelings with external forms," his verb *to mark* is nicely ambiguous about the agency of relation: "to note" something already given (though dimly) in the external order; or conversely, "to inscribe" in the intention of ordering.[24] In the background of this ambiguity is Locke's argument that all language is "a voluntary imposition, whereby such a word is made arbitrarily the mark of such an *idea*"—"not by any natural connection," but by "a *perfectly arbitrary imposition*" (Book 3, ch. 2; 2: 132).[25]

For his part, Coleridge tends to use "dim similitude"—the opposite of "Divine Similitude"—to signal dubious explanations. As the poet of *The Destiny of Nations*, for instance, declares his belief that "Properties are God" (36), he describes another line of reflection taken by those who

> boldlier think
> That as one body seems the aggregate
> Of atoms numberless, each organized;
> So by a strange and dim similitude
> Infinite myriads of self-conscious minds
> Are one all-conscious Spirit, which informs
> With absolute ubiquity of thought. (39–45)

The method of "similitude" dims the analogical argument it would shape and the chiasmus it would anchor. One doesn't quite know how to take the irony of this same voice resorting to simile over the course of the poem to explicate its own dim or obscure apprehensions. The perplexity is Coleridge's as well: even as he notes that "different means to the same end seem to constitute analogy," he has to admit that "analogy always implies a difference in kind & not merely in degree" (December 12, 1804; *Notebooks* 2319), and he is never free from sensing the factitiousness that he despised in Bowles's dim analogies.

"Suspending the power of comparison"

The "difference" that simile, for better or worse, always implies helps explain the pervasive interest in Romantic poetics in events that call the power of comparison into question or suspend it altogether, canceling its efforts in the sensation of a totalizing unity. For Coleridge, the most intense apprehensions occur as imagination by simile is shown to be not only inadequate but impossible: if the "beautiful . . . in its highest perfection sustains while it satisfies the comparing Power," the "sublime" appears "in relation to which the exercise of comparison is suspended."[26] This suspense infuses his report of "a storm of wind" over the Lake of Ratzeburg, accompanied "during the whole night" by "the thunders and howlings of the breaking ice." Such sounds, Coleridge contends, are "more sublime than any sight *can* be, more absolutely suspending the power of comparison, and more utterly absorbing the mind's self-consciousness in its total attention to the object working upon it." The power of comparison returns only in aftermath, and only with the return of visual coordinates: "On the evening of the next day, at sun-set, the shattered ice thus frozen, appeared of a deep blue and in shape like an agitated sea" (*Friend* 1: 367). In the ice-skating episode from *The Prelude*, Book 1, that he appends to this report (368–69), we see Wordsworth's sympathy with this drama of comparing activity. Its similes describe action and sensation that are still in the realm of the familiar, but that are about to be propelled into alien registers:

> I wheel'd about,
> Proud and exulting, like an untir'd horse
> That car'd not for its home. . . .
>
> Meanwhile the precipices rang aloud,
> The leafless trees and every icy crag
> Tinkled like iron. (*Friend* 1: 369)

Even in these comparisons we sense Wordsworth's disdain of the merely picturesque "habit" of "giving way / To a comparison of scene with scene" (*Prelude* 11.157–58) and his deeper interest in moments when the mind is "absorbed in . . . being conscious of external Power at once awful & incommensurable." Like Coleridge's, his imagination is caught by events that baffle comparison, and his investment is the same: "whatever suspends the comparing power of the mind & possesses it with a feeling or image of intense unity, without a conscious contemplation of parts, has produced that state of the mind which is the consummation of the sublime" ("The Sublime and the Beautiful"; *Prose* 2: 353–54).

Crucial in Wordsworth's aesthetic is his trusting of this suspense to an abundant recompense—a possession from without by a sensation of "intense unity." Yet more often than not, it is the phase of transfer, rather than the consummation devoutly to be wished, in which he and Coleridge apprehend the sublime. This intermediary mental exertion produces a language of shifting comparisons—some potent, others potential and flickering, others patently inadequate, and often releasing the bridging rhetoric of *as if*. In the aftermath of the lake-freezing storm, Coleridge reports, "the fishermen stood pulling out their immense nets through the holes made in the ice for this purpose, and the men, their net-poles, and their huge nets, were a part of the glory; say rather, it appeared as if the rich crimson light had shaped itself into these forms, figures, and attitudes, to make a glorious vision in mockery of earthly things" (367). Wordsworth summons *as if* in the ice-skating scene to convey a similar sensation, when, by the sudden braking of a "rapid line of motion," he drops the narrative out of the field of familiar nature and into a

sensation of earthly things turned unearthly: "I . . . / Stopp'd short: yet still
the solitary cliffs / Wheel'd by me even as if the earth had roll'd / With visible
motion her diurnal round!" (369). The queasy effect of *still*, in which an initial
suggestion of stasis turns out to signify dizzying duration, is made queasier
still by its transferring of the verb that had described his skating past the
cliffs—"I wheel'd about"—to the action imagined of the cliffs themselves.
The comparative syntax that follows prolongs this dizziness with a peculiar
grammatical slide from an adverbial "even as" to a subjunctive "as if," shaping
a figure whose potency is its very contradiction to any actual fact.

The effort at comparison, even as the mind is drawn "to the point of total
attention to the object working on it," generates the sensation and the aesthetics of the sublime. This tension between willful imagining and rapt absorption is more interesting to Coleridge than the immediacy of a dream. Although dreaming, too, "consists in a suspension of the voluntary and therefore
of the comparative power," it differs from the workings of "illusion," which
solicit the cooperation of, rather than coopt, voluntary imagination: "in sleep
we pass at once by a sudden collapse into this suspension of Will and the
Comparative power: whereas in an interesting Play, read or represented, we
are brought up to this point . . . gradually, by the Art . . . and with the consent
and positive Aidance of our own Will" (*Lectures* 2: 266). In the art of poetry,
this positive aidance is the work of simile in releasing the aesthetics of the
sublime. For both Coleridge and Wordsworth, the effort to shape a simile at
the limits of imagination confirms the sublime, and the sensation of mental
power on the verge of suspense is as crucial to the effect as the overwhelmed
state of mind that follows. Thus, Wordsworth praises one of the notoriously
dilated similes in *Paradise Lost* for the way it at once images and evokes a sublime suspense adequate to "the motion and appearance of the sublime object
to which it is compared" (Preface of 1815; *Prose* 3: 31):

> As when far off at sea a fleet descried
> *Hangs* in the clouds
> . . .
> so seemed
> Far off the flying Fiend. (*Paradise Lost* 2.636–43, Wordsworth's italics)

The "sublime" in the "object" is doubled in the figurative extravagance of its
simile, a nearly Satanic rhetoric in the eyes of some orthodox pre-Romantics.
But to Richard Bentley's numerous objections to the logic of this simile,
Zachary Pearce was willing to admire how Milton, like Homer and Virgil,
"often takes the liberty of wandring into some unresembling Circumstance;
which has no relation to his Comparison" (66–67).

In this unresembling circumstance, what impressed Romantic readers was
the power of the rhetorical resemblance, of a hanging in poetic form that
doubled the vehicle of the comparison. Also mining figures of suspense in

Paradise Lost, Coleridge cites another passage in which shifting seemings and similes do not cancel the effort at comparison but leave the mind "hovering between images . . . unfixed and wavering" between intangible options, to yield a "sublime feeling of the unimaginable." This is Milton's "fine description of Death" (*Lectures* 2: 495–96), the same passage Burke cited as the epitome of an aesthetics where "all is dark, uncertain, confused, terrible, and sublime to the last degree" (*Philosophical Enquiry* 100–101):

> black it stood as Night,
> Fierce as ten Furies, terrible as Hell,
> And shook a dreadful Dart; what seem'd his head
> The likeness of a Kingly Crown had on . . . (*Paradise Lost* 2.670–73)

The first simile shows what Coleridge senses in comparisons conscripted into the sublime: "as Night" at once poses an image of blackness and evokes a massively impenetrable, all-encompassing effect—Death stood as a figure of Night. This effect is intensified by the next two similes, "Fierce as ten Furies, terrible as Hell," each vehicle as opaque as the tenor it would explain. As a total trope of representation, Milton's similes show comparative power being overtaken by the unimaginable—an effect starkly fulfilled in the devastating image toward which these all build: "what seem'd his head / The likeness of a Kingly Crown had on." Blake evokes this rhetoric of simile, and virtually tropes the scene of Milton's Death, when, to render Urizen's apprehension of a world in which "forms / Of life" teem with "vast enormities" (*Urizen* VIII: 1), similitude is surrounded by a rhetoric of stark identity:

> Frightning; faithless; fawning
> Portions of life; similitudes
> Of a foot, or a hand, or a head
> Or a heart, or an eye, they swam mis
>   -chevous
> Dread terrors! (*Urizen* VIII: 2; plate 23 [B])

In the poetics of the sublime, simile is the privileged trope of representational crisis.

Insofar as this crisis taints verbal power per se, simile emerges as the subscript of all figures, shadowing even that to which it is typically opposed, the symbol, and its claim of presence. Staging this consequence in *Religious Musings* ("A desultory poem, written on the Christmas eve of 1794"), Coleridge begins with a potent simile, one that appears to offer the most affirmative of associations:

> This is the time, when most divine to hear,
> The voice of Adoration rouses me,
> As with a Cherub's trump: and high upborne,

Yea, mingling with the Choir, I seem to view
The vision of the heavenly multitude,
Who hymned the song of Peace o'er Bethlehem's fields! (1–6)

But in the company of a tentative *seem*, the simile strains, and soon statements of presence are yielding to notes of absence. Referring to "the Great / Invisible (by symbols only seen)" (9–10), the poet concedes a gap between what the senses apprehend and what is, at best, qualitatively different, "invisible."

This is de Man's "rhetoric of temporality," in which the "translucence" of the symbol works as a "reflection of a more original unity that does not exist in the material world" ("Temporality" 192). But it is Coleridge's rhetoric, too, in moments when his symbolic figures occupy a language that thwarts, defers, and conceals, as much as it seems to present, reveal, and unite the material word and world. Consider this nearly contemporaneous passage from the opening of *The Destiny of Nations*, in which the poet celebrates the power God has given man to "view" him

Through meaner powers and secondary things
17 Effulgent, as through clouds that veil his blaze.
For all that meets the bodily sense I deem
Symbolical, one mighty alphabet
For infant minds; and we in this low world
Placed with our backs to bright Reality,
That we may learn with young unwounded ken
The substance from its shadow. (16–23)

If the simile "as" (17) promises an affirmative analogue and pedagogical clarity, the metaphor in the vehicle, "veil," is ambiguous, suggesting both an agent and an obstruction to true sight. While this is a paradox and potential instability in traditional religious symbolism, on the Coleridgean stage, the disjunctive strains are sufficiently forceful to make the rhetoric of "For all that meets the bodily sense I deem / Symbolical" seem merely formal. The lesson becomes increasingly entrammeled in its contradictions: what meets the bodily sense, it turns out, has to be mediated by something other than bodily sense; what is an alphabet may be opaque to the infant mind, which is unspeaking, pre-linguistic; and finally, if our backs are turned to bright Reality, then, as in Plato's Cave, we are in illusion, learning "the substance from its shadow." The grammatical perplexity of this *from* (in distinction from, or derived from?) aggravates the confusion, for the figure that constitutes a substance is also, with our backs turned to bright Reality, what obstructs it, casting a shadow. The shadow figures as both the reduced language for bodily sense in this low world, and as the symbolical alphabet for a bright reality beyond.

No wonder that even a non-deconstructive critic such as Humphry House (thinking of *The Rime of the Ancient Mariner* and *Kubla Khan*) can challenge

Coleridge's distinction of symbol and allegory: "all allegory involves symbolism, and in proportion as symbolism becomes developed and coherent it tends toward allegory" (93). House means to recuperate this difference on behalf of an ultimately synthetic imagination, but de Man presses Coleridge's distinction to find a synonymy in the field of temporal difference: as Coleridge's symbolism becomes more involved with distance and noncoincidence, he proposes, it tends toward allegory: "symbol and allegory alike . . . have a common origin beyond the world of matter," both designating a "transcendental source" ("Temporality" 192). For de Man, allegory unveils what symbol veils, mystifies, and suppresses: the inevitable distance of the sign "in relation to its own origin" that consigns all language to "the void of this temporal difference" (207). For Derrida, this is the general situation of language, which not only "always implies within itself the distinction between signifier and signified," but exposes the latter only and "*always already in the position of the signifier*" (*Grammatology* 11, 73, his italics).

The capacity of allegory to expose difference and distinction in both rhetoric and history suggests why Coleridge is drawn to it as a poetic mode.[27] Allegorical figures that themselves designate this chain of displacements intensify such striking similes as the one from "Constancy to an Ideal Object" that Brooks has admired: the poet imagines that his "Fond thought" will receive "life-enkindling breath" only "when, like strangers shelt'ring from a storm, / Hope and Despair meet on the porch of Death" (7–10)—when, that is, the temporality to which both Hope and Despair refer is no more. In Brooks's poetics, this simile "has something of the paradoxical quality of metaphysical poetry and it comes to the reader with a fine rhetorical shock," whose "aftershocks, reverberations of meaning . . . expand and deepen the total import."[28] It is suggestive that the New Critical Brooks and the New Historical McGann find common ground with the deconstructive interests of de Man and Derrida in Coleridge's poetics of allegory. Whether the issue is "rhetorical shock" (Brooks), "temporal difference" (de Man), or "ideas and institutions" (McGann), allegory, as a poetical form that Coleridge "associated with a divided or alienated consciousness," was "peculiarly adapted to expose and explore critically the world of illusions, divisions, and false-consciousness," and was troublingly attractive to an imagination "always subject to a negative dialectic of 'apparition and evanishment'" (McGann, *Romantic Ideology* 96–97).[29]

Coleridge's poetics of simile inhabit this dialectic as the self-conscious figuring of its mysterious transitions. In *Religious Musings*, he summons a simile to contemplate the flux and transformation of "dark Passions" through faith:

> Lo they vanish! or acquire
> New names, new features—by supernal grace
> Enrobed with Light, and naturalised in Heaven.
> As when a shepherd on a vernal morn

Through some thick fog creeps timorous with slow foot,
Darkling he fixes on the immediate road
His downward eye: all else of fairest kind
Hid or deformed. But lo! the bursting Sun!
Touched by the enchantment of that sudden beam
Straight the black vapour melteth, and in globes
Of dewy glitter gems each plant and tree;
On every leaf, on every blade it hangs!
Dance glad the new-born intermingling rays,
And wide around the landscape streams with glory! (91–104)

In a footnote (*Poems* 112), Coleridge reinforces explanation by simile: "Our evil Passions, under the influence of Religion, become innocent, and may be made to animate our virtue—in the same manner as the thick mist melted by the Sun, increases the light which it had before excluded." These similes, even as they would circumvent a negative dialectic, are also an analogical fiction, at best an allegory. "In the preceding paragraph [64–87], agreeably to this truth," this note continues, "we had allegorically narrated the transfiguration of Fear into holy Awe." The vehicle of the simile that unfolds from line 94, its spiritual tenor notwithstanding, does not presume a stable symbolist ontology. It elaborates a temporal moment that is also temporary, one that for all its glorious effects, is prone to immediate diffusion and defusion: the "dewy glitter" that "hangs" on everything will (like the pendant icicles of the manuscript "Frost at Midnight") evaporate, vanish, acquire new names, new features. Coleridge does not write this simile into such consequence. Instead, he begins a new paragraph that returns the poetics of identity and one name, along with a rhetoric of flat statement: "There is one Mind, one omnipresent Mind, / Omnific. His most holy name is Love" (105–6). Yet the abruptness of this shift and the contrasting rhetoric only heighten the value of the middle space of the simile and its poetics of willing, though temporary, suspension.

Religious Musings and *The Destiny of Nations* are early poems, but Coleridge retained his attraction to simile in the dialectic of presence and absence. "No simile," he remarks in a lecture of 1818, "is expected to be compleat in all points—Else it would not be a Simile, but an Instance" (*Lectures* 2: 48). "Recollections of Love" (1807–1817) plays darkly with this expectation by setting instance against simile in a figure that unfolds vertiginously toward a perpetually receding point of origin: "You stood before me like a thought, / A dream remembered in a dream" (21–22). Making "thought" the vehicle, Coleridge subverts the usual procedure of simile, in which thought itself would be given a vehicle, an image for its impulse. Instead, "You" remains a figure of indefinition that deepens and extends into the vehicle of a dream remembered in a dream. In the dramatic climax of "Constancy to an Ideal Object," Coleridge shows a poet using an extended simile to fill the space between the presence of a "she" as an object of thought and the absence that makes her only a figure of thought. The poet begins by addressing "yearning Thought! that liv'st but in the brain" (4):

> still thou haunt'st me; and though well I see,
> She is not thou, and only thou art she,
> Still, still as though some dear embodied Good,
> Some living Love before my eyes there stood
> With answering look a ready ear to lend,
> I mourn to thee . . . (11–16)

If the repeated *still* equivocates between duration and position, *as though* intensifies the equivocation by shifting self-consciously into a fully imagined hypothesis, a pre-similitic maneuver in the drama of this poem. Hans Vaihinger, a careful reader of the "strange combination" of *as though / as if*, observes that even as the comparative *as* is modified by its link to a term that assumes "something unreal or impossible . . . yet from this *unreality* or *impossibility* inferences are drawn"; the rhetoric is an "apperceptive construct" within which the case "is still formally maintained" (91–93). He argues that this syntax also bears the logic of "if . . . then": "concealed and suppressed," the apodosis "lurks between the 'as' and the 'if,'" with the conditional allowing the "impossible case" to be "assumed or posited for the moment as possible or real" (258–59). The syntax of Coleridge's "as though . . . / . . . before my eyes there stood" is poised as just such a rhetoric. Echoing to revise the "and though" (11) that resigns itself to actual absence and difference, "as though" tests an apodosis in yearning for a correspondence in the figures of poetry.

The actual simile of "Constancy," one of the most complexly beautiful passages in all of Coleridge's poetry, structures the poem's final paragraph in terms of this equivocation and implies the dependence of language itself on such dialectics of absence and presence. The poet asks of his "Fond Thought," "And art thou nothing?" and answers, in the same line,

> Such thou art, as when
> The woodman winding westward up the glen
> At wintry dawn, where o'er the sheep-track's maze
> The viewless snow-mist weaves a glist'ning haze,
> Sees full before him, gliding without tread,
> An image with a glory round its head;
> The enamoured rustic worships its fair hues,
> Nor knows he makes the shadow, he pursues! (25–32)

This chiasmus, "art thou nothing? Such thou art," mirrors the negative "She is not thou, and only thou art she," but revises it with a simile, a correlative figure for ambivalent constancy to an uncertain object. Appealing to an extraordinary natural phenomenon, the poet can use the hypothetical figure to imply relation between his constancy and the rustic's worship, and at the same time allow its rhetoric to convey a knowing irony. For the poet at least, the simile is self-consciously textual. As Arden Reed nicely observes, its imagery points "to its own status as a linguistic construction": weaving "suggests a metaphor for textuality or poetic language"; the mist, "besides figuring a text," is also "the blank sheet a text is written on, making this simile allegorical for the act of writing: the woodman's shadow inscribes a figure on the fog"; he is "surrounded by, indeed trapped in, his own linguistic and imagistic net" (97). Coleridge's placement of the comma in the last line is as potent as it is when the Ancient Mariner compares himself to the apprehensive one who "knows, a frightful fiend / Doth close behind him tread" (450–51). In both sentences, the comma marks the mind's entrapment by illusion. For the Mariner, it says both that he knows this fiend and he knows himself to be haunted by it. In "Constancy," that only the poet and not the rustic knows that the comma verges on a subordinate syntax ("the shadow that he pursues") tightens the grip of the illusion.

Part of the poignancy of the whole simile is the way its writing shows a poet at the border of the rustic's delusion, even as he signals an ironic detachment. In *Aids to Reflection* (1825), Coleridge summons this same "curious phaenomenon" of ice and light to gloss the unpredictable effect of apprehending "Genius" in others: "The Beholder either recognizes it as a projected Form of his own Being, that moves before him with a Glory round its head, or recoils from it as from a Spectre" (227). Then, in a note appended to "Constancy" in his 1828 *Poems*, he says that this is a "phenomenon, which the Author has himself experienced," and quotes the passage from *Aids to Reflection* to gloss the simile (see *Aids to Reflection* 227–28, 557). Yet as with some other of Coleridge's glosses, this mutual glossing overproduces, for neither "as"— "as a projected Form of his own Being"; "as from a Spectre"—is identical with the situation of the rustic, who neither recognizes the image as a glorified self-projection nor recoils from it as a disembodied other. And the simile-weaver escapes glossing, too, for his wistful comparison, though it reflects on rather than identifies with the unwitting rustic, cannot quite distill projection from delusion. His simile bends the alternatives into a figure that both tests and ironizes the affinity of the poet's constancy with the rustic's naive enamoration. Without having to answer the question, "And art thou nothing?" the poet summons a rustic's phantom to displace a desired "thou" and its equations to thought ("She is not thou, and only thou art she"), using the simile to put before himself and us a figure that simultaneously credits and resists the attraction of ideal objects. If, as Rajan writes, this is a poem that "gives itself and does not give itself to its own illusions," simile emerges as the privileged rhetoric of this painful dilemma (*Dark Interpreter* 204).[30]

The dilemma of double consciousness is the foundation of Coleridge's way

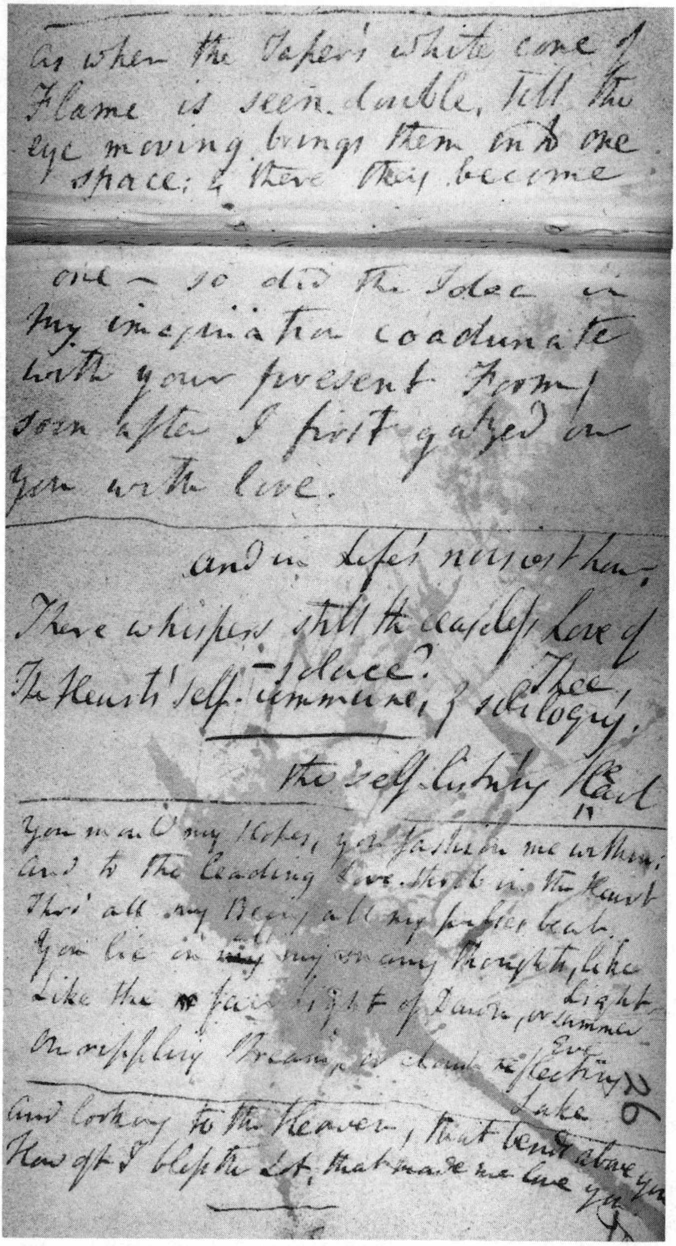

Figure 5. Samuel Taylor Coleridge. "As when the Taper's white cone of / Flame," a simile from Notebook 11: f. 25ᵛ–f. 26. British Library Add MS 47508. Reproduced by permission of The British Library.

with similes. A notebook entry from early 1807 (see Fig. 5) flirts with poetic form as it proposes the relation of "Form" to "Idea" in the form of an extended, doubled simile:

> As when the Taper's white cone of
> Flame is seen double, till the
> eye moving brings them into one
>   space; & there they become
> one — so did the Idea in
> my imagination coadunate
> with your present Form /
> soon after I first gazed on
> you with love. (my transcription of Notebook 11, f 26)[31]

The first part, in the overt form of "As when . . . / . . . so," argues for a true union achieved by an act of will; the second part, implied in the sonnet-couplet-like summation, uses the entire first part as a vehicle for a factitious union. In the first figure, the vehicle is a flame "seen double" in the eyes' relaxed apprehension, and made one by an intentional focus, a gaze that creates the unity of "one space." The tenors of "Idea" and "Form," always highly invested terms for Coleridge, unite by a similar intention, here called "imagination." Yet the play of this simile shows two acts: its argument uses the illusory division of the flame to imply the "real" unity of Idea and Form, and its rhetoric simultaneously displays the opposite, a genuine division coadunated by a factitious imagination that desires and so creates unity.

The second simile, the one implied by "soon after," is inflected by this double play. Subsuming the work of the first simile in coordinating his "Idea" with "your present Form," the poet courts "you" with similar intent, abetted by his punning from "eye" to "Idea" to "I." Yet even as his courtship is energized by these similes of sound and argument, it is also visibly mediated by such rhetoric, which situates the "you" addressed only, however vibrantly, as a "Form" of thought and a corresponding form of poetry. This double effect plays into the way the summary verb "gaze" flickers with two potential senses: the older sense, still current in Coleridge's day, is "look vacantly"—the tacit agency by which a flame is seen double; the more modern sense is "look fixedly"—the intentional movement of the eyes that coadunates the double image, or in the stated "gaze" of these lines, the desirous looking of the lover imagining his union with his beloved.[32] The risky wit of Coleridge's extended simile is the way "gaze" is almost seen double—as the implied verb for the unfocused look that produces false division, and, contradictorily, as the intentional look that brings two into one. The poetic energy of these lines is concentrated in the way they convert this potential semiological vertigo, by the arguments of their telescoping similes, into a poetics of desire that does not lapse into negativity.

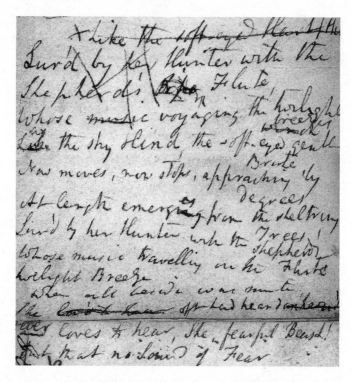

Figure 6. Samuel Taylor Coleridge. "Like the soft-eyed Hart (Hind)," a simile in Notebook 11: f. 45ᵛ–f. 45. British Library Add MS 47508. Reproduced by permission of The British Library.

To Lord Monboddo, who prefers "figurative words only by way of orna-ment," similes mark an unsophisticated linguistic culture whose speakers, "not being able to express a thing by its proper name . . . are naturally driven to tell what it is like" (3: 41). To modern theorists, this is the situation of all linguistic culture. Coleridge sensed the vital dependence of poetic writing on these very perceptions of difference. In the ideal of a symbol's simultaneity and unity, writing becomes redundant, silenced, absorbed; but simile stirs with a productive difference, even a Derridean "différance": "Without the possibility of différance," proposes Derrida, "the desire of presence [against absence] would not find its breathing-space. . . . Différance produces what it forbids, makes possible the very thing that it makes impossible" (*Gramma-tology* 143). This breathing-space and its latent power of inspiration are both the occasion and the subject of another notebook entry, this one from late 1806, tidied up in E. H. Coleridge's edition under the singular title, "A Simile." The notebook text (see Fig. 6; cf. *Notebooks* 2951) shows the beginning of a simile, first with the concentration of *like*, then with the more expansive expressive potential of *as*:

> X ~~Like the soft-eyed Hart (Hind),~~
> Lur'd by her Hunter with the
> Shepherd's ~~Pipe~~ Flute,
> Whose ~~music~~ voyaging the twilight
> > breezes
> As   ~~wind~~
> ~~Like~~ the shy Hind, the soft-eyed gentle
> > Brute,
> Now moves, now stops, approaching by
> > degrees
> > > es
> At length emerg~~ing~~ from the sheltring
> > Trees,
> Lur'd by her Hunter with the shepherd's
> Whose music travelling on the   Flute
> twilight Breeze
> > When all beside was mute,
> She ~~lov'd to hear~~ oft had heard ~~unharm'd~~
> & ever loves to hear, She, fearful Beast!
> but that no Sound of Fear. (my transcription)

This time in explicit poetic form, Coleridge begins a simile, and elaborates the vehicle without apparent purpose or tenor of argument. In his scenario of danger from a charming form of insidious intent, it is tempting to trace in its proto-simile a critique of the rhetoric of simile. But Coleridge's imagination is not so critically pointed. The simile seems indulged as an independent pleasure, recorded only as a potential resource whose tenor, as if in defiance of the danger at which it hints, is unknown and scarcely inevitable.

This indulgence, far from consigning Coleridge's attraction to simile to the trivial motions of an unfocused imagination, displays the vital involvement of his writing with a figure whose form defers even the most urgent demands of allegorizing or referential utility. The vehicle that is pure vehicle, the image that resists the totalizing forms of narrative or idealized symbol, is a compelling demonstration of how poetry can be generated by (and in this case, suspended within) its rhetorical structures. Coleridge's persistent turns and returns to simile are the signature of an imagination always given to reading its world, in various degrees, in formations of *like* and *as*. And the remarkable boldness of this signature is its projection of a formalist criticism worked through the instabilities of organic form and its ideological commitments.

Chapter 4

✖ Revision as Form

Wordsworth's Drowned Man

> Scattering thus
> In passion many a desultory sound
> I deemed that I had adequately cloathed
> Meanings at which I ha[rd]ly hinted thoughts
> And forms of which I scarcely had produced
> A monument and an arbitrary sign
>
>   that considerate and laborious work
> In That patience which admitting no neglect
> By that slow creation {which} imparts to speach
> Outline & substance even till it has give[n]
> A function kindred to organic power
> The vital spirit of a perfect form
>   resting not till. . . .
> —Wordsworth, DC MS. 33 (1798–1799)

>   I had forms distinct
> To steady me: these thoughts did oft revolve
> About some centre palpable which at once
> Incited them to motion and control'd.
> —Wordsworth, *The Prelude* 1805, Book VIII

> do you simply mean, that such thoughts as arise in the progress of composition should be expressed in the first words that offer themselves, as being likely to be most energetic and natural? If so, this is not a rule to be followed without cautious exceptions. My first expressions I often find detestable; and it is frequently true of second words as of second thoughts, that they are the best.
> —Wordsworth to R. P. Gillies, December 22, 1814 (*Letters MY*)

> you know what importance I attach to following strictly the last Copy of the text of an Author.
> —Wordsworth to Alexander Dyce, April 19, 1830 (*Letters LY*)

> Won't almost any theory bear revision?
> —Frost, "The White-Tailed Hornet"

The Textual Authority of Forms

It is rather early on in his autobiographical poem, newly extended by 1805 to thirteen books, that Wordsworth confesses one of its motivations: a hope

> that with a frame of outward life,
> I might endue, might fix in a visible home
> Some portion of those phantoms of conceit
> That had been floating loose about so long,
> And to such Beings temperately deal forth
> The many feelings that oppress'd my heart. (1.129–34)[1]

But a tendency to revision—Wordsworth's primary labor with this text across decades nearly coincident with his adult life—makes the hope all too prone to disruption in the play of an imagination in which floating and fixing compete for priority. Despite an intent to form a work that, in the words of its last book, would show "in the end / All gratulant if rightly understood" (13.384–85 / 14.388–89), years of revision subverted the rhetoric of *if* from its temporal promise into a perpetually conditional desire. Even as an illusion of mastery propels revision, the revisions work otherwise: if some fix the phantoms more securely, others often unfix the text with new uncertainties, new baffles to gratulant understanding. The process is not always additive but often contrary, dispersing authority across time and unseating any one moment as the limit of meaning.[2]

This process has another perverse productivity, its generation of debates about textual authority and its trouble to any formalist criticism depending on a unified, discrete, finished, stable textual object. No phenomenon more radically resists (or predicts the challenges to) these notions than Wordsworth's revisionary practices with the poem eventually titled (not by him) *The Prelude*. What kind of form do its plural texts, none published in Wordsworth's lifetime, define? What kind of formalist criticism is adequate to this formation and the whole business of genetic criticism on which it bears? In one long-standing tradition, revisions are read teleologically: they clarify an original intent and refine its "final" expression, each stage conveying the discipline and progress of a poet's mind. This evolutionary model is not the only one however, and *The Prelude*—perhaps more than any nineteenth-century text—poses a strong resistance to it. For many, there is a devolutionary tale: the revisions seem less to signify improvement than a hardening sensibility, the story of decline, default, and anticlimax that gets told about the career as a whole; correspondingly, earlier and earliest versions gain praise for their vitality and fidelity to the best "Wordsworth." Their recovery is the rationale of Cornell's expensive and elaborate editions: "Wordsworth's practice of leaving his poems unpublished for years after their completion, and his lifelong habit of revision . . . have obscured the original, often the best, versions of his work."[3]

This massive project is the consequence and archival detailing of a critical event in 1926: Ernest de Selincourt's unveiling of an 1805 text and his introduction of it in terms that, despite preliminary gestures toward a balanced appraisal of respective strengths and defects, wound up granting it creative priority. Although his preface ceded some improvements to the 1850 text—it "is a better composition"; its "weak phrases are strengthened, and its whole texture is more closely knit" in a way that "often gives form and outline to a thought before but vaguely suggested" (lvii)—he gave several demonstrations of "later deterioration" (lx–lxiii), and he concluded by boldly naming "the poet of the years 1798–1805" as "the authentic Wordsworth" (lxxiii). He first promoted the 1805 version in a parallel text edition that wasn't quite parallel: it appeared on the left side, as if it were the base text for 1850 variants. With this advance, de Selincourt then issued the 1805 text as an independent poem in 1933. His editions had considerable influence. Not only did other parallel-text editions follow, but the 1805 text gained such prestige that it became the standard for quotation and critical reference.[4] The evolutionary rubric of revision was being displaced (albeit not without controversy) by an archaeological excavation of original genius. By the 1970s, the case was settled for many. Geoffrey Hartman was describing *The Prelude* as a self-corrupting text, "the freshness of earlier versions . . . dimmed by scruples and qualifications, by revisions that usually overlay rather than deepen insight" (*Wordsworth's Poetry* xvii). "Moving backward to 1805 we find a distinct improvement," Herbert Lindenberger said more conclusively in 1984 (Gaull 3).

This backward movement was extended by the Norton Critical Edition, which in 1979 not only gave parallel texts of 1805 and 1850 (left to right) but included a "Two-Part" poem of 1798–99 that it promoted, stylistically and pedagogically, for the "small compass" of its extraordinary writing.[5] The formalism in such praise is revealing. Echoing de Selincourt's view that "Books I and II . . . form one vital and self-contained whole" (xlvii), Jonathan Wordsworth and Stephen Gill, two of the Norton editors, called it "a separate and internally coherent form" ("Two-Part *Prelude* of 1798–99" 503). J. Wordsworth admired the "simpler and more concentrated form" of its recollections ("Two-Part *Prelude* of 1799" 570), and J. R. MacGillivray observed "a much more unified theme and a much stronger sense of formal structure" compared to later texts (236). The poem that New Criticism had avoided thus returned in acceptable New Critical form. Meanwhile, Mark Reed was editing *The Thirteen-Book "Prelude"* for Cornell, with decidedly post-modern effects. His edition not only places the principle manuscripts for the 1805 text amidst a swirl of related ones but constructs yet another "principal new manuscript" (2: 5), the C-Stage revision of 1818–1820 (DC MS. 82). Designating this as a manuscript "stage" that is "incomplete, often unreliable," Reed avoids any claim that it has "achieved a practically finished form" (2: 6), presenting it merely—but dauntingly—as more evidence in the unfolding story of the poem's composition.[6] However one is inclined to take its information, the C-Stage text thickens the field to be negotiated.

From de Selincourt's unveiling there was no recovery, and controversies over textual authority and authenticity of poetic vision erupted and persisted, agitated by wider discussions of the theory and principles of textual editing.[7] Advocates of the 1850 text, invoking the credit usually accorded latest versions and revisions, argued for its authority as "a finished and free-standing product" under the control of a "supervising idea," and they cited the aesthetic refinements: its "tightened . . . style," "improved . . . diction," increased "clarity and precision," and more coherent "dramatic effects." [8] Advocates of the 1805 text admired the power and more authentic tidings of its "struggle toward definition" (Lindenberger, *On Wordsworth's "Prelude"* 298); and some even preferred the elemental energy of the earliest drafts. Yet, ultimately, neither career narratives nor editorial ideology are adequate to the full compositional history. Despite what Wordsworth himself optimistically described as his "theme / Single, and of determin'd bounds" (1. 669–70 / 641–42), its several distinct but interrelated textual forms, as Jack Stillinger remarks, leave open to question whether revisions are in the business of "clarifying [an] original idea" or of "expressing a different idea" (*Multiple* 93). *The Prelude* defies description by a single authorized text. In the eighth decade of debate about which version represents the true "Wordsworth," the terms have become as repetitive as they are irresolvable.[9] And they seem beside the point, for the poem's history cannot be undone.

More productive approaches have turned from the polemical privileging of one text or another, to respond instead to what is conceded by the Norton Critical Edition's naming, on both its cover and title-page, of "Authoritative Texts"—namely, the very *large* compass of the poem's composition and the challenge that this poses to theories of textual authority. If the New Critical practice was to slight "variants" in the belief that "the existence and the exhibition of such genetic vestiges is not intrinsic to the confrontation of our minds with the poem" (Wimsatt, "What to Say" 231), later critics, as well as editors, have included such vestiges and versions. Stillinger and Reiman (despite the latter's scholarly and aesthetic preference for the 1850) have elaborated proposals by James Thorpe and others to advocate new principles for representing works such as *The Prelude*. Arguing that to privilege a text is only to state a preference, Stillinger urges "the legitimacy and interest . . . of *all* the versions" (*Multiple* 94). Reiman supports this plurality for historicist principles as well. Resisting such speculative constructions as Owen's admittedly "eclectic" text of the fourteen-book poem (which, whatever its merits, has no discrete textual or historical existence), Reiman urges editorial "versioning," that is, making available "enough different *primary* textual documents and states of major texts" to enable comparisons—a project critical for works involving "two or more radically differing versions that exhibit quite distinct ideologies, aesthetic perspectives, or rhetorical strategies" ("Versioning" 169). All of us now welcome two *King Lear*s and two endings to *Great Expectations*,[10] and Romanticists have long accepted more than one version of Coleridge's *Rime*.[11] First prompted by Jerome McGann and David Simpson, we've also renewed attention to "La Belle Dame sans Mercy," the ballad by Keats that Hunt published in the *Indicator*, with important differences from the letter-draft version titled "La Belle Dame sans Merci" that editors have canonized. We also have two texts of *Frankenstein*, 1818 and 1831.[12] The Norton Critical *Prelude* and the cross-referenced Cornell editions do no more than formalize a multi-textual fact and facilitate intertextual attention. Whether one revels in or regrets the resources, there is no revoking their existence and no profit in resisting their challenge.[13] Wordsworthian revision, as both an activity of reflection and as a mode of composition, requires an account of poetic authority and poetic form adequate to its plural texts.

A decentered *Prelude* may even court description as a Barthesian "text," a methodological field and "*an activity of production.*"[14] Yet such productivity does not necessarily entail "the death of the author" and the corresponding "birth of the reader." If we recast Barthes' famous story for *The Prelude*, we discover a *re*birth, by reading, of a different kind of author. Barthes radically democratizes the text, canceling meaning from the domain of authorial intention or historical possibility and deeding it over to the reader's play. But insofar as Wordsworth's autobiographical situation interplays reading with writing, it prefigures this dissemination, and his revisionary text often intuits it. As poetic activity recollects, reviews, interprets and reinterprets its phantoms of conceit, poetic composition produces revision as the enactment as well as the report of these processes. Scanning the surfaces and depths of time past, the "considerate and laborious work" of writing returns Wordsworth to manuscripts past, to reperuse the surfaces and gaps of their texts.[15] Manuscripts as well as memories constitute his past, and textual revision reduplicates, perpetuates, and enters into recollection. In this involute, revision is not just compositional; it is the very trope of autobiography, a resistance, in events large and small, to arresting and fixing phantoms of conceit in a final frame of autobiographical argument.

In this respect, to read the network of Wordsworth's texts is to extend his activity as reader in the network of recollection. Formalist criticism, if it is to be relevant, has to enter into this network and follow its temporal process. As a local site for testing this possibility, I take the textual array, or a text in array, of a drowning in Esthwaite's Lake, a recollection from the poet's boyhood.

To summarize the events: Roving alone along the lakeside near a new home, Wordsworth noticed a heap of garments on the opposite shore and assumed that they belonged to a swimmer; evening fell, the garments remained; the next day, he watched as the lake was dragged and the corpse of a man recovered. Here are the principal versions:[16]

The Two-Part *Prelude*, 1798–1799 (ed. Parrish); *First Part*:
MS. V 7ᵛ–8ʳ

Ere I had seen

Eight summers (and 'twas in the very week
260   When I was first transplanted to thy vale
Beloved Hawkshead! when thy paths, thy shores
And brooks were like a dream of novelty
To my half-infant mind) I chanced to cross
One of those open fields which, shaped like ears)
265   Make green peninsulas on Esthwaite's lake
Twilight was coming on, yet through the gloom
I saw distinctly on the opposite shore
Beneath a tree and close by the lake side
A heap of garments as if left by one
270   Who there was bathing: half an hour I watched
And no one owned·them: meanwhile the calm lake
Grew dark with all the shadows on its breast
And now and then a leaping fish disturb'd
The breathless stillness. The succeeding day
275   There came a company, & in their boat
Sounded with iron hooks and with long poles
At length the dead man 'mid that beauteous scene
Of trees, and hills, and water bolt upright
Rose with his ghastly face. I might advert
280   To numerous accidents in flood, or field
Quarry or moor, or 'mid the winter snows
Distresses and disasters, tragic facts
Of rural history that impressed my mind
With images, to which in following years
285   Far other feelings were attached; with forms
That yet exist with independent life
And, like their archetypes, know no decay.
    There are in our existence spots of time
Which with distinct pre-eminence retain
290   A fructifying virtue, whence, depressed
By trivial occupations and the round
Of ordinary intercourse, our minds,
(~~Especially the imaginative power~~)
Are nourished, and invisibly repaired.

295   Such moments chiefly seem to have their date
       In our first childhood. I remember well . . .

The Prelude, 1805, *Book V*: AB-Stage (ed. Mark Reed)

450   Well do I call to mind the very week,
       When I was first entrusted to the care
       Of that sweet Valley; when its paths, its shores,
       And brooks, were like a dream of novelty
       To my half infant thoughts; that very week
455   While I was roving up and down alone,
       Seeking I knew not what, I chanced to cross
       One of those open fields, which, shaped like ears,
       Make green peninsulas on Esthwaite's Lake.
       Twilight was coming on; yet through the gloom,
460   I saw distinctly on the opposite Shore
       A heap of garments; left, as I suppos'd,
       By one who there was bathing: long I watch'd,
       But no one own'd them: meanwhile, the calm Lake
       Grew dark, with all the shadows on its breast,
465   And, now and then, a fish, upleaping, snapp'd
       The breathless stillness. The succeeding day,
       (Those unclaim'd garments telling a plain Tale)
       Went there a Company, and, in their Boat,
       Sounded with grappling-irons, and long poles.
470   At length, the dead Man, 'mid that beauteous scene
       Of trees, and hills, and water, bolt upright
       Rose with his ghastly face; a spectre-shape
       Of terror even! and yet no vulgar fear,
       Young as I was, a Child not nine years old,
475   Possess'd me; for my inner eye had seen
       Such sights before, among the shining streams
       Of Fairy Land, the Forests of Romance:
       Thence came a spirit, hallowing what I saw
       With decoration and ideal grace;
480   A dignity, a smoothness, like the works
       Of Grecian Art, and purest Poesy.
              I had a precious treasure at that time,
       A little, yellow canvass-cover'd Book,
       A slender abstract of the Arabian Tales . . .

The Thirteen-Book *Prelude*, 1805, *Book V*: C-Stage Reading Text
(ed. Mark Reed)

              Well do I call to mind the very week,
       When I was first entrusted to the care
445   Of that sweet Valley; when its paths, its shores,

And brooks, were like a dream of novelty
To my half infant thoughts; that very week
While I was roving up and down alone,
Seeking I knew not what, I chanced to cross
450   One of those open fields, which, shaped like ears,
Make green peninsulas on Esthwaite's Lake.
Twilight was coming on; yet through the gloom,
Appeared distinctly on the opposite Shore
A heap of garments; left, as I suppos'd,
455   By one who there was bathing: long I watch'd,
But no one own'd them: meanwhile, the calm Lake
Grew dark, with all the shadows on its breast,
And, now and then, a fish upleaping, snapp'd
The breathless stillness. The succeeding day,
460   Those unclaimed garments drew an anxious crowd
Of friends and neighbours to the fatal spot.
In passive expectation on the shore
These stood, while others sounded, from a Boat,
The deep—with grappling irons and long poles.
465   At length, the dead Man, 'mid that beauteous scene
Of trees, and hills, and water, bolt upright
Rose with his ghastly face; a spectre-shape
Of terror even! and yet no vulgar fear,
Young as I was, a Child not nine years old,
470   Possess'd me; for my inner eye had seen
Such sights before, among the shining streams
Of Fairy Land, the Forests of Romance:
Thence came a spirit, hallowing what I saw
With decoration and ideal grace;
475   A dignity, a smoothness, like the works
Of Grecian Art, and purest Poesy.
        I had a precious treasure at that time,
A little, yellow canvass-cover'd Book,
A slender abstract of the Arabian Tales . . .

The Prelude, 1850, *Book Fifth*: W. J. B. Owen's reading text (base text
MS. D)

        Well do I call to mind the very week
When I was first entrusted to the care
430   Of that sweet Valley; when its paths, its shores,
And brooks were like a dream of novelty
To my half-infant thoughts,—that very week,
While I was roving up and down alone,
Seeking I knew not what, I chanced to cross
435   One of those open fields, which, shaped like ears,

Make green peninsulas on Esthwaite's lake.
Twilight was coming on, yet, through the gloom,
Appeared distinctly on the opposite shore
A heap of garments, as if left by One
440 Who might have there been bathing. Long I watched,
But no one owned them; meanwhile, the calm Lake
Grew dark, with all the shadows on its breast,
And, now and then, a fish upleaping, snapped
The breathless stillness. The succeeding day,
445 Those unclaimed garments, telling a plain tale,
Drew to the spot an anxious Crowd; some looked
In passive expectation from the shore,
While from a boat others hung o'er the deep,
Sounding with grappling irons and long poles.
450 At last, the dead Man, 'mid that beauteous scene
Of trees & hills & water, bolt upright
Rose with his ghastly face: a spectre shape
Of terror, yet no soul-debasing fear,
Young as I was, a Child not nine years old,
455 Possessed me; for my inner eye had seen
Such sights before, among the shining streams
Of fairey land, the forests of romance;
Their spirit hallowed the sad spectacle
With decoration and ideal grace;
460 A dignity, a smoothness, like the works
Of Grecian Art, and purest Poesy.
    A precious treasure I had long possessed,
A little, yellow, canvas-covered book,
A slender abstract of the Arabian tales . . .

I'll briefly indicate the range of forms shaping this map of revisions by noting two features—one small and unrevised, one big and extensively so. For the first: Wordsworth seems to have wanted to keep within the form of a single poetic line his abrupt juxtaposition of the twilight vigil and the next day's search: "The breathless stillness. The succeeding day" (MS. V 7^v: 274; C: 459; 5. 466 / 444).[17] Using the same syntax and number of syllables on either side of the period, and crossing it with an iamb ("ness. The"), he joins one scene to the next through the form of his poetic line, rather than a verbal narrative. This poetic form implies the agency of the boy's privately tensed perception in producing the next day's public search—and more: it requires us to fill in the blanks in a manner analogous to the boy's intuition.

Wordsworth's continuing confidence in this local form contrasts with his emphatic "re-vision" of how to form this episode in his story of a poet's mind. And with this revision comes a host of related alterations: tinkerings with syntax and punctuation, recastings of metaphor and invocation, expansions or elisions of narrative detail, as well as important rearrangements of the preliminary context. The effort to secure "perfect form" is never secure from the pressure of "second thoughts." All these reworkings, in both the text and context, involve uncertainties about the story of the poem as a whole, for some revisions support, while others contradict, or even subvert its plot. Writing as an autobiographer, Wordsworth summons this memory into textual recollection with a powerful sense of import; but writing in poetic form acquires its own subversive agency, bearing information that eludes rhetorical mastery and thwarts exact imaginative supervision. In the rest of this chapter, I investigate what is at stake in this revisionary contest and the various poetic formations it affects: the contexts that situate the episode of the drowning; its immediate frames of introduction and ensuing evaluation; and the text of the episode itself.

Form and Context

That Wordsworth would revise this episode is half predicted by its multiple indeterminacies. Each version suspends its narration between premonition and surprise: its very site is likened to "a dream of novelty," seemingly new but latent in the boy's mind. With a similar finesse, Wordsworth represents the events as *chanced* (not claiming, as elsewhere, that he was "led" or "guided"), but also mitigates this impression by noting that the lake peninsulas were "shaped like ears," as if with the attention described in the next day's business—the search party's "sounding" of the lake.[18] In between these faintly sensory registers, the boy's own focus "through the gloom" on an object that appears "distinctly" to sight, a "heap of garments," conveys a probing in the direction of a narrative, his guess that someone was "bathing." The persistently "unclaimed garments" extend this initial narrative attention, generating what Willard Sperry calls a "quickened subjectivity" (27)—both in the boy and, by force of Wordsworth's power of telling, in the poem's reader. The only revision he seems to have made in MS. V (save punctuation) occurs at this point: he first wrote "still lake" (7^v: 271) then made the adjective *calm*. This prevents a repetition by "breathless stillness" a few lines on but also adds a resonance: *calm* bodes *still* with a paradoxical hint of superficial illusion. Implied is another, fatally breathless stillness in the lake's "breathless stillness." The only interruption is the occasional "leaping fish." Like the ear-y peninsulas, this may also be a chance detail; but in the play of ensuing events, it gets invested with an aspect of prefiguration, a sign of "the dead man" who will rise "bolt upright" from the lake's surface. Wordsworth's definite article, *the*, designates something already known and identified.

His finesse with these details—at once tuned to imply the outcome and implied to have been produced by the boy's perspicuous imagination—affiliates this episode with the poem's larger questions about retrospective self-reading: to what degree are the events "determined by various narrative and discursive requirements"?—as Jonathan Culler phrases the issue in his analysis "of a certain self-deconstructive force in narrative and the theory of narrative" (*Pursuit* 186–87). Or, as Wordsworth himself admits,

> I cannot say what portion is in truth
> The naked recollection of that time,
> And what may rather have been call'd to life
> By after-meditation. (3.646–50 / 3.613–16)

Confessing the perplexity that Culler analyzes and that de Man sees as endemic to autobiography,[19] Wordsworth plays it out in shifts of interpretation, ones registering noticeably in his several contextualizations of the events at Esthwaite's Lake.

In 1799, the narrative emerges in a train of recollected boyhood adventures prompted by the mysteriously charged, intention-laden question that launches the autobiography: "Was it for this" (MS. V 2ʳ). Though the pronominal referents are opaque, the metrical emphases, the syntax, as well as the literary antecedents evoked by the rhetoric, all announce a crisis in reckoning, a sense that the present is incommensurate with the promise of the past.[20] The recollections that follow are summoned to close this gap by demonstrating and "tend[ing] . . . / To the same point, the growth of mental power / And love of Nature's works" (7ᵛ: 256–58). But even as the autobiographer advances this "argument," he finds his writing arrested by "such effects as cannot here / Be regularly classed" (255–56). It is under this sign of resistance to the dominant naturalizing scheme that the story of the drowning is hailed into the verse. The apostrophe "Beloved Hawkshead!" (261) tropes the rupture, for its turn away (*apostrephein: to turn away*)—in this case, from argument to recollection—is only the first of several uncertain, rhetorically tensed turns of verse. Why this rhetoric attracts Wordsworth at this moment is illuminated by Culler's fine essay on the trope. Apostrophe, he argues, often interrupts a temporal or argumentative progression, to call attention to the presence of writing. This interruption matters in Wordsworth's call to Hawkshead, for by summoning past affection for a place against the uncertain trammelings of a present argument, he attempts, in Culler's words, to remove "the opposition between presence and absence from empirical time" and locate it "in a discursive time," producing thereby "a play of presence and absence governed not by time but by poetic power." Culler is not thinking of Wordsworth (whom he sees characteristically refusing apostrophe in favor of lyrical forms that work "synecdochially or allegorically," acquiring significance like a narrative [e.g., "lyrical ballads"]). But Mary Jacobus applies Culler's terms to *The Prelude* to show how its processes are driven by a tension between "narrative time" (its story) and "discursive time" (the compositional present in which apostrophe plays): "Regarded as a digressive form, a sort of interruption, excess, or redundancy, apostrophe . . . becomes the signal instance of the rupture of the temporal scheme of memory by the time of writing"—the force and signature of "a radical discontinuity."[21]

Such rupture looms in another turn of the recollective verse, one allied linguistically and conceptually to apostrophe: advertency. This possibility appears as the episode subsides into the autobiographer's musing that he "might advert / To numerous accidents . . . / . . . tragic facts / Of rural history that impressed" his boyish mind (MS. V 8^r: 279–83). Might, but does not. He speaks instead of "images" and "forms" that "yet exist with independent life, / And know no decay" (284–87) and then a theory about "spots of time" that "retain / A fructifying virtue" by which the mind is "nourished, and invisibly repaired" (288–94). These terms, echoing the introduction of this episode as yet another event in "the growth of mental power / And love of Nature's works" (257–58), seem to secure this interpretation. But in elaborating this frame, Wordsworth reverts to deathly facts of personal (if not rural) history. The "spots of time" that follow concern himself at age five stumbling on a mouldered gibbet mast where a murderer was hung (8^v: 307–13), and at age thirteen impatiently waiting for his father's horses to fetch him and his brothers home from school for the Christmas holidays, during which time this father died, leaving his sons orphans (8^v–9^r).[22] If his frame of argument is the growth of mental power, this frame of figures is its rejected shadow, a sequence of forms in the mind which retains the information, signs, and characters of death. As Wordsworth sets the death at the Lake as a text for the mind's life and growth, the mind's "imaginative power" (8^r: 293) seems, ghoulishly, to require new deaths to sustain the "independent life" of his poem. This is a fatal link that Wordsworth's revisions labor to undo.

His principal reworkings reconceive context and commentary to sever the story of the drowning from these deathly affinities. In the "Five-Book" version planned and abandoned in 1804, he puts the drowning in Book 4 and situates the "spots of time" at the end of 5, to follow the ascent of Mount Snowdon and to participate thus in the poem's concluding claims and promises. In the 1805 and 1850 texts, these spots are further distanced, to Books 11 and 12 respectively.[23] With their repetitions thus attenuated, Wordsworth reframes the story of the drowning and revises his reading of its import. From 1805 on, it is set in Book 5, installed in a tract about the education of children by the wise spirits of Nature and the nurture of their imagination by books.

Where the 1799 text multiplies its death, the new context translates the literal corpse into a literary figure, tempering and derealizing its life in the mind by assimilating its impression to forms of reading.

This is not so much a revision as an emergence, for a literary gloss was latent in the poet's proposed advertence in 1799 to other "distresses and disasters, tragic facts / Of rural history," terms that textualize events into literary categories and genres. Book 5's revision takes this textualizing in earnest and goes further, shifting the genre from tragedy to romance, the idealizing discourse of "purest poesy." Its verse immediately moves into a recollection of an actual book in the genre, a potently exotic "abstract of the Arabian Tales." Substituting for the memory of a father's death that follows soon after the account of the drowning in the 1799 poem, this recollection seems even to restore such loss. In the 1799 text, the memory of returning home to the father's house at the holidays is also the memory of his death. In Book 5, the recollection of the Arabian Tales opens a scene of paternal presence and plenty:

> when to my Father's House
> Returning at the holidays, I found
> That golden store of books which I had left,
> Open to my enjoyment once again
> What heart was mine! (5.501–5 / 479–83)

The capitals of "Father's House," following the lightly satirical drama of a "covenant" with a friend to realize the "promise scarcely earthly" of possessing "this Book" and of their religious preserving in this vow "spite of all temptation" (491–98 / 470–77), even cast this return, with some gentle wit, into the paradigm of a spiritual resurrection.

That the method of Book 5 so visibly excludes what the 1799 sequence intensifies helps us appreciate Jonathan Wordsworth's spirited case for the "much more concentrated power" effected by the "much smaller scope" of the earlier poem ("Two-Part *Prelude* of 1799" 568). Yet the more capacious text of Book 5 gains another kind of power in its new affiliations. While Wordsworth's claims that the child who reads "doth reap / One precious gain, that he forgets himself" (368–69 / 347–48), other passages of Book 5, in reviving the specter of death without any protective intercession, show that nothing is ever really forgotten. If the boy who saw the dead man had seen such sights before in his books, Wordsworth's books of autobiography incorporate this sight with a difference. Far from hallowing the corpse with "decoration and ideal grace," their contexts return the information of death in analogous images, figures, and rhetorical events. One is the chronologically later but textually earlier recollection of his encounter as a young man with the "Stiff . . . upright . . . / . . . ghastly" figure of a discharged soldier (4.407–11 / 393–96), an episode whose position near the close of Book 4 makes it a shady neighbor of the lake's corpse (they may even have cohabited in Book 4 of the "Five-Book" poem).[24]

I'll return to the bearing of this nearby figure on Wordsworth's self-construction as a reader and writer of tales; for now, I want to note how this passage, by its resonance and contiguity, forms part of an extended framing for the text of the drowned man, retaining the disturbances that the poet denies to the boy's book-hallowed view of the corpse. Book 5 itself, moreover, begins with a meditation on death and the perishability of books, the repository of "all the meditations of mankind" (37 / 38). Not only does this initial frame reverse the boy's translation of death into books, but Book 5 repeatedly implicates books with death. A book inspires a dream of an Arab frantic to save two books from destruction by universal deluge—one of which, the symbolic book of poetry, scarcely tempers the knowledge of death but prophesies it. The poet's ensuing diatribes against book-ridden education and the book-corrupted child prodigy evoke the spiritual death of the children of the earth forecast by the dream. And his reflection on his own boyhood reading conducts to a sense that its books are now "dead in [his] eyes" (574 / 553). Book 5 also contains two of the dead: the poet's mother; and another lake side figure, the Winander Boy.[25] And, after the drowning of Wordsworth's brother John at sea in February 1805, Book 5, though never noting this death, always bears it as a referential contingency in its recollection of a drowning.

Despite the determined assignment of the drowned man to Book 5, then, the new contexts echo old information. Amidst these returns is one particularly complicated tangle of revision having to do with Wordsworth's varying reports of his age at the time of the drowning. Each revision makes it later and thus more proximate to a major crisis—his mother's death and his consequent removal from the vale of his early years to the vale of the Hawkshead Grammar School.[26] The actual drowning occurred in June 1779, a month after he entered this school (Norton Critical 8, nn. 9 and 1), two months after his ninth birthday, and so on the cusp of his *tenth* summer—a year and three months after his mother's death in March 1778. In the 1799 text, Wordsworth dates the drowning "Ere I had seen / *Eight* summers"—that is, at the start of summer 1777 (his eighth) and several months *before* his mother died. In this aspect, the memory of the drowned man usurps and replaces the memory of her death, or, in the retrospect of twenty years, figures as its obscure anticipation. Then, in Book 5, Wordsworth says he was "not *nine* years old"—dating the drowning after his eighth birthday in April 1778, and thus just a few months after his mother's death. That this calendar is still a year ahead of the actual drowning shows the autobiographer refiguring the tragic facts of rural history into a fiction that assists his own tragedies into oblique representation.

Wordsworth's figurative reconstruction writes what Freud calls a "screen memory," one that blocks and conceals another memory but retains "mnemic residues" that signal its latency—such as the shifting dates in Wordsworth's records above, or, as we shall see, some recurrent imagery.[27] This screening function, both a concealment and a cryptic signifying of such concealment, is evident in the way that the deeper memory, of the mother's death, presses more visibly into the verse several hundred lines on in the 1799 text, in another report of loss and searching:

> For now a trouble came into my mind
> From   causes. I was left alone
> Seeking this visible world, nor knowing why
> The props of my affections were remov'd
> And yet the building stood as if sustain'd
> By its own spirit. All that I beheld
> Was dear to me and from this cause it c[am]e
> That now to Nature's finer influxes
> My mind lay open (MS. V 18ʳ: 320–29)

The contemporaneous MS. U fills the blank space with *obscure* (Parrish ed. 299n.), and by 1805 it becomes *unknown* (2.292 / 278); but the original blank signifies all on its own as a graphic screen of desertion.[28] In the texts of 1805 and 1850, Wordsworth places this report in Book 2, so that when the episode of the drowning is told, the images and figures seem already invested by it. Distanced before or after, the record of trouble in these lines shimmers within the account of the drowning, evoking the lost mother as a repressed referent for the sudden, but obscurely anticipated, death in the lake. In the 1799 text, for instance, the apostrophe that summons the memory is one that more specifically opens the verse to Nature's influx: "'twas in the very week / When I was first transplanted to thy vale / Beloved Hawkshead! . . . thy paths, thy shores" (V 7ᵛ: 259–61). The address projects a sentience and, as *beloved* suggests, affection. Book 5 relinquishes this claim, but it also deepens the suggestion of latent presence by expanding the boy's tracing of the vale: where the 1799 text moves directly from the poet's apostrophe to the boy's chance crossing of the peninsula, the revision interpolates two lines—"that very week / While I was roving up and down alone, / Seeking I knew not what" (454–56 / 432–34)—that affiliate his actions, in both verbal echo and historical particularity, to the era of the solitary, obscurely intentional, motions of "Seeking this visible world, nor knowing why."

One of the most revealing traces of these affiliations in all three texts is the faintly maternal figure of the lake that draws the boy and claims the man: "the shadows on its breast." In this thoroughly Wordsworthian signature, Wordsworth even considered writing *her* for *its*.[29] In the aggregate of Book 5, this figuration of a ghostly mother in the scenario of boyhood seeking bears the fatal trajectory of the episode that precedes it, about the Boy of Winander who internalized "the visible scene . . . / . . . receiv'd / Into the bosom of the steady Lake" and, as if answering its summons, "died / In childhood" (409–15 / 386–92). The "spots of time" that follow in 1799 likewise focus, first obscurely, then directly, on a memory of a parent's death. Each episode records feelings of abandonment and a confrontation with deathly signs. A boy disjoined from his "guide" by "mischance" stumbles onto a scene of death, and an older boy, anxiously awaiting his father's horses, will return to school an orphan. It is suggestive of an obscurely motivated perplexity in the moment of composition that the first recollection, like the account of the drowning, enmeshes Wordsworth in a confusion of historical references. As the Norton Critical notes (9 n. 8), his account conflates a recent hanging of a murderer at Penrith with a hanging a hundred years earlier at Hawkshead, of a man who poisoned his wife. This conflation traces a logic analogous to that of the screen memory, in which another death at Penrith, Wordsworth's mother's, lurks beneath the recollection of another death at Hawkshead, the drowning. The depths exposed in these episodes suggest succinctly but forcefully why *The Prelude* needs to be read as a process of several texts, revisions, and contesting representations.

If the framing of the drowning in Book 5 detaches it from the original text of graveyard plots and their shades of parental deaths, the contents of Book 5 retrieve the information—sometimes as a suppressed referent, sometimes a legible one.[30] Sometimes, even, as a direct reference: this is the only place in his poem where Wordsworth cites his mother, doing so in a composite of her death and his grievance: "she who was the heart / And hinge of all our learnings and our loves; / She left us destitute" (257–59 / 259–61). The Boy of Winander passage plays a part in this grievance. Lines added to its text in Book 5 describe his grave as forgotten by the social presence in whose "silent neighbourhood" it abides (428 / 406)—a presence whose gendering as female and maternal is only partly conventional:

> Even now, methinks, I have before my sight
> That self-same Village Church; I see her sit,
> (The throned Lady spoken of erewhile)
> On her green hill; forgetful of this Boy
> Who slumbers at her feet. (423–27 / 401–4)

Her forgetfulness contrasts his work of remembrance, the voice that says over and over, "Well do I call to mind." These hints of severed or forgetful supervision resist the argument of favored and fostered growth that the autobiography is at pains to develop, a strain aggravated by the original autobiographical status of this Boy and his location in the scene of the drowning: the "green / Peninsulas of Esthwaite" (MS. JJ S^r). The draft alternates its temporal scheme between past and present, absence and presence—and along with this, shifts its rhetoric between elegiac narrative and urgent apostrophe. It begins with a third-person figure and a nonspecific, legendary past, as if to situate this as a text of another time and another person. At the same time, its past imperfect tenses imply an abiding mythic presence, and the rhetoric of apostrophe means to summon a conversational presence:

> There was a boy ye knew him well, ye rocks
> And islands of Winander & ye green
> Peninsulas of Esthwaite many a time
> When the stars began
> To move along the edges of the hills
> Rising or setting would he stand alone
> Beneath the trees or by the glimmering
> lakes
> And through his fingers woven in one
> close knot
> Blow mimic hoot[ings] to the silent owls
> And bid them answer him. (MS. JJ Sʳ; Parrish ed., 86–87)

As these suggestive but uncertainly tensed orientations of rhetoric and temporality shift suddenly into the first person, the legendary account becomes historically specific:

> And they
> would shout
> Across the watry vale & shout again
> Responsive to *my* call (ibid., my italics)

With this first-person reference, the account turns into a chapter of autobiographical history, implicitly past and closed.

This self-reference haunts the version of these lines published in the 1800 *Lyrical Ballads*, which not only explicitly closes the Boy's (now third-person) history with the news that he "died," but allows the poet's contemplation of his grave to suggest a kind of death for the living at the end of boyhood. When this tale enters Book 5, the contiguous reference to the drowning at Esthwaite deepens the autobiographical implication, displaced into third person and distorted in its dating as it is. While the final line of the poem in the 1800 *Lyrical Ballads* says that its Boy "died when he was ten years old" (32), this information shifts to "*ere* he was ten years old" by 1805 (*LB* 140, my italics), also the term of 1805's Book 5 ("ere he was full ten years old" [415])—died, that is, at the same age that the young Wordsworth actually discovered the drowning. This too-suggestive historical affinity perhaps accounts for Wordsworth's loosening of it in his revisions of 1818–20, which now have the Boy die "ere he was full twelve years old" (C 5: 408; cf. 1850: 5.392), two years older than the boy who actually discovers the maternally shadowed death in the Lake, and at least two years older than his textual representations.

Wordsworth's ambivalent affiliations of the Winander Boy's death with his grieving for and grievance against his mother weave into larger ambiguities in Book 5 on issues of supervision: by mothers, by Nature, by tutors, and by books. In the verse that joins the elegy for the mother to the Winander Boy, both figures are tendered as examples of education without books. But the coda to the account of the Boy evokes a "race of real children" (436 / 413, italicizing *real*) taught by books as well as nature:

> Though doing wrong, and suffering, and full oft
> Bending beneath our life's mysterious weight
> Of pain and fear; yet still in happiness
> Not yielding to the happiest upon earth.
> Simplicity in habit, truth in speech,
> Be these the daily strengtheners of their minds!
> May books and nature be their early joy!
> And knowledge, rightly honor'd with that name,
> Knowledge not purchas'd with the loss of power!
>   Well do I call to mind the very week . . . (441–50 / 419–28)

The book-mediated recollection of the drowning that ensues, however, severely tests this economy of knowledge "not purchas'd with the loss of power," for in its knowledge, nature becomes a place of "pain and fear," and books are forced into the role of antidote, even agents of denial of what Nature teaches. Hence, when the poet recollects his childhood library, blessing the authors as "Forgers of lawless Tales . . . / . . . in league" with forces able to "make our wish our power, our thought a deed, / An empire, a possession" (548–53 / 526–31), the illicit gain is precisely that of desire over nature, of textual power over natural deed.

The language Wordsworth uses in this praise is set deliberately against the institutional power and supervision of those "who have the art / To manage books" (373–74):

> the Tutors of our Youth,
> The Guides, the Wardens of our faculties,
> And Stewards of our labour, watchful men
> And skilful in the usury of time,
> Sages, who in their prescience would controul
> All accidents, and to the very road
> Which they have fashion'd, would confine us down,
> Like engines, when will they be taught
> That in the unreasoning progress of the world
> A wiser Spirit is at work for us,

> A better eye than theirs, most prodigal
> Of blessings, and most studious of our good
> Even in what seems our most unfruitful hours?
>   There was a Boy, ye knew him well, ye Cliffs
> And Islands of Winander! (376–90 / 355–67)

This diatribe against the book-masters of the educational establishment points to a strange suppression of historical fact in Wordsworth's account of the drowning: the victim was a schoolmaster, not only undone by an accident of natural power, but undone in the last "ghastly" lesson he thus figures by the overlay of the boy's books.[31]

This quasi-judgment notwithstanding, Wordsworth is not categorically opposed to all instruction, for a hundred lines before he had praised his mother's faith that God-given "instincts" bear "his great correction and controul" (274–75 / 276–77). And in fashioning his own book, he values both the prescience and the road-building that he denounces in the Tutors: his sense of purpose strengthens when he can say, as he does at the end of his Book 1, "The road lies plain before me; 'tis a theme / Single, and of determin'd bounds" (669–70 / 641–42). At the same time, however, more than a few accidents happen on this road, including the double accident (of event and discovery) at Esthwaite's Lake. And throughout, the poem's most powerful moments of imagination, from earliest drafts to late revisions, are triggered by recollections that defeat control by imagination and containment by poetic form: moments of shock, mischance, chance, and surprise that "plant, for immortality, images of sound and sight, in the celestial soil of the Imagination," and yet threaten the possibility of coherent self-knowledge.[32]

Forms with Advertence

In the 1799 text, the recollection of the drowning inhabits a framework of argument that is nothing if not equivocal. Just before turning to it, Wordsworth stands back to survey the contours of his verse thus far:

>   It were a song
> Venial, and such as if I rightly judge
> I might protract unblamed but I perceive
> That much is overlooked, and we should ill
> Attain our object if from delicate fears
> Of breaking in upon the unity
> Of this my argument I should omit
> To speak of such effects as cannot here
> Be regularly classed, yet tend no less
> To the same point, the growth of mental power
> And love of Nature's works.

                        Ere I had seen
Eight summers (and 'twas in the very week
When I was first transplanted to thy vale
Beloved Hawkshead! . . .) (MS. V 7ᵛ: 248–61)

Although the "point" emerges at the end of the protracted sentence that concludes the prefatory paragraph, its path is tortuous. On the one side is Wordsworth's attraction to subjects that, in the regularity with which their effects may be classed, promise to protract the song happily underway; on the other, an uncertainty about sustaining unity of argument in this way. Although he says that the former attraction is merely "venial" and its impulse might be "unblamed," both adjectives court the judgments they would dispel. *Unblamed* raises the question of blame, and *venial* refines its degrees, indicating an excusable but not an innocent action: a venial sin, while less than a mortal one, is still a sin; hence Iago's cynical description as a "venial slip" an error whose appearance courts more scandal than it may warrant (*Othello* 4.1.9). Wordsworth's "venial" means to evoke the opening of Book 9 of *Paradise Lost*, where Milton elegizes the freedom with which "God or Angel Guest" used to permit man "Venial discourse unblam'd" (1–5). Yet where Milton is speaking about errant speculation, Wordsworth means something almost opposite: the argument whose unity is a delicately guarded artifice of omission is the discourse to be blamed; genuine integrity must risk disruption. And the sentence that poses this issue also enacts it, for its syntax is repeatedly self-interrupting. Much "is overlooked" in both contradictory senses of the verb.

The story of the drowning thus enters the verse of 1799 in perplexed alignments, classed with effects that resist the unity of argument, yet leagued with an argument nonetheless: "the growth of mental power / And love of Nature's works." This equivocation recurs right after the climax of the narration, the revelation of the dead man's "ghastly face." Without missing an iamb, Wordsworth writes,

                    I might advert
To numerous accidents in flood, or field
Quarry or moor, or 'mid the winter snows
Distresses and disasters, tragic facts
Of rural history that impressed my mind (MS. V 8ʳ: 279–83)

"I might advert" recalls "I might protract unblamed": though both *might*s are being resisted, they are both described in detail—a rhetoric that blurs the distinction of attraction and denial. And the very category of proposed reference above aggravates the category crisis, for "numerous accidents" names both a common denominator and uncommon events.

These uncertainties about formal unity inflect an even more precise sense of *numerous*: "numerous verse" is blank verse, the form alternately praised as liberty or suspected of abetting errancy, or at least overflow, of imagination. Wordsworth's reference to "numerous verse" early on in Book 5 is leagued with extravagant songs in "native prose" (201 / 202). The allusion is to Milton's description of Adam and Eve's praise of "Thir Maker, in fit strains pronounct or sung / Unmediated": "prompt eloquence / Flow'd from thir lips, in Prose or numerous Verse" (5.148–50). It is critical, however, that such numerous verse find fit strains by its inspiration and occasion, for without such ground, numbers may turn wayward. No less an arbiter than Dr. Johnson is divided on the question. About Young's wildly popular *Night Thoughts*, he suggests that its "wilderness of thought in which the fertility of fancy scatters flowers of every hue and of every odour" makes it "one of the few poems in which blank verse could not be changed for rhyme but with disadvantage. The wild diffusion of the sentiments and the digressive sallies of imagination would have been compressed and restrained by confinement to rhyme" ("Young" 395). Yet he worries that the "exemption which blank verse affords from the necessity of closing the sense with the couplet, betrays luxuriant and active minds into such self-indulgence that they pile image upon image, ornament upon ornament, and are not easily persuaded to close the sense at all"—and his own mimetically discursive expansion dramatizes the case ("Akenside" 417).

That Wordsworth would accrete "numerous" verse by "distresses and disasters" is a further complication, for as he was working on the 1799 text, he was also taking a stand against poetry exploiting such matter. His half-advertence to "numerous accidents in flood, or field / Quarry or moor" is an implicit self-measuring, by force both of overt echo and a weirdly accidental homonym (another "anti-pun")[33] of *moor* and *Moor* that summons Othello, an autobiographer whose repertoire in this genre of the tale beguiles Desdemona and turns a suspicious Venetian court into rapt and sympathetic listeners. Prompted (like Wordsworth) to give "the story of [his] life, / From year to year . . . / . . . from my boyish days / To the very moment" of its telling, Othello spins tales of "most disastrous chances, / Of moving accidents by flood and field" (1.3.129–35).[34] Wordsworth's affinity with such discourse is ambivalent. In the Preface to *Lyrical Ballads* he disdains "craving for extraordinary incident" as a degradation of literary taste (*LB* 746), and in the late 1790s he enlists more than a few of his narrators to the resistance. The poet of *The Ruined Cottage* promises "a common tale / By moving accidents uncharactered" (MS. D 50ᵛ: 231–32); the poet of "Hart-Leap Well" declares, "the moving accident is not my trade" (97); and the poet of *Michael* offers a story "ungarnish'd with events" (19). Yet the 1790s also accumulate a Wordsworthian inventory that patently trades on the appeal so disdained: *Adventures on Salisbury Plain*, *The Borderers*, *The Somersetshire Tragedy*, "The Three Graves," and "The Thorn."[35]

Wordsworth masters this advertence in his 1799 text by subjecting the imaginative productivity of all such accidents to a larger frame that, in effect, imposes regular classification. The "growth of mental power" is to be known and owned to the extent that the immediate emotional affect of these distresses can be shorn off, drained away, and disowned through time: all such tragic facts, the poet insists, "impressed my mind / With images, to which in following years / Far other feelings were attached" (MS. V 8ʳ: 283–85). This plot not only revises, but re-verses the original impression: landscapes of death and loss yield to "forms / That yet exist with independent life / And, like their archetypes, know no decay" (285–87). Yet even as numerous accidents are reduced to this common denominator, the productivity of verse evokes the feelings that its argument would discard. If the argument is that the mind's forms and images "know no decay," as if by independent agency, the word *decay* has a counter-agency that evokes the corpses—drowned man, murdered wife, executed murderer, dead father, all. What the mind's images know, with another form of "independent life," is that they can "know not" their original information of death.³⁶ And it is this not-knowing that the poetic forms of these images oddly contest and subvert.

Even what they contain may be no more knowable, if "spots of time"— the theme of the ensuing verse paragraph of the 1799 text—is the interpretive template. The odd discontinuity by which original impressions are alienated from their historical origins and allied with "other feelings" is read through a scheme, at once spatial and temporal, of invisible relations becoming legible over time. But its master-trope, "spots of time," contests this narrative, for a spot is self-contained, autonomous, and independent, however partitive *of* may be. In one conclusion tested for the first part, subsequently discarded in favor of a scheme in which latent contents are later "called . . . forth / To impregnate and to elevate the mind" (MS. V 10ᵛ: 425–26), Wordsworth even wondered whether to describe "those recollect hours that have the charm / Of visionary things" as "islands in the unnavigable depth / Of our departed time" (MS JJ Qᵛ).³⁷ And even here, he is uncertain whether to say *visible* or *visionary*, *thoughts* or *things*: are these recollections substantial and accessible or phantasmic and lost? If, like a "spot of time," an island is connected to a deep, invisible stratum, Wordsworth's adjectives, *unnavigable* and *departed*, interdict approach even to what is visible. In the landscape of memory as well as in the composition of verse, a "spot of time" may be less a radiant center for the growth of the mind than a site akin to what Freud describes as "the dream's navel, the spot where it reaches down into the unknown. The dream-thoughts to which we are led by interpretation cannot, from the nature of things, have any definite endings; they are bound to branch out in every direction into the intricate net-work of our world of thought" (5: 525).

Forms in Revision

Wordsworth's forms of revision involve the literal sense of seeing again and differently. His chief substantive revision to the text of the drowning, drawing on the concern of Book 5 with books, is a new reading of its place in the mind. Canceling the advertence proposed in 1799 to other "tragic facts" of life, he recruits its latent literariness to a turn to the salutary effects of childhood reading—the memory, indeed the education, of which, he claims, yields images that superimpose themselves, as if by independent agency, on the sight of the corpse. No sooner does he report the sensational resurrection of "the dead Man" from the lake "bolt upright / . . . with his ghastly face; a spectre-shape / Of terror even!" (470–73 / 450–53) than he disclaims its terror for the boy—insisting that "no vulgar fear" (1805 and MS. C), then "no soul-degrading fear," and finally, "no soul-debasing fear" (1850)

> Possess'd me; for my inner eye had seen
> Such sights before, among the shining streams
> Of Fairy Land, the Forests of Romance:
> Thence came a spirit, hallowing what I saw
> With decoration and ideal grace;
> A dignity, a smoothness, like the works
> Of Grecian Art, and purest Poesy. (475–81 / 455–61)

Imagination displaces death and death is redeemed by imagination. While the work of artifice stirs in the 1799 text (it is cast as a tale—"Ere I had seen / Eight summers"—and affiliated with literary genres: tragedy, history, as well as Othello's repertoire), the emphatic revision is the effect ascribed to it. In 1799, the narrative associations are to tragedy, and despite the repair to an argument about "spots of time," other deaths and disasters crowd into composition. In Book 5, it is an incongruously "beauteous scene" that signals and even prefigures advertence: the images and even the syntax of "the dead Man, 'mid that beauteous scene / Of trees, and hills, and water" are repeated in "Such sights . . . among the shining streams / Of Fairy Land, the Forests of Romance." The transposition of *scene* and *sights* in these sites helps the slide from one to the other. Wordsworth uses the aesthetic term *scene* to refer to phenomenal sight and makes *sights* refer both to this and—punning on the "scene" of the outer eye—to what had been "seen" before by the "inner eye" of book-informed memory. Coleridge, always the desynonymizer, objected to this inclination to use *scene* (he is thinking of the similarly punning phrase, "the visible scene," from "There was a Boy") "without some clear reference, proper or metaphorical, to the theatre"; even this usage, he protests, is too "equivocal" in evoking both "scenery" and a unit of dramatic action (*Biographia* 2: 103). But equivocation is exactly what Wordsworth is after in the "beauteous scene" of the drowning; the word predicts an improper (super)imposition of artifice.

The translation of sight into scenery emerges in every version from a train of prior specular events: in 1799, "Ere I had seen / Eight summers," "I saw distinctly," "half an hour I watched" (V 7ᵛ: 258–59, 267, 270); in 1805, "I saw distinctly," "long I watch'd" (460–62); in 1850, "Long I watched," "some looked / In passive expectation" (440, 446–47). The revisions develop the readerly aspect of such visual attention. In the 1799 text, the heap of garments evokes a tentative surmise that is like reading—"as if left by one / Who there was bathing" (269–70). Book 5 makes this scene a text: "Those unclaim'd garments, telling a plain Tale" (467 / 445). This tale—denoted with a capital *T* in 1805 and promoted from the parentheses in 1850–gains a further charge in Book 5 from the earlier figure of books as "garments" shed at death by "the immortal being" (22–23 / 23–24). The episode of the drowning literalizes the trope: the heap of unclaimed garments is read as if a book, and its tale is of its status as the posthumous remnant of an absent body.[38] This bookishness takes another turn when the body appears from the lake, for the boy reads it back into books. The 1850 booking of this body goes further yet, for the corpse is not merely hallowed with a "decoration and ideal grace" bestowed by books but, in a revision of 1805's "what I saw" (478), it becomes a "sad spectacle" (458)—a term that gives what was "seen" a literary staging, its "spectre shape" converted, with etymologic affinity, into an aesthetic "spectacle."

The aesthetic melioration applied by revision exposes the strain of its construction, however, not only in view of the intertextual evidence, but even in its own too obvious labors, as if these were a reaction formation of protesting too much. Stillinger is not alone in judging Wordsworth's summary "explanation" so "lame" that the poet might have been better off resisting the impulse "to interpret or theorize" (*Selected Poems* 551–52). Wordsworth's gloss looks "tack[ed] on" to David Perkins, though he is interested in the tacking as a sign of the poet's "need to reassure himself": "the very violence of [his] fears may be what compels [him] to assert that the incident could be blunted, the fears managed" (*Quest* 17). "No vulgar fear" and "no soul-debasing fear," like "unblam'd," display what they disclaim, bearing a "paradoxical power to create as a shimmering mirage lying over their explicit assertions the presence of what they deny," as Hillis Miller writes about the rhetoric of Wordsworth's praise of London from Westminster Bridge ("Still Heart" 306). The textual productivity of Wordsworth's revisions is such that even what he denies may become more explicit. Where the 1799 text, for instance, gives the corpse a "ghastly face" (279), Book 5 elaborates the image with terms of impression and effect: it is "a spectre-shape / Of terror even!" (472–73 / 452–53). The contradiction between the sensationalism of this report and the disclaimer of "vulgar fear" may account for the slight tempering in the 1850 text, where the excited insistence of *even!* is dropped and the more rigorously supervisory phrase, "soul-debasing," takes up the adjectival space. But the full text of these cancellations and revisions shows the degree to which, within the would-be purified aesthetic control applied by the rubric of Book 5, Wordsworth's writing finds its inspiration by contending with sensations that simultaneously urge formal control and resist its sway. His revisionary text typically works less to refine and stabilize an original intention than to enact a revisionary dialectic of confrontation and containment.

Not only does this dialectic attenuate the authority of the gloss for the corpse, but the textual field of the longer poem bears other, darker glosses—for example, the episode of the discharged soldier that closes Book 4, which echoes within the episode of the drowning in more than few chords.[39] The half-dead soldier is not only another specter shape of terror in the mind of the autobiographer; he is also another dark double for both the boy of immunized imagination and the autobiographer he would become. Recalling a figure seemingly left behind in the 1798–99 text, he speaks as a kind of English Othello grown old and impotent, unable to trade in the moving accident, despite an ample repertoire. His is a "strange half-absence . . . / . . . as of one / Remembering the importance of his theme / But feeling it no longer" (475– 78 / 442–45)—a figure weirdly akin to the child prodigy of Book 5, so dulled by his education that "fear itself, / Natural or supernatural alike, / Unless it leap upon him in a dream, / Touches him not" (315–18 / 308–11), or the self-forgetting boy reader (368–69 / 347–48), or the romance-shielded boy at the lake.

Such insulation is not just numbing; it may also, as Wordsworth knows, engender illusions and delusions, a romancing of personal and social upheaval.[40] The boy's easy conscription of the corpse into the literature of "Fairy Land" and "Romance" is refigured in the man's later description of the French patriot Beaupuy, who maintained his composure during the the Revolution's convulsions by casting their historical immediacy into idealizing and meliorative literary genres:

> He thro' the events
> Of that great change wander'd in perfect faith,
> As through a Book, an old Romance or Tale
> Of Fairy, or some dream of actions wrought
> Behind the summer clouds. (9.305–9 / 298–302)

If Wordsworth's own initial enthusiasm for Revolutionary France showed the "attraction of a Country in Romance," with "Reason" itself a "prime Enchanter" (10.696–99 / 11.112–15), the equivocal bearing of his lines above wonder about such enchantments. While he voices no overt judgment of the strategies one uses to survive war, the notation of wandering, by dint of literary tradition (Dante, Spenser, Milton), courts reading as a figure of potential error. The two analogies for this wandering recognize the extremity of the translation. Not only does Beaupuy's eye refigure the world as a book—the very books that the boy of Hawkshead calls on to mediate his lone image of death—but it seems to half-create that world in the second analogy's vocabulary of displacement and insubstantiality: "dream," "wrought," "summer clouds."

By far the most attractive literary model is the one to which Book 5 turns right after the melioration of the drowned man: The Arabian Tales. A repetition links the book-hallowed corpse to this Romance: the reciprocal of the claim in the 1850 text that no fear "possessed" the boy (455) is the recollection of a book he "possessed" (462). Yet Wordsworth's account of his boyhood romance with this book destabilizes the framework that summons it by evoking a proliferation beyond the control of any one imagination. The "slender abstract" of the Tales, in the unknown and unowned volumes it signifies, bodes uncontainable possibilities; it is "but a block / Hewn from a mighty quarry" (487–88 / 467), more like nature than art, a primer of something ever more about to be.[41] Whatever the boy is able to possess is not enough to make him lord and master of the whole. The teller of the Tales, Scheherazade, evokes such desire and frustration with the very structure of her narratives, for as their frame reveals, her task is to keep the Sultan on the stretch of curiosity in order to prevent him from executing her at dawn. The narrative expansions propelled by her forms of suspense recall the mode from which Wordsworth has never quite adverted: the moving accident, her stock in trade as well as Othello's. But Scheherazade's is a moving accident with a saving difference, for if her tales are as seductive as Othello's, she reverses his fate. Othello adeptly fashions himself as a figure of romance adventure, but he is also undone by others' plots. Scheherazade loves wisely and well: the Sultan not only releases her from the sentence of death, but has her tales written down and published throughout the realm—the highest earthly hope of any author, any poet.

But does her success come to terms with death, as Wordsworth demands of his own writing? Or does it merely forestall considerations of it? Wordsworth's struggle with this question of aesthetic agency often sets his revisions against themselves, its denials paired with greater emphases on what they deny, its forms and anti-forms spurring each other on. Some revisions elaborate signs of control over the specter of death. If the 1799 text situates the boy as one "transplanted to" Hawkshead, in Book 5 he is "entrusted to the care / Of that sweet Valley"—a rewriting with several important elements. The new phrase of conveyance, "entrusted to the care," smoothes out *transplanted*, which bodes disruption as well as purpose. Its dative projects responsive attention and nurturing, a world in which "chance" wanderings are more protected than they might seem; and the new capital of "Valley" inscribes this mythopoesis.[42] "*That* sweet Valley," referring to the valley of the Boy of Winander's privileged childhood, implicitly confers on the boy of Hawkshead the same prodigal blessings and wise supervision. Yet within this more secure framing, other revisions imply a random eventfulness and give fuller play to the boy's anxiety. Canceled are the personification and second-person address that in the 1799 text projected sensate receptivity; instead, there are signs of otherness—"its . . . its"—that imply an inaccessibility, even to autobiographical retrospection. Under these signs, there is also a fuller staging of the boy's restlessness. In the 1799 text, the valley is said to impress his "mind," that object "fram'd" by "Invisible workmansh[ip]" (MS. V I^v); in the revision, there is an active agency of "thoughts" and motions to suggest their pressure—the boy's "roving up and down alone, / Seeking I knew not what" (455–56 / 433–34). This new map of "up and down" also bears a linguistic anticipation of the signs, events, and aftermath of the drowning that it eventually discovers. In 1799, the Lake's surface is broken by a "leaping fish"; Book 5 changes the adjective to "*up*leaping," visibly prefiguring the rising of the dead man "bolt upright" (465, 471 / 443, 451). The C-stage revisions of 1818–20 extend this grid with the detail of the boat party sounding the "deep" (464), and the 1850 text elaborates it even further with the boat's searchers looking "o'er the deep" and the poet's claim that no "Soul-*debasing* fear" possessed the boy (448, 453).

This new verbal texture conveys a deeper sense of the mystery and anxiety that Book 5 would legislate into textual control. Even the "heap of garments," though endowed with a more legibly bookish function, is more enigmatic in each revision. The 1799 text writes this object into the sort of prosaic map we recognize in other of Wordsworth's spot-obsessed poems—"on the opposite shore / Beneath a tree and close by the lake side"; and the conjecture, "as if left by one / Who there was bathing," is voiced as a casual guess anyone might make (7^v: 267–70). The 1805 text drops the prepositional grid and expands the act of noticing to "left, as I suppos'd" (461)—the "I" stressing individual attention. The C text then increases the tension both by giving more signifying agency to the heap and less certainty to the boy's surmise. Instead of the previous syntax of subject and object, "I saw distinctly . . . / A heap of garments," we read "appeared distinctly . . . / A heap," with the predicate preceding the subject (453–54; cf. 1850: 438–39). Not only does this produce the frisson of action before agent, but the syntax lets *appeared* signify ambiguously: it implies "appeared to my sight"; but it also has a suggestive glint of independent emergence and beckoning.

Wordsworth applies a shift in verbal mood in the 1850 text to enhance this semiotic uncertainty: "as if left by One / Who *might have* there been bathing" (439–40). Although the *as if* of 1799 returns, the newly tenuous *might have* prevents any matter-of-fact deduction: one might have been bathing or might have abandoned his clothes and sought the Lake for another reason. The hesitation is subtle, but portent enough to invite conjecture and align this effect with other revisions that dilate the interval of the boy's anxiety. Where the 1799 text records only a chronometric "half an hour I watched / And no one owned them" (7ᵛ: 270–71), Book 5 writes in a strained act of attention, "long I watch'd," that expands the shimmer of implication and heightens its tension by substituting *but* for the merely sequential *and* (462–63 / 440–41). The new term of subjective measure, *long*, furthermore, initiates a train of echoes in the "long poles" that the search party uses and their success "at length," each repetition investing the boy's initial vigil with a sign of prophetic apprehension.

The double effect of these revisions, extending the inscriptions of anxiety within a seemingly more secure frame of interpretation, is also at work in the report of the events of the succeeding day, as the boy's twilight anxiety is translated into a public search. The communal gathering stages the issue of context in the recollection itself, with the revisions again destabilizing the formal charge of context as containment. On the one hand, a group of adults in the light of day vindicates the boy's lone, twilight uncertainties with a matter of plain public fact, defining a chapter of rural history rather than of mere individual trauma. This sense is conveyed by the rather flat notations of the 1799 and 1805 texts—"There came a company" (7ᵛ: 275) and "Went there a Company" (468)—and it is enhanced in the 1850 text by the erasure of 1805's subjective registers for the boy's initial attention: "I saw" and "I suppos'd" (460–61, the first canceled in C). But if Wordsworth uses this company to frame the boy's misgivings with common knowledge, his revision of other textual elements magnifies the initial mystery of agency, even more emphatically in C and the 1850 text. He now endows the garments with a magnetic power that multiples their force on the boy the evening before: in C, they "drew an anxious crowd / Of friends and neighbours to the fatal spot" (460–61); and in 1850, a suspenseful understatement names the fatality: the garments "drew to the spot an anxious Crowd" (446). Rewriting 1805's merely reportorial "Company" as an "anxious Crowd," moreover, gives the boy's apprehensions a communal register. As early as his revision of MS. A, Wordsworth is staging a shared anxiety (the crowd "lookd awhile . . . searchd the deep"), and he elaborates it in subsequent drafts:

> In anxious expectation on the shore
> These stood, while those were busy (rev. WW, C stage; Reed 2: 625)

> In passive expectation on the shore
> These stood, while others sounded (C: 462–63)

> some looked
> In passive expectation from the shore,
> While from a boat others hung o'er the deep,
> Sounding with grappling irons and long poles. (1850: 446–69)

The Norton Critical editors say that these last lines "place the solitary experience recorded in *1799* and *1805* in an untypically social context" (177 n. 3), but this isn't quite right: both *1799* and *1805* bring a company to the Lake. What is striking is that the social context operates less to counter and contain the boy's anxieties than to multiply and expand them. Those gazing from the shore in passive expectation reprise his watch the evening before and prefigure, in their distance, the way he will compose the scene into a sad spectacle. Those who "hung o'er the deep" probe actively, trying to penetrate the surface reflections of a "beauteous scene." With darker tension, they repeat the story of the Winander Boy, who when he "sometimes, in . . . silence . . . hung / Listening," received "a gentle shock of mild surprize" (1850: 383–84) amid his own scene, named variously but resonantly in Book 5 as a "beauteous . . . spot" or a "fair . . . Spot" in the vale (1805: 416; C: 409; 1850: 393). The language of the 1850 text also returns its o'er-hanging probers of the deep to the seemingly distanced text of "spots of time." When Wordsworth writes that the garments "drew to the spot an anxious Crowd," his replacement of the simply indicative *there* of the 1799 and 1805 with *the spot* retrieves the episode's original associations with 1799's death-haunted "spots of time"; his phrase is "the fatal spot" in C (461). And, although its elements are configured differently, some of the language of the first spot of time, "a *bottom* where in former times / a murderer . . . was *hung* / In *irons*" (8ᵛ: 308–10, my italics), carries further verbal echoes to reaffiliate these sundered texts.

A more immediate textual affiliate, one about textuality itself, is drawn in by the language that Wordsworth uses in the 1850 text to describe the probers of Esthwaite's Lake. This is the epic simile of his previous book (or the same, in the fleeting five-book poem), launched to image the perplexed epistemology of writing and reading autobiography:

> As one who hangs down-bending from the side
> Of a slow-moving boat, upon the breast
> Of a still water, solacing himself
> With such discoveries as his eye can make,
> Beneath him, in the bottom of the deep,
> Sees many beauteous sights, weeds, fishes, flowers,
> Grots, pebbles, roots of trees, and fancies more;
> Yet often is perplexed, and cannot part
> The shadow from the substance, rocks and sky,
> Mountains and clouds reflected in the depth
> Of the clear flood, from things which there abide

In their true Dwelling: now is crossed by gleam
Of his own image, by sun-beam now,
And wavering motions, sent he knows not whence,
Impediments that make his task more sweet—
Such pleasant office have we long pursued,
Incumbent o'er the surface of past time (1850: 4.256–74)

Not only do readers here preview the metaphors, even the very words, sounded in the text of the drowning—"the breast / Of a still water," its "shadows," its "beauteous sights"—but they find themselves situated in relation to these, drawn into lake-scanning and the analogized reading of "past time" by an inclusive "we" (273). A casual grammatical perplexity—"and fancies more" (262)—even presents them with an analogous phenomenology. In the train of nouns, "fancies more" appears as the summary term for "beauteous sights" and their extended discovery. But it also disrupts the chain of substantive sights by recasting all as "fancies"—projections of the eye's delights, even its whims. This disruption is abetted by a double grammar that lets "fancies more" seem part of a compound predicate, "Sees many beauteous sights . . . and fancies more," a syntax in which the eye first sees and then more than half-creates what it perceives.[43]

This perplexed epistemology, a pleasant office here, is not just recalled by the text-saturated imagery of the lakescape from which the dead man emerges a few hundred lines on; it is recreated by the form of the poem, in which this extended juxtaposition produces a memory of reading this passage about reading. The "surface of past time" becomes in this reverberation a simultaneous figure for the experiential object of the poet's consciousness, for the textualized past of his recollective processing, for the textual past of his writing—and, not the least, for his and our reading of it. When we see the lake-reading of Book 4 repeated in the text of the far less pleasant office of corpse-pursuit of Book 5, the information of the two passages plays into and implicates them with one another. In the poem's forward trajectory, the poetics of autobiography as an uncertain scanning of the surfaces and depths of past time re-emerges, refigured, as a rediscovery of death in, and by, nature. In the text of retrospect, this recollected discovery exposes its affiliation to the motive of autobiographical writing itself.

There is another kind of death that is always impending in autobiography: the fact that its text escapes revision only when its writer dies. Wordsworth intuits this end of revision in lines first drafted in 1804, as he was expanding his autobiography. Its textual site has to do with a frustrated imagination in the Alps—a set of pages that also contains his first effort to reframe the recollection of the drowning with the reference to books.[44] The lines in question turn meta-revisionary as they produce an epic simile describing the entry of a traveller (one of the poem's master-tropes for its autobiographer)

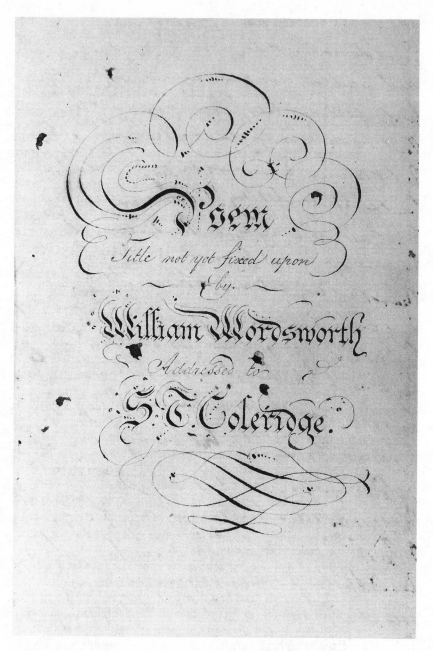

Figure 7. "Poem / Title not yet fixed upon / by William Wordsworth / Addressed to S. T. Coleridge," 1805 title-page of the poem later named *The Prelude*, Ms. B (Dove Cottage Ms. 53):4ᵛ. Reproduced by permission and courtesy of The Wordsworth Trust, Grasmere, England.

into a cavern whose visual field, a ferment of "Shapes and Forms and Tendencies to Shape," achieves the stability and perfection of a "written book" only
as it is drained of life. Here is the form of this simile in 1805, when Wordsworth moved it to Book 8:

> As when a traveller hath from open day
> With torches pass'd into some Vault of Earth,
>
> . . .
>
> He looks and sees the Cavern spread and grow,
> Widening itself on all sides, sees, or thinks
> He sees, erelong, the roof above his head,
> Which instantly unsettles and recedes
> Substance and shadow, light and darkness, all
> Commingled, making up a Canopy
> Of Shapes and Forms, and Tendencies to Shape,
> That shift and vanish, change and interchange
> Like Spectres, ferment quiet, and sublime;
> Which, after a short space, works less and less
> Till every effort, every motion gone,
> The scene before him lies in perfect view,
> Exposed and lifeless, as a written book.
> (1805: 8.711–27; cf. WW 26ʳ–27ᵛ [Reed 2: 255–57]; 1850: 560–76)

Once a specter shape is given a definite form and is turned into a simulacrum
of a literary artifact, the life of the subjective eye and I, produced by motion
and ferment, dies. Long before de Man articulated the negativity behind language, Wordsworth staged as much in passages such as this: mastery is death.[45]

But as the flux of his revisions demonstrates, mastery is also an illusion
that inevitably dissolves into the ferment against which it asserts itself, and
revision—that ceaseless play of shifts and vanishings, changes and inter-
changes—coincides with life, the energy that postpones death and quickens
the mind, and writing, with a hope for limitless adventure. Let this traveller
"pause a while, and look again," Wordsworth writes,

> And a new quickening shall succeed, at first
> Beginning timidly, then creeping fast
> Through all which he beholds: the senseless mass
> In its projections, wrinkles, cavities,
> Through all its surface, with all colours streaming,
> Like a magician's airy pageant, parts,
> Unites, embodying every where some pressure
> Or image, recognis'd or new, some type
> Or picture of the world; forests and lakes
>
> . . .
>
> A Spectacle to which there is no end. (1805: 728–41)

Drawn into this perpetual pressure toward newness is the image of the drowned man, its sad spectacle seemingly lodged in the safe house of books, but with another look, revealed to play within the mind in an endless spectacle of reading and rereading (and here the placement of "end" at the end of the line and verse paragraph opens, by visual pun, into the space of the page).

Wordsworth's revision of forms yields a form of revision in *The Prelude* that, in effect, theorizes form *as* revision. If revision sustains the illusion of formal stability, it also persists in postponing that achievement as each review of the hoped-for "perfect view" disrupts the possibility of closure. Revision is thus an endless opening of poetic form, not simply because any vision is open to numerous, potentially infinite interpretations and organizations, but because each review discovers within itself new motions and forms of reading. The drowned man, dead as he is in the boy's eyes, gains a life in Wordsworth's autobiography that the pursuit of his second death—the corpse's abstraction into the corpus of art and purest poesy—at once suppresses and sustains. The only name Wordsworth himself ever gave his poem, inscribed on the title page of its 1805 drafts, refers to an unfixed future where there will be time yet for another revision: "Poem / title not yet fixed upon / by / William Wordsworth / Addressed to / S. T. Coleridge" (see Fig. 7).[46]

Chapter 5

🦢 Heroic Form
Couplets, "Self," and Byron's *Corsair*

The measure is *English* Heroic Verse without Rime, . . . an example
set, the first in *English*, of ancient liberty recover'd to Heroic Poem
from the troublesome and modern bondage of Riming.
   —Milton, on the verse of *Paradise Lost*

Thy Verse created like thy Theme sublime,
In Number, Weight, and Measure, needs not Rime.
   —Marvell, rhyming on *Paradise Lost*

I have attempted not the most difficult, but, perhaps, the best adapted
measure to our language, the good old and now neglected heroic
couplet . . . not the most popular measure certainly.
   —Byron, on *The Corsair*

The problem of form in the poetry of our day . . . is before all a problem of meter. We have lost the repetitive harmony of the old tradition,
and we have not established a new. We have written to vary or violate
the old line, for regularity we feel is meaningless and irregularity
meaningful. But a generation of poets, acting on the principles and
practice of significant variation, have at last nothing to vary from. The
last variation is regularity.
   —J. V. Cunningham, "The Problem of Form"

Byron's poetry is the most striking example I know in literary history
of the creative role which poetic form can play.
   —W. H. Auden, *"Don Juan"*

Laws and Outlaws

Ever since Scott noted the "careless and negligent ease" of Byron's pen
(186), and Arnold, citing Scott's phrase without his praise, deemed this "style"
just "bad workmanship"—"so slovenly, slipshod, and infelicitous" as to seem
"the insensibility of the barbarian" ("Byron" 225, 222–23), attention has lin-
gered at this pass: loved or lamented, admired or abhorred, the workmanship
does not seem to bear, or to repay, scrutiny for poetic art. Not that the appearance of "ease" is insignificant: as with Wordsworth's ideal of a poetic lan-

guage no different from prose or ordinary conversation, Byron's casual style, whether by aristocratic license or in "sins of vulgarity" and "commonness" (Arnold again, 224–25) bears an argument—about poetic diction, about the ratio of aesthetic labor and discursive grace that a poetic object ought to exhibit, and about the bearing of these matters on lines of commerce between a poet and his readers. Yet even in these terms, the aspect of negligence is misleading, for no Romantic poet is more conscious of style and form, in both social and literary registers, than Byron—and this sensibility involves an often scrupulous, often experimental, use of poetic form as an instrument of critical investigation.

This statement may seem to be counter-intuitive, for the famous energy of Byron's style—its forward press, its expansive passions, its indulgence of digression, and its flow of conversation—seems just the opposite. His poetry, we are used to thinking, is no well wrought urn but, in his own famous description (late 1813), "the lava of the imagination whose eruption prevents an earth-quake," and even in this expression, lesser than "the talents of *action*" (*BLJ* 3: 179). With this cue, reading Byron has seemed to demand equivalent speed, as if the text's service, both to its writer and reader, were to convey a sensation of action that would be betrayed by ways of reading given to careful or patient attention to detail. I want to show that when this attention is paid, Byron's poetry shimmers with a complex interplay of formal commitments in which the energies of freedom and eruption are set against the demands of constraint and conservatism. My case for this claim is *The Corsair*, a text chosen in no small part for its famous speed of formation, both as a composition and as a product—written, by Byron's own account, "in ten days" (*BLJ* 4: 77) and devoured by readers, selling rapidly and widely. What is the point of arresting this speed and paying closer attention to the nuances of form and verse? I'd like to put this question another way, beginning with how poetic form in *The Corsair* and the narrative's mirrorings of formal issues arrest attention even as the pace of the narrative and its formal enhancements drive attention forward. The brilliant intricacies of lyric compression as well as its electric talents of action, I shall argue, are deeply allied calls to attention that put the poem's formal agency in the widest possible text of social and historical performance.

My more particular focus is on how Byron uses a seemingly perverse choice of form for *The Corsair*—the canonically stamped heroic couplet to render a tale of an outlaw—to develop an ambivalent staging of questions about subjective autonomy, systems of political power, and protocols of gender.[1] As we shall see, Byron works out important complements to the social couplings that affect the hero's autonomy and self-possession—with Medora his bride, Seyd his captor, and Gulnare his liberator—in the semantics of his couplets. These forms, too, expose the hero's oscillations between power and constraint, especially in relation to women. This formalist intelligence is further intensified by reverberations in the world beyond the poem—for, as we shall also see, its sensitivities tap into Byron's own performances of self against, and within, the formations of his social existence. Such interplay corresponds to what Jerome McGann nicely terms the "double act of reflection" by which Romantic poetry "'reflects'—and reflects upon—those individual and social forms of human life which are available to the artist's observation, and which are themselves a part of his process of observation" (*Romantic Ideology* 12). Yet the argument to which McGann attaches this dynamic, I think, needs adjustment for Byron. McGann contends that "the Romantic Ideology," even as it fosters the idea that a "poet and his works" can escape or transcend a "corrupting appropriation" by social forms, cannot save the poetry itself from the "contradictions" of this illusion. What is called for, he says, is an act of reading that can turn "this experiential and *aesthetic* level of understanding into a self-conscious and critical one" (13). I shall show how Byron, for one, uses the aesthetic materials of poetic form not to forge an un- or pre-critical illusion, but to produce just this "self-conscious and critical" level of understanding, for himself and for his readers.

In the preface to *The Corsair*, Byron advertises his attempt to revive "the good old and now neglected heroic couplet," admitting that it is not a "popular measure" (*Poetical Works* 3: 149). Coleridge illuminates the incongruity of heroic and popular in his remark, a few years later in *Biographia Literaria*, that a "descent to the phrases of ordinary life" is to be "hazarded in the heroic couplet" usually with "ill effect" (1: 80). Both Byron's and Coleridge's remarks report an atmosphere in which the formal prescriptions of this measure seemed the epitome of paltry mechanical form. Thus Hazlitt, in an 1815 essay in *Examiner* defending Milton's verse, sneers that "Dr. Johnson and Pope would have converted his vaulting Pegasus into a rocking-horse" (*Works* 4: 40), an image that Keats may have remembered when, in his review of the recent literary hegemony in *Sleep and Poetry*, he sneers parodically at the neoclassical Frenchified "foppery" of poets who "sway'd about upon a rocking horse, / And thought it Pegasus" (186–87), their prosody wed

> To musty laws lined out with wretched rule
> And compass vile: so that [they] taught a school
> Of dolts to smooth, inlay, and clip, and fit,
> Till, like the certain wands of Jacob's wit,
> Their verses tallied. (195–99)

Keats's dig at the mechanical metrics ("numbers" that must tally) uses language that is politically self-conscious—laws, rule—and pointed at the classism in neoclassicism.[2]

Because Byron's description of his choice of measure and its critical implications are not only class-inflected, but also situated in, and shaped by, a history of politicized debate about the proper management of heroic measure, we need to review the outlines. What these discussions expose more than anything else are the symbolic politics at stake in mimetic theories of poetic form. Dryden's Neander at first speaks on grounds of aesthetic ideology to argue that if "Couplet Verses" are "rendred as near Prose as blank verse it self, by . . . running the sence into another line," the result will make "Art and Order appear as loose and free as Nature" (*Essay* 71). The political implication is clearer in his summary: "Verse . . . is a Rule and line by which [a Master-workman] keeps his building compact and even, which otherwise lawless imagination would raise either irregularly or loosly" (80). These terms ally or, as in *Rule* and *lawless*, apply equally to art and politics, and it was possible to raise the stakes. Admiring Pope's neoclassical couplets, Kingsley would tell Victorians, "There is a beautiful and fit order in poetry, which is part of God's order . . . to offend against which is absolutely wrong" (457). Certainly in Byron's day, a poet who loosened his couplets risked charges of moral looseness verging on political subversion, at least in conservative reviews. In August 1818, *Blackwood's* "Z" (to take one well-versed critic) informed readers that although Keats's *Endymion* and some of the poems of 1817 appear to be in "English heroic rhyme," they really evince "the loose, nerveless versification . . . of the poet of Rimini"—a reference to Leigh Hunt and the manifold corruptions promoted by his "Cockney school of versification, morality, and politics," calculated to evoke the French licentiousness that courted the Revolution (521–22). Even before Z, Lord Kames's much republished manual linked enjambment, a French term, to French "license" and neglect of rule[3]— a post-Revolutionary French betrayal of the standards of Keats's target in *Sleep and Poetry*, *L'Art Poétique* of Boileau. Correspondingly, liberal defenses of Keats's practice, such as *The Nation*'s retrospect from the post-Reform 1840s, read a symbolic release from the *ancien régime*: "In his hands, [the heroic couplet] has all the freedom . . . of blank verse," showing a welcome liberation from the neoclassical "French fashion" that had "chained the free movements" of English verse and "put a strait waistcoat upon the English muse" (3: 858)—in effect, a confirmation of Keats's own critique.

Tweaking at such ideological alliances, of orderly verse with orders divine and social and of liberal verse with political liberty, Byron gleefully reports to Thomas Moore in early January 1814, "I have got a devil of a long story in the press, entitled 'The Corsair,' in the regular heroic measure. It is a pirate's isle, peopled with my own creatures, and you may easily suppose they do a world of mischief through the three Cantos" (*BLJ* 4: 16). This naming of "regular heroic measure" seems a patent anomaly amid these several figures of transgression: the story is "a devil," its hero a pirate, its promised subject a world of mischief, and the poem itself a version of its geographic base, "a pirate's isle." The opening lines seem an anthem to such energies:

> O'er the glad waters of the dark blue sea,
> Our thoughts as boundless, and our souls as free,
> Far as the breeze can bear, the billows foam,
> Survey our empire and behold our home!
> These are our realms, no limits to their sway—
> Our flag the sceptre all who meet obey.
> Ours the wild life in tumult still to range
> From toil to rest, and joy in every change.
>
>   .   .   .
>
> Oh, who can tell, save he whose heart hath tried,
> And danced in triumph o'er the waters wide,
> The exulting sense—the pulse's maddening play,
> That thrills the wanderer of that trackless way?
> That for itself can woo the approaching fight,
> And turn what some deem danger to delight;
> That seeks what cravens shun with more than zeal,
> And where the feebler faint—can only feel—
> Feel—to the rising bosom's inmost core,
> Its hope awaken and its spirit soar? (1.1–8, 13–22)

These couplets seem launched to reform the measure's negative associations with fit order and restraint. Even with their caesural pauses and terminal punctuation, they are quickened by alliteration and invigorated by the irregular rhythms of spondees and anapests. In sound and sense, they bristle with freedom, energy, and the boundless power of thought and soul. Writing for the reform-minded *Edinburgh Review*, Francis Jeffrey was moved to a kind of republican praise for Byron's handling "the regular heroic couplet, with a spirit, freedom, and variety of tone, of which . . . we scarcely believed that measure susceptible."[4] Byron even reforms the rhyme's famed "bondage" by making thematic capital out of its links—*sea / free*, *sway / obey*, *range / change*, *fight / delight*, *zeal / feel*, *core / soar*—forging a series of semantic and cognitive alliances that show how, as Hopkins put it, "parallelism in expression" may beget "parallelism in thought." The "bridging, associating, linking function of rhyme is a dialectical turn upon its ability to handcuff," John Hollander says in elaboration of this revision of Miltonic logic.[5]

Like the *Edinburgh*, many contemporary reviews of *The Corsair* cast their literary evaluation of Byron's form and style in politically toned remarks. Yet as notable as these tones are, just as notable are the overall and even the individual inconsistencies. The widely read and influential *Christian Observer*, not prone to reviewing secular poetry, let alone devilishly secular poetry, thought the pirate anthem "one of the worst applications of the heroic couplet" in the whole poem: it was either an injudicious experiment in "irregular" meter to convey "the jovial ribaldry of a savage piratical crew" or a travesty of "the regularity of these measured lines in the mouths of lawless banditti" (246–47). *The Theatrical Inquisitor* made this complaint with a class-conscious inflection when it criticized Byron's rhymes and "forms . . . of metre" for their lack of "assiduous study of the best models" and failure to "appeal to classical authority" (106). But the elusiveness of a consolidated judgment of Byron's formalism is apparent enough in the way that the *Observer*, despite sharing *The Inquisitor's* criticism of the slant, strained, and feminine rhymes in the heroic couplets, admired the general heroism of the poetry: banditti aside, they found the "change of measure" from Byron's earlier Eastern Tales "suited to the stately and heroic scale of his own mind" (246). The liberal *Eclectic*, in effect if not in intent, chimed the class tone of Byron's remark about the measure's current status as "not the most popular" when it gave extensive praise to his display of its "majesty, and force" in the "expression of thoughts of the highest class" (417). And still other reviews revealed how, in this key of high class, heroic style and heroic scale could be aligned with traditional standards of form, social and literary. With its class-invested, conservative line on literary style, the *Monthly Review* "congratulate[d] Lord Byron on his return to the standard heroic measure" (73: 190); the Tory *British Review* said that at least it was an "improvement" over the four-foot measure of previous Tales (507); and Scott, reviewing for the Tory *Quarterly*, read Byron's very facility with the form as a class act, the natural performance "of a man of quality" (186).

The divided attention of these appraisals—to irregularity (whether lawless or liberal) on the one side; to class-invested measures (heroic-aristocratic) on the other—reflects the degree to which the couplets of *The Corsair* are testing the question of formal semantics. The politics of their form are especially tricky. For as striking as the theme of freedom in the pirates' anthem is the lexicon of conventional political forms—*empire, realms, sway, triumph, obey, sceptre*—and Byron's formal parallel in the elements of "regular" heroic couplets: periods, caesurae, syntactical balances, and the very binding of the key thematic words—*free, range, change, wide, soar*—into a canonical rhyme pattern. This contradiction between the poem's formal laws and the pirates' "lawless train" (1.179) prompts William Keach to suggest that Byron's rhymes ironize the pirates' claims of freedom, an irony explicit in their boast of superiority to the ordinary man who, while "he faulters forth his soul / Ours with one pang—one bound—escapes controul" (1.31–32)—except the control of the full-stop couplet rhyme.[6] Keach's sensitivity to this tension reminds us of the other half of the debate about couplet rhyme, namely, that even with enjambment, it is not as free as blank verse. The reciprocal to Neander's case for the law and order of rhyme is that of its most famous English subverter,

Milton, whose headnote to *Paradise Lost* cast the issue as "bondage" versus "liberty."

Even Dr. Johnson, no fan of blank verse, waxes liberal over Milton's "versification, free . . . from the distresses of rhyme" ("Milton" 139), and he emphasizes the connection to political freedom when, elsewhere, he happily quotes Thomson's praise of Philips as "the second" after Milton, "Who nobly durst, in rhyme-unfetter'd verse, / With British freedom sing the British song"; "Milton, the unrhymer, / singing among / the rest . . . / like a Communist," William Carlos Williams would later put it.[7] These politics of form still impressed the social consciousness of Regency England. Recall Hazlitt's 1818 retrospect on the poetry of the 1790s, which cartoons a revolution in form going "hand in hand" with "the change in politics": rhyme "was looked upon as a relic of the feudal system, and regular metre was abolished along with regular government" ("Living Poets"; *Works* 5: 161–62). Yet the allegory is an unstable one, for like the reviews of *The Corsair*, the history of discussion shows aesthetic and political orthodoxy not necessarily holding hands. John Dennis, generally advocating art as a force of cultural order, welcomed the rejection of rhyme: it appeals chiefly to "Vulgar Readers," is "barbarous," and an enmity to "Liberty" and "Majesty."[8] Conversely, the radical Joseph Priestley complained in conservative tones about Milton's multiple "offen[ses] against" the "rule[s]" of versification: not only should "a pause in the sense . . . coincide with the metrical pause," especially "at the end of a couplet," but "in violation of this rule, . . . the liberty of drawing on the sense from one blank verse to another hath been greatly abused" (304–5).

Against this background, Byron's production of *The Corsair* in English heroic verse *with* rhyme is both an historicized and a politicized action, one that, in Donald Wesling's terms, uses its understanding of rhyme as "a product of history, not of nature," to test "how the device is limited and enabled by previous work" (*Chances* 50). The complexity and fluidity of this history prevent any facile mimeticism, calling attention instead to the way poetic form may not always sustain but may recast, or even put into question, relationships and systems of understanding taken to be stable, grounded, and culturally guaranteed. The text of *The Corsair* reflects this variability: some of Byron's couplets trope constraint, and in some versions, with more subtlety than any Miltonic story of "vexation, hindrance, and constraint" on poetic "liberty"; but in other couplets Byron contests their famed enmity to heroic verse, or keeps both operations going, or reconfigures them, or shapes critical examinations of the whole question.

We can open a view on these interactions with an event at the start of Canto II that restages the issues of form figured in the pirates' anthem at the head of Canto I. Conrad (the Corsair), disguised in the "form" of a dervise

(2.59) who has escaped from the pirates to the safety of Pacha Seyd's court, gives this tale of his former plight:

> I only marked the glorious sun and sky,
> Too bright—too blue—for my captivity;
> And felt—that all which Freedom's bosom cheers
> Must break my chain before it dried my tears.   (2.85–88)

In both phonics and semantics, these couplets perform a resistance to restraint: the weak alliance of *captivity* and *sky*, by eluding the full capture of rhyme, evokes the asymmetry of the two, and the enjambed "cheers / Must" claims freedom by breaking through the chain of the poetic line. Yet the poem's larger plot reverses and ironizes this performance with Conrad's subsequently real capture. Following his stunning "change of form" into a "bounding" corsair (2.143–45), he is then rebound by Seyd's host, "Within a narrower ring compressed, beset, . . . / Hemmed in" (245–48, the pentameter compressing "narrower ring" into the sound of *narrowing*), and then arrested in "heaviest chain" (312). This capture, moreover, is the result of his binding by another form: a code of chivalry to the "defenceless beauty" of "female form" (218, 203) that prompts him to defer quick escape to save Seyd's harem from the burning palace.

Byron theorizes such complicities of poetic and embodied form in a stanza of *Don Juan* that sets the demands of rhyme amid other institutions of restraint. His point of departure is the traditional conflict of rhyme and reason, the way the sensory demands of rhyming, as Wimsatt puts it, may "impose . . . a kind of fixative counterpattern of alogical implication" on meaning, or "an amalgam of the sensory and the logical, or an arrest and precipitation of the logical in sensory form."[9] Here is Byron's version of this process:

> Besides Platonic love, besides the love
>   Of God, the love of Sentiment, the loving
> Of faithful pairs—(I needs must rhyme with dove,
>   That good old steam-boat which keeps verses moving
> 'Gainst reason—Reason ne'er was hand-and-glove
>   With rhyme, but always leant less to improving
> The sound than sense)—besides all these pretences
> To Love, there are those things which Words name Senses;—
>
> Those movements, those improvements in our bodies . . .   (9.74–75)

Dryden's boaters agreed that rhyme should be "so properly part of the Verse, that it should never mis-lead the sence, but it self be led and govern'd by it" (*Essay* 14), and Pope famously urged, "The *Sound* must seem an *Eccho* of the *Sense*" (*Essay on Criticism* 365). Byron's stanza tacitly notes and thwarts such harmonics, not only by opposing sound and sense but by making the exact sense of *sense* elusive. First allied with "Reason," it then shifts to "Senses— / / Those movements, those improvements in our bodies / . . . / . . . our Sensations." This extension strains the initial opposition of rhyme and reason by implying the sensory motivation of "all . . . pretences." In "the simple use of *sense* the judgement and the sensation are . . . quite different," remarks William Empson; but in complex usages (such as Byron's, I am arguing) the reader is made to "think *about* the senses in connection with a word for good judgement," where "*sense* holds on to a reaction of some kind as a means of interpreting or finding profundity in the mere use of the senses." [10]

A complex manipulation of a system is not a release from it, of course. If, as Empson argues, sense informs judgment and interpretation, Byron, both in *Don Juan* and *The Corsair*, is alert to the way this sort of information can lead to a sense-dominated rule. The "loving / Of faithful pairs" figured by rhyme, the poet of *Don Juan* jokes, may figure a kind of political imperative as well: "The rhyme obliges me to this; sometimes / Monarchs are less imperative than rhymes" (5.77). Although enjambment, here and in the stanza from Canto 9, loosens the imperative, the form of obligation remains. [11] This obligation is apparent in the metaphors for rhyme that Byron summons and Wimsatt repeats—*arrest, obligation, imperative, limits, capture*—as well as the arguments that these convey, and it haunts the couplets of *The Corsair* and its definition of the romantic outlaw. This is a poem in which fixing, arrest, and capture are political and thematic concerns as well as formalist ones. Poetic form is critically implicated in the representation of a hero whose liberty variously resists and reinscribes the forms of power with which he contends.

These shifting alliances of form and subject are forecast by contradictions in Byron's dedicatory preface to Moore (*Poetical Works* 3: 148–50). As in the character of his hero, the function of form in his own self-definition is slippery. Byron is trying to synthesize his politics of liberal reform with his performance of social character, but the two are not always congruent. The politics are signaled by his remark that in "the East" (the locale both of *The Corsair* and a poem that Moore was writing) are to be found "the wrongs" of Ireland, a point sharpened by esteem for Moore himself as one whose name is "consecrated by unshaken public principle" and whom "Ireland ranks . . . among the firmest of her patriots." But the reference to Irish grievances is overloaded, for it is also tuned to remind readers (if any needed) of Byron's recent career in the House of Lords, during which he gave a spirited speech for Catholic emancipation. When his publisher, John Murray, worried about harm to Moore by these remarks, Byron sarcastically reported to Moore: "The fact is, he is a damned Tory" with "something of *self* . . . at the bottom of his objection, as it is the allusion to Ireland to which he objects" (*BLJ* 4: 18).

This view of Murray is more than a little ironic, however, since Byron's own politics were highly "self"-interested. His mentor, the Whig moderate Lord Holland, remarked that Byron's maiden speech to the House of Lords in 1812 (againt making frame-breaking a capital offense) was a patent self-display, "full of fancy, wit, and invective" and "not exempt from affectation . . . nor at all suited to our common notions of Parliamentary eloquence" (123). Byron did not dispute the assessment. Admitting that he had been "perhaps a little theatrical," he also knew the appeal, especially to "the papers": "I have had many marvelous eulogies repeated to me since in person & by proxy from divers persons *ministerial — yea ministerial!* as well as oppositionists. . . . Lord G remarked that the construction of some of my periods are very like *Burke's*!! . . . . & if I may believe what I hear, have not lost any character by the experiment" (*BLJ* 2: 167). Byron was cultivating a performative character as much as a political one. "I spoke very violent sentences with a sort of modest impudence, abused every thing & every body, & put the Ld. Chancellor [Eldon] very much out of humour," he boasts.[12] It is this spirit, according to Engels, that impressed his character outside the Lords, on "the workers": "Byron attracts their sympathy by his sensuous fire and by the virulence of his satire against the existing social order" (273).

From his viewpoint within the existing social order, Scott could discern the concern with style in Byron's opposition. Having heard "Lord Byron" hold forth in a "high strain of what is . . . called Liberalism" in the spring of 1815 "in Mr Murray's drawing-room" and at "parties and evening society" around town, he guessed that the performance of "displaying his wit and satire against individuals in office" was more inspiring than "any real conviction of . . . political principles." Indeed, to Sir Walter, the politics seemed a "peculiar" anomaly, a "contradictory cast of mind" in one so "proud of his rank and ancient family," very "much an aristocrat . . . a patrician on principle" (Lockhart, *Life* 5: 39–40). Hazlitt, not often inclined to agree with Scott, concurred on this point: "Lord Byron, who in his politics is a *liberal*, in his genius is haughty and aristocratic" (*Works* 10: 70–71). The doubleness of this performative politics and political performance is less a personal contradiction than a proto-critical reflection, on Byron's part, of how the "character" of one's politics is shaped by the contradictions of one's social existence. His Regency life was invested on both sides. Along with his reform politics and his trenchant analysis of the frame-breaking riots as a product of a social system, he is proud to be in the House of Lords and does not question the revenue and rents due to him as *Lord* Byron; he enjoys the banquets spread at Holland House and cultivates the aristocracy. The combination of interests is nicely revealed by his role in the passage of the bill on "the Catholic question." Byron's passionate oration in its favor was not matched by his appearance at the final vote; he had to be "sent for in great haste to a Ball which," he concedes, he "quitted . . . somewhat reluctantly, to emancipate five Millions of people" (*BLJ* 9: 28).

Byron's attachment to aristocratic style amidst his popularity is reflected in the apparatus of *The Corsair*. Its untranslated epigraphs are for the elite, and the dedicatee (for all his oppositional patriotism), is named by the title of gentry, "THOMAS MOORE, ESQ." The description of the heroic couplet as "good old" and "not the most popular" is of a piece. For in the midst of Restoration views of rhyme as a relapse to barbarism, the status of this measure as a sign of both high style and high class persisted. Thus Dryden's Neander, disputing a claim that blank verse is the form "nearest Nature," calls it "too low," and argues that any knowledgeable poet wanting to represent "the minds and fortunes of noble persons" and to portray these appropriately "exalted above the level of common converse, as high as the imagination of the Poet can carry them, with proportion to verisimilitude," will employ "Heroick Rhime . . . the noblest kind of modern verse" (*Essay* 74). Moreover, the "persistent order" of its formal elements, argues one modern student of the form, William Bowman Piper, suited the task of defining issues and balancing arguments for creditable public discussion—qualities that inspire Piper to claim that "the great and central achievements in closed-couplet literature from its very beginnings are . . . articulations of public communication . . . the impression of some kind of a public voice and, beyond this, of a significant public milieu" (24). Byron himself had worked this code with a vengeance in his early couplet satires (even if, as he says in the preface, he had lived to "regret" their "circulation").

It is this involvement of poetic form with public character, public performance, and public circulation that sponsors the nearly seamless shift in his preface from issues of form to issues of "Self": "May I add a few words on a subject on which all men are supposed to be fluent, and none agreeable?—Self" (3: 149). Byron's punning of *subject* and *Self* plays at the transitional and somewhat tensed senses of *subject* in his day: an autonomous agent; an object for others.[13] Evoking the equivocal inspiration of his political postures—as genuine positions and as public displays—this double "subject" also invests the two appearances of the verb *deviate* in this text, both concerning forms of self-presentation. Byron insists, first, that in his earlier Tales he "did not deviate" into other measures "from a wish to flatter what is called public opinion"—as if claiming an integrity of self in all poetic performance. The second instance is also defensive, but in a different direction. It follows a recognition of having "been sometimes criticised, and considered no less responsible for" the "deeds and qualities [of his poetic "personages"] than if all had been personal." Byron's surprise that within a month of publication "odd" reports were circulating "that *I* am the actual Conrad, the veritable Corsair" (*BLJ* 3: 250) seems disingenuous, especially given the hero's address as "Lord Conrad" (1.158).[14] More telling is his marking of this issue in the preface as deviance. Conceding the appearance of having "deviated into the gloomy vanity of 'drawing from self,'" he uses both *deviated* and *vanity* as if in judgment of such method, but lets the phrase *drawing from self* represent a double value: drawing his poetic character out from, as if tapping, the reserves and impulses of a private self, and drawing it from the lines of a publicly constructed, displayed, and commodified self.

This double evocation concedes the necessary involvement of structures of "self" with social existence. And on the level of poetics, it allies the patent and aristocratically invested form of the heroic couplet with the poetic "self" that, like "Conrad's form," "at times attracted, yet perplexed the view" (1.195, 210). The *Antijacobin* saw the critical issue, but missed the rhetorical point. No friend to "popular measures" itself, it still felt compelled to lecture Byron that "it ill becomes a man, who so frequently addresses himself to the public, to affect a contempt of public opinion—for [to] that opinion," it reminded him, "he must be indebted for the circulation of his works" (221). *Affect* is the right verb, however, for what was in the making was "Byronism" and, as Byron and his publisher had already discovered, its pose of aristocratic disdain and its evocation of a private self withdrawn from "public opinion" was proving, paradoxically, to be a common romance. The spectacularly popular appeal of *Childe Harold's Pilgrimage. A Romaunt* turned out to be its commerce with a private aristocracy of the spirit, alienated from the material constraints of social existence, that readers of any class could join.[15] Mark Rutherford, recalling how his "father, a compositor in a dingy printing office, repeated [its] verses . . . at the case," speculated that the force of Byron's style was exactly its ability to tap "any latent poetic dissatisfaction with the vulgarity and meanness of ordinary life" and give it "expression . . . awaken[ing] in the *people* lofty emotions" (131–32). He reproduced this effect in one of his novels with a reader of *The Corsair*.[16] If, as we shall see, the popularity of Byronic performance in its forms of alienation from what was merely popular defines the political ambivalences, and extremes, of *The Corsair*, commercially the question was not in dispute. In a pace of business that must have stunned the *Antijacobin*, the poem sold 10,000 copies on the day of its publication (February 1, 1814), and went on to exhaust six more editions (25,000 copies) by the end of March; it sold out an eighth edition by the end of the year; a ninth appeared in 1815 and a tenth in 1818.[17]

The Corsair bore a generative symbolic energy as well. Within a month of publication, Murray received a poem by "some pious person" called "Anti-Byron"—the "object" of which, Byron notes with amusement, "is to prove . . . that I have formed a promising plan for the overthrow of these realms their laws & religion by dint of certain rhymes . . . of such marvellous effect that he says they have already had 'the most pernicious influence on civil society'" (*BLJ* 4: 82). He wasn't able to convince Murray to print the piece but he remained confident that someone would, bragging to Moore a few weeks later that a poem was "coming out, to prove that I have formed a conspiracy to overthrow, by *rhyme*, all religion and government, and have already made great progress!" The symbolic reading of "rhyme," especially by its adversaries, was playing a part in constructing and sustaining Byron's public figure of self, for he added, "I never felt myself important, till I saw and heard of my being such . . . as to induce such a production" (4: 93).

In the Regency regime of prosecuting writers and publishers for sedition, there were more provocations in Byron's "rhyme" than its form. Yet his specific naming, in both the letters above, of *rhyme* (rather than, say, "poetry" or "poesy") as the force to "overthrow" various hegemonies suggests his and his readers' alertness to how the conduct of poetic form as well as its statements could be allegorized for other theaters of operation. As Hazlitt joked, these things went "hand in hand." Let's see in more detail how these forces occupy the couplets of *The Corsair*.

Heroic Form and Forms of Heroism

The "central ideological focus" of the "personal myth" conveyed by *Childe Harold*, argues McGann, "involves the question of personal and political freedom" with "the social and political context in which the individual is placed" ("Book" 261). This question figures into the forms of *The Corsair*, where heroic style, both in the representation of character and in the management of verse, is a site of contest—personal, social, literary, political. If its hero is a self-styled outlaw, the tale is cast in a traditional literary form, and its author announces his return to this form with a sense of himself as a self-drawn personality, a member of the aristocracy, and a public figure.

This intersection of autonomy and public form is reflected in the hero's entry into the verse, simultaneously the site of the poem's first enjambed couplet. Byron heralds him with a question that he does not answer, but instead expands across a verse that resists rule by the traditional protocols of heroic couplets:

> But who that CHIEF? his name on every shore
> Is famed and feared—they ask and know no more. (1.61–62)

In this preliminary naming of his hero, Byron has the syntax and meter overrun the end-rhyme *shore*, itself a term of a boundary, to hit the more audible chime of *name* and *fame*(d), just before the caesura at the alliteratively stressed *feared*. This play against couplet constraint is a transient effect, to be sure, but in the protocol of neoclassical heroic couplets, the introduction of the hero in such form carries semantic value. If, as Paul Fussell argues, the "decisions a poet makes about enjambment" express "an attitude toward the amount of flux he feels appropriate to the treatment he brings to his subject" (114), then these decisions are especially relevant in a poem whose title and eponym derive from the Latin *cursarius*: "running swiftly." While the conservative Piper berates such transgressions for abandoning the "elements of order and lucidity" in closed heroic form (53) and thus the "common sense and common judgment . . . the dependence on widely shared experience, widely discussed opinion, and widely communicable understanding, which radiates from the poetry of Dryden and Pope" (55), the terms of his complaint are instructive: to subvert this "order" is to produce form—and the encoded values—as a subject for critical reflection. In a domain of heroic couplets, enjambment gains effect and signifying potential precisely from the way end-rhymes are still visible and fleetingly audible as prescriptions against which to read and measure a transgressive, forward rushing syntax.

Even when the couplet form is not subverted, Byron shows how its legible construction can work a critical point. Look at the verses that represent the political structure of corsair society:

> Such hath it been—shall be—beneath the sun
> The many still must labour for the one!
> 'Tis Nature's doom—but let the wretch who toils
> Accuse not, hate not *him* who wears the spoils.
> Oh! if he knew the weight of splendid chains,
> How light the balance of his humbler pains! (1.187–92)

The enjambed syntax of the first couplet is opposed by the effect of a "double grammar" in which the pause at *sun* works to shape two potentially independent, apposite sentences.[18] Far from issuing the symbolic liberty of enjambment, the rhyming double grammar yields a rephrasing that enforces a precise analogy between solar system and social system, a formal complement to the mystique of the privileged one profiting from the labor of many. This caustic critique is sustained by the orderly manner of the ensuing couplets, each managing its rhymes (*toils / spoils*; *chains / pains*) to link the work of many to the rule of one. The fact that these rhymes, as Piper might argue, operate as a "device for asserting stability and unity" (13) is a critical point. The formal methods of Byron's verse urge attention to the way "Lord" Conrad's supposedly outlaw society subscribes to the same structures of power as the entrenched aristocracy, the common ideology being the attribution of such systems to "Nature's" law. The hero of *The Corsair* is striking, remarks Daniel P. Watkins, "not because he is free of all determinations, but—precisely the reverse—because so many determinations combine to form his character" (80); "even while he protests, and even while he cultivates his heroic stature, Conrad remains wholly attached to and governed by the codes of conventional society" (81).[19] It is perfectly consonant that corsairs are not revolutionaries, but opportunistic pirates. They depend on the economy they raid—its authorization, its established currencies, commodities, routes of trade, networks of transaction.[20] (And such operatives could also target literary property, as Byron would discover with *The Corsair* itself.)[21]

The dependence of the outlaws on larger economies of production enters

The Corsair as a poetics that defines the self in relation to inherited and ideologically nuanced forms of expression. By casting the hero in heroic couplets, Byron suggests that his power is less a mystery beyond discernment of "vulgar men" (1.200) than a mystification worked in the materials of an established formal inventory. As Conrad "sways" his crew "with that commanding art / That dazzles, leads, yet chills the vulgar heart" (177–78), Byron's couplet graphs such *art* in the way that this word literally inhabits its rhyme partner, *heart*—the answer in advance of the question that follows: "What is that spell, that thus his lawless train / Confess and envy, yet oppose in vain?" (179–80). This force of character through the spell of form is the legible text of several couplets on the methods of Conrad's power:

> What should it be? that thus their faith can bind?
> The power of Thought—the magic of the Mind!
> Linked with success, assumed and kept with skill,
> That moulds another's weakness to its will;
> Wields with their hands, but, still to these unknown,
> Makes even their mightiest deeds appear his own. (1.181–86)

The actions named in the couplets—*bind, linked, kept with skill, moulds*—are also the actions of the couplets. A significant element is the extension of the *will / skill* rhyme (183–84) into the medial accent of *still* in the next line (185), a subtle link correlative to the secret skills of Conrad's art. The rhyme of 185–86 reflects the method: *own* is a rhyme literally inhabiting *unknown*—a version in poetic form of Conrad's skill in appropriating the labor of others to self-interest. The semantics of this rhyme pairing underwrite Byron's inversion of it in the couplet that reports the crew's ignorance of Gulnare's (not Conrad's) murder of Seyd:

> had they known
> A woman's hand secured the deed her own,
> She were their queen. (3.508–10)

The deed that is "her own" remains suppressed, verbally as well as cognitively, in what is outwardly "known."

This is one of many rhyme repetitions showing how Byron's formal effects play across a wide textual field, as if in reform of the famously local intensities of the neoclassical couplet. More than once, rhyme echoes give a formal charge to the reversals of fortune that shape the plot. The verse of Conrad in prison, beset by a "withering sense of evil unrevealed, / Not cankering less because the more concealed" (2.352–53), draws part of its effect from reversing a key rhyme in the passage often cited as a locus classicus of the Byronic hero:

> And oft perforce his rising lip reveals
> The haughtier thought it curbs, but scarce conceals.

> Though smooth his voice, and calm his general mien,
> Still seems there something he would not have seen:
> His features' deepening lines and varying hue
> At times attracted, yet perplexed the view,
> As if within that murkiness of mind
> Worked feelings fearful, and yet undefined;
> Such might it be—that none could truly tell—
> Too close enquiry his stern glance would quell. (1.205–14)

Here, *reveals / conceals* links these words as antonyms in a carefully managed display; the verses are a model of classical decorum (even the enjambments are curbed by syntactic parallels). So, too, the couplet reporting how Conrad's power requires that his workings of "mind" remain "undefined" by others (211–12) uses a rhyming shorthand, as does the next, about the domination of what others would *tell* by Conrad's cunning power to *quell*. These verses are no neutral vehicle; Byron is working their forms to evoke the cagey devices of Conrad's power, using his poetic "lines" to write falsely neat formulas that perplex a reader's analysis, and so reflect the methods of a leader whose power derives from his ability simultaneously to compel and perplex the attention of those who would read him.

Byron echoes, with a stark contrast, this rhymed linking of the leader's power of "mind" to its remaining "undefined" by others in another textually extended repetition, when Conrad is in prison. Here "mind" is not a self-possessed interiority, but a psychological prison, and poetic form tightens the sensation of constraint:

> There is a war, a chaos of the mind,
> When all its elements convulsed—combined—
> Lie dark and jarring with perturbed force,
> And gnashing with impenitent Remorse;
> That juggling fiend—who never spake before—
> But cries, "I warned thee!" when the deed is o'er. (2.328–33)

The binding of sound in the end rhymes—*force, Remorse,* be*fore,* is *o'er*—joins this chord to the medial, but initial and key-word *war* (328) and its dim echoing in *warned* (333)—a ring of resounding that evokes the agonized mental prison of remorse.

Byron even brings enjambment into the poetics of bondage, reversing its Miltonic troping as liberty. Look how he uses it to ironize Conrad's stance of heroic-Satanic opposition to authority, human and divine:

> his deeds had driven
> Him forth to war with man and forfeit heaven. (1.251–52)

While the syntactic drive past the linear boundary and the weak rhyme of *driven* with *heaven* loosen the couplet, the grammar keeps Conrad in thrall, the object of actions and forces of which he is the agent but not the author (like a commodified "Byronic hero"). The stronger chimes of *forth, war, forfeit* are an internal pulsation that evokes with ironic difference the inner arts by which Conrad exercises power over others. It is significant that Byron replays this *driven / heaven* rhyme and its enjambed syntax when he depicts Conrad in prison, showing the material fact reinforced by a psychological subjection, as his "soul reviews" (2.340)

> The hopeless past, the hasting future driven
> Too quickly on to guess if hell or heaven. (2.346–47)

Far from graphing a power in defiance of restraint, the flow of line and the quickly driven syntax of both the couplets report a mind in the grip of forces beyond its control.

Forming Gender

These formally intensified fluctuations of power and enslavement, of autonomy and dependency, in Conrad's career are exacerbated by their interaction with feminine figures, feminine subject positions, and "feminine" rhymes. The *driven / heaven* pairs above are two of the poem's eight feminine couplets, a form atypical in neoclassical heroic-couplet tradition.[22] The same rhyme describes Medora forlorn:

> "He's gone!"—against her heart that hand is driven,
> Convulsed and quick—then gently raised to heaven. (1.499–500)

And four other feminine rhymes, almost too aptly, all report men in positions of supplication—always in relation to the arbitrary chances assumed of "heaven" and always with those chances leagued to female agency. Here they are. In prison, Conrad anguishes,

> Oh were there none, of all the many given,
> To send his soul—he scarcely asked to heaven? (2.290–91)

And the poet sympathizes with his loss of

> more than doubtful paradise—thy heaven
> Of earthly hope—thy loved one from thee riven. (3.238–39)

When Conrad is caught by Gulnare's tears, the poet cites Cleopatra's "weapon":

> Yet be the soft triumvir's fault forgiven,
> By this—how many lose not earth—but heaven! (2.551–52)

Finally, when Gulnare murders Seyd, Conrad realizes that

> she for him had given
> Her all on earth, and more than all in heaven! (3.529–30)

In all these cases, a feminine rhyme, allied with the powers of heaven, frames Conrad (or an analogous chief) as the passive object of forces by which he is contained and directed. Part of the impression of these couplets (as with enjambment in a field of couplets) derives from the way the bisyllabic feminine rhymes evoke a potential, but deferred, masculine rhyme. The rhymes were deliberate decisions not to contract these words into masculine monosyllables.[23]

In Byron's formal tropes of gender and power, even masculine rhymes may fail to master the feminine figures. Of Seyd's imperial rage at Gulnare, the poet remarks,

> Ah! little recked that chief of womanhood—
> Which frown ne'er quelled, nor menaces subdued. (3.196–97)

Neither in sound nor meter does the iamb *subdued* subdue the dactyl *womanhood*, which as word and class retains its potential insurrection. The most emphatic rhyme in these verses, moreover, is the hard "masculine" foot of the female name in the next couplet:

> And little deemed he what thy heart, Gulnare!
> When soft could feel, and when incensed could dare. (3.198–99)

Part of its effect derives from the way the surprising link with *dare* emerges from an "ad hoc semantic field" (Hollander's phrase, *Vision and Resonance* 120) in which *Gulnare* is paired first, and most often, with the conventional term for woman's passive affect, *fair* (Medora is ever "still and fair" [3.603]). Thus in Conrad's gallant rescue, Byron's couplet is:

> Brief time had Conrad now to greet Gulnare,
> Few words to reassure the trembling fair. (2.225–26)

Here, *fair* is not even an adjectival attribute, but a noun of identity, and the rhyme pair is set (though unstably) against the consonant rhyme of the next line, which situates this greeting as a "pause [of] compassion snatched from war" (227). The next rhyming of *Gulnare* reinforces the script of chivalry by its link to a word that simultaneously names the occasion of her trembling and Conrad's potency:

> that dark-eyed lady, young Gulnare,
> Recalled those thoughts late wandering in despair. (2.259–60)

Byron's use of *young* instead of *proud* (*Poetical Works* 3: 179 n.) stresses her powerlessness and helps establish Conrad's commitment to the codes it evokes.

It is thoroughly consistent that when Gulnare appears in prison, he first apprehends her as a

> form, with eye so dark, and cheek so fair,
> And auburn waves of gemmed and braided hair;
> With shape of fairy lightness . . . (2.402–4)

In the rhyme key, *fair* (echoed in *fairy* and then amplified by a rare triplet), the mystery of this form is pre-solved:

> Through guards and dunnest night how came it there?
> Ah! rather ask what will not woman dare?
> Whom youth and pity lead like thee, Gulnare! (2.406–8)

Yet the difference, and disturbance, is the addition, in sound and idea, of *dare* to this "fair" scheme, the same rhyme that will report Seyd's insecure position with her (3.198–99, quoted above). Byron shows Conrad resisting the information of this new rhyme—the new balance of power in his status as prisoner and Gulnare's as potential liberator—and clinging to the forms of understanding that join woman only with forms of "fair":

> What is that form? if not a shape of air,
> Methinks, my jailor's face shows wond'rous fair? (2.433–34)

Byron stresses Conrad's predisposition not only by making "shape of air" rhyme with *fair* (and echo "shape of fairy" [404]) but also by distilling the feminine keyword *fair* from its latency in "*of air*."[24]

This normative sounding of the female *fair* draws on well-known texts in the Byron canon. Zuleika in *The Bride of Abydos* (1813) is a "fairy form" eager to seat herself at her beloved's feet (1.285–86); we are assured that the Maid of Saragoza in *Childe Harold I* (1812), although "all unsex'd" in battle, is essentially a "fairy form, with more than female grace" (54–55), and that, in general, "Spain's maids [are] no race of Amazons, / But form'd for all the witching arts of love" (57).[25] The Corsair's straining for *fair* as the only chord he can imagine for *Gulnare* gives this argument by codes of rhyme, a poetic form that Byron uses to reflect habitual forms of social understanding. Thus Conrad says that he doubted that Medora had any equal in "form"

> —till thine appeared, Gulnare!
> Mine eye ne'er asked if others were as fair. (2.489–90)

And Byron has Gulnare measure herself against Medora not only with the rhyme Conrad wants to suppress, but against the one he favors:

> Though fond as mine her bosom, form more fair,
> I rush through peril which she would not dare. (3.298–99)

Gulnare's declaration of identity is precisely her opposition to Conrad's scheme of *fair*.

Along with this intrusion of the word *dare* into the female field of *fair* rhymes, another pressure is the latent rhyme of the word *Corsair*. Byron keeps it latent, never playing it as an end rhyme, never even a medial one. Yet its link always seems potential, a kind of shadowy textual affiliation of the hero with his female alter-ego and masculine-rhyme partner, "Gulnare." What both words have in common is a mutual exclusion in the poem's famous closing lines from the *fair* accorded to Conrad's dead bride:

> Long mourned his band whom none could mourn beside;
> And *fair* the monument they gave his bride:
> For him they raise not the recording stone—
> His death yet dubious, deeds too widely known;
> He left a Cor*sair*'s name to other times,
> Linked with one virtue, and a thousand crimes. (3.691–96, my italics)

This epigrammatic rhetoric and its syntactically emphasized terminal rhymes mute, but do not erase, an internal echo of the "Corsair's name" in the field of *fair*.

If this potential is not realized in the form of *fair* rhymes, there are feminine forms, as the feminine rhymes suggest, that do extend to Conrad—including the master-term, *form*. The repeated alliance of female *form* and *fair* (even the moon is of "fair face" and "glowing form" [3.36]) displays *form* itself as a keyword to the poem's social and cultural processes. In its Latin feminine gendering (*forma*), *form* bears strong ideational associations for literary tradition, with men as forming and women (such as Spanish maids) "form'd" for their desires. Much of *The Corsair* hits these marks. As Marina Vitale remarks, *form* is the poem's frequent "synonym for 'woman'" (84). It is also so for the social value, "feminine." Patient Medora is a "form" for Conrad's active passion—the "form he madly pressed, / Which mutely clasped, imploringly caressed" (1.476–77)—or his desire, "the form he panted to embrace" (3.588). In his absence, she abides a "meek fair form" (3.95) or lapses to a "fainting form o'er which [all] gaze" (120). The harem pluralizes such "female form," provoking Conrad's chivalry (2.203). No wonder that when Gulnare appears to him in prison, he first apprehends her as "an earthly form with heavenly face" (2.397): "That form ... so fair, / ... With shape of fairy lightness" (402–4); "What is that form, if not a shape of air"? (433). Thinking in these terms, he worries that his link with her will "blight [Medora's] form" (489). And when he rejoins his crew and daring Gulnare is reduced to a once more dependent, "dark-eyed slave" (3.531), the lines of form and gender follow suit: she swoons and sinks into his embrace as a "form so fair" (3.550). These female passivities of mere "form" correspond to masculine formative power. Byron makes Conrad's control of form a synecdoche of his political sway. His crew are "the breasts he formed and led" (3.127), and his first utterance is literally a command to form: "'Now form and follow me!' . . . / / And all obey" (1.78–80). In this cult of power, "Conrad's form" (195) is even asymmetrical to his sway, a set of illusory "outward signs" (227) that mystify what they hide: "Around his form his loose long robe was thrown, / And wrapt a breast bestowed to heaven alone" (2.59–60). When his power is displayed, it is with a "change of form" that "appalled the sight" (143).

It is this masculine command of form, along with the inscriptions of passive form as feminine, that underwrite Conrad's feminization when his power is lost. Beset by Seyd's host, his men "form—unite—charge—waver—all is lost!" (2.244), and after he too is lost, he is chained in "links that bound / His form" (3.388–89). When, on a stormy night, he drags this fettered body to the grate and prays for "one pitying flash to mar the form it made" (3.265), his subjection is underscored by the self-identification as a *form*. It matters that Byron withholds this word from a redeeming alliance with an available enough rhyme, *storm* (249, 267). Instead, we read it as an unrealized link, or muted medial chime at best. These feminizing formations collaborate in Byron's text with a recurrent term of feminine sensibility: softness, itself denoting susceptibility to external forming. Again, there are orthodox codes. Conrad hopes that Gulnare's "softening heart" will keep her from murdering Seyd (3.407), and his horror at the view of her "so wildly nerved in hate" abates only when he reminds himself that she is "soft in love" (538).

The *Monthly Review* confirmed the ideological formation when (just before welcoming Byron's "return to the standard heroic measure") it noted "in the character of Gulnare" an ultimate "return to that natural softness which must ever form a prevailing feature in the female character" (189–90). Unlike that of *fair*, however, Byron does not limit the discourse of *soft* to the female character. "His heart was formed for softness" (3.662), we hear of Conrad late in the poem, but the sensibility was always legible. Returning to Medora's tower, he is arrested at the portal,

> for wild and soft
> He heard those accents never heard too oft. (1.343–4)

Helped by his line break, Byron gives "wild and soft" a grammatical ambiguity that implicates Conrad with the feminine world: the adjectives seem to describe the enrapt listener as well as the accents that captivate him. So it is hardly anomalous that as Gulnare softens, Conrad loses "firmness" (3.540); or that grieving for Medora, he is "so feeble" that he succumbs to "his mother's softness" (648)—another grammatical ambiguity, suggesting both a reference to and incorporation of this maternal quality. Byron makes softness a term of ideological tension in the definition of his hero, his virtue and his weakness: "quickening round his heart, / One softer feeling would not yet depart"; "'gainst that passion vainly still he strove, / And even in him it asks the name of Love!" (1.281–82, 285–86).[26]

These affiliations of softness, passion, and threatened self-possession by female influence are deftly organized in the couplet forms in which Byron plays out the agon of Conrad's pained departure from Medora to rejoin the company of men:

> From crag to crag descending—swiftly sped
> Stern Conrad down, nor once he turned his head;
> But shrunk whene'er the windings of his way
> Forced on his eye what he would not survey,
> His lone, but lovely dwelling on the steep,
> That hailed him first when homeward from the deep:
> And she—the dim and melancholy star,
> Whose ray of beauty reached him from afar,
> On her he must not gaze, he must not think,
> There he might rest—but on Destruction's brink:
> Yet once almost he stopped—and nearly gave
> His fate to chance, his projects to the wave;
> But no—it must not be—a worthy chief
> May melt, but not betray to woman's grief.
> He sees his bark, he notes how fair the wind,
> And sternly gathers all his might of mind.   (1.505–20)

The Christian Observer, finding the "soft sympathy" of this "affectionate adieu" hard to reconcile with Conrad's general ("monstrosity of") character (248), sensed an important effect but missed the point. Peter Manning sees what is at stake: "the passage pictures no confident hero but a man fearfully and desperately denying a threat to his self-definition as a 'worthy chief': it is not until Conrad is safely on board that he again 'mans himself' [1.584] and 'feels of all his former self possest' (1.532)."[27]

Just before the lines Manning quotes, there is a polarized couplet, involving the key rhyme *soft*: as he descends to the shore, Conrad's eye marks

> more than all, his blood-red flag aloft,
> He marvelled how his heart could seem so soft.   (1.529–30)

The whole sequence of this departure spells a tensed psychodrama, as the couplets alternate swiftly alliterative enjambments that push forward ("swiftly sped / Stern Conrad down") with ones that lead back to Medora ("the windings of his way / Forced on his eye what he would not survey"), and use terminal stops to heighten the conflict: "On her he must not gaze, he must not think, / There he might rest—but on Destruction's brink." One of the most antithetically tensed rhymes would seem to be the aphoristic formulation that follows this couplet, "But no—it must not be—a worthy chief / May melt, but not betray to woman's grief." Yet the rhymed antithesis is muted both by enjambment and by the competing medial chime of *may* / *betray*, making the emphatic *must not* seem imposed on commitments that already "betray" (itself a complicated grammar)[28] equivocation. And in this crisis, Conrad's legendary "might of mind" gets no more than an off-rhyme with the "wind" that inspires it.

Such ambivalence even affects the shift from feminine to masculine rhymes in the verses of departure. Conrad turns one last look to Medora:

> Alas! those eyes beheld his rocky tower,
> And live a moment o'er the parting hour;
> She—his Medora—did she mark the prow?
> Ah! never loved he half so much as now!
> But much must yet be done ere dawn of day—
> Again he mans himself and turns away.   (1.579–84)

The first rhyme of this lingering look at Medora's world, *tower* / *hour*, hovers between masculine and feminine sounding, an ambiguity perpetuated by its echo in the next pair, *prow* / *now*. While this rhyme is masculine, its phonic alliance to *tower* / *hour* looks back to the feminine figures (of sound and sense) from which it emerges. Its pivot is just as crucial, however, for Medora is now figured as a form in the mind, and the next rhyme (583–84) is emphatically masculine in its report of Conrad's manning himself in independence of her. Byron makes Conrad's turn away from the feminine not just an act of heroic resolve, but also the action of the masculine heroic couplets.

The force of the gendered verb *mans* is enhanced by earlier links of *manned* rhymes with Conrad. Greeting his boat, the pirates cry, "'Tis manned—the oars keep concert to the strand, / Till grates her keel upon the shallow sand" (1.101–2)—*manned* launching and grounding the rhymes of the couplet, controlling its form even as the men control their feminine vehicle, the ship. This gendering shapes Byron's later use of *manned* to anchor two couplets, both describing Conrad's possession of himself as a text. The first reports his entry into Seyd's palace, in a tactical disguise:

> Submissive, yet with self-possession manned,
> He calmly met the curious eyes that scanned.   (2.61–62)

The power to manipulate the gaze of others is defined as masculine. The second instance of this rhyme concerns Conrad's self-reflections in Seyd's prison.

While he is physically overpowered, his resistance and integrity are evoked by the repetition of the earlier rhymes:

> Alone he sate—in solitude had scanned
> His guilty bosom, but that breast he manned. (2.372–73)

In both these couplets, *manned* controls the potential for adverse reading denoted by *scanned* and emphatically genders the hero's self-possession.

Repetitions of rhyme also limn significant reversals of gender. Look at the rhymes with which Byron has Gulnare reveal her designs to (and on) the prisoner:

> Corsair! thy doom is named—but I have power
> To soothe the Pacha in his weaker hour.
> Thee would I spare—nay more—would save thee now,
> But this—time—hope—nor even thy strength allow;
> But all I can, I will: at least delay
> The sentence that remits thee scarce a day. (2.460–65)

These rhymes play back to the tensed pairs in Canto I's verses about Conrad's near unmanning in leaving Medora (583–84, above). The *tower / hour* pair that earlier spelled her hold ("Alas! [his] eyes beheld his rocky tower, / And live a moment o'er the parting hour" [579–80]) echoes in the *power / hour* pair that here stresses a dependency on another woman. The rhyme pair of "his Medora—did she mark the prow? / Ah! never loved he half so much as now!" (581–82) that pointed the tension in his identity (husband or Corsair?) shadows the *now / allow* rhyme in Gulnare's marking of his present weakness. And the *day / away* pair that confirmed his release from Medora's sphere ("But much must yet be done ere dawn of day— / Again he mans himself and turns away" [583–84]) is now a *delay / day* rhyme in a design totally controlled by another female will (and deftly imaged in the literal way *delay* preemptively draws out *day*).

These reversals continue in the rhymes of Gulnare's departure from Conrad, for these replay his own departure from Medora, only now with him in the feminine position. In the first parting, Byron tells us that Conrad

> Felt—that for him earth held but her alone,
> Kissed her cold forehead—turned—is Conrad gone?
>
> "And is he gone?"— (1.480–82)

Now, in a mirroring and inversion, Gulnare "noiseless as a lovely dream is gone" and it is Conrad who focuses the question, "And was she here? and is he now alone?" (2.537–38). The helpless passivity that had before defined Medora is now his, and Byron's repetition of the earlier rhymes underscores the realignment of gender positions.

Conrad's feminization is also a formation in the rhymes that convey his release from prison. As Gulnare boasts of her power in this event and its necessary murder—

> 'Tis done—he nearly waked—but it is done.
> Corsair! he perished—thou art dearly won (3.430–31)

—her repetition of "done . . . done" encloses the deed in sound and sense and links it to *won*, the verb that thereby claims Conrad. These rhymes, moreover, are a patent repetition, in different genders, of Conrad's former command:

> "Do this!"—'tis done.
> "Now form and follow me!"—the spoil is won.
> Thus prompt his accents and his actions still,
> And all obey and few enquire his will. (1.77–80)

His new control by Gulnare's voice and action is intensified by the ensuing couplets in which Byron casts their escape. Of Seyd's agents, she reports:

> The few gained over, now are wholly mine,
> And these thy yet surviving band shall join:
> Anon my voice shall vindicate my hand,
> When once our sail forsakes this hated strand. (3.434–37)

In this declaration of power, the action of rhyme plays a part: the weak rhyme of *mine / join* lets the internally initiated, and semantically potent, link of "thy . . . band" to "my hand" sound more audibly, and its rhyme echoes in the first line of the next stanza, "She clapped her hands" (438).

The agent of murder and release is now in command. In this release, Conrad's passivity and dependence ironize his unbinding, both in its dramatic and formal actions. Gulnare's vassals

> stoop, his chains unbind;
> Once more his limbs are free as mountain wind! (3.440–41)

The off-rhyme does not loosen the couplet so much as it sounds the difference figured by the simile, calling attention to the nonequivalence of the freeing verb and the free wind. *Unbind*, moreover, is formally end-bound and grammatically end-stopped, an irony consonant with the unchanged bondage of Conrad to Gulnare's commands and his persistent sensation of oppression:

> But on his heavy heart such sadness sate,
> As if they [the vassals] there transferred that iron weight. (3.442–43)

This hard rhyme and tight couplet stress the captivity in which Conrad's heart—described earlier as the seat of his "power" (1.306)—is the efficient and grammatical object of Gulnare's actions. In this transfer of bondage, it is significant that the verb *betray*, a key one in reporting Conrad's resistance to Medora ("a worthy chief / May melt, but not betray to woman's grief" [1.517–18]) is amplified in a later, Gulnare-oriented couplet by a pointed rhyme about her power over him:

> And Conrad following, at her beck, obeyed,
> Nor cared he now if rescued or betrayed;
> Resistance were as useless as if Seyd
> Yet lived to view the doom his ire decreed. (3.448–51)

The ensuing *Seyd / decreed* couplet verges on an even tighter quatrain rhyme. This semantically potent phonic link reinforces the *as if*: obeying Gulnare, Conrad, whom "all obey[ed]," feels a psychological equivalence to his former imprisonment by Seyd.

This position is the end point of the hero's progressive feminization in terms of the social codes by which he has lived. His assault on Seyd has resulted in his capture and subjection in a state like that of the harem: "In the high chamber of his highest tower, / Sate Conrad, fettered in the Pacha's power" (2.366–67); "bound and fixed in fettered solitude" (3.222), it is also a position that refigures Medora's patient arrest in the tower that becomes her actual tomb. These alignments of Conrad's powerlessness with an orthodox feminine position are amplified by Gulnare's evolution into a figure of masculine potency in female guise. His failed attack on Seyd is bettered by her success, and her liberation of him reverses his rescue of her.[29] Murray recognized the sensation, gracing his 1814 edition with an engraving of Conrad abjectly chained, looking up at Gulnare, grasping a dagger by her waist (Fig. 8). The caption is her exasperated voice: "But since the dagger suits thee less than brand, / I'll try the firmness of a female hand" (3.380–81). This is a reversal of agency that Byron pointedly situates in the field of rhymes. Not only will Gulnare boast, "Anon my voice shall vindicate my hand" (436), but her *brand / hand* pairing evokes Conrad's lost power: we first perceive him "In pensive posture leaning on the brand, / Not oft a resting-staff to that red hand" (1.131–32; the "red hand" now Gulnare's); his first utterance is the order, "Be the edge sharpened of my boarding-brand, / And give its guard more room to fit my hand" (163–64); and in prison, he ruefully laments, "My sword is shaken from the worthless hand / That might have better kept so true a brand" (2.483–84).

The transformation of gender codes gets a formal register in *The Corsair* beyond the couplet, in the poem's only two sonnet-stanzas—a form whose history routinely involves positions of male authority and female objectification.[30] One of these stanzas is Gulnare's rescue of Conrad (Canto III: 12: "She clapped her hands" [438–51]), and as the verses I have already quoted above show, it tells of female agency and male subjection—an inversion of

BUT SINCE THE DAGGER SUITS THEE LESS THAN BRAND;
I'LL TRY THE FIRMNESS OF A FEMALE HAND —

Figure 8. Illustration for *The Corsair*, Canto III, 380–81, painted by Thomas Stothard and engraved by E. Engleheart (London: John Murray, 1814; facing p. 78). Courtesy of Yale University Library.

gender forms well in advance of *Don Juan* and *Sardanapalus*.[31] This inversion is cast into relief by the way it plays against the poem's first sonnet-stanza (Canto I: 3), which presents a traditional figure of feminine subjection in a man's world. Its event is the pirates' ecstatic greeting to one of their returning ships:

3.

"A sail!—a sail!"—a promised prize to Hope!
Her nation—flag—how speaks the telescope?
No prize, alas!—but yet a welcome sail:
The blood-red signal glitters in the gale.
Yes—she is ours—a home returning bark—
Blow fair, thou breeze!—she anchors ere the dark.
Already doubled is the cape—our bay
Receives that prow which proudly spurns the spray.
How gloriously her gallant course she goes!
Her white wings flying—never from her foes—
She walks the waters like a thing of life,
And seems to dare the elements to strife.
Who would not brave the battle-fire—the wreck—
To move the monarch of her peopled deck? (1.83–96)

While this is a heroic female figure, the display of its pride and power is contained by an instrument of male gazing, the telescope; it is a vehicle for men ("she is ours"; and in the next stanza, " 'Tis manned" [101]).

The formal and ideological decorum of this stanza supports the establishment of the "blood-red signal" as the sign of men. Thus the scandal of Gulnare, especially to Conrad, is her display of the "spot of blood" that should only have "flowed in combat, or [be] shed by men!" (3.426–29)—or, in various drafts, "reddened on the Scarfs and Swords of men"; "flowed a token of the deeds of men."[32] The transgression is named as "soul deforming" in one of these drafts, and this fate is explicit in the summary couplet of the stanza following the sonnet of Canto III.12, its rhymes tensely polarized to convey the shock to the system of gender by which Conrad has lived:

He thought on her afar, his lonely bride:
He turned and saw—Gulnare, the homicide! (3.462–63)

Homicide is more than tensed with the possessive "his . . . bride," for while it names a deed, it also implies a potential assault on the male social order. This apprehension multiplies in the gaze of the crew, in which Gulnare is rhymed with the term of uneasy wonder she inspires:

With many an asking smile, and wondering stare,
They whisper round, and gaze upon Gulnare. (3.512–13)

This "stare," a male gaze that cannot subject its subject, in effect superimposes Gulnare on the inscrutable Corsair who "attracted, yet perplexed the view" (1.210).

At this critical climax, Byron dissolves the perplexity of Gulnare's power by undoing the inversion. And he does so with couplet form as much as with any ideological form. First, as Conrad reboards his she-ship and rejoins his pirate crew, his masculine identity is reinstated: he "wrings with a cordial grasp Anselmo's hand, / And feels he yet can conquer and command!" (3.504–5)—the last word both a summary rhyme with the renewed sign of masculine fellowship, *hand* (e.g., "When hand grasps hand uniting on the beach" [1.104]) and an echo of *manned*, the poem's most emphatically gendered verb. Immediately after the perplexity summed in *Gulnare / stare* (above), the next couplet reins her in to masculine authority. The crew stare at her,

> And her, at once above—beneath her sex,
> Whom blood appalled not, their regards perplex. (3.514–15)

If Gulnare is in ideological trouble for evoking the paradox of a woman at once above and (thereby) beneath her sex, what balances this is her vulnerability to their stares.

Byron's ensuing verses quickly restore her to the "proper" figure of her gender, and the couplets are cast with correspondingly proper neoclassical decorum:

> To Conrad turns her faint imploring eye,
> She drops her veil, and stands in silence by;
> Her arms are meekly folded on that breast,
> Which—Conrad safe—to fate resigned the rest.
> Though worse than phrenzy could that bosom fill,
> Extreme in love or hate, in good or ill,
> The worst of crimes had left her woman still! (3.516–22)

Byron has Gulnare compose herself into passive, silent, feminine dependence, as if to recover the forms on which Conrad's admiration depends. The drafts show Byron's effort to get this reinscription just right, emphasizing her withdrawal from action: in line 516, he first had Gulnare actively "plead" with rather than merely turn a faint imploring eye; in line 517, he decided not to have her "str[i]de" but stand silently; and in 520, he chose to keep the word *worse* rather than the more ambiguous *"more* than phrenzy" (*Poetical Works* 3: 207). The couplets enforce this static submission to orthodox codes: ordered with clear rhymes and end-stopped syntaxes, they display a patently conservative style.[33] The triplet that closes the stanza strengthens the point by effectively submitting the danger posed by Gulnare's energetic transgression to resolution in "woman still"—a reinforcing rhyme-word that folds duration into stasis, of energy stilled into a conventional female form: Medora is so "still and fair" in life that her appearance in death scarcely works a change (3.603). Jane Austen certainly felt let down: "I have read the Corsair, mended my petticoat, & have nothing else to do.—" she wrote in a litany of female weariness to her sister (2: 379).

*

Despite this stilling of Gulnare, or what Austen's idiom might call the mending of a petticoat, Byron's tale leaves its hero incompletely restored. The frame of the narrative's non-closure suspends the hero's fate, signaling the unresolvable conflicts in the structure of his social relations, both inside and outside the law. These conflicts are also evoked, indeed keynoted, in the internal frame of the epigraphs of Byron's cantos, all from Canto V of *L'Inferno* and all involved with Francesca, yet another feminine gloss for the Corsair. The epigraph for Canto III, "Come vedi—ancor non m'abbandona," is from her confession of her still enduring capture by love:

> Amor, ch'a nullo amato amar perdona,
>   mi prese del costui piacer sì forte,
>   che, come vedi, ancor non m'abbandona. (V. 103–5)

> Love, who to none beloved to love again
>   Remits, seized me with wish to please so strong
>   That, as thou seest, yet, yet it doth remain.[34]

Byron's text places his hero in the palimpsest of this famous female fate, one impelled, governed, and punished by power—erotic and political. Francesca is first subjected to her father's politics, then seized by passion, then killed by the vengeance of a powerful husband, and lastly controlled by Dante, who sets her into the infernal fate of his text.

Yet Byron's casting of these allusions in fragments of conversation unaided by translation also complicates the authority of the captors over their captives. In the text of *The Corsair*, Francesca's voice floats free of Dante's Inferno, expressing the hold of her fatal passion as if it were the timeless fate of passion. In his closing couplets, Byron gives his hero a similar parole from judgment. These verses concern the afterlife of fame in the social world of the poem— that is, its construction of "the Corsair"—against what cannot be judged and recorded. The poem's own epitaph matches this tension with a set of couplets that evokes a name and its socially known links alongside the mysteries, traces, and gaps that haunt this social formation:

> For him they raise not the recording stone—
> His death yet dubious, deeds too widely known;
> He left a Corsair's name to other times,
> Linked with one virtue, and a thousand crimes. (3.693–96)

In a peculiar way, this conclusion anticipates Byron's reaction to the reception of *The Corsair*. He vows to "resign my person—politics and poesy" to "the conflict of journalists" vying for authority over his public name, and with this resignation, to protect those "other circumstances which in the words of the wary—are 'best known to oneself' and best kept there" (*BLJ* 4: 58). This simultaneous release of the public person and keeping of the private self is, in effect, how Byron's summary verses leave his Corsair: he vanishes, and his social form, "a Corsair's name," remains, the fugitive hero caught and arrested in the fame of (what would become) one of Byron's most memorable set of heroic couplets.[35] With this haunting contradiction, Byron forges a final link between the energies of rebellious individualism and their expression, and per-petuation, in the conventional forms of heroic style.

Chapter 6

✿ Teasing Form
The Crisis of Keats's Last Lyrics

O monstrous forms! O effigies of pain!
—*Hyperion*

A little time, and then again he snatch'd
Utterance thus.—"But cannot I create?
Cannot I form? Cannot I fashion forth . . . ?"
—*Hyperion*

          nor could my eyes
And ears act with that unison of sense
Which marries sweet sound with the grace of form.
       .   .   .
Still fix'd he sat beneath the sable trees,
Whose arms spread straggling in wild serpent forms.
—*The Fall of Hyperion*

  Thou, silent form, dost tease us out of thought
As doth eternity.
—"Ode on a Grecian Urn"

Formalism and Passion

When Eliot cited "Ode to a Nightingale" as a case of the "impersonal" art that he elevated over the Wordsworthian effect of expressing a "personality" (*Selected Essays* 9–10), he was repeating Keats himself, who stated this value in his much-cited description of the "poetical Character" as a "camelion." This is a creative agency that, unlike "the wordsworthian or egotistical sublime," has "no self" or "Identity" (*KL* 1: 386–87)—the lack that enables "Negative Capability" (1: 193), a term often glossed as an ability to negate self-interest.[1] Eliot's view evolved into the New Critical ideal of poetic form, in which Keats's "Great Odes" continue to figure, as the ordering of emotional content, the "integration of intellect and emotion" (Brooks, "Artistry" 251). It is thus remarkable to see this Keatsian effect "self"-subverted by the poems written after the Great Odes, from late 1819 to early 1820, for and about his passion for Fanny Brawne. These include three sonnets, "The day is gone,"

"I cry your mercy," and a version of "Bright Star"; two odes, "What can I do?" and "To Fanny" ("Physician Nature"); and the enigmatic fragment, "This living hand."[2] During these months, Keats was not only desperately in love but also despairing of success as a poet and struggling with financial difficulties and failing health. With no idea of publication, he was using poetic form to grapple with a passion, so he confessed to Fanny Brawne herself, that he sensed had turned him "selfish," that is, self-occupied (*KL* 2: 123; 223).

The results have proved a problem for Keats's readers. Other than "Bright Star" and (more recently) "This living hand," these poems are barely noted in critical studies, then usually by excuse of biographical necessity. Attention seems embarrassed by their tortured confessions and regrettable falling-off from the aesthetic mastery of the so-called Great Odes.[3] The only reader to have theorized this awkwardness is Jerome McGann, but not without some partiality of his own, due to the virtual capture of Keats by New Critical formalism. In his influential essay, "Keats and the Historical Method in Literary Criticism," he argued that the problem with the late lyrics is not Keats but critical tradition: our attention should not be text-centered but should refer to radiating contexts of composition and textual history. A "purely formal or stylistic reading" of these late lyrics introduces "a special bias into the critical act," he insisted, because such poems "are, by virtue of certain pre-emptive definitions created out of their historical circumstances, formally and, as it were 'by nature,' biographical works" ("Keats" 47). The total "biographical nexus . . . reveals the forceful presence of larger, socio-historical frames of reference," which require analysis in "the controlling framework of a general socio-historical methodology." This is the only way that the "dialectic between [Keats's] erotic feelings for Fanny Brawne and his sublimated devotion to his (also feminine) 'Muse'" can receive "its complete set of analytic possibilities" (48).[4]

This is a good caution, but its own bias of subordinating all "formal or stylistic reading" to a general sociohistorical framework may miss how some events of form and style can themselves contribute to a framework of critique. Attention to these contributions is no "special bias" for a poet such as Keats, whose "Muse" bears a history of poetic forms and styles, as his very first effort, an "Imitation of Spenser" in Spenserian stanzas, shows. It matters deeply that this poetic self-definition—emerging from traditions of form and their performative value in specific historical moments, and practiced and refined over a career of writing—is one of the things thrown into crisis by his passion for Fanny Brawne. The "accomplish'd shape" (a recurrent noun) on which masculine desire would describe itself to itself is both female and poetry, and frustration recoils in images of fragmentation, sometimes pathetic, sometimes resentful and hostile. If, as McGann contends, the late lyrics demand an "understanding of Keats's utter commitment to the life of imagination and a poetic career, and of the conflicts which these pursuits engendered both in his attitudes toward the quotidian world around him and in his feelings for Fanny Brawne" (48), then understanding the reciprocal is important, too: we need to see not just how being a poet comes into conflict with being in love and being in the world, but how these conflicts are registered in without being fully contained by poetic form.

One sign is the degree to which writing as a poet is conflated for Keats with writing as a lover. "This moment I have set myself to copy some verses out fair. I cannot proceed with any degree of content. I must write you a line or two and see if that will assist in dismissing you from my Mind," he tells his "dearest Girl," adding, "I cannot exist without you. . . . I cannot breathe without you" (*KL* 2: 223–24). This arrest, in the midst of even so mundane a poetic business as fair-copying, followed by a compulsive redirection of writing and attention to this "Girl," exposes her power in Keats's "Mind" at, and as, the intersection of his identities as "Poet" and "Lover." Not just a person, she is a personification of erotic passion in conflict with poetic self-possession and autonomy. Any argument about Romanticism and form must address this complication to the common notion of Romantic gendering, that the primacy given by male poets to the self and imagination entails actions that dominate and internalize an "otherness . . . frequently identified as feminine."[5] What makes the formalist poetics of Keats's late lyrics so compelling is their simultaneous investment in and betrayal of this account. The cry to "Physician Nature"—"let my spirit blood! / O ease my heart of verse and let me rest / . . . till the flood / Of stifling numbers ebbs from my full breast" ("To Fanny" 1–4)— epitomizes the crisis. Does a plea *in* verse to be eased *of* verse name a cure, or enact a cause? Is a verse whose numbers are anything but numbing a source of spiritual ease or an aggravation of disease?[6]

Keats wrote this ode most likely in February 1820, when Fanny Brawne was living next door and he was recovering from his first major hemorrhage. The prescription for his anguish seemed clearer in September 1818, when he was the physician, nursing his dying brother and seeking relief with work on *Hyperion*: "This morning Poetry has conquered—I have relapsed into those abstractions which are my only life—I feel escaped from a new strange and threatening sorrow.—And I am thankful for it" (*KL* 1: 370). By 1819, the abstraction of emotion into "Poetry" had nearly become an aesthetic principle.[7] This charge to poetic form, as the antithesis of and antidote to passion, has charted mainstream formalist theory and its high regard for the Great Odes. Helen Vendler devoted a book to their "formal meaning" (12), celebrating the last, "To Autumn," as the culmination of Keats's "apprenticeship to . . . form." Yet her elaboration of this claim uses a term with peculiar irony for his writing to Fanny Brawne: "The deliberateness of [his] compositional work in this ode, and his serenely powerful orchestration of all his means, bring to a classic perfection his sustained engagement with the genre of the ode, in a great *crystallization* of culture and language" (14, my italics). When, just a month before composing "To Autumn," Keats tells Fanny Brawne that thinking further of her "would uncrystallize and dissolve" him (*KL* 2: 142), we see how precarious the perfection is that Vendler admires and what this bodes for any formalism that is given to say, "the tighter the organization of the poem, the higher its value" (Wellek and Warren 243). Although Keats's last lyrics strenuously appeal to this value, their forms operate less as signs of success than as reflections of crisis. "What is Keats?" Arnold asked and stayed to answer: "A style and form seeker, and this with an impetuosity that heightens the effect of his style almost painfully" (*Letters* 100–101). Though scornfully, his terms diagnose the contingency, and urgency, of poetic form in Keats's late lyrics. Keats appeals to traditions of poetic form to articulate and read his emotional pain, only to find himself implicating the forms themselves in what he sought them out to manage.

This is a remarkable coda to a career devoted to an impersonal mode and a rapid mastery of poetic forms, but it is not a local disturbance. It reflects the basic debates about form that have been the subject of this book—about form as aesthetic mastery, about lyric self-possession and autonomy, about poetry and gender. On the first issue, the high Formalists in our century enlist as their progenitor Coleridge-the-theorist, voicing such arguments as "Strife is necessary" to achieve "the perfect Form" of "harmonized Chaos": "Beauty [is] not in the absence of the Passions, but on the contrary—it is heightened by the sight of what is conquered" (*Lectures* 2: 224). In *Biographia Literaria*, published the year before this lecture of 1818 and read by Keats, Coleridge names poetic imagination as the agent: "This power, first put into action by the will and understanding, and retained under their irremissive, though gentle and unnoticed controul . . . reveals itself in the balance or reconciliation of opposite or discordant qualities"—among these, "a more than usual state of emotion, with more than usual order; judgement ever awake and steady self-possession, with enthusiasm and feeling profound or vehement" (2: 16–17).

What attracts modernist formalism to Coleridge are less the excesses than the balancing act. In a clearly selective reading of Coleridge, Eliot derives his value of "impersonal" poetry from the conditions that Coleridge defines for the "genius" of creating images "modified by a predominant passion" (*Biographia* 2: 23), namely, "subjects very remote from the private interests and circumstances of the writer himself" and his "personal sensations and experiences" (20). Shakespeare is thus praised for "the alienation . . . the utter *aloofness* of the poet's own feelings, from those of which he is at once the painter and the analyst" (22). After the age of sensibility and the passions of the Revolution, this alienation was not only an aesthetic value; it also pressed on the authority of aesthetic representation as political and social interpretation. Kingsley's mid-Victorian critique of Romantic poetics emanates exactly from this demand for aesthetic authority. Hardening the Coleridgean standard of disinterest, he also rejected Coleridge's organicism:

What becomes of artistic form in the hands of such a school? Just what was to be expected. It is impossible to give outward form to that which is in its very nature formless. . . . For on such subjects thought itself is not defined; it has no limit, no self-coherence, not even method or organic law. And in a poem, as in all else, the body must be formed according to the law of the inner life. . . . But where the thought is defined by no limits, it cannot express itself in form. (464)

More than aesthetics was involved for him; a poetry lacking "clear and sound form, even organic form" (460), "would stand us in little stead if we were threatened with a second Armada" (459).

Even without an appeal to national security, the theoretical difficulty of designating emotion as a formal principle is clear. When, in the early 1950s, Brooks insisted that "form and content cannot be separated" and that "form is meaning," this was keyed to a New Critical tenet that "the primary concern of criticism" had to be "with the problem of unity—the kind of whole which the literary work forms or fails to form, and the relation of the various parts to each other in building up this whole" ("Formalist Critics" 72). At the same time, it is clear that Brooks knew unity was a "problem" and that some literary work "fails to form" along such lines. In 1957, his collaborator in *Literary Criticism*, Wimsatt, more directly faced this issue in terms of poetic practices that conflate form with emotional content. He closes his chapter on "Imagination: Wordsworth and Coleridge" thus: "As organization is a form of intelligibility, it is a basic question of poetic theory whether in fact emotion as such can become the formal or organizing principle of a poem without the disappearance of the principle" (408–9). A loaded question to be sure, one that senses the shadow of, or even forecasts, a formalist criticism in which "failure" and "disappearance" rebound as a fundamental critique of unity.

This shadow falls across the reception of Keats's late lyrics, in the wake of the praise lavished on his "Great Odes" by readers from Marshall McLuhan in the 1940s to Brooks in the 1950s to Vendler in the 1980s. The "high place which the odes have held in the regard of those who care for poetry," McLuhan argues, "is owing to qualities which they do not share with the bulk of Keats's poems—qualities of intense organization arising from the strict discipline of a critical intelligence" (167). The late lyrics are inevitably an awkward affair. When Douglas Bush explains that he has put them in his edition "partly as poems, partly as personal documents" (359–60), he names the crux and the usual apology. In the same documentary spirit, Richard Monckton Milnes put all but "This living hand" (of which he was ignorant) in *Literary Remains*

(1848), commenting on only one, "What can I do?" as "an interesting study of the human heart" (2: 33). Most editors, biographers, and critics, from Milnes's day to our own, read these poems as aesthetic failures, biographical documents, or not at all.[8] Sympathy is about the best response, and this plainly contends with harsher judgments. H. W. Garrod, for example, declares that "upon whatever page of Keats' poetry there falls the shadow of a living woman, it falls calamitously like an eclipse" (*Keats* 59).

The chief fault of these poems, all say in one way or another, is their formal treason against both the poet and the man. Agreeing with Garrod, E. C. Pettet, the least forgiving diagnostician, particularly despises "To Fanny" (usually the most disliked):

Never before, either in his letters or his poetry, had he so nakedly and emphatically confessed his "torturing jealousy" as he did in the *Ode to Fanny*; and it is the entire indulgence in this unlovely, deliquescent emotion, without pride, rebellion, anger, cynicism, or other bracing attitude, that makes this poem so distastefully mawkish. We are forced to admit its biographical interest, but it is certainly one of Keats's poems that we wish he had seen fit to destroy in the cool light of some morning's afterthought. (246)

If Keats himself had no such thought, Pettet's wish is granted by the critics. W. J. Bate's massive *John Keats* gives only a paragraph and a few footnotes to them all, and only with the routine noting of their echoes of letters to Fanny Brawne and a judgment of them, in the wake of "To Autumn" and *The Fall of Hyperion*, as a sign of manhood in decline: "flaccid," "somewhat jumbled as well as tired and flat" (620 n. 13; 617–18).[9] De Man tries to work positively with this effect, suggesting that the "radical change in tone" (*Keats* xxvii) in these poems—at once wrapped in intimacies of "self" and anguished by "an acute sense of threatened selfhood" (xxix)—shows that Keats was about to add "another dimension to a poetic development that, up till then, had not been altogether genuine" (xxvii). Like Morris Dickstein, I question this equation of genuineness and threatened selfhood (it seems a de Manian mythology), but I also think Dickstein's corresponding skepticism about Keats's ability to make "great poetry out of so contingent and existential a sense of selfhood" (262) too quickly adopts Eliot's polarization.

I have reviewed this reception not to discredit the studies that map it but to show the difficulty that many capable readers have had in assessing Keats's late lyrics as anything other than documents in agony and a sorry falling off from the Great Odes. We need to replace the measure of what these poetic forms are not in order to see what they are: self-critical enactments of compositional contingencies that form, as an idea, is usually taken to mystify or evade.

The Resources of the Sonnet

By 1819, Keats was experimenting with poetic forms to see if an idea could be "amplified with greater ease and more delight and freedom" than either the "pouncing rhymes" of the Italian sonnet or the stanzaic boxes of the English allow (*KL* 2: 26, 108), so his return to sonnet-writing later the same year is compelling.[10] In this return, Keats is not simply reviving a long practice in the form, he is summoning its history and performative patterns as a man so painfully in love with Fanny Brawne as to feel the vanishing of all his former ease, delight, and freedom. A sense of the historical implication of the form with these pressures appears in one of his first published poems:

> Should e'er unhappy love my bosom pain,
>   From cruel parents, or relentless fair;
>   O let me think it is not quite in vain
>   To sigh out sonnets to the midnight air! ("To Hope" 25–28)

Although "To Hope" is not itself a sonnet, it is a close reference to the form (each stanza is an *ababcc* sestet in iambic pentameter). The signifying appeal of the sonnet is its traditional prestige as the shaper of lovers' petitions: "I have a sonnet that will serve the turn / To give the onset" to love, boasts a Shakespearean suitor, troping the productive "turn" with the virtual anagrammatic turning of "onset" from the efficacious form, "sonnet" (*Two Gentlemen of Verona* 3.2.92–93). At the same time, and particularly for Keats in 1819, sonnet-writing involves those "cold chains" of compositional "discipline" that he describes to Shelley (*KL* 2: 323)—in this case, the demand to turn "imbalance" into art, and to contain expression in 140 syllables in fourteen rhymed lines.[11]

The involvement of these formal demands with a sensation of the imbalance of being a man in thrall to love is a part of the convention to which Keats was particularly sensitive in 1819. This is a gendered contest of power, of masculine poetic skill exerted against a loss of self-possession to a woman. The issue of gender is clear enough in a meta-sonnet Keats wrote earlier that year, one revealing both for its self-possessed formal innovation ("Incipit altera Sonneta," Keats says)[12] and for its glossing of this skill with an allusion to a story of a *female* in thrall:

> If by dull rhymes our English must be chain'd,
>   And, like Andromeda, the Sonnet sweet
>   Fetter'd, in spite of pained loveliness;
> 4   Let us find out, if we must be constrain'd,
>   Sandals more interwoven and complete
>   To fit the naked foot of Poesy:
>   Let us inspect the Lyre, and weigh the stress

8   Of every chord, and see what may be gain'd
        By ear industrious, and attention meet;
          Misers of sound and syllable, no less
      Than Midas of his coinage, let us be
12   Jealous of dead leaves in the bay wreath crown,
      So, if we may not let the Muse be free,
        She will be bound with garlands of her own.

Karen Swann notes how everything bears a mobility that "must be constrained"—"our English," "Andromeda," "the Sonnet sweet," "the naked
foot of Poesy" ("already a 'foot,' a measured unit"), and poets themselves—
and she sees Keats using a female gendering of the sonnet to suggest how,
within this condition of "unoriginated, inescapable limits," the mobility of
desire "may be translated into happy capitulation." Through "the enthralling
power of feminized forms," Keats is even seduced into imagining himself as a
woman who loves seduction by force ("Harassing" 91).

This is a sharp mapping of the force fields of Keats's experiment, but I
think his formal practices show less a capitulation than a negotiation—by a
self-consciously male poet, aware of the power of sexual tropes—of how
constraint may be manipulated into creative reform.[13] Take the first rhyme:
chain'd and *constrain'd*. With the hard consonance of words that themselves
name constraint, these frame a quatrain. But the medial enjambment of
"sweet / Fetter'd" keeps *sweet* from being fettered, and line 4, although it halts
at *constrain'd*, is kept moving by the syntax. Resisting chains, Keats pushes his
lines past the terminal designators, *constrain'd* and *complete*, to complete the
sentence at *Poesy* (6). Yet even in this completion, this sentence also initiates a
chord of exhortations ("Let us . . . Let us . . . let us") that drive the syntax
against the formal pattern that is the bay wreath crown of sonnet tradition:
Keats ends his sonnet not with a sestet or a couplet, but with a quatrain that
conspicuously mutes its rhymes. His enjambment of "let us be / Jealous" amplifies the chord of "Let us" from 4 and 7, and by overriding the stress of *be*
even extends it into a rhyme with *Jealous*, giving a kind of Midas-pleasing
return to the recommendation. The pattern rhyme of *crown / own*, though
coincident with terminal syntaxes, is not only not a strong phonic counterpart,
but Keats exploits its atonality for a sight-rhyme pun: even as the two-line
syntax of his last sentence mimes a Shakespearean couplet, its summary words,
"her *own*," are staged as a lexical release from and reform of the dead "c*rown*"
of sonnet tradition.

It matters in these dynamics, if we weigh the stress and attend to sound
and syllable, that this masculine escape-artist leaves his female-gendered and
feminine-foot *Poesy*, though garlanded by rhymes, unrhymed—or only lightly
fettered. Only *Poesy* is free from the *abc* rhyme pattern of the first ten lines;

and even if we feel that its unstressed *y* at last links up to *be* and *free* in lines 11 and 13 (which, however, chime more audibly with the more proximate chord of *leaves, wreath, we, She,* and *be*), no other rhyme is so distant, suppressed, asymmetrical. This display of formal unfettering is involved in a larger scheme of gender that bears further inspection. Keats's feminizings of English, the sonnet, Poesy, and the muse are conventional, but they are not merely so. In 1819, his sonnet-writing was focusing increasingly on Fanny Brawne, an interest that resonates with the story of Andromeda, who has been fettered for destruction by a serpent (a penalty for her mother's boasts of her beauty) and is liberated by the avatar of the poet, Perseus riding to rescue on Pegasus. She is successively an object: first of her mother's boasts, then a sacrifice chained to a rock, and finally of amorous desire, delivered by Perseus and then to him, along with a kingdom and a dowry. This allusion implicates a masculine poet's power to shape, clothe, bind, and unbind the form of "Poesy," to claim it as his own. The full story of Perseus has even more to do with this power than Keats's brief, almost casual, allusion lets on. Andromeda's succession of pained and sweet fetterings is but one episode; the chief event is Perseus's earlier slaying of Medusa, the epitome of demonic female power—power, moreover, that turns its antagonists into mere forms, stony paralyses of themselves. Perseus makes a trophy of Medusa's head, the agent of her petrifying power, and assumes control of its spell; it is no slight detail that his steed, Pegasus, the emblem of poetic inspiration, is born from her severed trunk.

The extended allusion of Keats's sonnet is a provocative horizon for his intent to have his way with its feminized form, and suggests why he resummoned it to write of Fanny Brawne. Yet the myth is just as revealing for its slippages. If in Perseus's history, pliant Andromeda succeeds the petrifying Medusa, the career of Fanny Brawne in Keats's psychomythia is otherwise. The cause and occasion of his love poetry, she also resists mastery or even containment by the poet's designs on her. She is a muse with a difference, not bound to Keats's desire but the seeming antithesis of poetic self-possession and creative autonomy: "I cannot exist without you. . . . You have absorb'd me," he protests to her in October 1819 (*KL* 2: 223). The ideal of a "camelion" poet from the year before haunts this confession, for if such a poet aspires to "no self . . . no Identity," Keats now experiences the existential liability. Even as a disembodied idea, Fanny Brawne produces "a sensation" of "dissolving," so Keats writes to her, "I should be affraid to separate myself far from you. . . . I have no limit now to my love. . . . I could die for you. . . . You have ravish'd me away by a Power I cannot resist; and yet I could resist till I saw you" (223–24). Constraining him with a force interwoven and complete, Fanny Brawne is invested in Keats's mind with a "Power" that subverts both the myth and the mastery that he had shown off in the sonnet on sonnet-writing. Within a few days, he tells her, "I must impose chains upon myself—I shall be able to do nothing—I sho[u]ld like to cast the die for Love or death . . . my mind is in a tremble, I cannot tell what I am writing" (224). In this urgency to be self-chained, Keats reverses the sonnet's politics of gender. He is now the chained one, unhappily feminized in an embodied negative *in*capability, in which he remains in doubt of liberation, either by Fanny Brawne or by a capacity to tell of himself in and through what he is writing.

"I am almost astonished that any absent one should have that luxurious power over my senses which I feel," Keats writes to her in July, his *astonished* giving Medusan power not even to her presence but her absence. Underneath an intent to say the opposite, a misspelling in his next sentence reinforces this arrest: "Even when I am not thinking of you I receive your influence and a tender nature *steeling* upon me" (*KL* 2: 126, my italics). The terms recur within a few weeks and persist into alienating self-division: "I am indeed astonish'd to find myself so careless of all cha[r]ms but yours" (2: 133). A few more weeks on, he defends himself, claiming a mind "so unsoften'd so hard . . . as to for-get" female charms: "My heart seems now made of iron," he insists, substituting his mettle for her influence (2: 141). But these enforcements occupy a letter that begins with different metaphoric codes: "I see you through a Mist. . . . The thousand images I have had pass through my brain—my uneasy spirits—my unguess'd fate—all sp[r]ead as a veil between me and you" (140). The "very sound of vale," Keats says about the homonym in Milton's "vales of Heaven" (*Paradise Lost* 1.321), "is a sort of delphic Abstraction, a beautiful thing made more beautiful by being reflected and put in a Mist" (Cook ed. 338). But if, as erotic concealments, mists, vales, and veils heighten desire, they also frustrate it with a barrier.

The sonnet that patently stages this crisis and attempts to modulate it into a formalized scene of self-possession is "The day is gone." Its very form re-ports the initial crisis with repetitions and anaphora that all but overwhelm the structure of the rhyme:

> The day is gone, and all its sweets are gone!
> Sweet voice, sweet lips, soft hand, and softer breast,
> Warm breath, light whisper, tender semi-tone,
> Bright eyes, accomplish'd shape, and lang'rous waist!
> Faded the flower and all its budded charms,
> Faded the sight of beauty from my eyes,
> Faded the shape of beauty from my arms,
> Faded the voice, warmth, whiteness, paradise,
> Vanish'd unseasonably at shut of eve (1–9)

Following the metrically stressed *gone*s of line 1, the trochaic anaphora of *Faded* prevails over the poet's represencing evocations; the mostly atonal and sonnet rhymes are no match. He himself is only disintegrated parts ("my eyes," "my arms"), which themselves register loss. And *paradise* and *eve* (8–9), by a contingent formal charge, link up along a vertical axis that, through the homograph *Eve* and the historical evocation of "paradise lost," affiliates the local elegy with the most famous poetic tale of primal loss through female betrayal and male enamoration. This link may be an echo as well as a formal contingency, for in Book 9 of *Paradise Lost*, Eve reports overhearing Adam and Raphael when she returned to their shady nook "at shut of Ev'ning Flow'rs" (278).

Yet against these notes of loss, something compensatory takes shape at the end of the third quatrain, by force of another verbal scheme:

> the dusk Holiday—or Holinight—
> Of fragrant curtain'd Love begins to weave
> The woof of darkness, thick, for hid delight (10–12)[14]

As Keats's end-rhymes replace the pattern of anaphora, they do so with a crucial dramatic and meta-formal effect: *Holinight / delight* pulls in its strain a chord heretofore submerged—*light* (3), *bright* (4), *sight* (6), and *white*ness (8)—which "hid delight" caps simultaneously in sound and sense. This chord also shifts the poem from notations of absence to ones of textual presence. That Keats first wrote "texture thick of darkness" enhances the tacit cross-lingual Latin punning on this emergence (*texere*, *to weave*) and its promise of composure by textual self-consciousness. The closing couplet—"But, as I've read Love's Missal through to-day, / He'll let me sleep, seeing I fast and pray"—reconceives his master-passion, love, as a personification who is also a writer, and whose book compensates for the vanished shape of the beloved.

This summary does not quite balance the books, however, for its economy turns the lover into a text himself—a figure in the conventions of Love—granted repose at the cost of individuality and self-possession. Keats's couplet might have been Surrey's or that of any practiced petitioner, so utterly pre-scripted is its voice and stylized its sentiment. The lover may speak the sonnet, but the codes speak him, as their latest iteration. This preemption is partly an effect of a paradox that is central in sonnet tradition: although declarations of love evoke autonomy, authenticity, and spontaneity, they are also a product of literary and performative culture. Keats attempts to resist the absorption of authenticity into artifice with a wry self-consciousness about what Jameson calls "our possession by language, which 'writes' us even as we imagine ourselves to be writing it."[15] But his alertness to the decentering effect is evident enough when, "plunged so deeply into imaginary interests," he asks Fanny Brawne "whether 't is not better to explain my feelings to you [in a letter], than write artificial Passion" (*KL* 2: 141). Any explanation, epistolary or poetic, has to treat with artifice of course, but the self-defining artificiality of the sonnet shows with a vengeance what happens if one takes too much to heart

Eliot's axiom that poetic composition "is not a turning loose of emotion, but an escape from emotion . . . not the expression of personality, but an escape from personality" (10). One poet's escape route leads to another poet's prison.

If sonnet tradition seems a Jamesonian prison-house to the self-defining poet, the extremity of Eliot's rhetoric in his argument against personality—"turning loose," "escape"—evokes the counter-urgency of another fettering, one that Keats recognizes when he says that he has "escaped from" Tom's illness and "relapsed into those abstractions" which constitute "the feverous relief of Poetry" (*KL* 1: 370). His terms blur the distinction. We see this fevered form in the sonnet, "I cry your mercy." It is a far cry from the form of "the sonnet swelling loudly / Up to its climax and then dying proudly" that he celebrated in "To Charles Cowden Clarke" (60–61). Keats's cry here is a dilated sentence whose syntax and pulsing repetitions are no plotted swell, but a warping of the sonnet at the limits of its form. Its deceptively casual greeting, "I cry your mercy" (an idiom equivalent to "I beg your pardon"), participates in this drama, for it bears a tortured rhetoric of suspicion from Othello's sarcastic response to Desdemona's protest of chaste and honest love: "I cry your mercy, / I took you for that cunning whore of Venice" (4.2.90–91).[16] In Keats's crisis—he might well say with Othello, "perdition catch my soul, / But I do love thee" (3.3.91–92)—his sentence nearly courts this perdition as it courts its object of passion.

Keats's cry seems at war with the form, as his syntax ruptures, his grammar contracts and disjoins, his meters halt and fracture:

> I cry your mercy—pity—love!—aye, love,
>   Merciful love that tantalises not,
> One-thoughted, never wand'ring, guileless love,
> 4   Unmask'd, and being seen—without a blot!
> O, let me have thee whole,—all,—all—be mine!
>   That shape, that fairness, that sweet minor zest
> Of love, your kiss, those hands, those eyes divine,
> 8   That warm, white, lucent, million-pleasured breast,—
> Yourself—your soul—in pity give me all,
>   Withhold no atom's atom or I die,
> Or living on perhaps, your wretched thrall,
> 12   Forget, in the midst of idle misery,
> Life's purposes,—the palate of my mind
> Losing its gust, and my ambition blind.

When in September 1818 Keats described his conflicting allegiances to nursing "Poor Tom" and to nurturing his "Poetry," there was an intervening third term, a "woman" (maybe Fanny Brawne) by whose voice and "shape" he felt not unpleasantly "haunted" (*KL* 1: 370). Now a woman is the all-absorbing force. In the story of Endymion's love-sick desire, "the fair form" of woman had been subjected, even if intermittently, to critical reading, and in *Lamia*, the "beauty of the bride" as a "fair form" was given over to, exposed, and destroyed by a philosopher's "brow-beating" (2.245–48). But in this late moment of sonnet-writing, Keats's desire for a woman's fair shape is a devastating love-sickness in which poetry figures as one more symptom, not an antidote.

Coleridge anticipated this consequence when he argued that in order for an artist to grasp the "Form and Figure" of his subject, he had to insure that "the Idea that puts the forms together . . . not be itself form" (*Lectures* 2: 223). But what if it is? Coleridge sometimes experimented with a formalist mimetics of emotion, as in "To Asra" (an anagram of Sarah, to whom he presented this sonnet, never thinking to publish it). Here is its apostrophe:

> Dear Asra, woman beyond utterance dear!
> This Love which ever welling in my heart,
> Now in its living fount doth heave and fall,
> Now overflowing pours thro' every part
> Of all my frame, and fills and changes all,
> Like vernal waters springing up through snow,
> This Love that seeming great beyond the power
> Of growth, yet seemeth ever more to grow,
> Could I transmute the whole to one rich Dower
> Of Happy Life, and give it all to Thee,
> Thy lot, methinks, were Heaven, thy age, Eternity! (4–14)

That the "frame" is both body and sonnet gives the rhythm of this single-sentence syntax an organic logic in the "heave and fall" of the poet's emotion. In the still-visible Shakespearean scheme, we see formal limits impending and resisted—end-rhymes impressed by a flux of internal verbal repetitions and repetitive participles, as well as three enjambments into the preposition *Of*—all enacting the "overflowing" of Love.

Like Coleridge in "To Asra," Keats attempts to swell the form of his sonnet with desire. Yet where Coleridge's overflowing sentence possesses the sonnet form, Keats's sonnet seems to conspire against him. Its verbal fragments are the language of loss and frustration—a Petrarchan fate that Keats's writing in Shakespearean form does succeed in avoiding. In the Petrarchan story, Nancy Vickers argues, the project is to dissolve the totality of the chimerical woman into words and signs that the (male) poet may manipulate as rhetorical counters—a representational mode that not only "safely permits and perpetuates his fascination," but unifies his poetic self ("his text, his 'corpus'") in "the repetition of her dismembered image" (102–3). Yet in more than a few texts this agenda yields merely "a collection of imperfect signs, signs that, like fetishes, affirm absence by their presence . . . 'I' speaks his anxiety in the hope of finding repose through enunciation, of re-membering the lost body, of effecting an inverse incarnation—her flesh made word"; but even in such "fictive experience . . . successes are ephemeral, and failures become a way of life" (105). This is Keats's fate with Fanny Brawne. That the key term of incarnation in the sonnet, its reiterated *all*, gets absorbed both as word and idea by its rhyme partner *thrall* spells a treachery of form by which the poet's plea for total possession—"all,—all—be mine!"; "give me all"—recoils into a sign of the self as totally possessed ("your wretched thrall").[17] Evoking the woman by parts does not gain her "whole" or command her "all"; atomizing her is no stay against confusion and self-loss.

A similar fate by form haunts Keats's rhetoric of apostrophe. Invested as "a figure of vocation," a poetic voice intent "to summon images of its power so as to establish its identity" (Culler, "Apostrophe" 142), Keats's "calling" is betrayed by an irrevocable absence. It is no small irony that his initial vocative, "I cry," releases a rhyme form of this fate, echoing at the end of line 1 as "aye love!"—an exclamation that in both performing the cry and punning its "I" leaves the self only self-answered. The whole iamb, moreover, reaches a delayed, but treacherous, rhyme in line 10's terminal "I die" (a chord claimed by the weakness of its formal rhyme with *misery*, 12). These forms are the verbal swirl of an interiority in which the mind is both subject and object, blind to all but the circle of desire upon itself. The rhyme of *love* solely with its own repetitions (end-rhymed and internal) is another treacherous echo, repeating the isolation that Keats betrays in his couplet-verse epistle to Reynolds when the endword of the line "Away ye horrid moods" finds no partner except its echo at the start of the next line "Moods of one's mind!" and a reverberation in "horrid moods" and "detested moods" (*KL* 1: 262–63). In the sonnet, moreover, the echoes of *love* play into syntactic and logical confusions: *love* is all at once a term of address, the object cried for, and the action desired.

To Stuart Curran, "Keats's condensation of uncontrollable passion" by means of "a breathtaking technical mastery" creates "a virtuoso display as an end in itself. . . . Such a polished representation of frenzy, in which the polarities of plentitude and emptiness are discovered to be the same, strains the sonnet form to the utmost and bears intimations of decadence" (*Poetic Form* 54). But "decadence" may be too arch for this rueful deconstruction: to the extent that Fanny Brawne inspires visions of loss and sensations of self-loss, the poet's form is invested and strained as a self-reflecting presence. When Keats confessed to her in August 1819, "it seems to me that a few more moments thought of you would uncrystallize and dissolve me," he also knew the antidote: "I must not give way to it—but turn to my writing again—if I fail I shall die hard" (*KL* 2: 142). In thoughts that uncrystallize and dissolve, a turn to poetic form promises self-possession, saved from decadence by the threat with which it contends.

And the promise frequently proves ironic. The sonnet can betray this salvational turn, as the appearance of a sonnet-stanza in "What can I do?" demonstrates. The ode begins in desperate questioning, expanded and elaborated for thirty lines: "What can I do to drive away / Remembrance from my eyes?" (1–2); "What can I do to kill it and be free / In my old liberty?" (5–6); and (echoing Troilus), "How shall I do . . . ?" (18–23). All petition leads to a summary re-petition: "Where shall I learn to get my peace again?" (30). If the existential answer is (always already) nowhere, Keats uses poetic form to answer with a presence: a sonnet-stanza in iambic pentameter, twelve lines in couplets, traced along a quasi-Shakespearean trajectory to a powerful summation: [18]

> 30   Where shall I learn to get my peace again?
>   To banish thoughts of that most hateful land,
>   Dungeoner of my friends, that wicked strand
> 33   Where they were wreck'd and live a wrecked life;
> 34   That monstrous region, whose dull rivers pour,
>   Ever from their sordid urns unto the shore,
>   Unown'd of any weedy-haired gods;
>   Whose winds, all zephyrless, hold scourging rods,
>   Iced in the great lakes, to afflict mankind;
> 39   Whose rank-grown forests, frosted, black, and blind,
>   Would fright a Dryad; whose harsh herbaged meads
>   Make lean and lank the starv'd ox while he feeds;
>   There flowers have no scent, birds no sweet song,
>   And great unerring Nature once seems wrong.   (30–43)

Evoking his earlier complaints about the constraint of the form, Keats now motivates it: this sonnet conceives the whole world as a vivid scene of frustration. It is a poignant detail that of its two uncoupled lines, the first (30) rhymes only in faint echo of "happy men" (27) and line 33 forgoes its *life*-rhyme for a wrenching repetition of "wrecked" in a texture of alliterations. De Man, noting a biographical allusion in this line ("the great lakes" is the scene of emigrant brother George's financial straits), reads it as the "landscape . . . of Keats's real self" confronting "the bleakness of a totally de-mythologized world" (*Keats* xxxii). Yet with the sonnet form in mind, it would be more accurate to say that this world is divested of one kind of mythology (Keatsian pastoral: zephyrs, dryads, and so forth) and simultaneously reinvested with another ("Nature" as dungeoner), in figures no less extreme.

In these remythologizing motions, Keats involves another trope of form, hinted at in Miriam Allott's note that the vision of erring Nature seems to be "glancing lightly" (688) at the famous close of the first epistle of Pope's *Essay on Man*:

> All Nature is but Art, unknown to thee;
> All Chance, Direction, which thou canst not see;
> All Discord, Harmony, not understood;

All partial Evil, universal Good:
And, spite of Pride, in erring Reason's spite,
One truth is clear, "Whatever is, is RIGHT." (1.289–94)

Keats's is more than a light glance, however. His lines audibly "re-verse" the Popean couplet to write a bitter satire of its complacencies. The purest parody is his use of an epigrammatically tight final couplet ("seldom a pleasing effect" in sonnets, he said [KL 2: 108]), as the vehicle to revoke Pope's rationalizing tautology. Before this, he turns the unerring symmetries of the Popean couplet to darkly expressive enjambments. In "that wicked strand / Where they were wreck'd and live a wrecked life" (32–33), for instance, *strand* is no terminus, but a site across which play wicked twists and turns of alliteration and half-rhyming echoes. The lines "dull rivers pour, / Ever from their sordid urns" (34–35) evoke this action with syntactic flow and an ooze of sound poured into an alliteration of *r*s and the accented assonance of *pour, sord*id *urns*. And the phonic tortures and jarring rhythms of the translinear syntaxes of "rank-grown forests, frosted, black, and blind, / Would fright a Dryad" and "harsh herbaged meads / Make lean and lank the starv'd ox" (39–42) convey the sensation of a relentlessly pulsing antagonism. Explaining his "detestation of couplets running into each other," Wordsworth said that "reading such verse produces in me a sensation like that of toiling in a dream, under the nightmair," protesting that "the Couplet promises rest at agreeable intervals" that ought not to be "mocked and disappointed" (July 6, 1819; *Letters MY* 2: 547). Keats's toiling in a bad dream of the Popean couplet not only ironizes the order of this form but uses the sonnet container as the crux through which the initial pleas for release from remembrance are turned to global defeat, forced into reverse, and finally made to serve the subject of remembrance itself. "To dissipate the shadows of this hell," the poet has to invoke a new "spell" of verse to conjure his vanished queen back into present desire (44–45).

For McGann, Keats's "Great Odes" exemplify "the Romantic Ideology" at "the heart of all Romantic poetry": "Its entire emotional structure depends upon the credit and fidelity it gives to its own fundamental illusions," and "its greatest moments usually occur when it pursues its last and final illusion: that it can expose or even that it has uncovered its illusions and false consciousness" (*Romantic Ideology* 134). In his last sonnets, Keats works out this ideological critique for—and against—himself, and not as a protraction of illusion, but in actions of writing that provoke the deconstructive agency of the poetic forms he had always trusted.

Love Verses / Versus Rhyme

"I do not pass a day without sprawling some blank verse or tagging some rhymes," Keats writes to Fanny Brawne in the letter that begins with his astonishment over his susceptibility to her "tenderer nature steeling upon" him. Whether the business of writing can effect his own steeling against her is in some doubt on this occasion, however, for he completes his sentence "on that subject" to "confess," "I love you the more in that I believe you have liked me for my own sake and for nothing else—I have met with women whom I really think would like to be married to a Poem" (*KL* 2: 126–27). But if Keats is mildly satiric about women prone to this romance, his protected self is no less vulnerable to being trapped by writing, as "What can I do?" shows. The problem is framed by the shifts of rhyme and rhetorical orientation in its opening:

> What can I do to drive away
> Remembrance from my eyes? for they have seen,
> Aye, an hour ago, my brilliant Queen!
> Touch has a memory. O, say, love, say,
> What can I do to kill it and be free
> In my old liberty? (1–6)

The nexus of meanings in *Remembrance*—a capacity to remember, actual remembering, a bearing of memory in the mind, the substance of the memory itself, a memorial remnant—exposes the mere rhetoric of the petition for banishment.

Correspondingly, the address to "my brilliant Queen!" becomes an apostrophe—that figure, Culler argues, which displaces a temporal sequence in which "something once present has been lost or attenuated" with "the power of its own evocativeness" ("Apostrophe" 150). Keats's poetic form assists his apostrophe, for *Queen* is joined to *seen* not just by grammar but also by rhyme. Beyond remembrance, the binding of *seen* and *Queen* formalizes the bondage sounded by the internal links of *I / eyes / Aye*—the self, its captivity, and its emotional cry. Against these chords, the weak, asymmetrical rhyme of *free* and *liberty* (resounding the opening question) spells the loss. There is a similarly telling dissonance when Lamia informs Hermes that she is keeping his desired nymph "free / To wander as she loves, in liberty" (*Lamia* 1.108–9)—a precarious liberty she will betray as soon as it suits her. In "What can I do?" the formal alliance of *free* and *liberty* is further strained by a competing sub-formal alliance of *liberty*, in meter and sense, to *memory*. If, as Winsatt argues, rhymes "impose upon the logical pattern of expressed argument a kind of fixative counterpattern of alogical implication" (*Verbal Icon* 153), the case is (over)loaded when, as here, the argument itself is about being imposed upon or fixated. For then rhymes apply a parallel logic.

These tensions of rhyme forecast the conflicts of form that drive the ode: enjambment against pattern; long lines of exhortation against short, nearly breathless retreats; constraints of "Remembrance" against a longing for a muse "ever ready . . . to take her course / Whither I bent her force" (12–13). In the semantic of *force / course*, Keats reflects ruefully on a much remarked

career of willfully bending his subject to his rhymes.[19] But the ode closes still
playing rhymes that would drive away remembrance against invocations that
revel in it:

> O, let me once more rest
> My soul upon that dazzling breast!
> Let once again these aching arms be placed,
> The tender gaolers of thy waist!
> And let me feel that warm breath here and there
> To spread a rapture in my very hair,— (48–53)

As the pronouns shift from *that* to *thy*, remembrance becomes present and the
difference between "here and there" becomes blurred. In this fantasy of possession, the one possessed is not she, but her would-be gaoler, who confesses
his rapture and whose poem concludes in the same space in which it began,
the only difference being that the initial petition for release has become its
opposite:

> O, the sweetness of the pain!
> Give me those lips again!
> Enough! Enough! it is enough for me
> To dream of thee! (54–57)

Again is both a strong rhyme link and a reduced invocation. An ally of pain, it
both resounds and puns "a gain" in "Enough! Enough! it is enough." But if
this urgent repetition would recast painful lack into bare sufficiency, the effect
is to refigure the absence and restless half-life that produces the poem's initial
anguish: *me* and *thee* join only in rhyme, linked across the vague tone of the
(metrically stressed) fantasy bond, *dream*. If, as McGann contends, odes such
as "To Autumn" argue "for an art that can imagine the sufficiency of the
imagination" ("Keats" 60), Keats's art here reverses the illusion of sufficiency
into a prolonged disease of imagination.

Enactments of this plight are also part of poetic tradition, as in the reversals of form in relation to feeling that Donne (for example) plays out in
"The Triple Fool":

> I thought, if I could draw my pains
> Through rhyme's vexation, I should them allay.
> Grief brought to numbers cannot be so fierce,
> For, he tames it, that fetters it in verse. (8–11)

The off-rhyme of *fierce* and *verse* poses a small irony to the thought of secure
fettering. As the title indicates, the delusion will be exposed: in saying his pain
or hearing it sung by another, the poet finds (in a Keats-like echo of "pains")
that he "frees again / Grief, which verse did restrain" (15–16, lines that
caught Coleridge's attention [Brinkley 520]).

An analogous sentiment is voiced by the poet of Sidney's *Astrophil and Stella* 34, in confused dialogue with himself:

> Come let me write, "And to what end?" To ease
> A burthned hart. "How can words ease, which are
> The glasses of thy dayly vexing care?"

The project of *Lyrical Ballads* inherits such contradictions. Wordsworth's Preface stresses the value of poetic form, including "the general power of numbers," in easing and allaying the pain of words: "if the words . . . are in themselves powerful, or the images and feelings have an undue proportion of pain connected with them," then the "co-presence of something regular . . . cannot but have great efficacy in tempering and restraining the passion" (*LB* 755). Yet some of the poems not only render such efficacy ambiguous but, at extreme pitches of passion, suggest how the forms charged with regulating, tempering, and restraining passion may become involved in it—for instance, the ballad beginning "Strange fits of passion." In this "fit of imagination" (as Wordsworth elsewhere terms a strange sensation, *LB* 398), a poet is seized by a fear that the maid he loves may have died. His ballad stages this fit "by fitting to metrical arrangement" and rhymed quatrains its language of "vivid sensation" (in the terms of the opening paragraph of the Preface, *LB* 741), shaping thereby "continual and regular impulses of pleasurable surprise" (756). While this artistic *fitting* is a different semantic from the psychic fits named in the ballad, there is a punning connection by virtue of *fit* as an archaic term of metrical division.[20]

This is the sense revived by Byron, who having sent Childe Harold on a wandering therapy for "his moping fits" (1.28), calls Canto I "one fytte of Harold's pilgrimage" (93), and he continues to play out the kind of extended pun with which Wordsworth signaled psychic errancy: "Then came his fit again. . . . / / Self-exiled Harold wanders forth again" (3.15–16).[21] It matters that across these verses *again* echoes as a dead repetition, aptly rhymed with "The very knowledge that he lived in vain" (16). Byron himself worried (like Shakespeare's Theseus) that poetic imagination is "so near" to madness that the usefulness of "rhyme" may be "in anticipating & preventing the disorder" (*BLJ* 3: 179). For him and for Wordsworth, the punning tension between the psychic fit and its form of expression strains the control of the poetic "fitting." Wordsworth's balladeer conveys the impression in "Strange fits" that while his meters may be fitting his passion to continual and regular impulses, the pulsation may be working less to temper and restrain than to revive the originary fit and its sensation of a fated sequence. Meter becomes another element of passion, amplifying what Geoffrey Hartman has termed the ballad's "poetics of error," which, in "mood, style, and subject," expose, and perhaps defeat, its palpable "defense against ecstasy." Barbara Johnson reads the very phrase

"Strange Fit of Passion" as "a summary of Wordsworth's poetic project: poetry is a fit, an outburst, an overflow, of feeling; and poetry is an attempt to fit, to arrange, feeling into form." It is the power of ballads such as this that these senses do not contradict one another so much as enact their own strange fit: the way form bears passion, even as passion threatens form.[22]

The fits of passion in Keats's last lyrics enter into this strain in repeatedly testing whether poetic form is mastery. This is a formalism that, far from serving "organic" mystification, is painfully inadequate to such work and nervously alert to the agency of form in exposing the illusion. The exposure is critical in "To Fanny" ("Physician Nature!"), the only poem in which Keats writes the name "Fanny" and tries to secure it, and her, in a scheme of rhyme. Confined in the apartment next to the Brawnes after his hemorrhage of February 1820, he frames his anxiety about their separation and her social life without him. His first stanza concludes in a dream of recovery ("I come—I see Thee, as Thou standest there, / Beckon me out into the wintry air") that contrasts the sadness of his own arrest: "My dear Fanny," he wrote in a note to her, "When I send this round I shall be in the front parlour watching to see you show yourself for a minute in the garden. How illness stands as a barrier betwixt me and you!" (*KL* 2: 263). On her side of the divide, Keats worries, his "dearest Love, sweet home of all my fears / And hopes" (9–10), is attracting other eyes than his:

> Who now, with greedy looks, eats up my feast?
>   What stare outfaces now my silver moon!
> Ah! keep that hand unravished at the least;
>   Let, let the amorous burn—
>   But, prithee, do not turn
>   The current of your Heart from me so soon:
>   O save, in charity,
>   The quickest pulse for me. (17–24)

The name *Fanny* enters the ode at the top of a stanza in which these entreaties not only intensify with repeated possessives and self-pleadings but escalate into accusations of coldness and infidelity. Keats addresses a fantasy to her of her in a social whirl of dances and parties, forgetful of him:

>   my Fanny! . . .
>   Put your soft hand upon your snowy side,
> Where the heart beats: confess—'tis nothing new—
>   Must not a woman be
>   A feather on the sea,
>   Swayed to and fro by every wind and tide?
>   Of as uncertain speed
>   As blow-ball from the mead? (33–40)

The rhetoric of the question is patently false to its grammar: "Must not?" states an accusation deploying a generic discourse about "woman." This is a striking expansion of fantasy—or perhaps less so, if we see it propelled by another young, vivacious woman whom Keats loved named Fanny, who did abandon him: his mother.

Although this Fanny Keats had a "doting fondness" for all her children, John was her favorite, so George recalls: she "was extremely fond of him and humoured him in every whim," he remarks, adding, "of which he had not a few" (*Keats Circle* 1: 314; 288). Thus, it is odd that Keats gave Joseph Severn the impression (probably in his last days) that "his greatest misfortune had been that from his infancy he had no mother" (quoted by Sharp 5 n). Her erratic behavior may explain the denial. A little more than two months after the death of his father in 1804, when John was not yet nine years old, she remarried, unhappily: disappearing mysteriously soon afterwards, she did not return until 1807, ill and consumptive. John took charge of her care, nursing her, reading to her, fixing her meals, and guarding her door as she slept. She died in 1810, when he was fourteen. These extremes of doting fondness and abandonment—the first inexplicable, the second mortal—may have knotted what his favorite son would later describe as his "gordian complication of feelings" about women (*KL* 1: 342): his devotion betrayed to pain and anger at her disappearance; his relief and hostility at her return; his guilt over her debilitation, a turn for the worse that could be seen as the effect of an angry desire to punish her; grief and anger aggravated by guilt at her death—at once a final punishment and another, radical abandonment. The retrospective fiction of "no mother" eradicates an insoluble complication at its source. Keats mentions her only once in all his letters, in a note to a letter in which he complains to the other Fanny, "You cannot conceive how I ache to be with you: how I would die for one hour" (2: 132–33). Two months later he will phrase his resistance to this longing as an intent to rid himself of maternal dependency: he says he is trying to "wean" himself from her (2: 160).

Fanny Brawne, Keats's "dearest girl," is thus fated for an already haunted psychic territory, read into mythologies that alternately charge her with and defend her from his worst imaginings.[23] Little wonder that "To Fanny" casts her doubly, as an object of bitter suspicion and of sacred worship, as if Keats were using the latter ("Let none profane my Holy See of Love" 51) to control the hostility aroused by the former. This oscillation is registered by the ode's very form. Most of its stanzas begin with three lines of pentameter (*aba*) that expand an expression of pain, desire, reverence, or suspicion. A trimeter couplet (*cc*) yields a pause or suspense before the verse returns to pentameter (*b*), almost always, to complete a syntactic unit. The stanza then concludes in a second trimeter couplet (*dd*). This stanza form seems designed to organize a flux into accomplished pairings and completed patterns.

Yet the name *Fanny* proves a problem for this frame. In a self-answering to his taunting question to her about the wayward character of "woman," Keats elaborates:

> I know it—and to know it is despair
>   To one who loves you as I love sweet Fanny,
> Whose heart goes fluttering for you every where,
>   Nor when away you roam,
>   Dare keep its wretched home:
> Love, Love alone, has pains severe and many;
>   Then, Loveliest! keep me free,
> From torturing jealousy. (41–48)

In the pattern of previous stanzas, *many* should rhyme with *Fanny*. But the rhyme is strained by being both feminine and imperfect—an effect that Keats decided to retain after having drafted the lines variously without rhyming *Fanny*, even discarding the name altogether, before deciding to keep it and retain its dissonance (see Stillinger, *Poems* 495 and *Facsimile Edition* 230–31). It is as if he meant to recognize what his form reports: as the feminine measure, *Fanny* teases at but resists the control of his rhyme, so its referent, Fanny Brawne, cannot be mastered by desire. It matters in this tension that the resistant rhyme of *Fanny* also involves *free*. By virtue of its metrical stress, *free* is the true anomaly. Simultaneously, another pattern of sound, that of emphatic repetition, forms an internal scheme of the poet's isolation: in the verbal flux of "I know it—and to know it is despair / To one who loves you as I love" (41–42) what the "I" does "know" and "love" is a self-enclosed repetition; the fact that *know* and *love* are unrhymed except with themselves emphasizes such isolation, especially in the repetition of the latter in the phrase "Love, Love alone" four lines later. When the poet calls Fanny "Loveliest" in the next line, the word echoes with a difference, for this epithet recalls but does not rhyme with *Love*—a verbal separation that implies the existential one between the poet "who loves" and the "Loveliest" one whose response remains under suspicion.

De Man's edition inexplicably truncates the ode to make this stanza its last (317), an effect enforcing the priority that he gives to Fanny Brawne as "a highly distinct and specific person whose presence awakens . . . an acute sense of threatened selfhood" (xxix). Keats's full text reveals this threat in a different way, however—one, as we shall see, that anticipates the logic of the last poem on which he is known to have worked, "Bright Star." Exhorting Fanny to fidelity—"if you prize my subdued soul" (49)—he closes with a couplet in which the rhyme links them in sense, or rather, in the erasure of painful sensation: "If not—may my eyes close / Love on their last repose!" (55–56). "My dearest Girl," he writes to her in August 1820, "I wish you could invent some means to make me at all happy without you. Every hour I am more and more concentrated in you" (*KL* 2: 311). His helpless fascination remains, and the letter concludes with desire given over to the fantasy of two equal surrenders: "I wish I was either in your a[r]ms full of faith or that a Thunder bolt would strike me" (313). He had already made plans to leave for Italy, and this seems to have been the last time he wrote to her.

But if Keats is "averse" to the painful seeing of Fanny Brawne herself (2: 312), his habitual remedy of verse continues to draw his imagination:

> If my health would bear it, I could write a Poem which I have in my head, which would be a consolation for people in such a situation as mine. I would show some one in Love as I am, with a person living in such Liberty as you do. Shakspeare always sums up matters in the most sovereign manner. Hamlet's heart was full of such Misery as mine is when he said to Ophelia "Go to a Nunnery, go, go!" (*KL* 2: 312)

Keats's *with* clause is doubly damning: "in Love with" such a person; "in Love, even as" such a person lives in liberty from its claim—hence the bitter (if unfair) echo of Hamlet (3.1). Maurice Buxton Forman hears echoes of "To Fanny" in this grievance (*KL* 2: 312 n. 5), but in context, it follows sentences that show Keats trying, once more, to summon a poetic form of potential consolation: "I cannot bear flashes of light and return into my glooms again. . . . To be happy with you seems such an impossibility! it requires a luckier Star than mine! it will never be."

Keats will bring this luckier star into being in the (re)vision of "Bright Star" that he composes during his voyage to Italy in the fall, entreating a kind of astrologic of transcendence:

> Bright Star, would I were stedfast as thou art—
>   Not in lone splendor hung aloft the night,
> And watching, with eternal lids apart,
>   Like nature's patient, sleepless Eremite,
> The moving waters at their priestlike task
>   Of pure ablution round earth's human shores,
> Or gazing on the new soft-fallen masque
>   Of snow upon the mountains and the moors—
> No—yet still stedfast, still unchangeable
>   Pillow'd upon my fair love's ripening breast,
> To feel for ever its soft swell and fall,
>   Awake for ever in a sweet unrest,
> Still, still to hear her tender-taken breath,
> And so live ever—or else swoon to death—

As if to summon Shakespeare's "sovereign manner," Keats appeals to a Shakespearean sonnet-pattern to modulate the deathwards progressing of desire.

This form, which is also an allusion, supports the central conceit, which transforms Keats's habitual ambivalence (whether his love is absent or present, false or true, to be possessed or not, dreamt of or forgotten) into a deftly elaborated, nearly oxymoronic coincidence of opposites. The poem begins with an address to a seemingly desirable ideal, yet by the second line, is defining this by subtraction. Even so, the detailing across the octave of what is ostensibly being rejected retains its attractiveness. So attractively does Keats particularize the bright star, in fact, and so filled with longing is his voice, that for some readers the divergence of rhetoric and effect subverts the logic of the whole; other readers are so seduced by the elaboration of the figure that they scarcely hear the framing negations—and some do not hear them at all.[24]

This contradiction of tone and argument seems stabilized in the synthetic figure of the sestet: the steadfast qualities of the stellar ideal are retained for the self but given a vital sensuous relation to fair human love. Yet this is the language of desire rather than of possession, of wish rather than fact—at best, an anticipation not yet secured. Moreover (as many note), the logic is problematic, for the ideal is a regressive figure of the self as blessed infant babe. If this is a consummation devoutly to be wished, in which there is no separation of self from his fair love or loss of vital inspiration from "her tender-taken breath," the catch in the poet's own breath in the last line ("And so live ever— or else swoon to death—") takes this perfect union to the verge of radical self-loss. This consequence is latent in the repetitions of *still* in lines 9 and 13: the former ("still stedfast, still unchangeable") would retain certain perdurable values for the self, and the latter ("Still, still to hear her tender-taken breath") would add a sense of eternal ease and perpetual inspiration. But from the perspective of line 14, all are betrayed to intimations of stasis and arrest, an immunity to flux won only by the surrender of consciousness to death.

The way that the final dash refuses a closure by form approaches the "act of irony" that de Man aligns with a "rhetoric of temporality"—a sense of form as "definitely not organic" but relating "to its source only in terms of distance and difference and allow[ing] for no end, for no totality" ("Temporality" 222). Whether as an aspect of technique or of informing idea, the forms that Keats evolved in the intimacy of his last poems render a world where both lovers and poems remain vulnerable to the radical insecurities of experience.

Formalism, Arrest, and Unrest

It is an index of the post-formalist climate of criticism that a fragment, "This living hand," has taken the place of the nineteenth century's candidate for "Keats's last poem," "Bright Star,"[25] and the career-closers favored by twentieth-century formalists and existentialists, respectively: the perfection of "To Autumn" and the suspended *Fall of Hyperion*. One tease of "This living

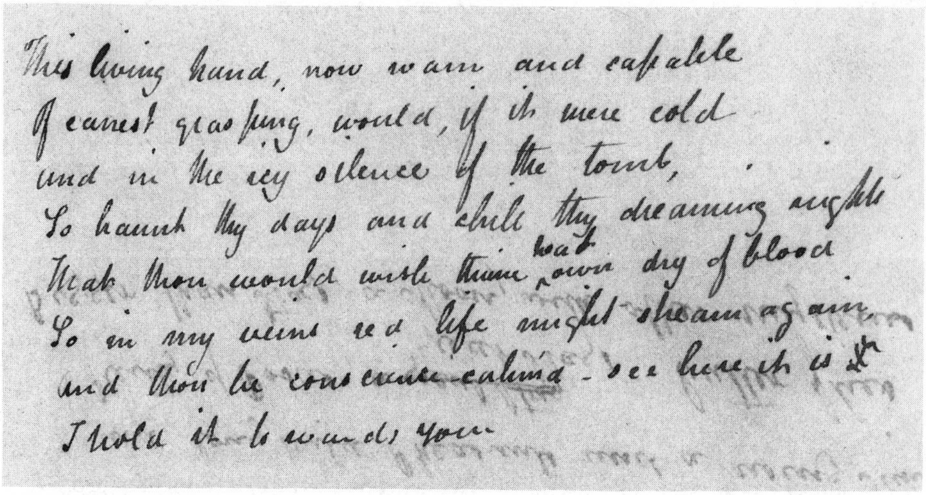
This living hand, now warm and capable
Of earnest grasping, would, if it were cold
and in the icy silence of the tomb,
So haunt thy days and chill thy dreaming nights
heart
That thou would wish thine own dry of blood
So in my veins red life might stream again,
and thou be conscience-calm'd - see here it is
I hold it towards you

Figure 9. John Keats, manuscript, "This living hand." Houghton Library Ms. Keats 2.29.2; published by permission and courtesy of the Houghton Library, Harvard University.

hand," involved with its form, is the undecidability of reference and the vertiginous play of its referents. The unknowability of circumstance, genre, speaker, and addressee yields a text that contends with the very rationale of poetic form (see Fig. 9):

> This living hand, now wa[r]m and capable
> Of ea[r]nest grasping, would, if it were cold
> and in the icy silence of the tomb,
> So haunt thy days and chill thy dreaming nights
>   hea[r]t
> That thou would wish thine own dry of blood
> So in my veins red life might stream again,
> and thou be conscience-calm'd – see here it is
> I hold it towards you—

These lines seem a canny Romantic prediction of one notorious post-formalist manifesto, Barthes' "Death of the Author"—but with the twist that what he states as "fact" Romantic poets sense as threat: namely, that the written text represents the author by substitution rather than expression; that the "future" of writing is reading, which comes into being "at the cost of the death of the Author" (148). Keats's own intuition of this economy accords with the decidedly Keatsian actors that play in Barthes' allegorical scene: the "modern" notion that replaces "the Author" is called a "scriptor," a figure for whom the "hand, cut off from any voice, borne by a pure gesture of inscription (and not of expression), traces a field without origin—or which, at least has no other origin than language itself, language which ceaselessly calls into question all origins" (146).

And yet as much as the fragmentariness of Keats's lines allegorizes Barthes' meditation, their rhetorical force has a peculiarly revivifying effect against the death so reported. It is true that the voice Keats scripts is one that imagines, and asks its listener to imagine, a hand cut off from the voice that speaks—and it is true that as readers, we encounter only this inscription. But the figure of origin is not so much effaced as perversely doubled and re-doubled. Ghoulishly parodying the "warm . . . welcoming hand" (the image in a letter to his [now dead] brother Tom; *KL* 1: 304), this voice exerts a power for readers beyond the merely nervous, grasping the imagination in a haunting poetics of presence.[26] To Culler, this is a refusal of apostrophe. The rhetoric is a direct address asking us to "believe that the hand is really present and perpetually held toward us through the poem. The poem predicts this mystification, dares us to resist it, and shows that its power is irresistible" ("Apostrophe" 154).

Part of this arresting power is produced by the verse form itself. Barthes wants to insist that "having buried the Author," the "modern scriptor" can no longer plead the pathetic old case that his hand is "too slow for his thought or passion and that consequently, making a law of necessity, he must emphasize this delay and indefinitely 'polish' his form" (146). The dead author cast by Keats's lines is alert to the way form can operate as more than a pathetic compensation. We sense this in the suspense of syntax across the lines—or in Milton's famous phrase for blank verse, "the sense variously drawn out": through apposition and subordination, Keats's first sentence dilates, displays, and defers the completion of its sense, slowly but relentlessly releasing a subjunctive contingency into a daunting consequence. The terse exhortation and declaratives that follow the dash after "conscience-calm'd" ("–see here it is / I hold it towards you—") sharpen the assault, seeming, in their epigrammatic summary, almost to parody the Shakespearean sonnet as they enforce an abrupt turn from the dilated subjunctive proposition ("would, if it were . . . that thou would") to concentrated actuality and immediacy, from stagey eloquence to sudden colloquialism, from an expansive iambic rhythm to a set of spare monosyllables.

That the conjuration of warm life into icy death is, in the rhetoric of these lines, both hypothetical in the present and prophetic of a future gives the fragment a peculiar enough intensity—and a shock-*affect* at stark variance to the final *effect* proposed with bitter irony: being "conscience-calm'd." It both recalls and ghoulishly empowers the Petrarchan poet of Vickers' account, who hopes to find "repose" in "re-membering the lost body, of effecting an inverse incarnation" (105). Keats may have intuited this reversal, but his fragment is more powerful yet for its accident in leaving us uncertain about our proper relation to the gesture of the text. If we were certain of a dramatic context, in which *I* and *you* designate characters whom we watch but with whose position we do not coincide, we might marvel at the effect (think, as Keats may have, of Lucius's cry to Titus's corpse: "O grandsire, grandsire, ev'n with all my heart / Would I were dead, so you did live again!" [*Titus Andronicus* 5.3.172–73]). But since the context can be only conjecture, and in any event forever unknowable, most of us, affected by the sensationalism of the gesture, take its proposal personally: lacking any reference to a visual stage or other dramatic frame, we enter a dynamics of reading similar to that of a personal letter or lyric poem whose author is absent, and with whose unspecified addressee, in the rhetoric of reading, we effectively, and affectively, identify. We take these lines as the trace of an absent speaker, its voice begging for admission to, or imposing itself upon, the present consciousness of the reader they project. Even in this orientation, however, a reader may be unsettled, for the parting lines, "see here it is / I hold it towards you," activate the question of reference by suspending the declaratives between a present moment, in which the speaker invites earnest grasping, and an event of imagination in which a cold hand, as promised, assaults the conscience. Do the two *its* refer to a living hand or a dead one?

The whole rhetorical thrust of the utterance not only confuses the question but makes it supererogatory. For what it manipulates in the reader is an act of imagination that conceives the present as past, the sensation of earnest grasping as the chilling grip of a nightmare, the actual as spectral, and the spectral as actual. The peculiar power of this solicitation has received fine attention from Lawrence Lipking and Timothy Bahti, both of whom confront the question of form only to write allegories of occlusion. For Lipking, the undecidability of reference—are we to imagine a living hand as dead, or an absent one as present?—provokes "two fully coherent yet mutually exclusive" readings (181). Noting Lipking's remark that "the very act of writing might be thought to confirm that a warm and capable hand is moving toward a reader" (182), Bahti figures out a way to coordinate these "radically contradictory" possibilities (219). He proposes that the poem's final lines represent

the living hand turned dead, written as dead in the poem's proleptic narrative, and "it"—the two letters of the neuter pronoun—is the *handwriting*, or "hand," of the "living hand": "it," and the whole text of "This living hand. . ." This dead or written hand, then, comes before us declaring itself "living" in the first line, and from our necessity of reading it as living it enacts its proleptic wish: that the reader(s) pour life into the "entombed" tomb of text so that it might live "again," as meaningful representation. (220)

In different ways, Bahti and Lipking take textual indeterminacy as a form to be made meaningful. Lipking sentimentalizes the parting gesture as signifying

Keats's investment of "hope in the reader's conscience, not in his own imperishable work"; for him, this is what makes the fragment fit "so snugly at the end of Keats' poems": "the process of his work can never be completed save by our own responsive acts of attention" (183). Bahti's point, essentially the same but conscripted into deconstruction, is that any poetics of reciprocity has to engage a reading of the living hand "as an entombed script or text that is 'living' only to the extent that it is animated by the reader's understanding ['earnest grasping' or comprehension], in accordance with the poem's narrative." The poet's "I" has to be reanimated, revived as living and capable of writing "This living hand . . . ," and fated, in the sequence already generated, to write itself back into the silence of the grave, thence to emerge again (220–21). This ceaseless involution of cause and effect, Bahti argues, makes the poem less a fragment than a textual moebius strip, a figure of "ongoing completion beyond which any continuation of the text would only cancel the meaningfulness at which it has arrived" (222). Or, as Lipking writes succinctly but with a similar sense of impasse, "In his presence [the poet] enforces a sense of absence, in his absence presence" (182).

Lipking's and Bahti's efforts to ascribe a rhetorical integrity to these lines demonstrate the longing, in the absence of a definite form, for some shape of reading, some principle by which to assimilate these lines to a Keatsian or a critical canon. Closure by form yields to a formal suspense of verse in mid-line, with the reader left in uneasy complicity with the fragment's last "heated" word, *you*, and forced to surrender to the writer in a radically charged economy of antagonisms—of friendship turned to haunting, of life to death. This is not so much Keats imagining the death of the author and the birth of the productive reader as it is the author's ghoulish rebirth through his text as the murderer of the reader. Even so, this writer, whose language will always remain suspended in petition, must surrender final authority to the reader. Sacrificing formal integrity to a projection of these violent transformations and transactions, Keats's fragment makes aggressive poetic capital out of the knowledge that anguishes his efforts to give form to his desire for Fanny Brawne.[27]

The canny, even hostile instability of form in this fragment and the crises of form that affect all of Keats's late lyrics align these texts to the movement of literary criticism in our own century "beyond formalism"—especially beyond the formalism once felt to be so capably at work, for both Keats and criticism, in the Great Odes. Stuart M. Sperry aptly remarks that the Odes seem almost "by nature ideally suited to the kind of close analysis that was the radical innovation of the New Criticism" (*Keats* 242)—its agenda tuned, in de Man's view, to "the necessary presence of a totalizing principle as the guiding impulse of the critical process" ("Form and Intent" 32). Even so, de Man observed, New Criticism tended to self-subversion: it was inclined not to "discover a single meaning, but a plurality of significations that can be radically opposed to each other," yielding "a discontinuous world of reflective irony and ambiguity. Almost in spite of itself," he argues, "this unitarian criticism finally becomes a criticism of ambiguity, an ironic reflection of the absence of the unity it had postulated" (28). And among its key, but evaded, intuitions is a sensation of form as "never anything but a process on the way to its completion" and of "completed form" as an illusion "in the mind of the interpreter"—whether poet or critic (31–32).

This account is reflected in readings of the Great Odes. In 1957, Brooks was still inclined to cite "Ode to a Nightingale" as an organic form, a "unity" encompassing the "interrelation" of its parts, its "formal elements" and its subject ("Implications" 62–63). Wasserman was less confident. In 1953, with a clear commitment to poetry as "a very special form of verbal communication" using "meter, stanzaic pattern [and] total structure" to shape "organic wholes" (*Finer Tone* 7, 10), he found the same ode to be a "turmoil" (178) of "disintegration," of "patterns flying apart, not coming together" (184), where its "forces contend wildly within . . . not only without resolution, but without possibility of resolution" (178), leaving us "no center of reference," merely "bewildering oscillations" (208). At the end of the same decade, in 1959, David Perkins's *The Quest for Permanence* bore a title that espied de Man's terrain and a critical perspective that released earlier New Critical binds of blindness and insight into indeterminacy: "None of Keats's lyrics can be regarded as a settlement or resolution of the central uncertainties" (284). Sperry's chapter on the Great Odes, appearing a few years after *Blindness and Insight*, is titled "Romantic Irony" and is focused on Keats's engagement with "a state of perpetual *indeterminacy*" (245, his italics)—a demonstration of his own American formalist interest in the rhetoric increasingly important to de Man.[28]

Such late New Critical readings of the Great Odes, those former verbal icons, suggest that what early apologists deemed the loose, unmasterful verse of Keats's late lyrics may be the emergence of a problematic of form already at play, and quite deliberately so, in the Odes themselves.[29] From having allied his own idea of "completed form" with Endymion's erotic yearning for "that completed form of all completeness" (1.606), Keats was moving through and beyond this kind of formalism into an investigation of poetic forms as factitious, temporary, and historically situated, thoroughly implicated with systems of experience and processes of language that they cannot transcend. It is not too much to say that in the formal charges of this later phase of writing Keats was discovering a new poetry, one in which the play of form is bound to a restless formalist criticism.

Chapter 7

✥ Social Form
Shelley and the Determination of Reading

The system of society as it exists at present must be overthrown from the foundations with all its superstructure of maxims & of forms before we shall find anything but disappointment in our intercourse with any but a few select spirits. . . . I wish to ask you if you know of any bookseller who would like to publish a little volume of *popular songs* wholly political, & destined to awaken & direct the imagination of the reformers. I see you smile but answer my question.

—Shelley to Leigh Hunt, May 1, 1820

But let us dismiss those more general considerations which might involve an enquiry into the principles of society itself, and restrict our view to the manner in which the imagination is expressed upon its forms.

—Shelley, second paragraph of *A Defence of Poetry*

The text only takes on life when it is realized, and furthermore the realization is by no means independent of the individual disposition of the reader—though this in turn is acted upon by the different patterns of the text. The convergence of text and reader brings the literary work into existence.

—Wolfgang Iser, opening paragraph of "The Reading Process"

Forms of Convergence

Shelley is nothing if not ambivalent about poetic form as a medium of transmission. In the affirmative motions of *A Defence of Poetry* he argues that poetic form, by revealing "the spirit of [earthly] forms," "redeems from decay the visitations of the divinity in man" (505). But other motions plea-bargain, reducing its claim to that of mere "instruments and materials," of a piece with "grammatical forms" which are "convertible with respect to the highest poetry without injuring it as poetry" (483).[1] Even the minimal form of a metrical line is no necessity (484). This ambivalence extends to Shelley's sense of a specifically "poetic" audience. His stated abhorrence of "didactic poetry" in the Preface to *Prometheus Unbound*—"nothing can be equally well expressed in prose that is not tedious and supererogatory in verse"—seems to dismiss poetic form per se as a means to stimulate the "reform" of other minds (135).

Yet the double negative implies a positive: when poetry *is* the expression, it communicates something that prose cannot. This is the tone on which Shelley rests his *Defence*, projecting poetry as a higher law whose form not only embodies visionary information but also signals visionary authority. The appeal is to an ideal commerce in which a poem is "the creation of actions according to the unchangeable forms of human nature, as existing in the mind of the creator, which is itself the image of all other minds" (485), and so is an element in and medium of a "social system" (486). It is in this spirit, and with a hope of political agency, that Shelley wrote to Leigh Hunt from Italy in May 1820, asking him to find an English publisher for "a little volume of *popular songs* wholly political, & destined to awaken & direct the imagination of the reformers" (*PSL* 2: 191).[2]

Yet these gestures coexist with Shelley's sense that his "passion for reforming the world" involved such "beautiful idealisms," as he says in the Preface to *Prometheus Unbound*, that "the highly refined imagination of the more select classes of poetical readers" was his best audience (135). Some of his actual routes of poetic communication were determined by this selectivity. He issued "Hymn to Intellectual Beauty" to the class who read the *Examiner*, as if to reconfirm the poem's radical and singular devotion to this "Spirit" in a venue of publication whose reform polemics in 1816–17 were alienating the sympathies even of Whigs and moderates.[3] He marked a no less ideologically narrow "class of readers" for *Epipsychidion* (1821)—"the esoteric few," Shelley tells his publisher, adding, in blunt contrast to the cast of his "popular" songs, "it would give me no pleasure that the vulgar should read it." His last lyrics, moreover, were oriented to a coterie who received them, if at all, as private letters, secret messages, gifts of intimacy.[4]

Whether projecting a radically public or a radically private audience, Shelley is constantly investigating the project of communicating with other minds in poetic form. This chapter juxtaposes two sets of texts projected at different senses of audience to show how poetic form in both is pressed into fundamental questions of social relations. The first set consists of some of the "political" poems that Shelley addressed to the public sphere in the heat of 1819, but which (perhaps predictably) remained unpublished until well after his death. The second are the lyrics of 1822 written for and about a domestic circle during the last months of Shelley's life. At these extremes of public and private, Shelley discovers a similar plight: even as he mobilizes his poetic forms to form his audience, his textual complications intuit the unknowability— and perhaps illusion—of this referentiality, and of a self-confirming social reception.

These complications are the signatures (if not always a critical processing) of two related indeterminacies: the translation of poetic form into social performance and reception, and the dispersal of authority when writing becomes reading. As a writer, Shelley manipulates poetic form as a prescription of reading. This is a rhetoric that draws, in ideal terms, on "the power of communicating and receiving intense and impassioned conceptions" (especially during political crisis, a "national struggle for civil and religious liberty")—the claim with which *A Defence* sums its argument for poetic authority (508). At the same time, he is aware of the agency of readers (and by extension, publishers, booksellers) over his texts. Thus, while his defense of poetry deems it "vitally metaphorical" in the way it "marks" previously "unapprehended relations" (482), his practice as poet senses that its forms cannot ultimately legislate reading by their marks, and that other self-devitalizing relations, unapprehended in the poet's conception, may evolve in the convergence of text and reader that brings a poet's work into existence.

Poetic Form and Political Reform: England in 1819

When Shelley asked Hunt to find a publisher for those "popular songs," he also imagined Hunt's reaction—"I see you smile." He was acknowledging a practical constraint, namely, press self-censorship for fear of prosecution for libel, sedition, or treason. The ironic phantom smile admits the unpublished fate of a reform polemic that Shelley had sent to Hunt eight months earlier for the *Examiner*, with either a guileless or a stubborn disregard of the risk to Hunt in indulging Shelley's self-performing desire for influence. This is *The Mask of Anarchy*, written in a fury over the "Peterloo Massacre." [5]

The prestige of *The Mask* as the epitome of political poetry strikes me as peculiarly idealizing (and idolizing). [6] But I think it is a valuable text of the *problem* of Shelley's "political poetry," especially in the conflicting investments of its poetic forms. For if such forms are calibrated to move and inspire a vast audience, they also expose a poetic self-absorption. "Ideally for Shelley," writes David Punter with sympathy, "the imagination was a source not only of poetic inspiration but also of political revelation; yet he was also painfully aware of how rarely such a synthesis actually worked" (165). This awareness involves another: the risk of political poetry seeming no more than an aesthetic processing of politics. This question—can poetry have political agency or is it "supererogatory" to political action?—energizes the contradictions of *The Mask*. What evokes admiration (however delayed the broadcast) is its daring equation of Anarchy and King, of mask and legitimacy; [7] its proto-Marxist analysis of labor and consumption; and the rhetorical dazzle of its call to the "Men of England" to recognize their claims (147–372; fully three-fifths of the poem). [8] Yet the larger social and historical fact is that the bolder aspects of this performance are exactly what rendered it unpublishable—and unable to affect the struggle it addresses. [9] Between its writing and its popular reading is a gap of over a decade in which its poet languishes as unacknowledged legislator (emerging in 1832 only as a belated, posthumous voice).

In this respect, *The Mask*, one of Shelley's most passionately charged "exoteric species" of poetry, is weirdly kin to the elitist visionary poem of the same period with which it is sometimes contrasted, *Prometheus Unbound*.[10] The "unacknowledged legislator" is a product, or byproduct, of a poetics that had a share in the adjective as well as the noun, and the outcome could not have been unanticipated.[11] Non-publication is not just an unlucky effect of state repression or exile in Italy; it is troped by the poem itself: the news "from over the Sea" (2) reaches its poet in a dream state from which he is never seen to awaken. While this modality—what *The Mask* calls "the visions of Poesy" (4)—is one that political appreciators tend to elide or to grant a license of prophetic vision, it is an awkward finesse.[12] This is "a public poem with revolutionary intentions having to face and cope with the fact that its generating consciousness, the poet's mind, is in no position to do more than write a poem," remarks Thomas Edwards (160). The effect is to make *The Mask* seem ultimately self-addressed, a masque in the mind of a poet dreaming about being a political orator and projecting this figure as a fantastic epipsyche.[13]

This inwardness is exposed by Shelley's full title—*The Mask of Anarchy: Written on the Occasion of the Massacre at Manchester*—for the occasion is not of his presence but of his reading, after the fact and a continent away. If the "infernal business" at Manchester had Shelley fuming in the voice of his incestuously raped and desperately patricidal Beatrice Cenci that "something must be done,"[14] his own best deed was to write, and to write, moreover, to recommend heroic restraint: "Let a vast assembly be . . . // Stand ye calm and resolute" (295 ff) in a kind of vast formation that would be public art. Doing his best with the possibilities of his own aesthetic action, Shelley puns his *Mask* in the aristocratic genre of "masque" and uses this pun to create a new force-field of forms: allegorical modes worked into ballad and broadsheet stanzas, political oratory investing highly literary conceptions, social critique in visionary figures, and so forth. Yet, if this vast literary assembly bears a symbolically revolutionary charge in its transgressive mixings and satirical tropings on traditional forms, the very extravaganza of forms also seems a symptom of the strain of trying to charge poetry as a comprehensive public discourse, "the centre and circumference of knowledge" (*Defence* 503). Both the extravagance and the strain of *The Mask* are generated by the charge to poetic form to produce new social forms. Can poetry inspire reform and insert its own forms into the process? Or is its work only a symbolic politics? Or even, a merely aesthetic self-satisfaction?

These questions come into sharpest focus, aptly, in the two moments where *The Mask* refers to concurrent social events. One is the internal orator's urgency that mothers and children "are dying whilst I speak" (171). The other seems quite opposite: the poet's dormancy, named in the opening lines, "As I lay asleep in Italy / There came a voice from over the Sea." The temporal incompatibility of these two "I"s—is the poem's immediacy in its oratory or its dormancy, its speaking or sleeping?—is seemingly reconciled by the key-note of the political allegory, a stanza that tropes a poet's pre-visionary sleep as a pre-revolutionary stage of consciousness:

> Rise like Lions after slumber
> In unvanquishable number—
> Shake your chains to Earth like dew
> Which in sleep had fallen on you—
> Ye are many—they are few. (151–55)

Shelley liked this reveille enough to repeat it as the close of the poem's internal oration, simultaneously the close of *The Mask* itself (368–72). But what of the simile that casts material oppression as ephemeral and insubstantial "chains . . . like dew"? A simile may be a cautiously figural form, but the stanzas that convey it are a patent displacement of the poem's formal frame—the slumber from which the poet does not rise—by the internal oratory.

What is displaced, even effaced, in this emergent performance is the opening scene of a poet's quiescence and self-imposed isolation from the distant political scene:

> As I lay asleep in Italy
> There came a voice from over the Sea,
> And with great power it forth led me
> To walk in the visions of Poesy. (1–4)

Poetic form may sustain the passion of the epipsychic oratory, but in this verse it bears a contrary power. The origin of its hypnotic, nearly claustrophobic single rhyme is not the first end-word, but "as*leep*" (itself oozing suggestively out of the initial *As I*). The quadruple end-rhyme is a dreamy extension of *sleep* into its site in *Italy*; the *Sea* across which lies England; the poet's sign of self, *me*; and the field of action, *Poesy*. Poesy, moreover, is not securely located in the syntax of "the visions of Poesy": *of* situates it both as the producer of visions and as object of envisioning. That this latter, specular seeming is not fully distinguishable from the status of the masquerade figures soon to follow already indicates the perplexed logic of Shelley's political poetics.

The Mask never really unmasks this dreamy origin. Its first verbal form, "*As* I lay asleep," imprints a syntax that binds its dream of political oratory, whose "words of joy and fear arose" (138)

> *As if* their Own indignant Earth
>
> . . .
>
> Had turned every drop of blood
> By which her face had been bedewed
> To an accent unwithstood,—
> *As if* her heart had cried aloud:
>
> "Men of England, heirs of Glory . . . (139, 143–47, my italics)

Echoing the initial *As* that conducts the poem to its visions of Poesy, these syntaxes of *As if* have a reflexive effect of restraining the political agency of the oratory to a dream. The words arise by inexplicable agency and are borne by fantastic illusion.

This dreamy shimmer is a tension that both sustains the poem's idealism and exposes the ideological bind of proffering poetry as the thing to be "done" in political crisis. *The Mask* does theorize the capacity of poetic form to inspire political "awakening," but not without exposing conceptual problems. One is the symbolic apparatus organized by its keyword *Mask*.[15] The political value of representing anarchy in and as a "Mask" is to provoke unmasking; the pun on *masque* assists by denoting an elaborate artifice with which a poet's art may or may not comply. Thus, in the reign of Charles II, Shelley remarks in his *Defence*, "all forms in which poetry had been accustomed to be expressed became hymns to the triumph of kingly power over liberty and virtue," demonstrating how in such epochs "the calculating principle pervades all the forms of dramatic exhibition, and poetry ceases to be expressed upon them" (491). In the "ghastly masquerade" section of *The Mask* (5–81), Shelley exposes this pervasiveness in the historical moment of 1819 by staging kingly power itself as a dramatic exhibition. This parade is a linguistic masquerade as well, an array of the discursive forms through which official power asserts itself and permeates social organization. In the trappings of kingship, anarchy is also a logos: "I AM GOD, AND KING, AND LAW!" (37); his "hired Murderers" echo, "Thou art God, and Law, and King" (60–61); the agents, "Lawyers and priests," whisper, "Thou are Law and God" (66–69); "Then all cried with one accord; / 'Thou art King, and God, and Lord'" (70–71)—an establishment vision of Poesy as a calculating principle proliferated and masked in different syntaxes and grammars. The "stifling repetition," remarks Stephen Goldsmith, "encourages belief that words are limited in supply, belong to a few, and can be combined only in prescribed, mechanical ways that endlessly reproduce the structure of power" (243).

Shelley's poetic form operates as a subversion. His couplet, "The hired Murderers, who did sing / 'Thou art God, and Law, and King'" (60–61), is frankly satirical in linking the embodied authority, *King*, to *sing*, its calculated hymn. Shelley's poetic staging of this masquerade sounds these chimes in increasingly bitter tones:

> Lawyers and priests, a motley crowd,
> To the earth their pale brows bowed;
> Like a bad prayer not over loud,
> Whispering—"Thou art Law and God"—   (66–69)

In this constricted quatrain chord, the dissonance of *God* exposes the strained conscription of God to party ideology. The poetic argument against this linguistic system is Shelley's designation of the Men of England as "Heroes of unwritten story" (148), whose consciousness he means to shape with new "visions of Poesy":

> What is Freedom?—ye can tell
> That which slavery is, too well—
> For its very name has grown
> To an echo of your own. (156–59)

In this didactic poetics, Shelley's punning of *groan* in *grown* and the absorption of *own* into *grown* spell the total claim on identity by economic oppression. He then produces a figure of outrageous equivalence for the oppressors' regard of their laborers:

> ye for them are made
> Loom, and plough, and sword, and spade,
> With or without your own will bent
> To their defence and nourishment. (164–67)

The proto-Marxist sting of "ye for them" is its very syntax: tools are not made "for" the laborers; the laborers themselves "are made" into tools "for the tyrants' use" (163).

Yet these political stings fade when the oration starts to employ allegorical figures:

> What art thou Freedom? O! could slaves
> Answer from their living graves
> This demand—tyrants would flee
> Like a dream's dim imagery. (209–12)

This call does propose an important linguistic politics—that the sheer naming of an idea of freedom gives it conceptual force and helps generate new ideas of social existence: "For the labourer thou art bread" (217); "To the rich thou art a check" (226); "Thou art Justice" (230); "Thou art Wisdom" (234); "Thou art Peace" (238); "Thou art Love" (246); "Spirit, Patience, Gentleness, / All that can adorn and bless / Art thou" (258–60). Yet the corresponding comparison of tyranny to "a dream's dim imagery" poses a difficulty related to the poem's master trope of "mask" as well as its mode of dream vision. Fighting tyranny with allegorical signs, "the sing-song of instructive nursery-rhyme or routine political oration" is a rarefied political poetics: "If the poem does not express a total loss of faith in politics," remarks Edwards, "it at best shows such faith sustained only by the mythologizing of political issues, making them rhetorical and symbolic 'properties' in a moral drama whose relation to the actual public case grows increasingly tenuous" (165, 168). In the mode of a dream, the battle is by representation and between representations.[16]

This inefficacy troubles not only this flat allegorical discourse but also the poem's aesthetically complex moments. Shelley intends his words and the poetic forms that bear them to pattern political action, and his epipsychic oratory urges a preliminary linguistic resistance to the anarchy of "God and Law and King":

> Let a vast assembly be,
> And with great solemnity
> Declare with measured words that ye
> Are, as God has made ye, free—
>
> Be your strong and simple words
> Keen to wound as sharpened swords,
> And wide as targes let them be
> With their shade to cover ye. (295–302)

A declaration "with measured words" is not only a speech act but also a poetic act: "measured" involves rational self-possession with poetic form as its prestigious expression ("poetry" is "measured" language, says *A Defence* [484]). With simple but insistent poetic measures—the chime of *e*-rhymes and tones (assem*bly*, *be*, solemni*ty*, *De*clare, *ye*, *ye*, *free*, *be ye*); the drumbeat of meter, the artful repetition of syntax—Shelley asserts the authority of poetry in this fantasy of political performance. As is often the case with his most invested imaginings, however, they seed their own subversion.

The seed here is the critical *poetic* figure in these verses, the analogy of words to weapons, with a troping of poetic form to sharpen the point: *words* are not just likened to and rhymed with *swords*, but are literally infused into them: s*words*. This semantic wit, however, is also the event that exposes the poetic self-service of Shelley's fantasy. For both the rhyme and the graphemic pun of *words/swords* are forms that register only in writing and reading rather than in speech and listening, where the rhyme is off at best, or inaudible.[17] The poetic forms that make Shelley's political point do not translate into oration, and other aspects of his verse even contribute to the obstruction: the rhymes that really chime are the ones initiated by *assembly be*—the icon of political action as static aesthetic spectacle.

Moving from the definition of "Freedom" to the agenda of "Let a great Assembly be / Of the fearless and the free" (262 ff), Shelley's orator first argues that the transition from the idea ("Freedom") to the political fact ("free") has to be expressed in "deeds, not words" (260–61). Yet Shelley's own medium of words soon makes them (a substitution for) deeds, and soon even deeds are being cast into the silent signifying of a readable text:

> Stand ye calm and resolute,
> Like a forest close and mute,
> With folded arms and looks which are
> Weapons of unvanquished war. (319–22)

The allegorical version and justification for this translation of deeds into mute spectacle is the sudden death of Anarchy. This is a phantasmic event initiated by a "maniac maid" who lies down before the onrushing army of tyrants—an outward action, or mask, that covers the identity that her voice claims: "her name was Hope, she said: / But she looked more like Despair" (86–88).

Shelley's point is that what looks like surrender is actually a potentially revolutionary performance, a political art. Prefiguring the later call for a mass demonstration of passive resistance, the maid's risk of martyrdom is redeemed by a miraculous epiphanic female intervention, an advent that simultaneously leaves Anarchy dead and releases the words to the "Men of England":

> between her and her foes
> A mist, a light, an image rose,
> Small at first, and weak, and frail
> Like the vapour of a vale:
>
> Till as clouds grow on the blast,
> Like tower-crowned giants striding fast
> And glare with lightnings as they fly,
> And speak in thunder to the sky,
>
> It grew—a Shape arrayed in mail
> Brighter than the Viper's scale,
> And upborne on wings whose grain
> Was as the light of sunny rain.
>
> On its helm, seen far away,
> A planet, like the Morning's, lay,
> And those plumes its light rained through
> Like a shower of crimson dew.
>
> With step as soft as wind it past
> O'er the heads of men—so fast
> That they knew the presence there,
> And looked,—but all was empty air.
>
> As flowers beneath May's footstep waken
> As stars from Night's loose hair are shaken
> As waves arise when loud winds call
> Thoughts sprung where'er that step did fall. (102–25)

This is a "vision of Poesy" as politics that bears a recognizable Shelleyan cast, of ideals at once sustained and attenuated by their mode of representation. Notwithstanding its ground in "Hope" and the array in quasi-military mail, the political work of this "Shape" in Shelley's rhetoric is both tentative and ambivalent. Some read a political allegory in the way the verse accumulates comparisons and analogies, a Shelleyan signature of visionary access.[18] Yet the central agency, the "Shape" (its visionary status marked with the capital *S*) is elevated and limited to an intangible, phenomenal "presence" that finally produces "empty air"—in other words, visionary poetry itself, rather than an analysis of how material change might be realized in the historical moment of 1819. When the *Athenæum* noted the publication of 1832, it felt compelled to explain that although *The Masque of Anarchy* (the title Hunt used when he published it) is "political" in subject, "Shelley was too much of a poet to be a good politician, and, with every wish to be simple and plain, he is much too lofty in his conceptions to be either," and it went on to alert readers that Shelley's "account of the Peterloo affair . . . is not in the customary style of reports" (262: 705).

Admirers of the poem's reform politics are certainly distressed by Shelley's summary appeal to "the old laws of England" (331), as if this social form transcended its modern abuse: "sold / As laws are in England" (231–32). Paul Foot tries to recuperate the contradiction and Shelley in general ("at the end of the poem, he seems to be openly advocating revolution"), but this seems a wistful gloss to his concession that for "much of the poem Shelley seems to be counselling the people to behave constitutionally, and to protest within the system" (*Revolutionary Year* 16). The contradiction that arrests Foot (who admits its presence in other of Shelley's political poems) has to do with the way passivity, even (or especially) in a heroic masquerade, can serve the interests of tyranny. While Shelley would never consciously put his art to such service, his anxiety about the historical processes of change is related to this effect. What the poem's contradictions contain, in both senses, is a specter of anarchy—not in the Crown, but in the Men of England. When, before he learned of Peterloo, Shelley worried to Peacock about the consequences of a radical monetary reform from which the working classes would benefit (shifting from the "fraud" of paper currency and the sinking fund to "paying in gold"), he was more than a little nervous about a radical insurgency that might destroy all social order: "England seems to be in a very disturbed state. . . . But the change should commence among the higher orders, or anarchy will only be the last flash before despotism. I wonder & tremble" (August 24, 1819; *PSL* 2: 115).

Some of this trembling appears in the contradictory elements that Shelley writes into the aftermath of the revolutionary Shape's advent:

> And the prostrate multitude
> Looked—and ankle-deep in blood,
> Hope that maiden most serene
> Was walking with a quiet mien. (126–29)

The prostrate multitude—that is, the political class that repeats and extends the maniac maid's political theater—sees two things: the quiet serenity with which this courageous maid survives, and the sea of blood (to recall Blake's image in *Gwin*) on which she survives. Michael Scrivener remarks that the ringing refrain, "Rise like Lions . . . / In unvanquishable number," is no appeal to "moral argument, but a political exhortation, an appeal to *physical* superiority" (209). The Tories, for their part, were quite alarmed by the specter of change seemingly signified by the working-class formation at St. Peter's Fields: a disciplined, carefully rehearsed, display of a grievance—a kind of embodied public poetry.[19] Shelley's caution is to be sensed in how he exhorts this class to value the work of poetry. The epiphanic female orator instructs the assembly that

> Science, Poetry, and Thought
> Are thy lamps; they make the lot
> Of the dwellers in a cot
> So serene, they curse it not (254–57)

This "delicious stanza," Hunt says in his Preface, produces "a most happy and comforting picture in the midst of visions of blood and tumult" (x), and he was happy to read its imagery as a striking "*political anticipation*" (his italics) of what could be judged, from the retrospective of 1832, as the right policy: "the Poet recommends that there should be no active resistance, come what might; which is a piece of fortitude, however effective, which we believe was not contemplated by the Political Unions; yet, in point of the spirit of the thing, the success he anticipates has actually occurred, and after his very fashion. . . . The battle was won without a blow" (x–xi).

The Reformists' view of success, however, is not equivalent to the sum of Shelley's ambivalent vision of Poesy, which wavers between a call to revolutionary resistance and an aesthetic fantasy of melioration. Or, to put this issue in the language of Shelley's contradictory imaginings, will anarchy be reformed by a visionary light that looks like "crimson dew" (117), or by a violence "ankle-deep in blood" (127)? Foot privileges what the framing rhetoric of the oratory also privileges by its repetition and its summary position: "Rise like lions after slumber." This is the activist language that the political unions did take up. The frame shaped by its two stanzas (151–55, 368–72) is the most critical formalist maneuver in *The Mask*, for it not only occludes but usurps the initial dream frame. It frames a substitute reality. That the poem remains in the rhetoric of its fantasized oratory (a draft does not even apply closing quotation marks, merely a prospective dash)[20] suggests Shelley's imaginative investment in this voice. At the same time, the suppression of the poem's initiating frame marks an aesthetic ideology that is as delimited as it is motivated by its challenge to political ideology. Shedding the dream frame, Shelley positions the fantasy oration for a potentially wider circulation, implying that a political action has emerged from visionary Poesy, that the dream song has scripted a voice for the "Men of England." If the frame were to return, it would cast the oration as an unreal event—a wish and a dream, a fantasy wrought by visions of Poesy—at the very moment that Shelley wants to insist on its political potency.[21]

A sonnet written later in the same year, one whose scope includes but extends beyond Peterloo, also tropes poetic fantasy as political—but with a sense of craft now cannily managing the strains as figures of the dilemma. Shelley did not delude himself about the prospect of publishing "England in 1819."[22] Yet, the conscious cancellation of an immediate audience leaves him in the peculiar position of writing a political poem whose chief interest seems to be that of self-arousal. It is under this tension that we must assess the sonnet's most dramatic event of form: the drive of its syntax toward a predicate that seems to yield a kind of symbolic poetics for the action it describes.

> An old, mad, blind, despised, and dying King;
> Princes, the dregs of their dull race, who flow
> Through public scorn,—mud from a muddy spring;
> Rulers who neither see nor feel nor know,
> But leechlike to their fainting country cling
> Till they drop, blind in blood, without a blow.
> A people starved and stabbed in th'untilled field;
> An army, whom liberticide and prey
> Makes as a two-edged sword to all who wield;
> Golden and sanguine laws which tempt and slay;
> Religion Christless, Godless—a book sealed;
> A senate, Time's worst statute, unrepealed—
> Are graves from which a glorious Phantom may
> Burst, to illumine our tempestuous day.

But arousal it is. With impressive skill, Shelley defies the formal patterns of both the Italian and Shakespearean sonnet, increasing the syntactic pressure of his list of ills and grievances toward the predicate, finally appearing in the blunt statement of line 13, "Are graves." Even here the syntax does not close, but initiates a couplet whose syntactic energy drives past the rhyme toward *Burst*.

Yet as forceful as this play against formal prescription is, it registers with uncertain effect, as three sample readings show. For Stuart Curran, the form negotiates a tensed ambivalence with an ultimately ironic result in relation to its very presence:

The sudden enjambment of the final couplet, with its ambiguous modal auxiliary—"may"—throw[s] the accumulated weight of the single-sentence catalog onto the active, explosive verb so long awaited. The melding of form and content appears seamless. Yet ultimately the appearance is a paradox, for the informing idea of this marriage is an impossibility: the subject, as Shelley conceives it, is pitted against the form itself. . . . Shelley pivots his poem on a syntactic potentiality—"may"—that yields to the bursting of its formal bonds in a movement parallel to the revolutionary explosion that will invert the anti-forms repressing contemporary society. The form symbolically consumes itself, as surely as does the society it catalogs. (*Poetic Form* 55)

For Curran, the emergence of *may* from the catalogue of oppression is a rhetorical feat that takes precedence over its ambiguous mode, but for F. R. Leavis, its sign of hesitation coincides with a "pathetic weakness" of both form and statement: the "oddly ironical stress" that "results from the rime position" of *may* exposes a politics (as in *The Mask*) governed by a Phantom of miraculous agency ("Shelley" 213). Yet Timothy Webb finds the stress on *may* tough-minded: "Shelley's intellectual honesty prevents him from even believing wholeheartedly in such an incarnation: the rhyme scheme insists that we underline the improbability of this redemption by stressing the word *may*. . . . A mere escapist would not have allowed that ironical and limiting stress on *may*. Surely the point is that Shelley's sense of evil is too strong rather than too weak?" (107–8).

What these divergent readings show is that the question that Webb poses rhetorically is one Shelley's formalist poetics produce as genuine and genuinely unresolvable. It is no overstatement to say that Shelley's sonnet stakes the force of its predicate—a force both conceptual and, more specifically, political—on a simultaneous apprehension of form and grammar. In the register of form, *may* has significance as a rhyme form weakened in the rush to *Burst*; in the register of grammar, it designates a merely tentative hope. Curran argues for the former, in effect a signifying form, and Webb and Leavis for the reverse, seeing weak rhyme conveying, for better or for worse, a limited confidence. There is, moreover, a semantic indeterminacy in the two incompatible senses of *may*. If it means "perhaps," it is tentative, whether optimistically or skeptically, in the way that Leavis and Webb recognize. But if it means "is enabled," or even "is empowered to," then it is energized in the way that Curran suggests.[23]

The array of signals in this climactic couplet—fantasy, hesitation, faint hope, affirmative prophesy—makes the question ultimately undecidable, and the charge to Shelley's readers is to see how his poetic form keeps the possibilities in tension. Even his letter to Hunt pivots interestingly on the point: "I do not expect you to publish it, but you may show it to whom you please," he said of the sonnet (*PSL* 2: 167). Publication would provoke two audiences, the oppressed for whom the sonnet articulates political grievance and the oppressors for whom it articulates a political threat. The compromise of giving it to Hunt with no demands, but with yet another calculated overload on *may*, places the agency on him: either with Shelley's permission, or as a possibility from his own judgment, he "may" show the poem to readers in England in 1819. In the poems he wrote to and about Jane Williams in 1821, Shelley attempts to control this selection himself, as well as the particulars of interpretation.

"Familiar forms" and the "Idle mask of author": Shelley's Last Invitations

The reception of Shelley's political poems of 1819—their canonization by Chartists and Socialists, or their suppression by the "angelists"[24]—is a posthumous history. Shelley's immediate sense of his audience was tending towards contraction. He instructs Ollier to publish "merely one hundred copies" of *Epipsychidion* "for the esoteric few" (February 16, 1821; *PSL* 2: 263); a year later he tells a friend that "Prometheus was never intended for more than 5 or 6 persons," and some weeks on, this Miltonic audience of fit though few has depleted any "motives . . . to write."[25] If the vision of social poetry retreats into a vision of poetry for a select society, Shelley's last lyrics retreat even further, concentrating on his relations with Edward Williams and his common-law wife, Jane, and implicitly, with Mary Shelley and Byron. Yet despite this seeming withdrawal from large imperatives, the immediacy of their concerns makes these lyrics in some ways the most intensely social of Shelley's poems, for in them he explores the smallest minimal units, or charges, that define social organization—charges of affection, rivalry, and manipulation.

"The social sympathies, or those laws from which as from its elements society results, begin to develope themselves from the moment that two human beings coexist," Shelley argues in *A Defence* (481). When in the same paragraph he proposes to dismiss a general "enquiry into the principles of society itself" in order to consider "the manner in which imagination is expressed upon its forms" (481), it was not because he thought these subjects antithetical. In the letter that tells Peacock of his concerns over the "disturbed state" of England (just before he learned of Peterloo), Shelley admits his dependence on social existence "in some form," a dependence that is also a textual figure:

Social enjoyment in some form or other is the alpha & the omega of existence.

All that I see in Italy—and from my tower window I now see the magnificent peaks of the Apennine half enclosing the plain—is nothing—it dwindles to smoke in the mind, when I think of some familiar forms of scenery little perhaps in themselves over which old remembrances have thrown a delightful colour. (August 24, 1819; *PSL* 2: 114)

Two years later, this preference for "familiar forms" had narrowed: "My greatest content would be utterly to desert all human society," he tells Mary;

"I would retire with you & our child to a solitary island in the sea, would build a boat, & shut upon my retreat the floodgates of the world.—I would read no reviews & talk with no authors.—If I dared trust my imagination it would tell me that there were two or three chosen companions beside yourself whom I should desire." Conceding the fantasy, he proposed an "alternative": "to form for ourselves a society of our own class, as much as possible, in intellect or in feelings: & to connect ourselves with the interests of that society" (August 15, 1821; *PSL* 2: 339). Half a year later, however, it was not Mary and their child, but another couple with whom Shelley would retreat, Edward and Jane.

Their small "society" of three focused a set of compositions in the last months of Shelley's life, as he was struggling with *The Triumph of Life*. Arriving in Italy in January 1821 at the urging of their friend and Shelley's cousin, Thomas Medwin, the couple became steady company, even sharing residences with the Shelleys, first in Pisa then Lerici, from October 1821 to July 1822, when Shelley and Edward drowned in a storm at sea. Shelley took to both and increasingly to Jane, who by early 1822 seemed "more amiable and beautiful than ever, and a sort of spirit of embodied peace in our circle of tempests."[26] By June, he was in love with her. Of his late lyrics, four are inscribed "To" her—"To Jane. The Invitation"; "To Jane. The Recollection"; "With a Guitar. To Jane"; and "To Jane" ("The keen stars were twinkling"); another untitled poem enclosed in a note to Edward (beginning "The Serpent is shut out from Paradise") shifts its initial address to him and her to Jane alone ("Dear friends, dear *friend*"); and two others concern her—"The Magnetic Lady to her Patient" and a fragment later titled "Lines written in the Bay of Lerici."[27] Except for the last (which appears in the manuscript of *The Triumph of Life*), all were sent with inscriptions or notes to Jane or Edward or both. The social context of these performances is more than a little complicated, involving not only Shelley's sense of himself as a *poet* in doubt of a public audience, but also his painful awareness of Edward's privileged place in Jane's affections, and so of Jane and Edward as audiences to be addressed with a difference, and of Mary as a rhetorically alienated reader. It is clear why William Keach finds Shelley's inscriptions and notes "hard to keep separate from the poetic texts to which they are attached" (217).

Nor should they be kept thus, despite a routine editorial practice of canceling them or reducing them to footnotes. These communications are fundamentally a composite form whose poetics are charged by Shelley's desire "to form . . . a society . . . as much as possible, in intellect or in feelings."[28] This social rhetoric is also the definition of their formal problematics. Cast (both as projection and as script) for social reception, Shelley's texts situate his reader as a necessary "supplement"—in the full Derridean duplicity of the term—to the poet's self-sufficiency.[29] For if the public poems seem haunted by their inefficacy, the private poems struggle with a dependency on social effect. By Romanticism's own lights, we have come to regard lyric as *the* form of self-sufficiency, a plenitude achieved not only in independence from but in defiance of a social audience: when Shelley takes his "estimate" in *A Defence* of "the manner in which poetry acts" and of "its effect upon society," he casts the poet as a figure unified in, and by, its privacy, singing "to its own solitude" rather than in consciousness of "auditors" (486–87). At the same time, the negative verbal forms that accrue to this situation—*unapprehended, unseen,* and famously, *unacknowledged* (486, 508)—court as potential what they here negate. Shelley's late lyrics evoke this tension by submitting poetic form to temporal, social, and historical contingencies of reading and reception—exactly that "bond of connexion" by "time, place, circumstance, cause and effect" that defines the mode of "story" and distinguishes it from that of "a poem," which is created "according to the unchangeable forms" of "universal" and "eternal truth" (485). Their involvement with the "story" of his love for Jane Williams heightens this doubleness, eroding their self-authorized aesthetics with urgencies of correspondence and response that take shape as a series of calculated performances.

These performances are self-dramatizing appeals to their actual and imagined audiences, with the poetic documents functioning not only as their stage of enactment also as a material part of it. The inventory includes the wounded deer and desperate patient of Petrarchan love-longing, Shakespeare's Ariel, Milton's tortured serpent, the social satirist, the carpe diem poet, the poet of elegy and epitaph, the melancholy abject lover—all played through "the idle mask of author" for sympathetic acknowledgment. Shelley's performances are not just a matter of these masks, however; they are also worked through his formalist practices—a convergence especially apparent in the untitled verses beginning, "The Serpent is shut out from Paradise," the source of the phrase, "the idle mask / Of author." Early in 1822, Shelley sent these verses to Edward Williams with a seemingly casual note (January 26; *PSL* 2: 384; the italicized words in the brackets are editorial):

> My dear Williams
>   Looking over the portfolio in which my friend used to keep his verses, & in which those I sent you the other day were found,—I have lit upon these; which as they are too dismal for *me* to keep I send them you [who can afford *deleted*].
>   If any one of the stanzas should please you, you may read them to Jane, but to no one else,—and yet on second thought I had rather you would not [*some six words scratched out*].
>   Yours ever affectionately,
>   P.B.S.

"A curious method of communication for one who lived two flights of stairs above," remarks Richard Holmes (698); he does not develop the point, but he hits the right word: *method*. The wavering about whether Edward is to share these stanzas with Jane, Stephen C. Behrendt suggests, seems "a calculated rhetorical and psychological maneuver designed more to ensure than to prevent" this result (244). Everything seems calculated—from the scenario of accidental discovery, to the friendly-resentful transmission of the verses' "dismal" mood, to the way that the visibly deleted words (so short a note could have been rewritten) produce what Wolfgang Iser calls a rhetoric of negation: one that writes in order to "cancel," allowing the cancellation to remain "in view" (*Act* 169) as a textual form to provoke "formulation" by "deciphering" ("Reading Process" 299). It is even possible that the gendered conventions of address that dictate the different intimacies of "Jane" and "Williams" are calculated, not only holding him at a distance but also suggesting indirectly that she was not really (legally) a "Williams," not really his.

Such manipulations shape the poetic performance itself. Not the least gesture is Shelley's sly suggestion that Edward "read" rather than show his verses to Jane. He thus gets to use Edward's voice as his own (hardly idle) mask for communicating to Jane, making Edward accommodate him and making both aware, in amusement or unease, of this superimposition. (In "The Magnetic Lady" he works the reciprocal, writing a script for Jane.) The first ottava-rima stanza of "The Serpent," despite a display of self-pitying helplessness, is a deftly articulated strategy:

> The serpent is shut out from Paradise—
> The wounded deer must seek the herb no more
> In which its heart's cure lies—
> The widowed dove must cease to haunt a bower
> Like that from which its mate with feigned sighs
> Fled in the April hour.—
> I, too, must seldom seek again
> Near happy friends a mitigated pain. (1–8)

Not only do the poet's words invade their Paradise, but in the phonic field of his couplet, which defers the renewal of "again," there is the ghost of the word that focuses his deepest desire, *Jane*.

Other poems chime *Jane*, explicitly and meaningfully, in chords of tentative harmony against the pressure of pain. After the title "With a Guitar. To Jane," *Jane* haunts the rhymes of the poet's initial petition to her to make his delighted spirit glow "'Til joy denies itself again / And too intense is turned to pain" (7–8) and of the reciprocal lines in which he imagines that the tree from which the guitar was wrought "Died in sleep, and felt no pain, / To live in happier form again" (55–56). The last line sounds the name itself as it commends the guitar "For our beloved Jane alone." In "The keen stars," as we shall see, not only are the monometric lines *Dear Jane* and *Again* a chord linking Jane as agent to a pleasurable recurrence of song, but Shelley's note on the manuscript uses rhyme-words that tease at her name, as if in coded communication to her: "I sate down to write some words for an ariette which might be *profane*—but it was in *vain* to struggle with the ruling spirit. . . . I commit them to your secrecy & your mercy" (*SPP* 451, my italics).

Both "With a Guitar" and "The keen stars" deploy rhymes of *Jane* / *again* not only as a phonic harmony but as its sign: the recurrent sound operates as an invitation to recurrence and its promise of a mitigated pain. In this intertext, it matters that the potential rhyme of *pain* is absent in "The keen stars," and that in "The Magnetic Lady" its alliances with *Jane* become part of the drama.[30] In this last poem, the Lady speaks in sympathy to Shelley—"Sleep, sleep on, forget thy pain— / My hand is on thy brow, / My spirit on thy brain" (1–3)—as Shelley's rhymes evoke a link to *Jane*. The rhyme itself emerges at the poem's close. The penultimate stanza sets the stage by sounding the rhyme field, as the Lady reiterates her sympathy for her patient:

> Like a cloud big with a May shower
>   My soul weeps healing rain
>   On thee, thou withered flower.—
> It breathes mute music on thy sleep,
>   Its odour calms thy brain—
> Its light within thy gloomy breast
> Spreads, like a second youth again—   (28–34)

Predicted by *pain*, *brain*, *rain*, *brain*, and *again* (the very trope of rhyme), the Lady's name, with disingenuous casualness, finally joins the spell of words that, implicitly, she has been inspiring all along:

> "The spell is done—how feel you now?"
>   "Better, quite well" replied
>   The sleeper—"What would do
> You good when suffering and awake,
>   What cure your head and side?"
> "What would cure that would kill me, Jane,
> And as I must on earth abide
> Awhile yet, tempt me not to break
>   My chain."   (37–45)

Part of the poem's sub-logic is its final pairing of *Jane* with *chain*, the term of torturing enforcement (to life, to Mary) against the final cure, and a strength quite different from the dew-like chains said to bind the Men of England in *The Mask of Anarchy*.

The calculated signifying of this *Jane* / *chain* rhyme to both Edward and Jane is related to the other key places in Shelley's text where her name appears: its designations of audience. At the top of the manuscript he wrote, "For Jane & Williams alone to see," then put it in a wrapper which, repeating the specification, advertises its privacy: "To Jane. Not to be opened unless you are alone, or with Williams" (Chernaik 257). The domestic intimacy of the couple and the Shelleys risked a reading by Mary, or perhaps even counted on it to communicate, indirectly and "accidentally," to her, too, as a sign of intimacies excluding her.[31] Both Mary and, once again, Edward are cast in a strange role by these addresses: the note solicits his attention, but in the poem itself this turns out to be an enforced awareness of his status as a marginal spectator to a scene of two, audience to a conversation between the Magnetic Lady and her Patient that imposes on him a consciousness of the latter as a would-be, if not actual, rival.

The gesture would become habitual. "Dear Jane," Shelley begins another note (*PSL* 2: 386–87),

> If this melancholy old song suits any of your tunes, or any that humour of the moment may dictate, you are welcome to it. Do not say it is mine to any one, even if you think so; indeed, it is from the torn leaf of a book out of date. How are you today, and how is Williams? Tell him that I dreamed of nothing but sailing, and fishing up coral.
>
> Yours ever affectionate,
> P.B.S.

It is clear that he has been dreaming of nothing if not Jane as the singer of his songs and of the secret bond ("Do not say it is mine to any one") to be wrought between him and her by his art—so that what she is instructed to "tell" Williams is a lie that enlists her in confederacy against him. By this script, not only will she operate in conscious duplicity, but Williams—told of Shelley's dreams by her—will realize that she and "P.B.S." have a sympathy of two.[32] This is the larger social plot of "With a Guitar," a lyric accompanying the gift to Jane of an Italian guitar. It opens with a notation, "Ariel to Miranda," that means to reverse the Shakespearean story, where Miranda never sees or speaks to Ariel. Shelley's heading signifies not just a direct address but also a shutting out of Ferdinand, notwithstanding Ariel's claim to be sending this gift by his "permission and command" (9). This exclusion even defines the site of composition. To write this poem, Shelley returned to the pine forest that inspired "The Invitation" and "The Recollection," records of a day with Jane *sans* Edward and from which Mary is erased (about which, more soon). On this later day, he was gone so long that Mary became alarmed and enlisted their friend Trelawny to help her find him. She grew tired, and Trelawny left her (almost too allegorically) "forsaken" and "wretched" at "the entrance of this grove, in despair," while he continued on. With the help of a local pinecone gatherer, he discovered "the Poet" deep within the grove, by "a deep pool of dark glimmering water . . . gazing on the dark mirror beneath, . . . lost in his bardish reverie"; nearby, was the fragment of a draft of verses in "a frightful scrawl" (Trelawny 72–78).

When these verses were presented "With a Guitar. To Jane," they were "beautifully written" (Chernaik 262; *SPP* 449). Shelley's care for the aesthetic object is continuous with the poem's dominant conceit, his image of himself as an instrument to be awakened by Jane, "the voice of one beloved singing to you alone" (as he imagined such correspondence in "On Love" [*SPP* 474]):

> Ariel to Miranda;—Take
> This slave of music for the sake
> Of him who is the slave of thee;
> And teach it all the harmony,
> In which thou can'st, and only thou,
> Make the delighted spirit glow (1–6)

Both the guitar and the accompanying poem signify a potentiality to be released in reception. Shelley solicits this reception by representing transmission as a finely tuned conversation:

> The artist wrought this loved guitar,
> And taught it justly to reply
> To all who question skilfully
> In language gentle as thine own. (58–61)

The reciprocal is the guitar's latency: what "it knows" from its artist-maker it "will not tell" (79)

> To those who cannot question well
> The spirit that inhabits it:
> It talks according to the wit
> Of its companions. (80–83)

Shelley presents both the guitar and himself as instruments for Jane's questioning, or, more precisely as answers, Ariel-like, awaiting liberation:

> sweetly as its answers will
> Flatter hands of perfect skill,
> It keeps its highest holiest tone
> For our beloved Jane alone.—— (87–90)

Shelley's lyrics "acknowledge and embrace the fact that their release from the prison of the page depends on human intervention," Barry Weller writes (924). I would tighten the terms: these lyrics also cast this intervention as Jane's particular role. The note Shelley wrote in June on the manuscript of another guitar-"ariette," "To Jane" ("The keen stars"), pointedly shifts its rhetoric from our beloved Jane to his Jane alone. A "ruling spirit," he says, "compelled me to speak of things sacred to yours & Wilhelmeister's

[Williams's] indulgence"; but the real indulgence courted is Jane's: "I commit them to your secrecy & your mercy." Shelley makes her his "ideal reader," one "who would understand perfectly and would approve entirely the least of his words, the most subtle of his intentions"—an intimacy that the first publishers of the poem felt to be indiscreet.[33]

The coy manipulation of Jane's attention and Edward's unease throughout these correspondences is unapologetically prescriptive in "The Serpent," where Shelley exhorts them to "know" him and to evoke him, by agency of his verses, in his absence:

> Therefore, if now I see you seldomer,
>   Dear friends, dear <u>friend</u>, know that I only fly
>   Your looks, because they stir
>   Griefs that should sleep, and hopes that cannot die.
>   . . .
>   When I return to my cold home, you ask
>   Why I am not as I have lately been?
>   <u>You</u> spoil me for the task
>   Of acting a forced part in life's dull scene.
>   Of wearing on my brow the idle mask
>   Of author, great or mean,
>   In the world's carnival, I sought
>   Peace thus, and but in you I found it not.
>   (17–20, 25–32, Shelley's emphases)

When Shelley boasted to Trelawny, "I have the vanity to write for poetical minds, and must be satisfied with few readers" (Trelawny 80), he was evading the secondary meaning of *vanity* as emptiness, or idleness.

In this poem, the sensation is near enough to become his own mask—a mask of author—and he holds Edward and Jane accountable for both redeeming him from and damning him to this charade. He plays his verse accordingly. He organizes line 31 to shape the phantom syntax of "In the world's carnival I sought"—a form that stages his alienated searching—and he doubly loads the *but* in line 32—I found peace not in the world, only (nowhere but) in you; I might have found peace in the world, except (but for the fact that) you have spoiled me for the task—to serve his charge to his friends.[34] In both cases, Shelley gets to say two things at once and to imply their relation. What his dear friends are exhorted to "know" resolves into what he would have them know of his way of knowing them. Included in this correspondence is a melancholy representation of his own marriage, summed by an account of a final cure:

> I asked her yesterday if she believed
>   That I had resolution. One who <u>had</u>

51   Would ne'er have thus relieved
              His heart with words, but what his judgment bade
            Would do, and leave the scorner unrelieved.—
54   These verses were too sad
              To send to you, but that I know,
            Happy yourself, you feel another's woe. (49–56, Shelley's emphasis)

Keach nicely observes that *thus* in line 51 is referable both to yesterday's conversation with "her" and to the present address to the Williamses (219). This
is only one of the equivocations: like a suicide tease, Shelley hints at what he
"would do."[35] But, as in the political poetics of *The Mask of Anarchy*, he
chooses a performance of "words." He equivocates about this, too, indicating
a sense of transgression in involving his friends in his distress, but then sending them his sad verses and implying that their happiness ought to be condi-
tioned by feeling his woe. Reiman and Powers say that *were* in line 54 is subjunctive, "to express a condition contrary to fact" (*SPP* 448 n. 5), but the
"fact" is that in January 1822 Shelley did send them these verses, and here his
"but" is both a self-pleading and a plea against his friends' self-contained
happiness.

"I only feel the want of those who can feel, and understand me. Whether
from proximity and the continuity of domestic intercourse, Mary does not.
The necessity of concealing from her thoughts that would pain her, necessi-
tates this, perhaps. . . . The Williams's . . . are very pleasing to me," he would
tell John Gisborne some months later, in June (*PSL* 2: 435). Indeed, by 1822,
as Keach writes, Jane became "Shelley's muse, lyric focus," and a "primary
audience" (203). She first pleased him as a kind of trivial poem—"an extremely pretty & gentle woman—apparently not *very* clever," he tells Mary's
step-sister, Claire Clairmont (his emphasis). Yet he enjoyed the easy pleasure:
"I like her very much. I have only seen her for an hour" (January 16, 1821;
PSL 2: 256–57). This abides, with improved value: "I like Jane more and
more," he tells John Gisborne in June 1822; "She has a taste for music, and an
elegance of form and motions that compensate in some degree for the lack of
literary refinement" (2: 435). This easy liking, however, was a complicated
sensation for Shelley, linked to the knowledge that Jane and Edward were the
Edenic pair of a Paradise shut to him. It must have been with considerable
pain that Mary Shelley edited for *Posthumous Poems* (1824) the pieces we now
know as "To Jane. The Invitation" and "To Jane. The Recollection."[36] For
even before Mary knew these intimate titles, she must have noted the singular superlatives devoted to Jane ("Dearest, best and brightest" [p. 149]), her
own erasure from the poems' scenes, and Shelley's pained, summary self-
inscription: "But less oft is peace in ———'s mind, / Than calm in waters
seen."[37] This loaded blank begs for comment, but first we need to attend to
the events of poetic form that predict this melancholy climax.

Cast in the social form of an invitation, "The Invitation" is also a motivated apostrophe—a rhetoric evoked by Jane's absence and intended to invoke
her presence. Its rhetoric is a fictive composition: Shelley is writing an imitation after the occasion.[38] This is, therefore, a subtly manipulative commemo-
ration, for it is a nostalgic reproduction intended to keep Jane in the circuit of
petition. The poem addresses her not only as an "ideal reader" but also as a
potentially responsive subject, and elaborates its desire by troping the text of
invitation in the summons of the "fair day" itself. In line with the reproductive
intent, the day commands by a temporal magic, a future unexpectedly present:

> The brightest hour of unborn spring
> Through the winter wandering
> Found, it seems, this halcyon morn
> To hoar February born. (7–10)

In this "brightest hour," the invitation to "Brightest" Jane—herself "Fairer
than this fair day" (2)—is calibrated with parallels to coerce her acceptance as
a natural logic. Modulating these parallels into mirroring images, Shelley
writes himself into the emotional tenor, as another site of restoration. This
halcyon morn

> like a prophetess of May
> Strewed flowers upon the barren way,
> Making the wintry world appear
> Like one on whom thou smilest, dear. (17–20)

The day is now not only a prophecy of May, but May, as personification, is the
counterpart of Jane, reviving and revitalizing the poet who petitions her.

These symmetries trope the harmony of the couplets, which schematize
correspondence and empower poetry to refigure it in a new social existence:

> Radiant Sister of the day,
> Awake, arise and come away
> To the wild woods and the plains
> And the pools where winter-rains
> Image all their roof of leaves,
> Where the pine its garland weaves
> Of sapless green and ivy dun
> Round stems that never kiss the Sun— (47–54)

Even the darkening rhyme of *dun* and *Sun* in this sylvan reflection is pastor-
alized, a prelude to the way the poem will finally mute *dun* internally and
release *Sun* to rhyme with the sign of unity, *one*:

> When the night is left behind
> In the deep east dun and blind
> And the blue noon is over us,

> And the multitudinous
> Billows murmur at our feet
> Where the earth and ocean meet,
> And all things seem only one
> In the universal Sun.— (62–68)

This fantasy seduces language itself into its unities: *multitudinous* does not merely rhyme with *us* but contains it in a punning "multitude in us"—an egalitarian version of Donne's conceit in "The Sun-Rising": "She'is all states, and all princes, I"; and "universal" advertises the role of verse in these illusions of all things seeming only "one."

At the same time, Shelley's poetic forms also project their own annihilation—not with the frustrated tortures of *Alastor*, *Epipsychidion*, and *Adonais*, but in an oppositely toned sentimentality that renders poetry supererogatory to the society of souls:

> To the silent wilderness
> Where the soul need not repress
> Its music lest it should not find
> An echo in another's mind,
> While the touch of Nature's art
> Harmonizes heart to heart.— (23–28)

This is as idealistic as Shelley gets about "Love" itself, that thirst of a subject "after its likeness . . . a soul within our soul that describes a circle around its proper Paradise which pain and sorrow and evil dare not overleap" (*SPP* 473–74). But the work of poetry is softly duplicitous: on the one hand, *find*, by semantic punning, does, formally, find an echo in its rhyme with *mind*; at the same time, it names an echo that is, in effect, an unheard melody. So while the verbal repetition, "heart to heart," seems to figure an ideal echo, even in the way "heart" is literally touched by nature's "art," it implicitly names the poet's art as a language of desire generated from a point of absence.

This link of poetic art to absence is more darkly visible in the rhyme frame that opens "To Jane. The Recollection / Feb. 2, 1822":

> Now the last day of many days,
> All beautiful and bright as thou,
> The loveliest and the last, is dead. (1–3)

Now at first seems to refer to the loveliest day, especially in its rhyme (the poem's first) with its presider, *thou*. But the flat declaration "is dead" deflates the illusion, even as *loveliest* seems contracted and contained by the reiterated "last . . . last." When *now* returns, it is in a considerably darker chord:

> Rise, Memory, and write its praise!
> Up to thy wonted work! come, trace
> The epitaph of glory fled;

> For *now* the Earth has changed its face,
> A *frown* is on the Heaven's *brow*. (4–8, my italics)

The rhymes plot even against the invocation of memory to "trace / The epitaph of glory fled," for the chime is already with *is dead*. "Glory" seems doubly dead, not only fled, but its very epitaph a receding trace. The patently allusive language of Wordsworthian elegy ("Whither is fled . . . / Where is it now, the glory . . . ?") seems tuned to evoke an efficacious "Recollection."[39] But another more immediate echo, or textual recollection, attenuates this allusive potential, namely the summary rhymes of Shelley's own "Invitation"—"And all things seem only one / In the universal Sun"—which haunt with a difference:

> It seemed as if the hour were one
> Sent from beyond the skies,
> Which scattered from above the sun
> A light of Paradise. (17–20)

In this repetition of *one / sun* is also repeated "seemed." In line 67 of "The Invitation" (above), *seem* is gently self-indulgent; here, its past tense stresses an illusion, so that even as the dead day is recalled, recollection turns into a prefiguration of the impending death:

> We paused amid the pines that stood
> The giants of the waste,
> Tortured by storms to shapes as rude
> As serpents interlaced. (21–24)

If, in the magic light of an illusory Paradise, Shelley fantasized himself as Adam to Jane's Eve (with Mary and Edward effaced), in the memory, the serpent has invaded paradise with knowledge that is death to the poem's hopeful invocation—"come trace!" As Shelley evokes the lost paradise as one wherein "There seemed . . . // A magic circle traced" (41–44)—a precarious poetic and imaginative form—*traced* is no simple repetition but a past tense tortured through an intermediary signifying chain of *waste, serpents interlaced,* and *mountain-waste*.

This chain of sound is only one example of how Shelley's poetic forms of recollection rupture the conceptual form into which he would enlist Jane's imagination:

> 31   As still as in the silent deep
>   The Ocean woods may be.
>
> How calm it was! the silence there
>   By such a chain was bound
> That even the busy woodpecker
> 36   Made stiller with her sound
> The inviolable quietness;
>   The breath of peace we drew

With its soft motion made not less
   The calm that round us grew.—
There seemed from the remotest seat
   Of the white mountain-waste,
To the soft flower beneath our feet
   A magic circle traced,
A spirit interfused around
46   A thrilling silent life,
To momentary peace it bound
   Our mortal nature's strife;—
49   And still I felt the centre of
   The magic circle there
51   Was one fair form that filled with love
   The lifeless atmosphere. (31–52)

Having described Jane as a "spirit of embodied peace in our circle of tempests" (January 12, 1822; *PSL* 2: 376), Shelley here draws the circle to exclude
the tempests and include himself, using links of rhyme as much as statement:
Bound/sound/round/around/bound. Yet the attendant notations of stillness are
of ambiguous effect. Marking a charged suspense in "still as in the silent deep"
(31), "Made stiller with her sound" (36), and "still I felt" (49) that resonates
with the silent action of *thrilling* (46) and *filled* (51), *still* also evokes a deathly
arrest in the magically "lifeless atmosphere" (a draft shows the adjective as
breathless [Chernaik 270]) that seems imaged to forestall or even preempt the
coming death of "glory fled."

   The positive investment of this still circle is the figure of poetry itself that
Shelley goes on to write into the landscape of memory, in the form of a perfect
containment whose very powers of idealizing illusion make it seem, paradoxically, transcendent:

We paused beside the pools that lie
   Under the forest bough—
Each seemed as 'twere, a little sky
   Gulphed in a world below;
A firmament of purple light
   Which in the dark earth lay
More boundless than the depth of night
   And purer than the day . . . (53–60)

But again, the frank (though evocative) notation *seemed* and what Keach calls
the "illogically extravagant comparative rhetoric [of] 'More boundless' and
especially 'More perfect'" (214) concede the illusion, and the very pressure of
extravagance—at least in a Shelleyan universe—guarantees a collapse: "Such
views . . . in our world above / Can never well be seen" (69–70), Shelley admits; this is the real "atmosphere without a breath" (75).

This retraction is worked figuratively into the temporality that betrays illusion in the scene itself:

> Until an envious wind crept by,
>   Like an unwelcome thought
> Which from the mind's too faithful eye
>   Blots one dear image out— (81–84)

The comparison of this envious wind to a disruptive presence in the mind is obscurely coded; the usual suggestion is that it refers to Mary (e.g., White 2: 343), effaced from the poem's "we" and its magic circle. Whatever the referent, what is most significant in Shelley's representation is that it is imagination itself (what abides, with Hamlet-like guilt, in the mind's eye) that blots out its dear image. As McGann puts it, "The 'envious wind' that wipes away the image . . . is itself a part of that vision" ("Secrets" 34). This internal agency, like the negative contained in illusion's keyword, "inviolable" (37), ultimately allies the verbal forms of recollection with what nostalgia would exclude— namely, the knowledge that undoes the poem's meta-trope, the magic circle.

Yet in the wake of this loss, Shelley tunes absence to a different key, a rhetoric that asks Jane to read and respond to a form that she might fill with love, a poetic form:

> Less oft is peace in ———'s mind
>   Than calm in water seen. (87–88)

By asking Jane to fill in his name, Shelley's script gets her, too, to trace the epitaph of the day, in sympathy with the disturbance of his recollection. Shelley understood this rhetoric well before Iser theorized the reader's role as one "marked by gaps in the text . . . the blanks which the reader is to fill in" in an act that pivots "the whole text-reader relationship" (*Act* 169). Iser, however, sees a Sartrean "hollow form" in these blanks, whether scriptive or cognitive, that functions "virtually as instructions," a dictation that reading must follow; and he stresses the writer's need to guide this relation "if the reader is to be maneuvered into a position commensurate to the intentions of the text" (212– 13). Shelley's texts display such intentions, but they are also alert to what desire cannot determine—an awareness nowhere more evident than in the textual situation that binds "The keen stars" and "Lines written in the Bay of Lerici."

Drafts of both appear in the manuscript of *The Triumph of Life*, dating them among Shelley's last compositions. More specifically, they appear (along with some monetary tabulations, sketches of boats, and other poetic fragments) on four pages that interrupt Rousseau's self-measuring against "the great bards of old who inly quelled // The passions by which they sung" (274–75):[40]

                                    —I
              Have suffered what I wrote, or viler pain!—
                              .   .   .
              And so my words were seeds of misery— (f. 33ʳ; 280)

Shelley's composition founders on two ambiguities: the temporal order of *suffered* and *wrote* and the prepositional meaning in "seeds of misery" (genitive
or partitive?).[41] When he resumed, he aligned and rhymed his image of words
as "seeds of misery" to "the deeds of others" (37ᵛ; 278–81). Before this, however, he filled the rest of 33ʳ with drafts that he then canceled, before turning
over the page to write about another voice, Jane's. This writing produces the
middle lines of "The keen stars" (from "then / To the strings without soul"
to "the dews of your melody scatter / Delight") and its last two lines, about
the ideal expressed: "When moonlight & music & feeling are one" (33ᵛ).

     These images reverse the scenario of Rousseau in every way: "seeds of
misery" are replaced by a scattering of delight, and words bearing suffering
from the past into the future are replaced by a wordless harmony of present
intoxication. "We drive along this delightful bay in the evening wind, under
the summer moon, until earth appears another world," Shelley writes to John
Gisborne about the inspiration; "Jane brings her guitar, and if the past and
the future could be obliterated, the present would content me so well that I
could say with Faust to the passing moment, 'Remain, thou, thou art so beautiful'" (June 18, 1822; *PSL* 2: 435–36). Postponing the damnation borne by
this last identification, Shelley's draft first used present tenses to set and reproduce the scene: "The keen stars are twinkling / And the moon is rising among
them."[42] His shift into the past tense after these lines, and later in them, is a
delicate concession to a passing moment:

              The keen stars were twinkling
              And the fair moon was rising among them,
                    Dear Jane.
              The guitar was tinkling
              But the notes were not sweet till you sung them
                    Again.— (1–6)

The participles also conspire, rendering the moment always a "passing moment." At the same time, however, Shelley tests the resources of poetic form
for prolongation. His draft has no terminal punctuation after *Jane* or *Again*,
with the effect of letting both words sound as syntactic links, even cues for the
repetition cued by "Again.—"[43] As for the participles, the sense of passing
that they evoke contends with a sensation of extension by sound: the initial
rhyme of *twinkling* and *tinkling* plays across *rising* and echoes in the *revealing/
feeling* of stanza two.

     By stanza two, moreover, Shelley is writing only in present and future
tenses, with an exhortation, half-rhymed with the participles, "Sing again,"

to convey one tense into the other. *Again* is his master-trope, a note played to subsume "the past and the future" into a repetition of present content. Rhymed with *Jane*, *Again* more specifically invokes recurrence by her agency, in time and rhyme. With a self-reflecting repetition of *again*, Shelley rounds out "To Jane," subsiding into an intimation of what Keats termed "happiness on Earth repeated in a finer tone" (*KL* 1: 185):

> Though the sound overpowers
> Sing again, with your dear voice revealing
>   A tone
> Of some world far from ours,
> Where music and moonlight and feeling
>   Are one. (19–24)

Scripting this recurrence with a text for Jane to sing—the note to her calls it "words for an ariette"—Shelley writes more than "an imitation of the song Jane might have played" (Chernaik 166); he calls for a performance in which his words and her voice will sound as "one," a blending signed by ampersands in the draft: "moonlight & music & feeling" (33ᵛ; 38ᵛ). This draft also shows related attention to the summary word: Shelley first wrote "Are won" (38ᵛ), as if the destination intimated by Jane's singing could be gained by striving. Revising to *one* retains the pun on *won* with further advantages to be realized in Jane's reading. One of these is the visual as well as homophonic punning of the rhyming line *A tone* into *Atone*, and by etymological recovery, its spectral reversal into *At-one*. While grammatically alogical, these puns operate as scriptive hints of the guilty scenario of "secrecy & mercy" that Shelley's note to Jane proffers. The slight atonality of *A tone* with the last line's *one*—semantically relevant in suggesting how "far from" the world of *one* is the world in which its *tone* is sung—is also redeemed by an extension of this visual punning. In the graphics of reading, Jane will see that the keyword of ideal unity, *one*, has been literally distilled out of the *tone* of her voice.

All this wordplay produces an odd but revealing contradiction to Shelley's report to John Gisborne about his pleasure in the Williamses' company: "Words are not the instruments of our intercourse" (*PSL* 2: 435). Shelley indulges a sheer form exceeding the *Defence*'s argument that the "harmonious recurrence of sound," without which a poet's language would not be poetry, "is scarcely less indispensable to the communication of its influence, than the words themselves" (484). The ariette for Jane, in consonance with her figuring throughout these lyrics as the "form" of poetry itself, would unburden words of referentiality, both to immediate meanings and to the larger social complications of life in the past and future. This suspension is undecidable as a political allegory. On the one hand, its aspiration for a pre- or non-referential effect cuts against the political mobilization of poetic language (as the visionary effects of *The Mask of Anarchy* demonstrate), and so escapes from Shelley's sense of failure. On the other hand, the very retreat from the sociohistorical regime of language is also a kind of unbinding of language from it. This unbinding releases language to play within a social world of the poet's own invention—and in this aspect serves to test a more free-floating kind of poetics.[44] The compositional tensions of Shelley's late lyrics sense these questions but resist a critical focus on them—in no small part because the release from referentiality itself is too prone to exposure as a fragile illusion. For within a couple of short paragraphs of describing the pleasures of his retreats with the Williamses, Shelley is reporting a different kind of arrest in "the present," one that feels like paralysis: "I write little now. It is impossible to compose except under the strong excitement of an assurance of finding sympathy in what you write. . . . I feel too little certainty of the future, and too little satisfaction with regard to the past, to undertake any subject seriously and deeply" (*PSL* 2: 436). Here "the past and the future [are] obliterated" with a difference.

Such suspensions, in their complex pleasures and pains, inform the arresting complications of "Lines written in the Bay of Lerici." Initially, Shelley drafted a voice reporting a recent loss, "She left me . . . ,"[45] a syntax he repeats eight lines on at the start of a line that terminates in *alone* (a rhyme word noticeably unsounded in the tonally akin rhymes of "The keen stars"):

> She left me, and I staid alone
> Thinking over every tone,
> Which though now silent to the ear
> The enchanted heart could hear. (f. 35ʳ; 19–24; cf. 15–18 in *SPP*)

While the second of these couplets, by the semantics of rhyme and a delicate scheme of letters, conveys the tones lost to the *ear* doubly into the "h*ear*t" that can "h*ear*," the first couplet resists this assimilation. This resistance is one of intertextual pressure, for its rhyme of *alone* and *tone* echoes with a devastating difference the final rhyme of Shelley's dedication of the guitar to Jane: "It keeps its highest holiest tone / For our beloved Jane alone."

Mediating these two *tone/alone* rhymes is a later variation of tones in "Lines" itself, recalling a time that is now perceived as illusion: "I lived alone, / . . . In the time which ~~was~~ is our own" (35ᵛ: 21–24; cf. 29–30 in *SPP*). Both lines place the sign of special sharing, *own*, in tension with the loss and isolation boded by *alone*. The very rhyming of these words to evoke this tension between a magically contained present and its recollection from a point of dissolution is also one haunted by intertextual differences. In "The keen stars," *own* (the soul that is Jane's "own") is rhymed with and distilled from the image of moonlight "thr*own*" over the sky. In the form of their iambic monometer lines, moreover, *Is thrown* and *Its own* predict the symmetrical forms in stanza two of *A tone* and *Are one*, with the grapheme *own* even a prefigurative anagram of the last line's initial word-choice *won*. The chime of *alone* in "Lines" is darkened not only by this difference but also by pernicious double senses. While one sense (that of "I lived alone") is "exclusively," the other, suppressed in this but primary in "I staid alone," is exactly subversive: "lonely, forlorn, solitary, desolate"—the scene of recollection, and of poetic composition, that follows forgetting. The next couplet—"The past & future were forgot / As they ~~would be~~ had been, & would be, not.—" (35^v:25–27; cf. 31–32 in *SPP*)—emerges in a tortuously compressed syntax and a rhyme allying the *not* that negates past and future with its effective mental action, *forgot*.

In the difficult pressures of desire and self-possession that these lines are trying to manage, any strategy in Shelley's mind to manipulate a social communication seems remote. He can scarcely articulate the import to himself:

> In my ~~weak~~ faint heart . . I dare not ~~tell~~ speak
> ~~The~~ My thoughts; but thus disturbed & weak
> I sate and watched the vessels glide
> Along the Ocean bright and wide
>
> .   .   .
>
> Like spirit winged chariots sent
> Oer some ~~diviner~~ serenest element
> For ministrations strange & far
> (36^r:1–12; cf. 35–41 in *SPP*)

In this oppression of thought, the simile opens a scene of imagination, borne forth by *As if* to elaborate a seaside pastoral of seemingly serene and restorative influence:

> As if to some Elysian star
> They [the vessels] sailed for drink to medicine
> Such sweet & bitter pain as mine.—
>
> .   .   .
>
> And the wind that winged their flight
> From the land came fresh & light
>
> .   .   .
>
> And the scent of sleeping flowers
> And the coldness of the hours
> Of dew, & the ~~light~~ sweet warmth of day
> Was scattered oer the twinkling bay
>
> .   .   .
>
> 51   And the fisher with his lamp
> And spear, about the low rocks damp
> Crept, and struck the fish who came
> To worship the delusive flame
> (36^r:13–20; 36^v:5–16; cf. 42–54 in *SPP*)

The flow of anaphoric *And*s shimmers in superimposed scenes of imagination and of watching, with a suspense dispelled, breathtakingly, at "And the fisher

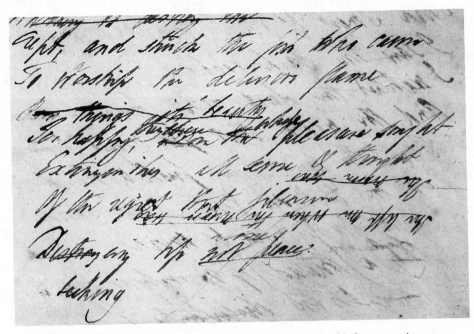

Figure 10. Percy Bysshe Shelley, detail from *The Triumph of Life* manuscript showing the last part of "Lines written in the Bay of Lerici." Ms. Shelley adds, c. 4, folio 36ᵛ detail, by permission of the Bodleian Library, Oxford.

with his lamp / And spear" (51–52 in *SPP*). Shelley first thought to cue this pivot—from medicine (pointedly an off-rhyme with *mine*) to death, from soothing to killing light—with a syntactic shift ("Which" or "I saw" [36ᵛ:9–11; 51 in *SPP*]), but decided on the more sinister effect of retaining the anaphora of *And*. Although *Elysian* medicine may have already signaled a cure by death, the catalogue evolved in the anaphora and their anapests ("And the *x*") seems pleasantly hypnotic. When the starker iambics of "And spear . . . and struck" emerge from this pattern with their lethal tenors, Shelley shows once again how a mind can subvert its refuges of imagination by a perversion of its very forms.[46]

No wonder that a few pages before in the *Triumph of Life* manuscript, after drafting a line of anticipation for "To Jane"—"Though the moon rise a full hour later tonight"—Shelley wrote out and underlined *Oh do not seek* (33ᵛ: 11). The composition of "Lines" halts at the point at which he could not assess the impulse against which he cautions (see Fig. 10 and transcription). The drive of writing is to extract a summary piece of wisdom from this reflection, but the sentence cannot consolidate the sententia:

~~Watching to destroy the~~

Crept, and struck the fish who came

To worship the de lusive flame

~~Poor things its beauty~~
          they ~~these~~ whose
Too h a p py, ~~who~~one ~~the~~ pleasure sought

Ex tinguishes a ll   sense & th o u g h t

~~The moon was~~

Of the regret that pleasure

~~She left me when the moon was~~

                alone
~~Destroy~~ing life   not peace:

Seeking

(Donald Reiman's transcription of 36ᵛ: 14–24; *Bodleian Shelley* 1: 207; cf. lines
55–58 in *SPP*)

The anterior resistance to this summary is the uncertain fate of pleasure. Its
unwritten predicate (21; some editors, remembering the reiterated "She left
me," suggest *leaves*) shows a perplexity about how to evaluate a pleasure so
absorbing as to extinguish consciousness of its impending evanishment: "too
happy in thine happiness," Keats's aching poet envied the nightingale, in an
ode that Shelley might have read recently.[47] The fragment of Shelley's last line,
with the couplet undevised, allows no more certainty than its opposition of
life and peace, while the pivotal verb, which the manuscript tests as *Destroying*
and as *Seeking* (editors argue), is perhaps truest as a palimpsest: at this point
Shelley could not decide whether it is unconscious instinct that draws life delusively but happily to its destruction, or whether it is conscious pleasure that
is itself the vital instinct, however prone to a regret that ruptures peace, until
the final peace of death. Unsure, that is, whether seeking always ends in destroying, or whether the desire that impels seeking will always resist closure,
Shelley stops writing. Blocking (in) a potential rhyme for *peace*, he did not yet
know what it could be—other than *cease*, its partner in "The Serpent is Shut
Out" (47–48).[48]

    The crisis on which "Lines" founders challenges, at a preemptive level,
the possibility of communication, even with one's own thoughts. Shelley con-

tinued to negotiate this crisis, but not in poetry. One of his last texts (maybe *the* last) was a letter to Jane, a social form of writing inspired by and projected toward its reader:

I fear you are solitary & melancholy at Villa Magni—& in the interval of the greater & more serious distress in which I am compelled to sympathize here, I figure to myself the countenance which has been the source of such consolation to me, shadowed by a veil of sorrow—

How soon those hours past, & how slowly they return to pass so soon again, & perhaps for ever, in which we have lived together so intimately so happily! — Adieu, my dearest friend—I only write these lines for the pleasure of tracing what will meet your eyes.—Mary will tell you all the news. (July 4, 1822; *PSL* 2: 445)

This projection also sets up Mary once again: in the "telling" that Jane is urged to solicit from her, she will again have to confront Shelley's exclusive intimacy with Jane.[49] The letter itself stages this intimacy: Shelley evokes "The keen stars" with a key *Jane*-rhyme, "soon again." And his "tracing what will meet [Jane's] eyes" recalls the "magic circle traced" in "The Recollection," now making explicit its writer's agency as the tracer of a perhaps more durable textual form. The trace of Shelley's "lines" is no chance of magic, but fashioned for reading and reception. "The event of reading," argues Fredric Jameson, "only partially obliterates that earlier event of the writing upon which, as in a palimpsest, it is superposed. Such is, I think, the social basis of Formalism as a method, insofar as the work is work solidified, the product the end-result of production" ("The Formalist Project," *Prison-House* 89). Shelley's last invitation to Jane is as inspired as his lyrics are by the imagination of this palimpsest. At the same time, however, he knew that the social form of the letter risked an indeterminacy of reading that no poetry—whatever "the manner in which the imagination is expressed upon its forms"—can ultimately legislate.

Formal Charges has been addressing the question of literary, and more particularly poetic, form in relation to what George Levine aptly describes in his introduction to *Aesthetics and Ideology* as "the radical transformation of literary study that has taken place over the last decade" (1). The value of broadening such study to include the multiple contexts in which literature is written and produced, read and evaluated, is not part of this question. What is questionable are two related effects of this transformation, both noted by Levine: a regard of literature as "indistinguishable from other forms of language (as against the dominant assumption of the now nefarious 'New Criticism')," and "a virtually total rejection of, even contempt for, 'formalism'" (2). Both these stances are typically accompanied by flattened descriptions of literary performance and cartoons of formalist criticism, especially in previous critical climates.

Levine and some of the contributors to *Aesthetics and Ideology* mean to refresh formalist criticism, but their sensitivity to a stigma is as apparent as Harold Bloom's setting himself (with different motives and a more heroic sense of opportunity) against the "impasse of Formalist criticism" (*Anxiety* 12). Derek Attridge's project is to "rescue" attention to literary form from a "fall into the dualisms of the aesthetic tradition," such as "the opposition form and content, which sets formal properties apart from any connection the work has to ethical, historical, and social issues"; the consequence of such a fall, he argues, is "a highly reductive account of the operation of these properties" ("Literary Form and the Demands of Politics" 245). His positive proposal is to consider how "meaning is both *formed* and *performed*" in language that puts "into play—while also testing and transforming—the set of shared codes and conventions that make up the institution of literature and the wider cultural formation of which it is part" (246). My work is sympathetic to this contextual interest (the interaction of aesthetic forms and cultural formations), but I question Attridge's judgment that arguments about how "sound echoes sense, form enacts meaning" can only be an "embarrassment," the shade of an outmoded, traditional aesthetics from which critical discourse needs to be redeemed as it progresses to "a consideration of semantic, and thus historical, political, and ideological matters" (245). This view assumes that formalist criticism can work only in traditional dualisms, with meaning and sense having a separate priority over a merely instrumental sound and form. My arguments have been concerned with the way sound is not secondary to but implicated in sense, the way meaning is not just the scriptor of poetic form but implicated in and even produced by it.

Attridge's discourse of "embarrassment" is a barometer of our present critical climate, however; its self-distancing finds a telling counterpart in Levine's seeming need, as a prelude to his "plea for a new kind of formalism" (23), to clarify his credentials by labeling "formalists" as "the most academically and politically conservative" critics, the polar opposite of the so-called critical "revolutionaries" (22). This identification seems to me as unfortunate as the trends about which Levine complains; it is an inaccurate account of the variety of formalist criticism—some of it from academically and politically left critics—animating critical, and literary, practice today. To be fair to Levine, he may have meant at this turn in his introduction only to convey an oft-told story, and this local moment does not accord with his overall commitment to refreshing the value of attention to literary form. A few paragraphs on, he urges a discussion of "the aesthetic" that will "push the pendulum back toward the formal elements that have for so long been denigrated as literary intellectuals complete their reaction to the excesses of the New Criticism" (23). And he invited some contributors (myself included) to show what could be done. But his preliminary linking of formalist criticism with formal*ism* and conservatism is a revealing, and perhaps rueful, nod to that part of the critical community that will always view formalist criticism, at least with a literary object, under suspicion.

This suspicion is not content to regard an interest in form as merely irrelevant, myopic, or naive. It links it to an "aestheticization of politics" that celebrates an "anti-affective, formalist coldness," as Martin Jay describes one repellent kind of formalism ("What Does It Mean to Aestheticize Politics?" 73); or it discerns a less overt and more insidious service to a discursive police state. Thus, the French sociologist Pierre Bourdieu's "Censorship and the Imposition of Form," one of the most influential of the essays in *Language and Symbolic Power*, can present its study of cultural forms ("the social and political conditions of language formation and use," in his editor's gloss [2]) only with a corresponding slam at formalist literary criticism as a practice complicit with, because detached from, the worst work of social form. This essay begins in Orwellian tones, describing a universal, transhistorical regime of censorship that produces "the form of expression" (138) as a kind of Freudian "compromise formation," the consequence of "imposing form as well as observing formalities" (137). In this scenario, there is no distinction between "form and content, that is, between what is said and the manner of saying it or even the manner of hearing it," because a "*dialectical* relation" (Bourdieu's emphasis, 139) of censorship and insidious internalization imposes and so "determines the form—which all formalist analyses attempt to detach from social determinisms—and, necessarily the content, which is inseparable from . . . and therefore literally unthinkable outside of the known forms and recognized norms" (139). "Formalist analyses," readable only as a story of culpable detachment, can do no more than an obfuscatory service. Bourdieu is not rejecting the importance of formal exegesis; he is only, but radically, subsuming questions of aesthetic form into the mega-form of "social determinism," leaving no space for symbolic productions to do other than serve and conserve its regime—no space, that is, for any work of resistance or critique, or nonculpable pleasure.

Formalist aesthetics fare no better in Michael Sprinker's *Imaginary Relations*. As his title indicates, his account locates itself within an Althusserian scenario (Althusser's famous statement is that "ideology represents the imaginary relationship of individuals to their real conditions of existence" ["Ideology" 152–55]). When Althusser describes this representational mode as an "imaginary form" (153), he, too, means to relate it to social formations. The question is the nature of the relationship, one which he addresses in his "Letter on Art." Here, he argues that as art refracts ideology into a "form of '*seeing*,' '*perceiving*,' and '*feeling*' (which is not a form of *knowing*)," it effects "a *retreat*, an *internal distantiation* from the very ideology" from which it emerges and in which it is held (204, his italics). Tony Bennett regards this "Letter" as granting to aesthetic forms a power to decenter the subject of ideology, disrupting the imaginary forms through which ideology operates on perception (122–23). Sprinker is less accommodating, however, seeing the argument of the "Letter" as containing aesthetic forms under the architectonic of ideological forms. By way of explanation, he cites Althusser's distinction between aesthetic modality and ideological function, a distinction, in effect, between two kinds of "form." In the "specifically aesthetic modality," writes Sprinker, forms are looked at as properties produced by aesthetic practice; but an ideological critique will view these forms as always produced, in turn, by "the formal structure of particular historical ideologies," namely, the social field that Bourdieu describes.[1]

What is curious about these stories is the way the (purported) New Critical reification of aesthetic form, overtly despised, returns as a more pervasive ideological formation. This is still formalism, shifted from aesthetic agency to social determination, and it seems to me as much a "form of fetishism" (Bourdieu's critique of the gesture that "unconsciously absolutizes . . . the dominant usage" ["Production" 52]) as the verbal icon of the radical literary formalists in the era that produced New Criticism. Ideological formation is the dominant trope in a number of influential studies of Romantic-era poetry—Jerome McGann's and Marjorie Levinson's, as we have seen, and also Alan Liu's study of Wordsworth. Liu's interest is in the necessary presence and value of "formalism" in historical criticism (new and old)—the way it subtends descriptions of "history," past and present. Thus, when he comments on form in specific literary sites, he can sound like Bourdieu. He reads Wordsworth's early poetry, for instance, under the sign of a picturesque tradition that "arrests" experience wholly in form, at the convenient and ideologically useful cost of forgetting narrative, the repository of social meanings. "If form arrests motive within the frame of a literary or pictorial text," he argues, "there must be a larger, cultural context motivating and supervising the arrest"; and this turns out to be the realm of that pernicious operation described by Bourdieu, a social field determined by "the *cultural* forms" that the picturesque would, but cannot, forget. The reason for this "arrest of form" is "not literary or pictorial formalism, but a historically knowable cultural formalism: institution" (*Wordsworth* 84–85), a supervision that makes the picturesque "in every sense a form of social control" (90).

Cultural formalism has replaced aesthetic formalism in these reports as the universal, always subsuming all other formalisms to itself. Yet, however much this process goes on, dictating, policing and arresting the forms that expression can take, Bourdieu and those who echo him seem unable to address, or even concede, the way that aesthetic form has always been experimental, potentially critical, even antagonistic—not, that is, always already determined by (or assimilated and conscripted into) "the structure of the [social] field" (as Bourdieu puts it ["Censorship" 139]), but capable of testing and resisting its limits. This is the more flexible operation in which Michel Foucault views social agency, even though he is often cited for planting the seed-bed of today's socio-historical critiques. Foucault does, of course, argue that the discourses by which we understand and represent our experiences are not transparent systems of reference, but "practices that systematically form the objects of which they speak" (*Archaeology* 49), and he urges criticism to study "the forms of exclusion, limitation and appropriation . . . how they are formed, in answer to which needs, how they are modified and displaced, which constraints they have effectively exercised, to what extent they have been worked on" (*Discourse* 231)—in short, the rules of "discursive formations." At the same time, however, he attends to the counter-dynamic, "how series of discourse are formed . . . in spite of," as well as "with the aid of these systems of constraint" (232). His larger analysis is thus concerned with "the effective formation of discourse whether within the limits of control, or outside of them, or as is most frequent, on both sides of the delimitation" (233).

Poetic form, I have been arguing, is sensitive to this frequent situation of "both sides": as a discursive formation identifiable by form itself, it is always, inescapably implicated in practices that systematically form: tradition, convention—what Foucault calls "pre-existing forms of continuity" (*Archaeology* 25). But each poem is also a specific event that is not equivalent to the dictates of tradition or their degree of force in the historical moment of its composition. Some poetry, usually not the most durable, may look like cookie-cutter products of systematic formations; but other texts, particularly when a systematic formation is a critical subject, take shape as creative work across the grain, putting—again, in Foucault's terms—forms of continuity "in suspense," not "rejected definitively, of course, but . . . disturbed" (ibid.).[2] To see all aesthetic form as only subordinate to an all-determining social form, I think, is to miss the dialectical interaction of aesthetic imagination and social information, to miss how the materialities of literary, and more specifically, poetic performance may resist, revise, or reform a prevailing social text. More than a few Romantic-era poems, as we have seen, show vexed affiliations of poetic form to historical thinking, lines of relation that are not readily assimilable to Bourdieu's analysis of the social and political forces that at once produce forms and reproduce them in the social and political subject. Bourdieu's critique is an antidote to any formalism still inclined to argue against referentiality. But to describe every writer as a social and political subject unwittingly, helplessly colluding in the structures of power by becoming a further agent of censorship, "censored once and for all, through the forms of perception and expression that he has internalized and which impose their form on all his expressions" ("Censorship" 138), is to tell a very partial story. Nor does Jean-François Lyotard offer much of an alternative in the heroics of a postmodern aesthetic determined to deny "the solace of good forms" and instead undertake a search for "new presentations, not in order to enjoy them but in order to impart a stronger sense of the unpresentable" (81).

Is there another possibility for language in aesthetic form? When society is "deformed" by social "habits and institutions" or when "the calculating principle" of censorship "pervades all the forms" of artistic expression, is it possible for writers who are "capable of *creating* in form" to be other than one more cog in its monolithic cultural machinery? The phrases in quotation are not Bourdieu's but Shelley's, in *A Defence of Poetry* (488, 491, 496, his italics). As self-contradictory as this document often is, its perpetual returns to the mutually challenging pressures of social and individual determinations remind us of why aesthetic performance is always an element of culture. I hope it is clear that my interest in poetry involves the way its forms are informed by personal motivations, domestic interactions, political developments, social and cultural contradictions, and receptions both actual and imagined. But I hope, too, that this book has been able to open up claims of cultural and institutional priority and anteriority by showing how the forms of poetry can have their own agency, and by demonstrating how close attention to these workings, rather than a priori pronouncements about them, can be a productive criticism.

"There are many ways to transcend formalism, but the worst is not to study forms," Geoffrey Hartman proposed in 1966 ("Beyond Formalism" 56). While the essay indulges some dated sexist allegorizing about critical procedures, the point itself remains valid. Such a study need not devote itself to autonomous formal icons of meaning; it can be developed with critical attention to the several kinds of meanings that form, both as a signifying performance and in its particular events, can enact in relation to ethical, historical, and social inquiry—and can do so by those very "acts of signification" with which critics such as Attridge would propel literary study beyond the embarrassments of traditional formalist criticism.[3] To see in literary performance a capacity for critical reflection on its forms is to engage what is most material in the formal charge, not to be hoodwinked by what is most abstract. Poetic form plays its part not by imposing any static aesthetic ideology, but by articulating a mobile set of practices and competing impulses, taking shape in different ways in different textual sites and within different contextual pressures. Cultural knowledge is not excluded but informed.

I want to conclude this book, however, by urging attention to form not only defensively, in terms of its potential agency within and against the cultural regimes that Bourdieu describes, but also affirmatively. That the formal actions of Romantic-era poetry can have such agency and that its performances can penetrate wider social and political formations has been a central argument in my chapters. But formal actions also involve a kind of density and intricacy that, I'm convinced, can neither be encompassed by theories of a totalizing cultural form nor be dismissed for a failure to address them. Reading the local particularities of events in form, we discover the most complex measures of human art—the terms of its durable social, political, and psychological interest. We also feel the charge of an historically persistent, forever various, aesthetic vitality.

Reference Matter

Notes

1. The phrase in quotation is James Breslin's description of his methodology for his superb study of the "antiformalist revolt" in American poetry in the late 1950s (xiv). "Formalist" criticism, as we both use this phrase and apply such criticism, names a concern with how poetic form is articulated and valued, "with the changing theories and practices of poetic form," in Breslin's words (ibid.). It is thus to be distinguished from "formal*ism*," which in critical and political tradition typically names an ideologically toned disciplinary commitment that prioritizes and privileges form in relation to other possible locations of value. As I shall be arguing, however, the liveliest and most alert formalisms, both in the historical moment of Romanticism and in our century, are not only aware of this investment but reflect this awareness in a simultaneous formalist criticism. Thanks to William Keach for urging me to refine and clarify this terminology.

2. René Wellek's "Concepts of Form and Structure in Twentieth-Century Criticism" offers a cogent overview of these definitions in their wider European scope and in their descent from the nineteenth century. He attends not only to the shared "recognition of the inseparability and reciprocity of form and content" but also to the "very different [practical] consequences . . . drawn from this insight" (55–56). See also John Carlos Rowe's succinct discussion of the shift from "form" to "structure" in twentieth-century linguistic theory (25–30), and Martin Jay's survey and assessment of the stakes in the contested situations of form in aesthetic modernism, ranging from "the fetishization of self-sufficient form as the privileged locus of meaning and value" to "a powerfully antiformalist impulse" ("Modernism" 147). For a discussion of the various meanings and historical permutations conveyed by *formalist*, *form*, and *formalism*, see Raymond Williams's *Keywords*, 138–40. R. S. Crane gives specific attention to the way notions of form were mobilized in the first decade of postwar criticism by Brooks, Wellek and Warren, Leavis, and Bateson, among others (92).

3. While Eagleton's early analyses remain influential, he himself has modified these stances. By 1986, he was arguing that "language is a specific *event*, which cannot simply be read off from the formal structures which generate it" (he means the general linguistic structure, *langue*, but the social application is relevant); "A literary text is in one sense constrained by the formal principles of *langue*, but at any moment it can also put these principles into question"—a "dynamic," he suggests, that may be "most evident in a poem, which deploys words usually to be found in the lexicon, but by combining and condensing them generates an irreducible specificity of force and meaning" (*William Shakespeare* 35–36). Although Eagleton does not extend this textual dynamic to poetic form, the designation of the poem as the generative site of this activity ought to include its forms.

4. Prose lines are "the work of the compositor and not of the artist; they are compositorial, not compositional," remarks Christopher Ricks (*Force* 89), whereas in poetry, the line is not just an "instrument" of expression but part of a signifying design (91). Ricks gives brilliant attention to the eventfulness of the line in Wordsworth's poetry; Wordsworth himself once remarked that a common "fault" of inexperienced poets is a tendency to misuse this resource; their lines are "not sufficiently broken" (*Letters LY* 2: 58). Boris Tomachevski, one of the Russian Formalists, also made this case: "La pratique européenne contemporaine garde l'habitude d'imprimer les vers en lignes arbitraires égales, et même de les rehausser par des majuscules; inversement, on publie la prose en lignes ininterrompues. . . . Ce morcellement de la langue poétique en vers . . . est évidemment le trait spécifique de la langue poétique [Contemporary European practice retains the habit of printing verse in arbitrarily equal lines, and even of setting them off with capitals; inversely, one publishes prose in uninterrupted lines. . . . This division of poetic language in verse . . . is obviously the specific characteristic of poetic language]" (155).

5. I quote from "On Poetic Language" (23) and "Poetic Designation" (68). Mukařovský argues that this "aesthetic function" is a "self-orientation" that is not self-enclosed, but particularly suited for reviving attention toward "the relation of language to reality" ("Poetic Language" 6). The Russian Formalists, with whom he was initially associated, also distinguished the functions of aesthetic and ordinary language, but Mukařovský, who eventually distanced himself from them and joined the Prague Circle, shared with the latter a sense of the historical relativism of such distinction and within this, of aesthetic function not as an essential property but as a manifestation "in a certain social context" (*Aesthetic Function* 3) and "the system of a *particular* national language" ("Poetic Language" 11).

6. I quote Arnold from "The Function of Criticism at the Present Time" (1864; *Prose* 3: 264) and the Preface to *Poems of Wordsworth* (1879), xiv–xv.

7. I quote from Brooks, "Formalist Critic" (72) and Jakobson, "Linguistics and Poetics" (321). Bradley's term "significant form" was soon taken up and given a mystical twist by Clive Bell, who designated visual art as an aesthetics of "pure form" (in both senses of "pure"), as opposed to works in which it is "ideas of information suggested or conveyed by their forms that affect us" (17). Super-

charging Bradley's notion into an intuitively and subjectively validated, but none-theless "universal and eternal" aesthetic of "Significant Form" (8, 11, 36), Bell in effect overruled Bradley's equation to elevate form as the dominant signifier, the identification of which (in a turn on Arnold) must be "the function of criticism" (9). Even if there is a referential aspect (i.e., "a representative form"), its value, Bell contended, will be "as form, not as representation. The representational element . . . is irrelevant" (25).

8. Russian Formalism emerged in the 1910s and prospered in the 1920s, energized by the work of Shklovsky, Tomachevsky, Jakobson, and others. Intent, like Anglo-American formalists, to defend the study of literature from usurpation by (or reduction to) psychological, sociological, or historical argument, these crit-ics claimed that the distinctive character of literature was its formal devices, or technique as art, and that its content (the text as representation) was an effect of the formal organization. Denying a mimetic function, they treated the text as structure, with meticulous attention to "literary" qualities: versification, meter, rhythm, rhyme, syntax, phonics, and style, as well as proto-structuralist analyses of narrative. For discussions of the development, theoretical foundations, and lit-erary practices of this movement, see Krystyna Pomorska, Victor Erlich, and Ewa M. Thompson; the last two assess some of the affinities of Russian Formalism and New Criticism. Jameson gives a critical appraisal of Russian Formalism in *The Prison-House of Language*. The earliest critique, focusing on the Formalists' pro-grammatic turn from social and historical frameworks, was M. M. Bakhtin / P. N. Medvedev's *The Formal Method in Literary Scholarship* (Russia, 1928). Excellent studies of the relation of Russian Formalism to Marxism are offered by Tony Ben-nett's *Formalism and Marxism* and Jameson's *Marxism and Form*. The first chapter of Donald Wesling's *Chances of Rhyme* offers a capacious survey of formalism from Romanticism through Russian Formalism to New Criticism.

9. See Jameson's fuller discussion and analysis of this theory in "The Formal-ist Projection" (*Prison-House*, esp. 43–54), wherein he notes the implicitly revo-lutionary agenda in "the enabling act which permits literary theory to come into being," namely, "distinguishing . . . the purely literary system" of defamiliariza-tion from "other verbal modes": if "the ultimate purpose of the work of art" is "the renewal of perception," with literary devices "ordered towards this end," the effect is to install a "permanent revolution" in the domain of art, marked by a history of "discontinuities," "ruptures," and "perpetual change"—a history "in-herent in the nature of artistic form itself, which once striking and fresh, grows stale and must be replaced by the new in unforeseen and unforeseeable manners" (52–53).

10. I take this last phrase from Catherine Gallagher's excellent discussion of formalism in different kinds of Marxist criticism (39) and, residually, in New His-toricism. Comparing Russian Formalists to New Critics, Jameson remarks that the former were "contemporaries of . . . revolutionaries both in art and in politics, whereas the most influential literary contemporaries of the American New Critics were called T. S. Eliot and Ezra Pound," this "split between avant-garde art and

left-wing politics" being only "a local, Anglo-American phenomenon" (*Prison-House* 45). Bennett notes that while the initial agenda of Shklovsky and his circle was to invest defamiliarization with a "purely aesthetic" rather than "ideological significance," their interactions with the politically motivated (Russian) Futurists (the quotation from *Mayakovsky* is from Shklovsky's summary of his lecture on Futurism), induced them "to revise their contention that the literary device was 'unmotivated'" and to consider the Futurist view of "defamiliarization as a means for promoting political awareness by undermining ideologically habituated modes of perception" (31–32). A recent seminar at the New School and a subsequent radical-press anthology on "the politics of poetic form" invoked a patently Shklovskyan vocabulary to argue that "laying bare the device" is a political act that submits "the established order" to a "*social* undecidability, a lack of successful *suture*" (Andrews 31, his italics; cf. 24). Eagleton emphasizes this connection in his own formalist vocabulary: noting Trotsky's claim that artistic creation is a "transformation of reality, in accordance with the peculiar laws of art," he observes the precedent of "the Russian formalist theory that art involves a 'making strange'" and sees it taken further by Pierre Macherey, for whom "the effect of literature is essentially to *deform*" (*Marxism and Literary Criticism* 50–51; his italics). Such analyses retain attention to form, even if in reform of earlier protocols. Thus, Jameson elaborates a "dialectical notion of the relationship between form and content," evolved on the analogy of literary aesthetics in Marx's political theory (and in this respect "something quite different from the older Aristotelian notion of form and matter"): "the essential characteristic of literary raw material or latent content is precisely that it never really is initially formless. . . . The work of art . . . transforms their initial meanings" (*Marxism and Form* 402–3).

11. Inaugural lecture in *The Place of English Literature in the Modern University* (London, 1913; quoted in Wellek and Warren 139).

12. The sociopolitical disparagement of formalism is a legacy of Russian polemics. As Bennett points out, "Formalists" was not a self-description (they called themselves "Specifiers"), but "a pejorative label applied to them by their opponents in the turbulent critical arena of post-revolutionary Russia" (18)—that is, the decade or so after October 1917. Eagleton's description of American New Criticism refreshes the label and sees it hiding a problematic "mere Romanticism": "From the mid-1930s to the late 1940s, American literary theory fell under the sway of a curious hybrid of critical technocracy and Southern religious-aesthetic conservatism known as the 'New Criticism.' Offspring of the failed agrarian politics of the 1930s, and aided by the collapse of a Stalinized Marxist criticism, New Criticism yoked the 'practical critical' techniques of I. A. Richards and F. R. Leavis to the re-invention of the 'aesthetic life' of the old South in the delicate textures of the poem. . . . Since a mere Romanticism was no longer ideologically possible, New Criticism couched its nostalgic anti-scientism in tough 'objectivist' terms . . . cut loose from the flux of history" ("Idealism" 49).

13. For representative distortions, see Jonathan Culler's charge that New Criticism, distinguishing what was external in favor of internal analysis, rejected

historical explanation (*Pursuit* 4); Paul A. Bové's contention that both New Criticism and deconstruction are "radically anti-historicist" ("Variations" 4); John B. Thompson's poorly informed but confidently totalizing description of the "difficulty that vitiates *all* 'formalist' approaches": "they take for granted but fail to take account of the social-historical conditions within which the object of analysis is produced, constructed and received" (introduction to Pierre Bourdieu's *Language and Symbolic Power* 28–29, my italics).

14. A former graduate student at Yale, my colleague Larry Danson, reports that in Brooks's seminars, the first half of the term was spent reading historical background, biography, and literary history, the second half reading the poetry. While the curriculum was not dialectical, it was also not exclusionary. As for the charge of mere technique: New Criticism was not really a technical formalism, at least in the Russian mode. As Wellek notes, it paid "little attention to what is traditionally called the form of a poem," focusing on the "psychological" organization of poetic structure, its orchestration of "tones, tensions, irony, and paradox" ("New Criticism" 618). Although New Critics tended to describe this structure as "poetry's form," its reflection of what they took to be "the structure of imagination itself" virtually conflated it with content (as Robert Con Davis and Ronald Schleifer remark [21]).

15. The obvious reference is to Marx and Engels (1: 328–29). The argument persists in Jameson's *The Political Unconscious*, in which he reads the production of aesthetic forms as an ideological act "with the function of inventing imaginary or formal 'solutions' to unresolvable social contradictions," indeed, "a purely formal resolution in the aesthetic realm" (79).

16. Cf. "Dead-End" 230–31. De Man's deconstruction, Tilottama Rajan remarks, was to read New Critical formalism "as a form of desire enmeshed in its own de-realization" and eliding "the radical difference between linguistic and organic structures" that Romantic poems themselves often register ("Displacing" 454). If de Man was thereby reading his own methodological desire as the subtext of New Criticism, a certain historical irony attends this affinity, for in a later turn, he voices their desires, with a touching tone of self-consciousness. In the preface to *The Rhetoric of Romanticism*, an anthology not of his own initiation, he confesses "misgivings" over the "fragmentary aspect of the whole"—the book's failure, in effect, to be a New Critical artifact: the "apparent coherence *within* each essay is not matched by a corresponding coherence *between* them. . . . They do not evolve in a manner that easily allows for . . . historical totalization" (viii, his emphases). De Man is aware that this result may be allied to a central question in "the historical study of romanticism" itself (ix).

17. In a late essay, de Man elaborates this application in sympathy with the aims of political critique, arguing that attention to "the linguistics of literariness is a powerful and indispensable tool in the unmasking of ideological aberrations, as well as . . . in accounting for their occurrence" ("Resistance" 11). In another late essay, "Aesthetic Formalization," he offers the sort of critique that interests historicist readers. For a sympathetic discussion of the political critique of aes-

thetic ideology in these essays, see Christopher Norris, *Paul de Man* 62–63, 116–24.

18. In *The Ideology of the Aesthetic*, Eagleton is "glad to observe a certain unexpected convergence" between his analyses and the political implications of de Man's, "*pace* those left-wing critics for whom de Man is merely an unregenerate 'formalist'" (10).

19. The first legacy is clear in Brooks's view of "the structure of a poem as an organism" (*Urn* 218); cf. "Irony": "the parts of a poem are related as are the parts of a growing plant . . . organically" (232); "this general concept of organic structure . . . has been revolutionary in our recent criticism; our best 'practical criticism' has been based upon it; and upon it rests, in my opinion, the best hope that we have for reviving the study of poetry and of the humanities generally" (237). The view persists in Elizabeth Nitchie's assertion, in 1957, that "surely form itself is good only if it is organically unified with content" (4). Crane emphasizes aesthetic agency in this project: in attempting to account for the way form operates in actual poetic composition (as opposed to theory), he complains that "contemporary critical language" offers no "means for dealing precisely and particularly with what *I shall call the forming principle or immediate shaping cause* of structure in individual poems" (140, my italics; as in Brooks, and in Wellek and Warren, Coleridgean language appears, but in this case the debt is suppressed).

20. I have in mind as examples of form-attentive Romantic studies of these decades W. J. Bate and Stuart Sperry on Keats; Earl Wasserman on Keats and on Shelley; Paul Sheats, David Ferry, and Stephen Parrish on Wordsworth; David Perkins on all three. Meanwhile, Harold Bloom was aggressively turning the "fallacies" itemized in New Criticism (that is, the various "extrinsic" and contextual approaches) into a new set of interpretive paradigms.

21. Wolfgang Iser's description of the fate of formalism in this kind of analysis is apt: these interpretations typically regard "form" as the means through which a "pattern of disturbance and mastery is organized . . . a defensive structure through which the turbulence of an awakened fantasy can be tamed and set at a distance. Form does not stimulate, but controls that which has been stimulated . . . channels the agitation" (*Act* 44).

22. See, for instance, Jameson's description of Marx's dialectics of social process: "Here form is regarded not as the initial pattern or mold" but as "the final articulation of the deeper logic of the content itself" (*Marxism and Form* 328–29)—an echo of the German and Coleridgean aesthetics of "organic" form realizing itself as it develops from within, in contrast to the *a priori* mechanic imposition from without.

23. "Coleridge on Wordsworth and the Form of Poetry" 214. Simpson argues that the organic aesthetic not only compensates for these material conditions; it tactically opposes mechanic form's display of "the signs of its own construction" and "the details of its own coming into being." Organic aesthetics are thus complicit with privilege-protecting political theories, such as Burke's, that represent "a contrived or constructed paradigm" as "innate," disguising "human agency . . . as a spontaneous evolution" (214–16).

24. Both cite Macherey's *Theory of Literary Production*. With Etienne Balibar, Macherey elaborates this argument ("On Literature as an Ideological Form"), training the question on the aesthetic structure of "realist" fiction. As Catherine Belsey paraphrases this argument, "the unconscious of the work is constructed in the moment of its entry into literary form. . . . The text is a bearer of ideological meaning, but only in so far as literary form permits the production of meaning" (135). McGann's representative and most influential critiques focus on Book 1 of *The Excursion* (*Romantic Ideology*) and "To Autumn" (1979; rpt. *Beauty*); Levinson's treat "Wordsworth's great period poems": "Tintern Abbey," "Peele Castle," the Great Ode ("Intimations"), and *Michael*.

25. I discuss my reservations about these tendencies more fully in "Questioning 'The Romantic Ideology'"; compatible views are given by Manning ("Placing Poor Susan") and Simpson (*Wordsworth's Historical Imagination* 14–15).

26. Stating his sympathy with current critiques of "the Romantic Ideology," Keach explores how this ideology (especially "formalism and the aspects of art and literature that constitute its focus") in its founding historical moment (the Romantic period) "poses questions about the cultural valuing of formal articulation that neither poststructuralism nor Marxism, with their opposed assumptions about history and about social and discursive totality and determination, have been able definitively to answer." Keach sees this analysis beginning in the work of the Bakhtin circle, Jameson's *Marxism and Form*, and Bennett's *Formalism and Marxism*, but he feels that much more is needed for "an adequate materialist understanding of formal values," which for him involves a return to the efforts, in the old Romantic sites, "to come to terms with that aspect of language that makes it a part of material reality and that gets foregrounded rather than denied in literary form and style" ("'Words Are Things'" 220–21).

27. Bové reads Brooks's project as one of invoking irony to recover a "world ordered not by logic but by analogy. . . . The ironic poem functions magically to 'represent' the unified perception of the order" that the poet and critic desire (see chapter 3 of *Destructive Poetics*; I quote from 104–5).

28. It is this affinity that sharpens de Man's insight into the deconstructive subtext of New Criticism as well as his sympathy with close reading, especially when these practices "put up a resistance to [their] preconceived aesthetic absolutes" and "privileged rhetorical tropes" (Norris, *Paul de Man* 39).

29. Culler offers a related analysis of how the poem's anticipation of responses shifts its rhetoric into a "structure . . . of repetition and proliferation rather than crystalline closure"—one in which Brooks's own analysis is implicated (*On Deconstruction* 202–5; I quote from 205).

30. Keats, "Ode on a Grecian Urn," stanza 5. The fullest treatment of such trans-segmental drifts of letters, in defiance of "the scripted, the visible, the graphemic form of words in sequence," is Stewart's *Reading Voices*. I quote from his prologue (30); for his work on Keatsian "ease," see 159–60. Such poetic slides coincide nicely with Hartman's witty double-definition of a pun "as two meanings competing for the same phonemic space or as one sound bringing forth semantic twins" ("Voice" 347).

Unless otherwise noted, quotations of Keats's poetry follow Elizabeth Cook's edition, only because she is more sparing of silent emendations to the accidentals of unpublished poems ("punctuation, capitalization, spelling, word-division and paragraphing") than Stillinger (Stillinger 17–18; cf. Cook xxxv–vi); one has to consult an appendix to discern Stillinger's emendations. In all cases, I have checked her texts against his, and in some cases I follow his reading (Cook's proof-reading can be careless). I note all cases in which I follow Stillinger on substantive matters, but I have spared my reader an itemization of my preferences for his reading of accidentals. I use Cook's edition as my base text merely for the expedi-ence of not having to footnote repeatedly my restoration of Stillinger's emenda-tions; I remain grateful to Stillinger for producing the most valuable, most in-formative edition of Keats's poetry to date.

31. New Critical formalism, Liu argues, would contain "the mobility of sub-versive plurality within a myth of organic wholeness" while deconstruction, having rejected this myth, uses formalism to contain "difference"; common to both is a delimiting of a text-centered place that sets aside "cultural history" ("Power" 739–40; cf. *Wordsworth* 37, 466; Liu exempts McGann from his critique, crediting him with chastening Romantic studies of such lapsing tendencies). Gallagher (44) agrees with the charge that New Historicism is "formalist in its assumptions" despite its principled resistance to formalism in such claims as "form papers over ideological gaps" (the chief critique of "the Romantic Ideology") and, contrarily, that form subversively "exposes ideology and thereby helps render it powerless" (the "left," post-Russian formalism often invoked by modernist and post-modernist criticism).

32. Bennett describes, on the one hand, arguments (e.g., by Macherey and Eagleton) that try to give Russian Formalist themes a historically material speci-ficity, showing how literature, "through its formal mechanisms, is said to work on the terms of seeing proposed by ideology so as parody, invert or reveal them"; contrarily there is a legacy (most pronounced in the work of Althusser) from aes-thetic criticism that tends "to define the 'literary effect' . . . as the result of some invariant set of formal properties which establish an eternal, ahistorical distinction between 'literary' works and other forms of writing" (*Formalism and Marxism* 108–9).

33. Vincent P. Pecora is frankly disturbed that despite the New Historicists' treatment of literary production "as no more than a version of ubiquitous pro-cesses of cultural semiosis," they indulge a "surreptitious revalidation of 'Litera-ture'" as a site of resistance to cultural absorption, "constructing the literary both as a more revealing, and potentially as a more oppositional, version of cultural production" (270–71). In this double-dealing he detects flirtation with "a new kind of formalism" (272), but I am inclined to see this persistence as a recognition both of literary value and of the value of form in defining it. It is interesting to find Liu in *Wordsworth*, even as he would annihilate "formalism in the old sense," feel-ing compelled to "acknowledge and make restitution" to "formalism" as a concep-tual category: "There is a vital need for the perennially new criticism that worships

forms: formalization of past or otherwise alien experience shapes the interval of similarity/dissimilarity without which neither critical reflection on the past . . . nor critical self-reflection on the present . . . would be possible" (37–38).

34. *The Evolution of Modern Drama* (1909), quoted by Eagleton in *Marxism and Literary Criticism*. Remarking that this "is not the kind of comment which has come to be expected of Marxist criticism," which "has traditionally opposed all kinds of literary formalism" as a reduction of literature "to an aesthetic game" (20), Eagleton cites Lukács as an instance of a Marxist criticism, with which he is sympathetic, that is interested in the complex shaping of forms by a relatively autonomous literary history, by "certain dominant ideological structures" in specific historical moments, and within these, by "a specific set of relations between author and audience" (26; see 20–34).

35. Cf. 128–29. Althusser argues that art deploys a formalist aesthetics of "internal distantiation" that gives a distanced and detached view of "the *ideology* from which it is born" ("Letter" 204–5). The tenaciousness of form as an analytical concept is implicit in Raymond Williams's comment that Marxist criticism has been most successful as a literary criticism, especially when it is treating literature as "decisive evidence of a particular form of the social development of language" (*Marxism and Literature* 53). See also Eagleton's remark that some relations "between historical fact and aesthetic value, overlooked by both formalist and sociologist," need, in effect, a form-attentive study, to see how conflicts within a "hegemonic formation" may throw its fault lines into partial relief, exposing "the impaction of value upon value, signification upon signification, form upon form" ("Marxism and Aesthetic Value" 180–81).

36. De Man describes a politics of form in Barthes that, like Russian Formalism, treats its conspicuousness as significant. In epochs when social and political freedom is "curtailed," an artist's "choice of form become[s] problematic," and form itself ceases to be "transparent" and becomes "an object of reflection"—a potentially "revolutionary action" ("Dead-End" 234).

37. Hans Robert Jauss insists on the role of formal device in constructing and constituting historical understanding (29–50). Like Barthes, he is interested in the way (in another famous Barthesian formulation) "any text is an intertext" whose affiliations involve "more or less recognisable forms" (Barthes, "Theory of the Text" 39).

38. I quote from "Marxism and Aesthetic Value" (166) and *Literary Theory* (206). In the former, Eagleton brackets the whole issue of literary aesthetics to call for its resituation "within the field of general cultural production" (166). His disparagement of formalism perpetuates the critique of (Russian) Formalism advanced by Bakhtin/Medvedev, with fuller attention to historical determinants: "born in the epoch of the dissolution of symbolism," Russian Formalism, "lacking a firm and creative social base" of its own, was unable to conceive of any project more valuable than "the purely negative work of the corruption of the forms established in the symbolist epoch" (70). Reacting to the mystical excesses of this epoch, high academic Russian Formalism polemically focused on technique in iso-

lation from content (not the habit of American formalism), and this led in turn to its discrediting by the social-realist ideology of the decade following the Revolution of October 1917. The formalist poetics of Romanticism were more visibly inflected by its own Revolutionary epoch and, far from reacting against a prior symbolist hegemony, interacted with a contemporary and vigorous symbolist aesthetics.

39. German Romantic theory tends to be concerned less with techniques of poetic form than with the value of poetry as the expressive form for a metaphysics of perpetual flux, infinite possibility, and inclusiveness. Friedrich von Schlegel famously argued that the "peculiar essence" of Romantic poetry "is that it is always becoming and that it can never be completed. It cannot be exhausted" (Aphorism 116 from *The Athenaeum*; Behler and Struc 140–41). On this scale, the "artificial or natural products which bear the form and name of poems" contrast with "the unformed and unconscious poetry" to be tapped in the spiritual energies that animate this flux (*Dialogue*, ibid. 53–54). This metaphysics obviously favors both an aesthetic of incompletion and the self-critical forms of "artistically arranged confusion," "chaotic form," and *"fantastische Form"* (Schlegel, quoted in Eichner 64, 66–67). Yet none of these terms, Eichner argues, denotes "genuine confusion"; rather they describe "the semblance of chaos, tempered by an underlying order" (68). Alice A. Kuzniar sees the German Romantics "mistrusting the schematization offered by a philosophy of history, a teleology, or the myth of organicism" with a "vigilance" that "almost approaches a systemization in itself. Friedrich Schlegel, for instance, writes of 'künstlich geordnete Verwirrung' [artistically staged disorder] and furthermore states that the highest order is that of chaos" (49). Walter Benjamin contends that the German Romantic ideal of the absolute infinitude of art involves "the articulation of a medium understood to consist of a 'continuum of forms'" (Weber 312–13). Benjamin calls this an "irony of form," deriving from the fact that "all art is 'subordinated' to the 'objective lawfulness' of a certain formality. This irony thus 'attacks' the 'illusoriness' of the form of a work" but does not abandon form (Weber 314, quoting Benjamin). For discussions of Schlegel's aesthetics, see Eichner, chapter 3 and, in relation to English Romanticism, Anne K. Mellor, *English Romantic Irony* 3–12.

40. Dryden, *Essay* (1668; *Works* 17: 79); Wordsworth's Prefaces of 1800 (*LB* 744) and 1815 (*Prose* 3: 34).

41. A recent moment of these debates is the emergence of the "New Formalism" among American poets in the 1980s, itself a reference to the "New Formalists" of the 1950s. Vernon Shetley reads a "cultural and political conservatism" (152) in both these movements, and at the time Diane Wakoski described the 1980s return to traditional verse forms and the corresponding denunciation of the free-verse revolution ("the fulfillment of the Whitman heritage") as "The New Conservatism in American Poetry," of a piece with Reaganite Republicanism and implicitly anti-American in cherishing European values over authentically American ones (*American Book Review*). In a subsequent essay, she suggested that the New Formalists had a "strange coalition" with their self-declared antagonists,

the language poets, in caring more for the display of form, whether traditional or avant-garde, over "subject matter or content" and in presenting "the surface form of language" that would escape from, deny, or refuse an authentically personal voice (*New Letters* 21–23). Alan Shapiro disputes the logic of political allegorizing (212–13), while Dana Gioia's review of the "encoded political debate" reverses it, saying that the New Formalists have "put free verse poets in the ironic and unprepared position of being the status quo, . . . the long-established, ruling orthodoxy" unexpectedly challenged by formalism (395–96). Also turning the political tables, Robert McPhillips appropriated the Left's rhetoric for New Formalism, calling it "an unexpected revolution" (73), and Paul Lake goes so far as to describe the New Formalists as rebels against post-1960s orthodoxies and revolutionaries against "the hegemony of free verse" (113).

42. Quotations of *Biographia Literaria*, here and subsequently, follow the edition of James Engell and W. J. Bate.

43. Wesling, in fact, speaks of Romanticism's modernity as a "' laying bare,' in the Russian Formalist sense as ironic exposure, of all the central Augustan devices" (*Chances* 10); Wellek and Warren comment briefly on this affinity (242).

44. The pre-Revolutionary ferment in which Russian Formalism emerged put a different value on defamiliarization, which worked not to unveil a vision of the extraordinary but to expose the structure of the ordinary, its devices and motivations. The usual line on this Formalist method, following Bakhtin / Medvedev, is that it is either apolitical or reactionary in sustaining an aesthetic ideology that resisted, even refused, reference to social reality. But more perceptive (especially in relation to Shklovsky), I think, is Bennett's demonstration of how the Formalists' work was more political, historical, and sociological, and less strictly formalist, than the stereotypes imply.

45. The Biblical references are given by Engell and Bate (*Biographia* 2: 7 n. 2).

46. See Cyrus Hamlin on the hermeneutics of form in the Romantic ode and J. Hillis Miller's discussion of the conflicting senses of the word *form* in classical poetics ("Still Heart"). In *The Romantic Ideology* (44–48), McGann shows how Hegel's theorizing of the defective commerce between principle and embodiment eventually strips "meaning and significance" from the "external form" of art: the struggle of "the spiritual idea" to find an "adequate form" in the sensuous matter of "the *symbolic* form" generates an energy of "self-transcendence within its own artistic sphere and artistic form," finally privileging a non-material interiority of the spirit (the quotations are from Jacob Loewenberg's translation of Hegel's "Introduction to the Philosophy of Art").

47. "Shelley's poetics everywhere resolves itself into the problems and consequences of integral form," remarks Wasserman (*Shelley* 208), who gives good attention to Shelley's uncertain weighing of the claim for poetic form as universal and eternal against its ties to historical conditions and values (208–10). In *Shelley's Style*, Keach provides a superb account of the shifting attitudes to be traced, both in the *Defence* and in Shelley's poetic practice, toward the formal commitments and verbal medium of poetry; he begins this book with the first of Wordsworth's

comments (in Christopher Wordsworth 2: 484). The second comment is reported by Trelawny (14).

48. With a dubious claim that this issue is "conventionally left unproblematized" (23), Easthope bluntly defines "English bourgeois poetic tradition . . . precisely as a regime of representation aiming to disavow enunciation ["the speech event"] so as to promote . . . the effect of an individual voice 'really' speaking by concealing the way it is produced as an effect" (46).

49. Owen and Smyser cite and quote briefly from this essay in their commentary on the Preface to *Lyrical Ballads* and identify the author as William Enfield (*Prose* 1: 173–74).

50. According to Kenneth MacLean, almost two-and-a-half million acres were enclosed in the last four decades (14). For statistics as well as a discussion of the controversy, especially of the impact of enclosure on the unpropertied laborer, see 12–26.

51. For my fuller discussion of how Romantic theory and practice contended with the problem of meter, see "Romanticism and the Measures of Meter." See also Brennan O'Donnell's comprehensive study of Wordsworth's metrical art, which appeared just as this book was going to press.

52. According to Wordsworth, Coleridge "attributed in part, his writing so little, to the extreme care and labour which he applied in elaborating his metres. He said that when he was intent on a new experiment in metre, the time and labour he bestowed were inconceivable; that he was quite an epicure in sound" (*Poems*, ed. E. H. Coleridge, 511 n. 1, citing Christopher Wordsworth's *Memoirs*).

53. I take this description from Shetley, who observes "the New Formalist faith in the power of traditional poetic forms to give valid shapes to subjectivity" (20).

54. Cf. Allen Tate's endorsement of Winters's polemic on "the fallacy of imitative or expressive form": "Formal versification is the primary structure of poetic order, the assurance to the reader and to the poet himself that the poet is in control of the disorder both outside him and within his own mind" ("Poetry Modern and Unmodern" 228). Cf. Nitchie's esteem for the "formal excellence" of Romantic poetry as a sign of "control" and "artistic discipline" (3, 5, 16).

55. Miriam Allott claims that the chief sense of *organic* by Keats's day was "organ-like" (293 n. 1), but Keats's sense would surely would have involved "organic form," a term Coleridge advanced in his lectures on Shakespeare (1812–1813), and "organic sensibility," the capacity that Wordsworth's Preface to *Lyrical Ballads* claimed for the poet (744). Owen and Smyser (Wordsworth, *Prose* 1: 170n.) remark that the latter means "belonging to or inherent in the organization or constitution of . . . a living being," and Wordsworth linked it to the poet's "mechanically" enacted habits of mind (*LB* 745). Even so, this use of *organic* for aesthetic production effectively reverses the older sense of *organic* as synonymous with *mechanic*, as "done by means of instruments, mechanical" (OED [1971], sense 2b). The oscillation of senses in Keats's phrase is a good example of how, as Williams writes, "earlier and later senses coexist, or become actual alternatives in

which problems of contemporary belief and affiliation are contested" (*Keywords* 22); for an account of these developments and their implications for social discourse, see "Organic" 227–29.

56. The neoclassical bias of this value may be measured by Joseph Priestley's contention that the pleasure of rhyme (compared to blank verse) derives "not merely from the chiming of the same sound at the end of the lines, but chiefly because to construct words in this manner is more difficult, and shows greater art and skill" (267).

57. Sidney Cox paraphrases Frost as saying, "You deliberately limit yourself by traditional, artificial rules. What you try for is effective and appropriate form. And success is measured by surpassing performance, including the surpassing of your former self" (70); if these are Frost's very words, they nicely play the changes from *form* to *performance* to *former*.

58. In *Institutio Oratoria* (9.1.10–11, 14), Quintilian reflects this ambivalence in describing the verbal "figure" as both a *forma sententiae* (the "form in which thought is expressed") and a formal *schema* (a reforming of language from its ordinary or simple form); he joins these senses in designating *figure* as "a form of expression to which a new aspect is given by art" (3: 352–55). Wordworth's library included Quintilian (*Prose* 1: 176).

59. See Milton's headnote on "The Verse" for the second edition of *Paradise Lost* (1674); Dryden's terms are from *Essay of Dramatick Poesie* (1668; *Works* 17: 65–66), the dedicatory epistle to *The Rival Ladies* (1664; *Works* 8: 101), *Essay* 70, and dedicatory epistle 99.

60. Dryden, *Essay*, *Works* 17: 70–71; Wordsworth, *Letters LY* 2: 58, and Byron, Medwin's *Conversations* 291, reflecting in 1821–22 on his various compositions. "I have spoken of the fatal facility of the octo-syllabic metre," he comments, evoking his considerable career, a decade or so earlier, in this form (e.g., *The Giaour, The Bride of Abydos, The Siege of Corinth, Parisina*); "The Spenser stanza [*Childe Harold*] is difficult, because it is like a sonnet, and the finishing line must be good. The couplet [*The Corsair, Lara*] is more difficult still, because the last line, or one out of two, must be good. But blank-verse is the most difficult of all, because every line must be good" (291–92).

61. While Dr. Johnson insisted that poetry could not be verse merely to the eye but had to keep its distinction from prose "by the artifice of rhyme" ("Milton" 192), Dryden suggested that even heroic couplets could be "rendred as near Prose as blank verse" by using enjambment, hemistiches, and variety of cadence (*Essay*, *Works* 17: 71). Thomas Sheridan's *Dictionary* thus insists on a "different manner to be used in the recitation of verse, from that of prose" (xlvii)—namely with a "pause of suspension" (xlix) at the end of the verse line in order to "mark the difference" from prose, for it should not be "to the eye only that metre is to be marked"; it should also be marked "distinctly" to the ear (xlviii) with "musical pauses" (li). Kames (Henry Home) agreed: for the ear to "distinguish verse from prose" there must be a slight "musical pause at the end of every line" (2: 354, 438). Richard Roe, not an admirer of Milton's enjambments, concurred (22–23), while

Hugh Blair wavered: "On the Stage, where the appearance of speaking in verse should always be avoided, . . . the close of such lines as make no pause in the sense, should not be rendered perceptible to the ear. But on other occasions, this were improper: for what . . . end has the Poet composed in verse, if in reading his lines, we suppress his numbers; and degrade them, by our Pronunciation, into mere prose? We ought, therefore, certainly to read blank verse so, as to make every line sensible to the ear," and he, too, urged "a slight suspension of sound" toward this end (*Lectures* 2: 215–16). The opinion of John Walker's *Elements of Elocution* was a distinct minority: conceding that Sheridan's advice is approved by "persons of great taste and judgment," he insists that to pause "where the sense does not require it" is an artificial constraint on verse meant to sound like "real prose" (1: 207; cf. *Rhetorical Grammar* 174); indeed, blank verse is often just "numerous or harmonious prose," he remarked (*Elements* 1: 210), and even Kames called Shakespeare's dramatic blank verse "a sort of measured prose" [2: 439]). For alerting me to a number of these texts, I am indebted to David Perkins's resourceful essay, "How the Romantics Recited Poetry," esp. 663–64. This debate about how to address the artifice of blank verse has to cast doubt on Easthope's claim that pentameter suppresses "recognition of the work of metric *production*—and so of the poem as constructed artifice"—in order to advance "a notion of the poem as spontaneously generated *product*" (67, his italics).

62. I quote Eagleton from "Marxism and Aesthetic Value" 187, 180.

63. In a way that Wordsworth's later sonnet-writing develops, this sonnet stanza, composed in units of 10½ / 3½, avoids a standard pattern: its only rhyme is the faint harmony of *ministry* and *I* in the final two lines (a shadow of a summary couplet); and the cadence is not uniformly iambic or even pentameter. This embedded sonnet reflects Wordsworth's pleasure in discerning the form in *Paradise Lost*, identifying some "fine fourteen lines" as "a perfect sonnet without rhyme"; disliking "the Italian mode" of "uniformly closing the sense with a full stop and of giving a turn to the thought" in the sestet, he preferred how in his actual sonnets "Milton lets the thought *run over*" (Henry Crabb Robinson; Morley 2: 484–85). In the "better half" of these, he remarked, "the sense does not close with the rhyme at the eighth line, but overflows into the second portion of the metre" (*Letters LY*, 2: 604). For discussions of Wordsworth's own embedded sonnets see Lee M. Johnson 174–80, and Clifford Siskin 116, 122, 192–93.

64. Karen Swann shrewdly analyzes the formalism of Wordsworthian subjectivity in the narratives rendered in Spenserian stanzas by the characters of *Adventures on Salisbury Plain*. The conspicuous formalism of the stanza, she argues, both makes "legible that which inhabits subjectivity as something foreign, archaic, and received" and, at the same time, and alternatively, signifies a literary field "which the subject inhabits as figure or trope" ("Public Transport" 819).

65. In a reading of Wordsworth in "Still Heart" (298–99), J. Hillis Miller views this deconstruction of form and substance as a shadowy legacy of Western metaphysics, registering with particular critical intensity on Romantic poetry, where the problem of form is not only thematized but is given to a figurative subversion of mimetic reference.

66. Reading within this canon (albeit not always canonical works) also gives me a chance to refine a view represented by John Hollander: "while the first generation of poets was more concerned with freeing poetry from the institution of eighteenth-century literature, the second was seeking new affirmations in re-engagements, stylistically speaking, with older voices. Keats, Shelley, and Byron contribute virtually nothing to any continuing discussion of formal theory" (*Vision and Resonance* 187). Hollander is a superb formalist, as poet and critic, and I have learned much from his work, so I want to repay the debt by attending to the contributions of the writers he too quickly discounts. One of the best comprehensive studies of the subject is Stuart Curran's *Poetic Form and British Romanticism*, which gives fine attention to how the "major forms of earlier poetry are resuscitated and transformed in the Romanticism of Great Britain" (12). A related discussion, at once broad-ranging and precise, of the Romantic "transformation" of the large-scale tendencies of Augustan formalism, is offered by Wesling's "The Transformation of Premises" (*The New Poetries* 29–69).

Chapter 2

1. Blake's note is a response to Reynolds's argument that "an artist becomes possessed of the idea of that central form . . . from which every deviation is deformity," and his effort, a few pages later, to accommodate the objection that "in every particular species there are various central forms" (Discourse III of *Discourses on Art*, in *Works* [1798] 60, 62; rpt. *BPP* 648). Hazard Adams provides an illuminating discussion both of the perplexities in Reynolds's case for "central form" and of Blake's unforgiving quarrels with this notion. De Man's remark is from a conversation with W. J. T. Mitchell, quoted by Mitchell, "Visible Language" 91.

2. Unless otherwise indicated, quotations of Blake's poetry and prose follow David V. Erdman's *Complete Poetry and Prose*; this edition incorporates Blake's emendations to *Poetical Sketches* after 1783. Unlike Erdman's transcriptions of the plates, however, mine observe and indicate the linear units on the plates, following their reproductions in Erdman's edition of *The Illuminated Blake*, to which all my citations of plates refer.

3. Critics usually put these poems into some historical narrative, reading them either backwards, in relation to literary history, or forwards, as prefigurations of "later Blake." Their relation to literary history has received detailed attention. As Robert F. Gleckner (who, after Margaret Lowery, gives the fullest account) comments, Blake's "early interest and wide reading in the English poetic tradition is abundantly evident" (1), with "one text allusively challenging another" (7); indeed, the volume may be read "as a series of essays on (not exercises in) the idea of imitation, a revealing mental fight with . . . predecessors out of which emerged Blake's unshakable conviction that true imitation is criticism" (148). The "immense power of assimilation" that T. S. Eliot sees in this "boy of genius" ("Blake" 276) also fuels the genius of the man, whose assimilation includes even his own early work: Gleckner shows how often the "phrasing and imagery of the *Sketches*

reappears . . . in later contexts, a habitual self-quotation and intracanonical allu-siveness that one comes to perceive quickly as a staple of Blake's mythopoeic method" (10); in Northrop Frye's succinct statement, *Poetical Sketches* gives "the main outlines of Blake's archetypal myth," the "major themes" of the canon in "embryo" (*Fearful* 182).

4. For all his complaints about the tyranny and littleness of imposed rules, Blake respects craft as much as art: "Mechanical Excellence is the Only Vehicle of Genius," he annotated Reynold's Discourse I (*BPP* 643). Anne K. Mellor gives a full study to Blake's critical negotiations with "the nature and value of form": even as he was "rejecting as a Urizenic tyranny the outline or 'bound or outward cir-cumference,'" Blake was developing a visual mode that was "above all a matter of outline, of an image realized almost entirely through a strong, clear, bounding line" (*Blake's* xv–xvi).

5. Of the hundreds of words tabulated in Erdman's *Concordance, form* is 34th in frequency (2: 2181), and words beginning with the syllable fill eight pages (1: 739–46)—a tally that does not include the plural, the verbal conjugations, or mor-phemes such as *deformed, unformed, transformed.*

6. The title page reads: "POETICAL SKETCHES. // By W. B. // London: Printed in the Year MDCCLXXXIII" (*BPP* 408).

7. The usual line on the visual aspects of *Poetical Sketches* does not concern this graphic quality, but treats what Osbert Burdett describes as the "pictorial quality" of the poetic figures (12). Endorsing Burdett, Lowery admires the way Blake's "visual imagery" compels "his readers' eyes to follow his" (196, 198).

8. The term "composite art" is best known from Mitchell's title; he cites prior usages by Frye and Jean Hagstrum (*Composite* 3). The visual aspect of Blake's po-etic forms is also suggested by Roman Jakobson's remarks on the "relational geo-metricity" ("Verbal Art" 8) of grammatical and rhyme patterns in "Infant Sorrow" (*Songs of Experience*): the "symmetry and palpable interplay" of these structures form a verbal art of "mythological power and suggestiveness" (10). Mitchell ana-lyzes Blake's "tendency to treat writing and printing as media capable of full pres-ence," especially in "the material character of the printed word in his illuminated books" ("Visible" 51, 80). More recently, Aaron Fogle has written perceptively on "morphemic patterning" in "London" (237–38).

9. This text is briefly noted by the Study Group (308, 323) and Nelson Hilton ("Becoming Prolific" 420).

10. See Johnson's "Milton" (193) and Milton's headnote to *Paradise Lost.* A superb study of blank verse in this aspect is Hollander's "'Sense variously drawn out': On English Enjambment" (*Vision and Resonance* 91–116).

11. That this sense of "performance" to an audience was habitual for Blake (despite his limited production of work for public sale) is evident even in private marginalia. At the front of his copy of Reynolds's *Discourses,* he writes, "The Reader must Expect to Read in all my Remarks on these Books Nothing but In-dignation & Resentment" (*BPP* 636)—as if imagining an audience were necessary to energize any commitment of opinion to paper. While the OED (1971) gives no citation of a performative sense of *sketch* in the eighteenth century, the Advertise-

ment for *Poetical Sketches* evokes it in its appeal to "a less partial public" than the poet's friends. Because Blake did not market the volume, this "public" was not a social fact until the 1860s, when the Pre-Raphaelites published and publicized *Sketches*. In 1863, Dante Gabriel Rossetti selected ten lyrics and passages of *King Edward* for Gilchrist's *Life* (2: 3–16), and in 1868, Richard Herne Shepherd scrupulously edited Pickering's reprinting of the entire volume from the 1783 typeset. Before then, its readership was limited chiefly to a coterie, with a few poems occasionally finding wider publication. For an account of the volume's reputation before the 1860s, see Michael Phillips's careful research in "The Reputation of Blake's *Poetical Sketches*."

12. There is no manuscript authority for the sequence in the printing arranged by Blake's patrons, the artist John Flaxman and Reverend Mathews. Lowery thinks that Blake had no part in preparing the volume for or seeing it through press (31), and Phillips guesses that Flaxman was the supervisor ("Printing" 13). Blake's role was to assemble the unbound printed sheets: he "folded the sheets of his poems and hand-stitched them in plain blue-gray wrappers" and presented these volumes to friends and acquaintances throughout his life; both the nature and the relatively small number of his corrections suggest, moreover, that he was pleased with the faithfulness to his original (Phillips, "Blake's Early Poetry" 2 and "Blake's Corrections" 41–43). There have been various attempts to thematize the printed volume's ordering. The classical trajectory of a poet's career is routinely traced: pastoral lyrics and love songs succeeded by epic and visionary pieces. Erdman refines this arc into a movement "from laughing songs . . . to grim prophesies" (*Prophet* 17). Elaborating, James McGowan sees a progress from "calm and confident lyric artistry, cosmic in scope (the season-day poems), to the uncertainties of increasing involvement in the secular world (the love songs), to the terrors of political chaos during a time of war and of the responsibility to be a public artist (the political fragments), to a state of discontent and frustration" in the prose sketches (143); but he (like others) notes a few aberrations. Construing an ideal sequence, John W. Ehrstine does Blake the favor of rearranging the contents "on the basis of complexity and growing thematic awareness" (3): he begins with "To the Muses" and ends with the season poems.

13. I quote from Hartman, "Blake" (193) and Culler, "Apostrophe" (142). Hartman is concerned with how the invocations individualize a cultural preoccupation with the "Progress of Poesy" in England and the West. Phillips, reading a code more biographical than cultural, finds in these exercises a "record of self in relation to its increasing sense of poetic vocation" ("Early Poetry" 2). All note a concern with vocation: "the prophetic or speaking out and the invocational or calling upon," remarks Hartman, "are more important than the conventional subject" (193). The chief concern is with "poetic tradition," suggests Culler: "devoid of semantic reference, the *O* of apostrophe refers to other apostrophes and thus to [their] lineage and conventions" (143).

14. A similar event occurs in "Imitation of Spencer," where the call—"And thou, Mercurius, that . . . / . . . laden with eternal fate, dost go / Down, like a falling star" (19–25)—exploits the turn of the line to mime the action described.

15. Punning on this etymology, Spenser's Perigot tells Colin, "How I admire ech turning of thy verse!" ("August" 191). Wordsworth puns similarly, with the graphic enhancement of enjambment, when he speaks in *The Prelude* of how "forms . . . circumfus'd" with "Visionary Power" may, "through the turnings intricate of Verse / Present themselves as objects recognis'd, / In flashes, and with a glory scarce their own" (1805, 5: 625–29).

16. Frederick Tatham, quoted in Bentley (215); Mark Schorer reacts similarly when he remarks that "the first seven poems in *Poetical Sketches*, while broken into stanzas, are unrhymed, and their cadences, as in 'To the Evening Star,' are more like those of the rhythmical prose passages at the end of the book than they are like the normal cadences of the iambic line they purport to emulate" (350).

17. Thanks to my student Joseph Accioli for sharp conversation about this effect.

18. In his preface, Shepherd "firmly protest[s] against the dangerous precedent" of Rossetti's editorial license: although he credits Rossetti's "genius and rare critical perception" and concedes the value of his emendations in "remov[ing] or ton[ing] down" "much ruggedness of metre and crudeness of expression," he complains of the "unwarrantable" intrusion of "tampering with [the] author's text" (ix). Swinburne and Rossetti derided Shepherd as an unimaginative drudge, but when Dante Gabriel's brother, William Michael Rossetti, assembled his edition, he accepted Shepherd's authority (see his p. 39), as did Yeats (his p. 6).

19. The stanza is "difficult and unpleasing; tiresome to the ear by its uniformity, and to the attention by its length," and its archaic diction "disfigure[s]" the lines with bad rhymes: "If it be justly observed by Milton, that rhyme obliges poets to express their thought in improper terms, these improprieties must always be multiplied, as the difficulty of rhyme is increased by long concatenations" (*Rambler*, no. 121; *Yale Edition* 4: 285).

20. To Lowery, the poem lacks "mastery" (90–91); Ostriker sees only juvenile "arrogance" in Blake's flouting of his model (he is "reluctant to obey the simplest rules of his craft" [33, 35]); "Blake at his worst technically," says Gleckner (161); Ehrstine confesses "confusion" at the "faulty" metrics and diction (64), and Schorer decides that Blake's refusal to be "correct" renders the poem "of no consequence *except* as it shows the young poet's impatience, even when he is deliberately imitating a formal pattern, with the structures of the pattern" (350). But both Phillips and Hollander see a point in the "perversity": for Phillips, it signals "disquiet within the convention" and a desire to "modulate the form in new ways" ("Early Poetry" 3); for Hollander, "conscious formal perversity" is the mastertrope: "every stanza is 'defective' if taken from one point of view, or 'adapted' if from another" (*Vision and Resonance* 205).

21. E.g., *The Faerie Queene*: "the hall . . . With rich array and costly arras dight" (1.4.6); "ere he could his armour on him dight" (1.7.8); Alma "to her guestes doth bounteous banket dight" (2.11.2); "damzels, in soft linnen dight" (4.10.38); "he . . . bids him dight / Himselfe to yeeld his loue" (6.2.18); "lusty *Spring*, all dight in leaues of flowres" (7.28). For Blake, *dight* is a conscious archaism; after wide medieval usage, it was nearly obsolete in the eighteenth century

before revival by Romantic poets and their nineteenth-century heirs (OED [1971] D: 352).

22. See Erdman's admirable account of how Blake addresses these poems to the urgencies of his immediate historical situation (*Prophet* 14–19) and more briefly, John Holloway 54–55.

23. For the echoes of Chatterton in this ballad, see Lowery 177–83.

24. At the end of *Paradise Lost* Book 4, Milton writes that in the face-off between Satan and the Angelic Squadron, all creation might have "gone to rack, disturb'd and torn / With violence of this conflict, had not soon / Th' Eternal to prevent such horrid fray / Hung forth in Heav'n his golden Scales . . . // Wherein all things created first he weigh'd" (994–99)—scales that now show the futility of Satan's resistance. Merritt Hughes's note details the Homeric precedents Milton was remembering in this image (301).

25. See also William Keach's brief but trenchant analysis of how *Gwin* and *King Edward the Third* focus attention on the images of violence that animate Blake's representation of revolutionary energy as a collective social conflict ("Blake" 26–28).

26. Holloway, noting the "patriarchal pastoralism" of the season poems, suggests that Blake's anti-war sketches are "largely, though not entirely, literary in inspiration" (56); but Erdman, with a wider sense of the "literary," shows that the prose histories available to Blake, even the most favorable, described Edward's reign as "filled with aggressive wars, cruel executions, and hypocritical manifestos" (*Prophet* 65, see 65–68), and linked the victory at Crécy to the siege of Calais (where Edward prevailed, but with great cruelty and with disastrous losses on his side), the Black Death which ravaged England soon after, and the perpetual conflicts of the Hundred Years' War (63).

27. Because the drama is left in suspense, readers tend to think the sketch "unfinished" and call it a "fragment": see Crabb Robinson's initial remark of this kind (1811; rpt. Bentley 163), followed (inter alia) by Damon (228–29), Lowery (112), Erdman (*Prophet* 18, 56, 63–64), Bloom (*BPP* 969), and Gleckner (96). For an illuminating critique of the "reception protocols" in both the publication and the reading of the "fragment" genre, see Marjorie Levinson's *The Romantic Fragment Poem*, especially her first two chapters.

28. In the wake of Milton's headnote to *Paradise Lost*, Dryden's debates in *Essay of Dramatick Poesie* and his own statement in the dedication of *The Rival Ladies*, and Johnson's complaints in "Milton," a political vocabulary continued to inflect commentary on blank verse—well into the nineteenth century, after its canonicity was secured and was even being challenged by freer verse. In his study of English prosody, George Saintsbury evokes a politics of blank verse when he suggests that it joins "the claims of Order and Liberty . . . as in no other metrical form" (1: 345). William Morris perhaps had such analyses in mind when, coyly summoning the law to restrain the illusory freedom of this form, he suggested that "the use of blank verse as a poetic medium ought to be stopped by Act of Parliament for at least two generations" (quoted by Watts-Dunton 248).

29. For the most part, unrhymed lyrics before Blake, notes Hartman, "were

obvious imitations of the classics or paraphrases of the Psalms, so that Blake's choice of verse may signify an 'ancient liberty recover'd' and evoke the prophetic portions of both traditions" ("Blake" 194). If, as Easthope remarks, the ascendancy of pentameter as *the* English meter relegated "older accentual metre to a subordinate or oppositional position"—"the appropriate metre for nursery rhymes, the lore of schoolchildren, ballad, industrial folk song" (65)—we can see Blake's resistance to this formal order (and Milton's investment in it) reflected in two ways. After *Poetical Sketches*, he rejects pentameter, and by *Songs of Innocence and of Experience*, he is mobilizing "low" forms as vehicles of political, philosophical, and aesthetic critique. Even so, he is haunted by what he resists. In the atmosphere of "real experimentation" in the *Sketches*, Hollander sees "the move toward freer accentualism" interacting with "a commitment to a traditional-sounding accentualism," and in *Jerusalem*, "a kind of traditional modality of meter" resembling "a transformed equivalent of the freest kind of blank verse" (*Vision and Resonance* 205, 208–9).

30. During the 1780s, the language of "chartering" was focusing ever sharper critical discussion. By 1792, Paine was insisting in *The Rights of Man* that "it is a perversion of terms to say that a charter gives rights. It operates by a contrary effect, that of taking rights away. Rights are inherently in all the inhabitants; but charters . . . leave the right, by exclusion, in the hands of a few"; "The only persons on whom they operate, are the persons whom they exclude" (458). Even his opponent, Burke, was noting the "fallacious and sophisticated" perversion of the rhetoric of "chartered rights," distinguishing public instruments such as the Magna Carta from the charters awarded to commercial interests: "*Magna Charta* is a Charter to restrain power, and to destroy monopoly: the East India Charter is a Charter to establish monopoly, and to create power. Political power and commercial monopoly are not the rights of men. . . . These Chartered Rights . . . suspend the natural rights of mankind." Paine's condemnation is noted by Erdman (*Prophet* 276–77) and Burke's remarks, from a document of 1784 abstracting his speech on the East India Bill, are quoted by Heather Glen (382 n. 62).

31. This perception notwithstanding, Erdman does suggest that "Blake's early intellectual growth is in part the story of his learning to see the larger web of commerce and war within which 'peace' was often mere hallucination" (*Prophet* 4), and he was one of the first readers of Blake to see the massive ironies of the sketch as a whole.

32. David Simpson notes that by the turn of the century such arguments were being promoted as a political expedient against unrest. Recanting his early support of enclosure, Arthur Young, for example, recognized in 1801 that if a man is allowed to "love his country the better even for a pig" (given land sufficient to keep a pig), he will feel that he "has a stake in the country," and therefore will be reluctant "to riot in times of sedition" (quoted by Simpson, *Wordsworth* 78 and MacLean 23). Simpson (ibid.) also cites *The Anti-Jacobin*'s support for this idea: such ownership "tends to connect more firmly the links of the social chain; and to encrease [sic] that attachment to *home*, which is the source of much individual com-

fort and of infinite public good" (3 [1799]: 458–59). And Erdman refers to the Ode of the Bard of Albion (William Whitehead), published June 4, 1778, "urging British troops to fight in France to 'guard their sacred homes'" (*Prophet* 70).

33. It is revealing of Blake's formal challenge that many readers try to recuperate these sketches as versions of (Blakean) blank verse. Ehrstine compares the general cadences of these prose sketches to that of blank verse (32); tuning more finely, Phillips remarks that in "its elevated style, its diction and diversity of rhythm," *Samson* resembles the blank verse of *Samson Agonistes* ("Early Poetry" 18). W. M. Rossetti even casts "Prologue to King John" and *Samson* in blank verse for his edition (see 33 n. 1, 33–34, 61–67); Jack Lindsay, to demonstrate the general debt of eighteenth-century prose rhythms to *Paradise Lost* and Blake's particular "bondage" to Miltonic measures, experimentally casts the opening lines of *Samson* in blank verse (18); and Lowery—either inattentively, or pointedly but without explanation—prints the second part of the youth's lament in "The Couch of Death" ("My hand is feeble . . .") in the form of a blank-verse sonnet (70).

Chapter 3

1. See, for example, Brooks, *Well Wrought Urn* 18–19, 26, 258, and *Modern Poetry and The Tradition*, ch. 1 ("Metaphor and Tradition") and 40–43; Wimsatt, *Verbal Icon* 81 (explicitly enlisting Coleridge to formalist criticism), and the oft-anthologized chapter from which I have already quoted, "The Structure of Romantic Nature Imagery" (103–11); Abrams, "Wordsworth and Coleridge," "Coleridge, Baudelaire," and "Structure and Style"; and Wasserman, "The English Romantics: The Grounds of Knowledge." Although all these essays are sensitive to instabilities in Coleridge's organicism, he is generally cited as its patron.

2. See my "Romanticism and the Measures of Meter," especially 236–39.

3. I follow the text of *The Morning Post* (September 11, 1802), because its language of form is more pervasive; the variants are given in *Poems* 376–80.

4. De Quincey observed the "unacknowledged obligations" to Brun in his first piece on Coleridge for *Tait's Edinburgh Magazine*, September 1834, just after Coleridge's death, but he softened the charge by describing Coleridge's poem as "an expansion" of Brun's, alike only in "the mere framework" but distinct in the way its "judicious amplification of some topics" and "its far deeper tone of lyrical enthusiasm" bring "the dry bones of the German outline . . . into the fulness of life. It is not therefore a paraphrase, but a recast of the original" (Wright 37). Brun's precedent is noted by E. H. Coleridge (376–77 n. 2) and by Barbara Rooke (*Friend* 2: 156 n. 2), who refers to A. P. Rossiter's discussion of the issue in *TLS* (September 28, 1951: 613). Norman Fruman elaborates the evidence of Coleridge's plagiarism from Brun, reading in it indications of a pathology of writing (26–30).

5. Cf. Lecture 3 (1818), where Coleridge defines "allegoric writing" as a mode in which "the difference is every where presented to the eye or imagination while the Likeness is suggested to the mind" (*Lectures* 2: 99). David Hartley also

finds a common poetics of likeness in simile and allegory: "If the Likeness extend to many Particulars, the Figure becomes implicitly a Simile, Fable, Parable, or Allegory . . . all Instances of natural Analogies improved and set off by Art" (*Observations*, part 1, prop. 82; 1: 292, 297). And Lord Monboddo called allegory "a lengthened simile" (1: 148).

6. For a comprehensive treatment of this figure, see Hans Vaihinger, *The Philosophy of "As if,"* esp. 91–95, 256–60. Coleridge's use of this figure is illuminated by those who have studied it in Stevens: Helen Vendler brings nicely nuanced attention to the way his *as if* syntax forms "a bridge between perception and reflection" in Stevens' characteristically "pensive" style (33); and in a brilliantly wide ranging study of Stevens and simile, Jacqueline Vaught Brogan (with reference to Vaihinger) sees the "logical division between the words 'as' and 'if'" coordinating "the unitive and disjunctive processes of language in a precarious threshold of impossible possibility" (126, 133; see 126–39). Eliot's J. Alfred Prufrock speaks at this threshold: even as he laments, "It is impossible to say just what I mean!" he still can add, "But as if a magic lantern threw the nerves in patterns on a screen. . . ."

7. John E. Grant, also giving poetic form renewed theoretical consideration, has a similar view of Coleridge's value: "a viable post-poststructuralist criticism will surely want to rehabilitate the concept of form, and to do so [it] will need to return to Coleridge"—in particular, his effort to acknowledge "irreconcilable elements within a work of art without . . . abandoning the premise of controlling form"; Grant considers Coleridge's place both within a history of ideas of form, especially "organic form," and in "alliance with prevailing antiformalist critical trends of our time" (113–14).

8. Cf. Blake's annotation to Reynolds's statement in the *Discourses* that it is "the same taste which relishes a demonstration in geometry, that is pleased with the resemblance of a picture to an original, and touched with the harmony of musick"; Blake counters, "Demonstration Similitude & Harmony are Objects of Reasoning" (*BPP* 659).

9. See also Freese's note (397). For Aristotle's centrality in ancient theories of comparison, see Marsh McCall 24–56 and Paul Ricoeur 24–27. Catherine Addison notes diverse views in these classical rhetorics, seeing Cicero and Quintilian diverging from Aristotle in positing simile as the basic structure of comparison under which metaphor, as a kind of implied or compressed simile, develops (402–3). To Derrida, the general preference for metaphor in classical theory is motivated by a desire to evade the facticity of simile: while "classical theory" prefers metaphor "as an 'economical' way of avoiding 'extended explanations': and, in the first place, of avoiding simile," this preference also evades what simile exposes— namely, that the substitutions that form metaphor are likewise, but less explicitly, not grounded, but part of a "circular" structure of signification: "all the concepts which have played a part in the definition of metaphor always have an origin and a force which are themselves 'metaphorical'" ("White Mythology" 20, 54). Ricoeur argues, however, that the formation of "resemblance" in metaphor is not

evasive, but "the site of the clash between sameness and difference" (196; re-marked by Addison 405).

10. Boswell, quoted by Whaler 1071; Kames, too, felt "an enlivening effect" and "gratification" in "discovering differences among things where resemblance prevails, and in discovering resemblances where difference prevails" (1: 350–51, 279).

11. *Table Talk* 1: 489–90 (June 23, 1834); cf. "Fancy" is "the bringing to-gether Images dissimilar in the main by some one point or more of Likeness" (1808; *Lectures* 1: 67).

12. See, for instance, John Dennis: an "imperfect *Rhyme* is, where there is a similitude with a Difference"; a "whole or perfect *Rhyme* is, where there is a si-militude of Sound without any Difference, . . . a thorough Identity . . . two Sounds which are Unisons" ("Of Prosody," chapter III: "Of Rhyme"; *Works* 2: 238–39).

13. Unless otherwise noted, quotations of *The Rime* follow the 1834 text in E. H. Coleridge's edition; references to prior versions in *Lyrical Ballads* follow Butler and Green. I discuss the ambiguities of interpretation that Coleridge stages in the poem and extends to the reader in "The Language of Interpretation"; for related discussions, see Frances Ferguson, "Coleridge and the Deluded Reader," and Raimonda Modiano, "Words and 'Languageless' Meanings."

14. See also L. D. Lerner: the Homeric simile evokes "a sense of context . . . the life of the community," a place where "readers were at home" (297; cf. George Whalley 768). Pöschl details the Virgilian sophistication of the Homeric trope in turning its reference from the world of visible relations to the work of establishing moods, interpreting states of mind, and intimating impending fate (81). In both deployments, the effect depends on a frame of reference assumed as knowable, representable, and relatable.

15. The 1798 text is the one Mary Shelley recalls, not quite accurately, in the 1818 *Frankenstein* (vol. 1, ch. 4; Macdonald and Sherf 88; I also quote from 87). The concentration of the *Rime*'s two epic similes on a single effect, an elaboration of a state of mind, makes their organization more nearly Miltonic than Homeric: comparing the structure of the Miltonic simile to that of the "similitudes" of Ho-mer and Virgil, Joseph Addison, for one, sees Milton working "his simile until it rises to some very great idea, which is often foreign to the occasion that gave birth to it"; he "runs on with the hint until he has raised out of it some glorious image or sentiment, proper to inflame the mind of the reader, and to give it that sublime kind of entertainment which is suitable to the nature of an heroic poem" (*Spectator* 303 [1711–1712], *Works* 1: 438). As Whalley remarks, Milton's similes, even more than Dante's and Virgil's, apply "with precision a multiplicity of comparisons within a single extensive image or action" (768).

16. It is significant that Whalley uses Coleridge to gloss the potential of the Miltonic simile for overwhelming singleness of effect with a multiplicity of elabo-ration: "This, in Coleridgean terms, could be described as a movement from Imagination to Fancy" (768). To Zachary Pearce, "*Milton* in his Similitudes, (as is the practice of *Homer* and *Virgil* too), after he has shew'd the common re-

semblance, often takes the liberty of wandring into some unresembling Circumstances; which have no other relation to the Comparison, than that it gave him the Hint, and (as it were) set fire to the train of his Imagination" (66–67). But to other eighteenth-century commentators, this was a movement into self-indulgence and error. Joseph Trapp said that "*luxurious Comparisons* that deviate from the Subject . . . neither deserve Commendation, nor are capable of Defence" (138). And Joseph Priestley cautioned that the "extended simile" can become "so remote from the principal object, that the mind cannot, at one easy glance, see the connection" and "the *unity of the whole* is lost. . . . It is a still greater fault to make so much of a simile, that the attention of the reader shall be more engrossed by it than by the principal and original figure" (175–76, his italics)—a practice that Shelley's poetry exploits as rhetorical strategy, not always to acclaim. John Walker advised that such digressions at least had to be marked off by voice: "A simile in poetry ought always to be read in a lower tone of voice than that part of the passage which precedes it" (*Elements* 2: 221; cf. *Rhetorical Grammar* 173). Modern critics recuperate the problem as a calculated rhetoric. Anne Ferry shows how the epic simile, seemingly explanatory in function, deploys an asymmetry "in which the known term of the comparison is elaborated far beyond its resemblance to the less-familiar term"; denying "(at the same time that it professes) the use of similes for comparison," the figure turns into a vehicle for authorial self-display (68)—the focus of a complaint about the deviation of the Miltonic simile, voiced in 1756 by "A Gentleman of Oxford" in *A New Version of "Paradise Lost"* (quoted by Ricks, *Milton's Grand Style* 123). With characteristic brilliance, Ricks comments on both the critical debates about Milton's similes and the textual events that inspire them ("Simile and Cross-reference," ibid. 118–50).

17. This is Reeve Parker's phrasing (64, 27). He does not study the poem's similes in this respect, but focuses on how, in a Baudelairean fashion, analogy gives Coleridge "the grammar for the language of symbols": his creative intelligence reveals "a strong analogical bent," animated by a general sense of "the common ground of nature and mind in One Life," with analogy "ultimately conceived in terms of Christian emblemism" (47, 52). As for Coleridge's early mentor, Hartley: Jerome Christensen (who offers an extensive study of Hartley's complex influence on Coleridge) argues that Hartley's appeal to the principle of analogy as a way to "justify philosophical invention" leads him eventually to submit "the reliability of analogy itself" to investigation (28).

18. To Alaric Watts, Nov. 16, 1824; *Letters LY* 1: 284. One may note Jean-Pierre Mileur's point about the "imaginative and temporal distance" that conditions "the privileged insight," but to say that this is a rhetoric of "skillful evasion"—of the absence of "conversation," of the "discontinuity" between mood and occasion (44)—is to miss the subtle links in the poem's syntax of "as."

19. See Barthes: "etymologically, the text is a tissue, a woven fabric" ("From Work to Text" 159), with the pleasure of etymology "not in the truth or the origin of the word . . . but rather the *effect of overdetermination* which it authorizes: the word is seen as a palimpsest" (*Roland Barthes* 85, his emphasis).

20. Pope's confessed pleasure at Homer's "manner of heaping a Number of

Comparisons together in one Breath, when his Fancy suggested to him at once so many various and corresponding Images" (*Poems* 7: 13), predicts the Romantic designation of "fancy" as the simile-maker. One of Wordsworth's *Poems, in Two Volumes*, "To the Daisy" ("With little here to do or see"), makes this association explicit: "Oft do I sit by thee at ease, / And weave a web of similies, / Loose types of Things through all degrees, / Thoughts of thy raising: / And many a fond and idle name / I give to thee, for praise or blame, / As is the humour of the game, / While I am gazing" (9–16); note, too, his later variants for line 10—"I sit, and play with similies"; "Beguild by sportive similies," as well as his classification of this piece with "Poems of the Fancy" in *1815*. The poet of *Don Juan*, unrolling a series of *likes* to convey "the evaporation of a joyous day," simultaneously concedes the futility and resists the concession: it is "like nothing that I know / Except itself;—such is the human breast; / A thing, of which similitudes can show / No real likeness,—like the old Tyrian vest / Dyed purple" (16.9–10).

More soberly, de Man considers the way such sport corrupts the work of analogy, which aspires "to transcendental totality": his case is Baudelaire's *Correspondances*, in which the ambiguity of *comme*—its sense of *like* shading into *such as*—displaces analogy into enumeration: "Enumerative repetition disrupts the chain of tropological substitution at the crucial moment when the poem promises, by way of these very substitutions, to reconcile the pleasures of the mind with those of the senses and to unite aesthetics with epistemology" (*Rhetoric* 250). Abrams, whose Romanticism de Man is always critiquing, not only insists on the cohesion of Baudelaire's *universelle analogie*, but sees its correspondence to the even more integrative process given in "Coleridge's exposition of the role of the creative imagination" ("Coleridge, Baudelaire" 114–20).

21. Wordsworth transferred this simile to Book 8 (1805: 711–27), where the vehicle—a traveller's passage "from open day" into a cavern—conveys the poet's sensations on first seeing London: "such a swell of feeling, follow'd soon / By a blank sense of greatness pass'd away" (743–44). I'll have more to say about this moment in my next chapter.

22. The eight lines of *The Eolian Harp* from "O! the one Life within us and abroad" (26–33), were intended for the text of *Sibylline Leaves*; they were supplied in the *Errata* and first included in the poem itself in 1828 (*Poems* 101).

23. For a fine study of Coleridge's various versions and revisions of these lines, see Paul Magnuson, who also reads the draft as enclosing the surmise in a series of "idle flitting phantasies," a context that makes it seem "merely one figure among other figures" (8).

24. V 15ʳ: 164–66 (*"The Prelude," 1798–1799* 286–87). Dorothy Wordsworth's *Journal* has examples of this inscriptive sense: "to mark" means "learning to write" (41, 44). As for the matter of marking analogical relations, de Man notes that in the late eighteenth century, analogical discourse gets replaced with more qualified terms of association—linking and dim similitude, for instance. While the new terminology does not change "the fundamental pattern of the structure, which remains that of a formal resemblance between entities that, in other respects, can be antithetical," terms such as "affinity" indicate "a gliding away from

the formal problem," for these apply to "relationships between subjects rather than to relationships between a subject and an object. The relationship with nature has been superseded by an intersubjective, interpersonal relationship that, in the last analysis is a relationship of the subject toward itself" ("Temporality" 195–96).

25. In *Shelley's Style*, Keach illuminates the influence of this essay on Shelley's attitudes about language. Foucault describes the ideal of language governed by similitude as "the sovereignty of the Like" (*The Order of Things* 43) and argues that the seventeenth and eighteenth centuries show a heightened sense not only of the "lost similitude" of words and things but of signs themselves as "never . . . anything but similitudes" (36, 41–42). See also Simpson's discussion of how post-Enlightenment philosophy sought to displace that "lingering theological version of analogy which posited the adequacy of all relational perception within the perfectly created cosmos" to stress, instead, the "making of ratios and similitudes as a *way* of conducting the rational activity; it is explicitly heuristic, and therefore less likely to be taken as 'reality'" (*Irony* 139). See also Wasserman: "the ubiquitous urge to find some moral or subjective analogue . . . reveals the anxiety to internalize the external and integrate the spiritual with the phenomenal. The resort to analogy only dodges the problem, since it both pretends to a relation between subject and object and yet keeps them categorically apart"—as Coleridge complains about Bowles ("Grounds" 20–21).

26. Shawcross 341; cf. Raysor 533. In this respect, both Coleridge and Wordsworth echo Kant, who names the sublime as "*absolutely great . . . beyond all comparison*" ("Analytic of the Sublime" 94); the aesthetic challenge for Kant is that the sublime is associated with objects "devoid of form" (90) and characterized by "formlessness" (93). For a fine discussion of Coleridge's debts to Kant's articulation of the sublime, and especially on the issue of comparison, see Modiano, *Coleridge* 101–37.

27. John Gatta, Jr., notes that the "inherently binary structure" of the allegorical mode has an appeal for "a sensibility peculiarly disposed toward dualistic vision and 'desynonymizing,' toward the development of binary distinctions"—such as Reason and Understanding, Imagination and Fancy, Imitation and Copy, and, not a little ironically, Symbol and Allegory—even if the articulation of these binaries is meant "as a necessary first step in the project of constituting an ultimate unity" (75). See also Brogan's study of Stevens's simile as an intermediary between the unitive impulses she sees in his metaphors and his awareness of the tendency of language, as a rhetoric of signification, to disjunction.

28. Brooks, "Metaphysical Poet" 153–54. As Patricia Ward remarks, Coleridge "employs allegory as a critical principle much more vigorously than he does the symbol," and in "discussing the language of poetry [he] seems more concerned with the fancy and arbitrary figures than with symbols" (30). He also employs allegory as a poetic principle: throughout the career we find such figures as Faith, Hope, Charity, Death, Love, Fear, Patience; "To An Unfortunate Woman Whom the Author Had Known in the Days of Her Innocence" appears as "Allegorical Lines" in manuscript (*Poems* 172) and in two letters (*Letters* 1: 314,

315), and is termed "an allegory" in a third (3: 322); some late poems, notably "Time, Real and Imaginary," "The Pang More Sharp Than All," and "Love's Apparition and Evanishment," bear subtitles designating an allegory; the last one, in fact, was revised to give "greater *perspecuity* in the Allegory," Coleridge says (6: 952, his italics) and was renamed "an Allegoric Romance" from "a Madrigal" (954). He also refers to that figure of the sublime itself, Milton's Death, as "half person, half allegory" ("Apologetic Preface" *Poems* 599), titles an early prose piece "An Allegoric Vision," and calls the opening essay of *The Friend* an "allegory" (1: 9).

29. Such "allegorical deconstruction" of "the most fundamental objects of the mind, the heart, and the soul itself," McGann remarks, is "negative pattern" that "grew more firmly rooted in the poetry even as Coleridge's prose developed a more confident . . . ideological focus"; "these sorts of ideological losses and surrenders are powerful and terribly moving precisely because their vehicular form is a poetic one" (*Romantic Ideology* 97–98).

30. Brooks, with a different critical interest, notes something similar even in the figure of analogy: within the limitations of language, the poet "has no one term," but "must work by contradiction and qualification . . . by analogies" (*Urn* 9).

31. Coburn wrongly, I think, transcribes these lines as prose (*Notebooks* 2994). My sense that they are poetry is encouraged by the fact that Coburn herself transcribes the next three entries as poetry (see Fig. 5; cf. *Notebooks* 2995–97). I think that across all these entries Coleridge is drafting a poem, which continues from "you with love," to link in near perfect iambic pentameter to:

<blockquote>
and in Life's noisiest hour,
There whispers still the ceaseless Love of
    —solace?   Thee,
The Heart's <u>Self-commune</u>, & soliloquy.

              ye
    the self-listning Hart
</blockquote>

<blockquote>
You mould my Hopes, you fashion me within;
And to the leading Love-throb in the Heart
Thro' all my Being all my pulses beat.
    all
You lie in ~~my~~ my many Thoughts, like
                 Light
Like the fair Light of Dawn, or summer
               Eve
On rippling Stream, or cloud-reflecting
              Lake
</blockquote>

<blockquote>
And looking to the Heaven, that bends above you
How oft I bless the Lot, that made me love you.
</blockquote>

---

32. See OED (1971) G 88: *gaze v.* 1, *intr.*: "to look vacantly"; "to look fixedly." Coleridge's poetic usages include both senses, but often with the vacant sense involving a visionary rapture and the fixed sense an erotic rapture; the fixed gaze, usually in eager longing, desire, or doting, often shades into the entranced, bewitched, or awe-struck gaze. Some of the best-known instances: "O dread and silent Mount! I gazed upon thee" ("Hymn before Sun-Rise" 13); the truly "blest" are those whose strong eyes "adore with steadfast unpresuming gaze" ("Religious Musings" 48); "Hope has fix'd her wishful gaze" ("Ode to the Departing Year" 20), "I have stood, / Silent with swimming sense; yea gazing round / . . . gaze till all doth seem / Less gross than bodily" and "While thou stood'st gazing" ("This Lime-Tree Bower" 38–41 and 73); "All this long eve, so balmy and serene, / Have I been gazing on the western sky, / . . . / And still I gaze" and "It were a vain endeavour, / Though I should gaze for ever" ("Dejection: An Ode" 27–30 and 42–43); "with steadfast gaze," the lover "worships" ("The Picture" 82–83).

Chapter 4

1. Unless otherwise stated, quotations are of the 1805 "AB-Stage" (based on MSS. A and B [DC MSS. 52 and 53]), in Mark Reed's *Thirteen-Book "Prelude"*; "DC" refers to the Dove Cottage archive in Grasmere. When there are two citations, these refer to AB and the comparable passage in the fourteen-book text in W. J. B. Owen's edition, based on MS. D (DC MS. 124) rather than the 1850 first edition. For fuller remarks on my choice of texts, see n. 16, below.

2. *The Prelude* occupies more than twenty manuscripts: for a census and description, see Norton Critical Edition 507–26; Stillinger provides a helpful tour of the compositional and publication history (*Multiple* 74–77). The manuscripts gather to three principal stages: the "two-part" poem of 1798–99 (JJ [DC MS. 19], RV [DC MS. 21], V [DC MS. 22], U [DC MS. 23], etc.); the thirteen-book poem of 1805 (chiefly A and B, but also W [DC MS. 38] and WW (DC MS. 43]); and the fourteen-book poem of the 1830s (D and E) that yielded the base text for the 1850 publication. Reed's edition gives a full account of the manuscripts from 1799 up to D and constructs a "C-Stage revision of 1818–1820" from base A (DC MS. 82). Jonathan Wordsworth, noting the poet's remark in early 1804 that he is "engaged in a Poem on my own earlier life which will take five parts or books to complete" (*Letters EY* 436), has speculated (in the absence of any fair-copy manuscript, but with reference to W) about the probable shape and contents of a five-book poem from early 1804, one that he likes for old-fashioned formalist reasons: it "is the most formally rounded of the *Preludes*" ("The Five-Book *Prelude*" 20; summarized in the Norton Critical 516–17). For reservations about some elements of this speculative reconstruction, see Robin Jarvis's essay.

3. I quote from the statement at the front of every volume of the Cornell Wordsworth, by the general editor, Stephen M. Parrish, who elaborates the case for attention to earlier versions and multiple intentions in his essay in *TEXT*. The Cornell project has issued three editions of *The Prelude*: "*The Prelude*," *1798–1799*, ed. Parrish; *The Fourteen-Book "Prelude,"* ed. Owen, and *The Thirteen-Book*

"Prelude," ed. Reed—every *Prelude*, that is, except the publication of 1850, *The Prelude, or Growth of a Poet's Mind: An Autobiographical Poem*. Advocates of the 1850 publication claim that this is the final text authorized by Wordsworth, but as Owen and other editors report, there are questions of accuracy raised chiefly, but not exclusively, by the readings of its two prior manuscripts, D and E (DC MSS. 124 and 145).

4. For citations, see Stillinger, *Multiple* 80. Major parallel-text editions include de Selincourt-Darbishire (1959); J. C. Maxwell's handy paperback, *The Prelude: A Parallel Text* (1971), and the Norton Critical (1979), again in a much-reissued, handy paperback.

5. The conveniently "small compass" of the 1798–99 poem made it, for a while and problematically, a pedagogical favorite: for practical reasons, it was the only version printed "in its entirety" in the 3rd and 4th editions of *The Norton Anthology of English Literature* (1974, 2: 196–218; and 1979, 2: 231–55, respectively)—an event that in 1974, as Jonathan Arac wittily observed, made it "the most extensively circulated new poem published that year, perhaps even of recent decades"; in the 5th edition, it is discussed in a headnote, but dropped as a text.

6. "Wordsworth's C-stage revisions . . . did not culminate in a fair-copy recension, approved by the poet, of a new state of the poem," Reed cautions; "he did not review [the] often obviously imperfect copy . . . attentively; and this stage of revision was not finally finished off, but was simply dropped. No C-stage text of the poem survives with authority equivalent to that of the approved recensions MSS. A, B, D, and E." Even so, Reed urges the claims of this text in any investigation of the poem's development: it represents "a distinctive stage . . . which deserves study in its own right, and neither its extent nor its individuality has been sufficiently recognized" (1: 81–82).

7. As Stillinger summarizes the issues: "Until fairly recently, all editorial theories . . . were based on a concept of . . . 'realizing'—approximating, recovering, (re)constructing—the author's intentions," usually equated with the "*final*" intention (*Multiple* 195). During the nineteenth century and for the first half of the twentieth, credit thus gathered to the latest version—either the last publication in an author's lifetime or the last text prepared under his or her supervision. In the 1950s, W. W. Greg and Fredson Bowers, questioning the degree of such supervision after the first edition, argued for the greater authority of the first published edition or a fair-copy base-text manuscript. The initial essays in this polemic were Greg's "Rationale" (1950) and Bowers' "Current Theories" (1950). Yet this reversion proved as controversial as the paradigm it meant to correct, not only because of its rationale but also because the whole issue of intention and authority was getting theorized. New Criticism opened the gates by formulating the "Intentional Fallacy" (denying statements of intention absolute authority over interpretation), and subsequent theories pressed further against authorial intention as a presence and court of appeal. For discussion of these issues and a relevant bibliography, see Stillinger's "Implications for Theory" (*Multiple*, esp. 194–202; 243–44).

8. The first set of remarks is by M. H. Adams (*Natural Supernaturalism* 76)

and the second by Donald H. Reiman, in a review for *Studies in Romanticism* (rpt. *Romantic Texts* 153–54).

9. For those unfamiliar with the terms: the keynote is de Selincourt's comparison, in his original introduction (rpt. in Darbishire's revised edition [lvii–lxxiv] and in Gill's new edition [xix–xxxviii]; some points, with a bias toward 1805, are elaborated in Norton Critical 522–23). Helen Darbishire's Clark Lectures (1949), though conceding some technical improvements (121), "deplored" the revisions "which overlay and obscure" and "often mar the poetry" of earlier expression (123), especially in the effort "to explain, to rationalize, to moralize" (133). The controversy climaxed, or anticlimaxed, in the "The Great *Prelude* Debate" at the 1984 Wordsworth Summer Conference, published in *The Wordsworth Circle* 17, ed. Marilyn Gaull. This debate reprises the themes, with some novel twists: Norman Fruman argues for the stylistic superiority of the 1805 text and Robert Barth claims that the 1850 text does not so much impose alien religious piety as amplify a religious dimension already strong in the 1805 text. For a recent, but largely familiar polemic against the principles of the Cornell series as well as the notion of Wordsworthian multi-text, see Zachary Leader, who insists on editorial and textual fidelity to "Wordsworth's explicit instructions" (his latest revisions), granting them "the rights of literary and material property" guaranteed in copyright law (677).

10. Stephen Orgel's "What is a text?" studies various problems of bibliography in Renaissance texts. Steven Urkowitz offers an important case for the 1608 first quarto and the 1623 first folio versions of *King Lear* as equivalent, "alternative texts created by a revising author" (5) rather than as partial keys through which one might divine a missing original. And George Bernard Shaw insisted on printing the original and the revised endings of *Great Expectations* in the edition that he supervised in 1937.

11. *The Rime of the Ancyent Marinere, In Seven Parts*, antiqued and unglossed, appeared anonymously at the head of the 1798 *Lyrical Ballads; The Ancient Mariner. A Poet's Reverie*, less antiqued, with some revision, and still anonymous, held a less privileged position in 1800; in 1802 and 1805, the subtitle was dropped and further revisions applied; *The Rime of the Ancient Mariner*, revised, with marginal gloss and a new epigraph, was issued with Coleridge's name in *Sibylline Leaves* in 1817. In 1961, Royal A. Gettmann published a parallel-text edition of the 1798 and 1834 poems; for readings of the implications of this textual multiplicity, see Frances Ferguson ("Coleridge and the Deluded Reader"), Anne K. Mellor (*English Romantic Irony* 137–50), myself ("The Language of Interpretation" 24–31), and Martin Wallen (unaware of this previous critical work). Stillinger offers an interesting tour through the multiple versions of this and several other of Coleridge's canonical poems, with the intriguing proposal "that Coleridge changed his texts at least partly in order to create the very instability that would make his poems and their meanings elusive"; the "conspicuous featuring of his poetry's instability" implies that his poems were "always in progress" and suggests "that the perfect poem was a chimera and that authority itself was therefore a fiction" ("Multiple Versions" 138 and 146; cf. *Coleridge and Textual Instability*).

12. For discussions of the texts of "La Belle Dame," see McGann on the *Indicator* text ("Keats and the Historical Method," esp. 31–42), and Simpson (*Irony and Authority* 14–23), who praises Douglas Bush (206 n. 27) for giving both versions equal representation in *Selected Poems and Letters* (199–202). For the two texts of *Frankenstein*, see the editions of D. L. Macdonald and Kathleen Scherf, and James Rieger. These print the 1818 text with the substantive variants of 1831. Rieger also supplies intermediary revisions, and advocates the merits of the 1818 text; for a rebuttal of his argument and a reassessment of the evidence, see Mellor's *Mary Shelley* (58–69) and "Choosing a Text." What is still wanting, as Mellor laments, is a parallel-text edition.

13. As Nigel Wood remarks, "the need for a unitary performance" obscures the fact "that there is enough evidence to suppose that there were several 'final intentions'" (8). In a brisk and shrewd reply to Jeffrey Baker's alarm that "the principles on which the Norton Edition is based [its aesthetic and ideological prejudice toward the earlier texts] constitute a danger for English studies" for failing to "see an object as in itself it really is" (86), Robert Young remarks that not only is the claim to objectivity itself an interested position (an "interpretation") but that Baker's singular *it* is a misrepresentation: "to see *The Prelude* as it really is is to see that it is not one poem at all but several poems—1799, 1805, 1850, and all the intermediate versions and stages as well"; in view of these "different forms," the critic's project should not be one of debating relative merits, "but rather the exploration of the complex and subtle intertextual relations and differences among the different poems. Instead of asking which is best, we should be asking what does this multiplicity mean, and what are its effects?" (87). The essay from which this present chapter evolved ("The Illusion of Mastery") is one such asking, as are my reviews of Owen's and Reed's editions (in *The Wordsworth Circle* and *Review*, respectively). Others who have analyzed revision, textual authority, and *The Prelude* include Peter J. Manning ("Reading Wordsworth's Revisions"), Theresa M. Kelley ("Economics of the Heart"), William H. Galperin (*Revision and Authority*), and Jack Stillinger ("Multiple Consciousness in Wordsworth's *Prelude*," in *Multiple*).

14. My references to Barthes' "theory of the text" and its enfranchisement of reading are drawn from "Theory of the Text" (esp. 36–37, 39, 42–43), "From Work to Text" (esp. 157 [his italics], 159, 161–62), and "The Death of the Author" (esp. 147–48). Nigel Wood's introduction proposes the usefulness of Barthesian models for theorizing how a reader might address the plurality of *The Prelude* (4).

15. The quotation is from DC MS. 33: 49^v (*Prelude 1798–1799* 163). Theorizing a textualized subjectivity that also refers to the writer as historical subject, Tilottama Rajan helpfully describes a "discourse of subjectivity," in which, say, the author of *The Prelude* "does not simply represent himself but also puts himself under erasure in the gap between his self-representations." This yields "two complementary movements": "the act of introjection by which a character in a text is claimed as autobiographical and the act of projection which involves the 'I' in a process of self-reflection and specularisation" ("Coleridge" 61–62).

16. One has to have base-texts for reference. I use ones that retain accidentals

or note, rather than leave unrecorded ("silent"), any emendations (accidental variants involve elements of spelling, punctuation, or capitals; substantive variants involve matters of wording, sequence, and so forth affecting sense—though it is clear that some accidentals, such as capitals, have substantive bearing). The Norton Critical's collation of several texts and manuscript drafts is handy and affordable, and probably the most widely read; but since the "punctuation in the printed texts of *1799* and *1805*" is "editorial" and silent (511)—including some significant capitals—the text is not as reliable as Reed's (and even Gill's own). In the episode of the drowning, moreover, Norton persists in reprinting a misleading typographical error at 5.480 (*words* for *works*), despite its editors having been informed of this mistake: MS. A 108ʳ clearly shows "works" (see Reed 1: 776).

For the "Two-Part" *Prelude* of 1798–99, I follow MS. V (Dorothy Wordsworth's fair copy of 1799), in Parrish's edition; the episode of the drowning appears on 7ᵛ–8ʳ; 256–59 (cf. reading text 49–50).

For the 1805 text, I follow Reed's "AB-Stage Reading Text" (based on MS. A, Dorothy Wordsworth's fair copy, and MS. B, Mary Wordsworth's duplicate). Reed's edition has photographs of A; the episode of the drowning appears on 107ʳ–109ʳ (1: 774–76) and is transcribed and interpreted in 2: 624–26.

For the "C-Stage revision," largely a collation of the corrections made on A through 1818–20, I follow Reed's "Reading Text" in vol. 2.

For the fourteen-book poem, I follow Owen's edition. He uses MS. D as his base text and so rejects the normal determination of the authoritative copy text for published works—in the case of *The Prelude*, a census of the first edition of 1850 and its base-text, the latest authorial manuscript, E. Although Reiman urges the credit of E as the manuscript "which Wordsworth approved before his death" (*Romantic Texts* 153), Owen queries the extent of supervision, because both it and the 1850 publication, he and others note, introduce several alterations of substantives and accidentals that were not clearly authorized by Wordsworth and perhaps reflect the interference of his executors. Owen's is thus an "eclectic" construction, favoring D (written by Mary Wordsworth in 1832 and revised at the end of the decade) and referring to E and *1850* only when their substantive readings patently supersede those of D. Owen believes that this construction corresponds to what "Wordsworth would have approved for his final version of the poem" (11); for a fuller account of his work, see his introduction or, more briefly, my review in *The Wordsworth Circle*. The 1850 publication, of course, has historical validity as the form in which the poem was read in the nineteenth century.

17. Only an 1804 draft tries out and then rejects a narrative transition: "Soon as I reachd home / I to our little household of the sight / Made casual mention"; see MS. W 31ᵛ (Reed 1: 388 and 2: 280).

18. In attending to the aural hint of *ears* and *sounding*, I share Hartman's sense of "strange currents of symbols, half formulated symmetries" (*Wordsworth's Poetry* 232) over Cynthia Chase's claim that the language of this episode (contrasting the way words elsewhere in Book 5 "resonate with symbolic meaning or imaginative significance") conspicuously effaces "figurative meaning," evincing a "spare liter-

alness" (15): "The principal quality of ears, their power of hearing, is without relevance, the word's usage here referring only to the accidental fact of their shape. The principal meaning of *sound*, its power of resounding, has no pertinence in this usage of the verb that borrows not its sense but only its letters" (20). It is true that the local name for one peninsula was Strickland-ears—fancifully derived, Wordsworth suggests in his *Tour* of the Lakes, from "the form & the manner in which it is attached to the shore" (*Prose* 2: 337; noted by Owen 105). It seems to me, however, not only that Wordsworth has taken advantage of this contingency but that Chase's very sorting of literal from accidental shows the power of semiotic ghosts. Christopher Ricks calls such effects "anti-puns," ghostly demarcations that the sense of the statement "positively precludes" but that the "pressure" of contiguous words calls up. Referring to Preface to *Lyrical Ballads*, Ricks proposes that the anti-pun "is one form which may be taken by the poet's 'disposition to be affected more than other men by absent things as if they were present'" (*Force* 99–100).

19. "We assume that life *produces* the autobiography as an act produces its consequences, but can we not suggest . . . that the autobiographical project may itself produce and determine the life and that whatever the writer *does* is in fact governed by the technical demands of self-portraiture? . . . Does the referent determine the figure, or is it the other way round: is the illusion of reference not a correlation of the structure of the figure, that is to say no longer clearly and simply a referent at all but something more akin to a fiction which then, however, in its own turn, acquires a degree of referential productivity?" ("Autobiography as De-Facement" 69). See also Tilottama Rajan: once "facts" enter a poem, their status as ground for "the meaning of the text" succumbs to the force of "their own figurative constitution" ("Displacing" 472).

20. For my fuller discussion of *The Prelude* in terms of its foundation of questions, see *Questioning Presence* ("The Interrogative Origins of Autobiography" [131–50]), and "Answering Questions and Questioning Answers: The Interrogative Project of *The Prelude*." The formula of this specific question, with antecedents in Virgil, Ariosto, Milton, Thomson, Pope (and its inevitable parody in Byron) works as an allusion to other such questioners in similar crises. The Norton Critical refers to "correspondence in *TLS* April–September 1975" detailing these antecedents (1 n. 2); Jonathan Wordsworth gives the Miltonic formula fuller consideration in *Borders* (36–37, 420 n. 3), and John A. Hodgson attends to the "allusively evocative" character of this question in a specific rhetorical tradition, concentrating on Virgilian instances and resonances.

21. Culler, "Apostrophe" 149–50; Jacobus, "Apostrophe and Lyric Voice" 171–72. Applying another phase of Culler's argument, Jacobus argues that Wordsworth exploits apostrophe throughout *The Prelude* (especially at such key moments as the "glad preamble") as "a form of self-constituting self-address": "The question of the poet's vocation, translated into invocation, becomes the question of poetic voice" (172).

22. Wordsworth's discussion of "spots of time" and the attendant memories appear first in 18A (DC MS. 16, which precedes the base-texts for the 1798–99

poem, MSS. U and V; see Parrish 20–21). Norton's house style both indents and puts spaces between verse paragraphs—a format that distorts the closer association of the episode of the drowning and the spots of time passage in Wordsworth's manuscript, where there is indentation only (see Parrish 258–59).

23. 11: 258–389 and 12: 208–335. In this position, the passage is invested with a dramatic function that enhances its claims. Following the books about Wordsworth's imaginative impairment by the specter shapes of Terror in France, the passage on "spots of time"—both as a tale of early memories transformed by later feelings and as an early text recalled in the poem's later stages of composition—enacts what it describes, as the poet repairs to earlier texts and times to inspire and sustain his present writing.

24. According to Jonathan Wordsworth, Book 4 of the five-book poem contained much of the material that would appear in Books 4 and 5 of the 1805 text: the dawn dedication, the discharged soldier, the meditation on the perishability of human works and of books in particular, the complaints about modern systems of education and the monstrosity of the child prodigy, the Winander Boy, and the general recollection of the poet's boyhood reading ("Five-Book" 10–15). Jarvis agrees that the drowned man and the discharged soldier were part of its fourth book and thinks that there is a "reasonable ground" for supposing that the Arab dream was intended for the five-book poem, too (but not enough for positing "There Was a Boy" as part of it) (539). For details of the compositional history of 1805's Book 5 and relevant manuscripts, see Reed 1: 11–39.

25. See Hartman's brief but resonant meditation on the affinity of this passage to that of the drowned man (*Wordsworth's Poetry* 232).

26. Editors feel compelled to "correct" Wordsworth: see de Selincourt-Darbishire (516, note on line 308) and the Norton Critical (8 n. 9).

27. I owe this reading of the drowning as a "screen memory" for the death of the mother to Richard Onorato's illuminating analyses (252, and a related reference on 208). See Freud 15: 200–1 and 23: 74.

28. The death of the mother as the suppressed referent of these lines is proposed both by the editors of *The Norton Anthology of English Literature* (4th ed. 2: 251 n. 3) and Onorato: the child's seeking the visible world is directed toward finding "a substitute for the mother, upon which many of the dependent needs endangered by her loss could be projected" (148).

29. See Reed 2: 624. Coleridge was the first to read the signature of "the bosom of the steady lake": coming on it in MS. JJ (the basis for "There was a Boy" in the 1800 *Lyrical Ballads*), he wrote to Wordsworth, "I should have recognised [the image] any where; and had I met these lines running wild in the deserts of Arabia, I should have instantly screamed out 'Wordsworth!'" (December 10, 1798; *Letters* 1: 452–53).

30. The dynamic of "suppression and retrieval" is illuminated by Theresa Kelley in "The Economics of the Heart," a study of Wordsworth's ambivalent confrontations with the sublime in the revisionary aesthetics of the "spots of time"

passage in the three major texts of *The Prelude*. Kelley applies these terms to the drowned-man episode in her paper, "Wordsworth's Figural Interventions," some of which appears in *Wordsworth's Revisionary Aesthetics* 93–95.

31. For the historical information, see Norton Critical (176 n. 4) and Maxwell (548 n): "T. W. Thompson, *Wordsworth's Hawkeshead* [1970], identifies the drowned man as 'James Jackson School-Master of Sawrey.'" Chase uses this fact to propose that the account of the drowned man extends the polemic against schoolmasters: "the exemplary educational episode consists in seeing a teacher as a dead man" in a text governed by "the duplicity of a gesture that simultaneously hallows the lost teacher and reinscribes his statuesque disfigurement" (31).

32. The phrase in quotation is from Wordsworth's comment on "There was a Boy" in the Preface to *Poetical Works* (1815), where it is the first of the "Poems of the Imagination." See *Prose* 3: 35.

33. See the reference to Ricks, n. 18, above.

34. Norton Critical notes the allusion (8 n. 2). For a subtle exploration of Wordsworth's affinities with Othello, see Manning, "Reading Wordsworth's Revisions."

35. For relevant discussions of this contradiction between ostensible program and imaginative practice, see Averill (147–87) and Jacobus (*Tradition and Experiment* 240–50). As Manning observes, moreover, even the first "spot of time," by recalling a place where a wife-murderer was executed, uncannily traces Othello's story into Wordsworth's own autobiography: the memory has a fitness of detail consonant with "the story of Othello glimpsed in the preceding episode. It is as if the outlines of a plot at first only shadowily glimpsed had been delayed, split off, and had now begun to emerge"; if Othello "can convert his stories of death into tales of love, he also becomes the murderer who kills the wife his tales have won" ("Reading Wordsworth's Revisions" 96, 92).

36. Here, I share the attention to rhetorical figure in Chase's incisive deconstructive reading: "the insistent literalism of *decay*," she argues, "refers back to the decay of the risen corpse. The statement becomes an assertion that forms or images cannot figure (cannot 'know') the literal decay that was a fact. Or, rather, the statement simply displays so conspicuously the 'decay' denied by its syntax that it compels repeated rereading" (25)—a dynamic also observed in Hillis Miller's reading of Wordsworthian negatives in "The Still Heart," cited later in this chapter.

37. See Parrish's text 80–81; Norton Critical 493.

38. Miller notes that in the first usage Wordsworth is transferring the traditional trope of "describing the body as the garment of the soul" to "books" ("The Stone and the Shell" 133). Considering the play of the word *garments* in Book 5— first a figure, then a literal fact—Chase takes this "divestment of figurative meaning in the literal recurrence of the noun *garments*" (16) as emblematic of the way Book 5 constitutes its text—its operation as context for the drowned man by means of an "atemporal repetition of *wording* from one passage to another, a repe-

tition at once overdetermined and contingent" (23). Andrzej Warminski's essay elaborates the shifty substitutions of this metaphor system and the significance of its analogical slippages.

39. For careful discussions of the parallels between Wordsworth's representations of the young man's encounter with the soldier and the boy's with the drowned man, see Onorato (252) and Manning ("Reading Wordsworth's Revisions" 98–99).

40. Contemporaneous texts with analogous figures, most notoriously the Pedlar who tells the story of the ruined cottage, yield consequences just as troubling in their aestheticizing of tragedy. Although these texts often ironize this attitude and relativize its authority, Wordsworth's repeated stagings suggest his irresolution. For relevant discussions, see Averill, especially chapters 4 and 7; Manning, "Wordsworth, Margaret, and The Pedlar"; Simpson, *Wordsworth's Historical Imagination*; Michael H. Friedman's study; and chapter 4 of my *Questioning Presence*.

41. Scholars have not been able to identify the "abstract" to the "four large Volume" set of the "Tales" to which Wordsworth refers. Even so, there were several multi-volume editions printed in England and Scotland in the eighteenth century. In 1706, A. Bell of London issued a four-volume edition of "Arabian nights entertainments consisting of one thousand stories, told by the sultaness of the Indies, to divert the sultan from the execution of a bloody vow . . . Tr. into French from the Arabian mss. by M. Galland [Antoine Galland] . . . and now done into English"; a 7th edition, in twelve volumes, was published in London by J. Osborn and T. Longman in 1728–30; a 14th edition, again in four volumes, was published by T. Longman in London in 1778 (most likely the one to which Wordsworth refers) and reprinted in 1789.

42. The capitalizations are not random accidentals; "What is the reason that our modern Compositors are so unwilling to employ Capital Letters?" Wordsworth complained in 1845 to John Moultrie, whose recent edition of Gray's *Poetical Works* did not reproduce the "substantives . . . written in Capital Letters" (*Letters LY* 4: 644).

43. Jon Cook's essay (31) helped me think about this grammatical doubleness.

44. An early version of the "Cave" passage appears in MS. WW (26^r–27^v), following lines about the realization that "Alps wer crossd" (26^r) and lines that would evolve into the famous apostrophe to "Imagination": "The vault before him lies / in perfect view / [? revived] [?] / by charm / But let . . . / that word must rest / A little while [?Imagination] crosd / me here / Like a[n] unfatherd vapour, & my / verse / Halts in mid course" (27^v–28^r; Reed 2: 255–57). The link of these lines to the period of composition in which Wordsworth was experimenting with a new frame for the drowning is revealed by other pages of this manuscript. Earlier in WW appears a sketch for the new coda for the drowning, with the account of the abstract of the Arabian Tales preceding, rather than following, the lines denying fear: the former concludes, "Till by joint saving we could gain our / ends / And

make this book our own / But perseverance brought us / enough"; the very next lines on the page are "no vulgar fear / possessed me for my inner eye had seen . . ." (see 18ʳ–18ᵛ; Reed 2: 244–45).

45. Words, unlike natural objects, are "engendered by consciousness," de Man remarks, and he assigns this beginning to a process of negation and difference from nature ("Intentional Structure" 4). Writing thus shifts ambivalently between its immediacy as event and its belatedness as record: "it can be considered both an act and an interpretative process that follows after an act with which it cannot coincide. As such, it both affirms and denies its own nature or specificity" ("Literary History" 152).

46. Photographs of the elaborate title page of MS. B (4ʳ) appear opposite page 1 of the de Selincourt–Darbishire edition, opposite xxxviii of Gill's, and on 1: 1168 of Reed's edition. J. Wordsworth and Gill report that this title also appears on MS. A ("Two-Part" 510), and Reed's edition shows a similar inscription on iii of MS. C; see 1: 1217.

Chapter 5

1. A summary may be helpful. *Canto I*: Conrad, the Corsair chief, returns between ventures with his crew to the pirates' isle, eager for a reunion with his devoted, patient wife Medora, his "one virtue" amid "a thousand crimes." With great difficulty, he wrests himself from an all-too-brief evening with her to launch his next assault, on his enemy the Pacha Seyd.

Canto II: Disguised as a dervise (holy man), Conrad enters Seyd's court, spinning a tale that diverts attention from the pirates' torching of Seyd's galleys. When the treachery is sighted, Conrad uncloaks, the pirates swarm over the court, and start to torch the palace and city along with the harbor. As victory seems certain, they hear the cries of the harem, whom they are moved to save, Conrad himself rescuing the queen, Gulnare. In this delay, Seyd's forces rally; most of the pirates escape, but Conrad is captured and imprisoned for execution. Gulnare secretly visits him, confessing her gratitude and promising to plot against Seyd, whom she hates.

Canto III: Four days later, Gulnare returns from an increasingly suspicious Seyd to Conrad, now declaring her love for him and with plans for his escape. Conrad is reluctant to let a woman help him thus, and although she reports that Seyd plans to impale him the next morning, he begs her to let him manage his own affairs. She vanishes, and when she returns, she tells him that she has killed Seyd in his sleep with her "secret knife"; she orders the guards, whom she has paid off, to release Conrad, leads him out of prison and on to a bark, which unites with the pirates' flagship. On board, Gulnare sees how appalled Conrad is by her actions and faints in distress; Conrad, in pity, embraces and kisses her. When all return to the home isle, Conrad discovers that Medora is dead, and he is heartbroken. The next morning, his crew looks for him, to no avail; the following morning they find a boat-chain, and although they search the seas for months, he is never found.

2. William Keach's "Cockney Couplets" gives an excellent reading to Keats's satirical performance in this passage as well as to the "complicated and even contradictory politics of style" involved in the Regency debate about Pope, Cockney poetics, and blank verse, whose most visible practitioner in 1814 was the increasingly Tory Wordsworth.

3. Kames of course prefers the freedom of blank verse to the cramps of rhyme, but in rhyme, he says, "if a couplet be a complete period with regard to melody, it ought regularly to be the same with regard to sense"—"rule . . . quite neglected in French versification," he adds in later editions (Mills edition 316). William Bowman Piper, a conservative formalist, heightens the charge when he blames Romantic poets (Moore, Byron, Keats, Hunt) for the "unhappy destruction of the great couplet tradition" in English verse, in the way they "degraded" it (4) with "that exasperating abuse of the form," the enjambed "romance couplet" (49). This form, he contends, "is an exact perversion of the closed couplet; not merely a careless loosening of its proper emphases and definitions but, to repeat, a perversion. The poet practicing this form abuses the means by which closed-couplet poetry gains force and lucidity" (52). (And, of course, Byron's later ottava rima often makes its summary heroic couplet mock- or anti-heroic).

4. Including Dryden in this praise and conceding the exquisite wit of Pope's couplets, Jeffrey remarked that "there is nothing in Pope of impetuous passion or enthusiastic vehemence." Byron has "proved that this, the most ponderous and stately verse in our language, could be accommodated to the variations of a tale of passion and pity, and to all the breaks, starts, and transitions of an adventurous and dramatic narration"; he has shown "that the oldest and most respectable measure . . . is at least as flexible as any other—and capable, in the hands of a master, of vibrations as strong and as rapid as those of a lighter structure" (23: 206). "The versification is thought highly of indeed," Murray was happy to report to Byron (February 3, 1814; quoted in Smiles 1: 224).

5. Hopkins, "Poetic Diction" (1865; *Reader* 80); Hollander, "Rhyme and the True Calling of Words" (*Visions and Resonance* 119). These remarks press at the semantic force of Dennis's application of the term *similitude* to rhyme ("Of Prosody," in *Works* 2: 238–39). Jakobson, raising the question of a "semantic propinquity, a sort of simile between rhyming lexical units as in dove-love . . . name-fame," cites Hopkins's essay, admiring its "prodigious insight into the structure of poetry"—namely, the way "rhyme is only a particular, condensed case of a much more general, we may even say the fundamental, problem of poetry, namely *parallelism*" ("Linguistics and Poetics" 312–13).

6. Keach's essay on Cockney couplets gives brief but valuable attention to Byron's *Corsair* couplets, which he finds "politically suggestive" in their work to "check—and also give contrasting point to—the poem's appeal to a restless, rebellious energy" (188–89). Christopher Ricks reminds me, along these lines, that the pirates' claim to dance "in triumph o'er the waters wide" cannot avoid the

formative power of natural forces: a life subject to wind and wave is both free and yet not free.

7. "Choral: the Pink Church" (*Collected Later Poems* 162). Thomson's *Autumn* (645–46) is quoted by Johnson in "Life of Young" (377). The verse is a bit devious in its formalist effects, however: in the first line, the metrically and syntactically stressed *durst* and *verse* almost rhyme, while the double-stressed *British* in next line and the near homonymy of *sing . . . song* produce a sensation analogous to rhyme. The forming of the verse, that is, verges on countering the unfettering that it praises.

8. I quote "Of Prosody" (*Works* 2: 240) and the preface to his blank-verse tribute, *The Monument* (1702), in which Dennis elaborates Milton's remarks, excoriating rhyme "not only as an Enemy to Art, and a clog to Genius, and a Debaser of the Majesty of Verse; but as a thing of barbarous Sound, and contrary to true Musical Delight" (1: 297). Two years later, in the Preface to another blank-verse offering, *Britannia Triumphans*, Dennis cited "the spreading Fame of *Milton* [as] a sure Prognostick of the decaying Reputation of Rime," speculating that "before this Century is half expir'd, Rime will be wholly banished from our greater Poetry" (1: 379).

9. *Verbal Icon* 153 and 165. "How now, sir? What are you reasoning with yourself?" Valentine asks Speed, who replies, "Nay, I was rhyming" (*Two Gentlemen of Verona* 2.1.135–36).

10. *Complex Words* 259–60. Johnson recognized the untoward constraint of sound and sense on certain kinds of imaginations—for instance, Thomson's "wide expansion of general views, and his enumeration of circumstantial varieties" in the *Seasons* "would have been obstructed and embarrassed by the frequent intersection of the sense, which are the necessary effects of rhyme" (299). The slippery senses of *sense* in the stanzas from *Don Juan* trope these effects in the rhymes themselves, which deftly examine their own hand-and-glove fittings. The most prescriptive of these, the poet pretends to lament, is *love / dove*, a pairing on which he had already dwelt at the top of Canto 5, to "denounce all amorous writing" (5.2):

> When amatory poets sing their loves
>   In liquid lines mellifluously bland,
> And pair their rhymes as Venus yokes her doves,
>   They little think what mischief is in hand. (5.1)

The stanza in Canto 9 recalls this yoke, but with mischief in hand. Sounded four times in a stanza that prescribes its yoking with *dove* (five, with the accented syllable of *loving*), *love* is cast as the dictator of sound over sense. The wit culminates in the way the needful rhyme of *love* with *dove* extends its chord to the meta-complaint that "Reason ne'er was hand-and-glove / With rhyme." Yet the poetic work of the rhyme partly subverts the complaint, for *hand-and-glove* at once "improv[es] / The sound" of the stanza and proves its "sense" by its reference to man-made fitting. The structuring of the rhyme is apt: even as a glove covers the hand it fits, *glove* adds a *g* to the word it fits, *love* (cf. similar wit in the rhyme of woman's love of "love" becoming "a habit" that "fits her loosely—like an easy glove" [3.3]). Byron embeds his complaint about the conventions of amatory poetics in a meta-rhyme that displays the factitious arrangements of sound and sense in all language.

11. In 1821, Byron sends verses to Murray and Moore that make a similar joke:

> Of [Turdsworth], the grand metaquizzical poet,
> A man of vast merit, though few people know it;
> The perusal of whom (as I told *you* at Mestri)
> I owe, in great part, to my passion for pastry.

He reminds Moore that "it was from Fusina that you and I embarked, though 'the wicked necessity of rhyming' [a turn on Milton's complaint] has made me press Mestri into the voyage" (*BLJ* 8: 68; cf. his letter to Murray 8: 66).

12. Malcolm Kelsall shows how Byron calculated his parliamentary discourse not only to communicate "principles, but [to draw] attention to the orator's education and verbal felicity" (*Byron's Politics* 36); for a fine discussion of the stylistic and performative character of Byron's speeches and their inflection by the discourses of patrician politics, see chapter two.

13. See Raymond Williams, *Keywords*: the meanings in contention, or interaction, involve the earliest English meaning of *subject*, "a person under the dominion of a lord or sovereign," with a newer one (much used by Coleridge) imported in the eighteenth century from German classical philosophy, "the active mind or the thinking agent (in ironic contrast with the passive subject of political dominion)" (308–10).

14. About his (temporary) decision to cancel the dedication, Byron tells Moore, "there was too much about <myself and> politics and poesy . . . ending with that topic on which <all> most men are fluent and none very amusing—one's self" (*Poetical Works* 3: 446). The parallels were political and well as personal. As McGann points out (3: 445) and Franklin (79) and Watkins (70) elaborate, Byron took the name "Conrad" from a Ghibelline aristocrat at the end of the thirteenth century who tried unsuccessfully to protect Italian Republicanism from the turn of popular favor to the despotic Neapolitan Guelphs, the ancestors of the present House of Hanover for whom "Guelph" is a "contemptuous code-phrase." Moreover, his "insistence on publishing 'Lines to a Lady Weeping' with *The Corsair* shows that he wanted [his readers] to make the connection between the alienated noble, Conrad, and the Whig leaders abandoned by their erstwhile patron, the Regent, in 1811" (Franklin 79).

15. See Peter Manning: *Childe Harold* and the Tales involve "the ceaseless mechanical reduplication of the Byronic hero in the sphere of commodities, the seemingly unique, sublime experience transmogrified into the desires and gratifications of a carefully manipulated mass market"; the "salient characteristics" of this hero were "repetition and reproducibility, not brooding uniqueness" ("Childe Harold" 182, 184). Cf. Jerome Christensen: gaining popularity, dubbed "Byronism," in "a stance of gloriously Romantic (Satanic, existential, Promethean, revo-

lutionary, etc.) or neurotically compulsive opposition," Byronic "opposition did not break with the literary culture that invented and profited from it" (*Lord Byron's Strength* 88–89, et passim).

16. In *The Revolution in Tanner's Lane* (1887), Zachariah, who had heard that Byron was known by heart among people "who were accessible to no other poetry . . . old sea-captains, merchants, tradesmen, clerks, tailors, milliners," picks up the poem skeptically; but "as he read his heart warmed, and he unconsciously found himself declaiming several of the most glowing and eloquent lines aloud. . . . Zachariah found in *The Corsair* exactly what answered to his inmost self, down to its very depths. The lofty style, the scorn of what is mean and base, the courage— root of all virtue—that dares and evermore dares in the very last extremity, the love of the illimitable, of freedom, and the cadences like the fall of waves on a sea- shore were attractive to him beyond measure" (quoted in A. Rutherford, *Byron: The Critical Heritage* 370). Manning notes John Wilson's similar remarks in *Edin- burgh Review* about *Childe Harold IV*, as he pondered the contradiction that "the morbid and melancholy lover of solitude, might act a conspicuous and applauded part on the crowded theatre of public fame": Byron works the "singular illusion, by which [his] disclosures . . . seem to have something of the nature of private and confidential communications . . . secrets whispered to chosen ears" and "the in- most recesses of [the] heart" rather than to "the careless multitudes around him"; the poetry seems "intended [for] kindred and sympathizing spirits, who discern and own that secret language, of which the privacy is not violated" (30: 90). "The shadow double of the splendid Byronic hero," remarks Manning, "is the alienated reader of the mass market. The Byronic text . . . separates man from his fellows, while reinforcing his sense of his own precious individuality" ("Childe Harold" 186).

17. *Childe Harold*, moreover, reached its 10th edition in 1815. For reports on the sales of *The Corsair*, see Leslie A. Marchand (*Byron: A Portrait* 162) and Mc- Gann, *Poetical Works* 3: 444–45. Murray wrote to Byron on February 3 about the "ferment": "a thing perfectly unprecedented—10,000 copies. . . . You have no notion of the sensation which the publication has occasioned" (quoted in Smiles 1: 223–24). Manning observes that sales were hot not because of the Byronic hero but "because presses could produce ten thousand copies, booksellers' dinners crys- tallized the market, the inclusion of such scandalous tidbits as Byron's 'Lines to a Lady Weeping' could be made known by judicious advance leaks to the news- papers, and the great quarterly reviews [Murray himself founded the *Quarterly Review*] formed and perpetuated taste" ("Childe Harold" 184). Manning's "Tales and Politics" explores the political ramifications of Byron's insistence on repub- lishing (and hence revealing his authorship of) "Lines" with *The Corsair*; first printed in the Whig *Morning Chronicle*, the poem sympathized with Princess Charlotte's public distress over the Regent's betrayal of his Whig allies. Kelsall elaborates the political agenda: loyal opposition to the Crown tended to gather round "the heir to the throne—the 'reversionary' interest—as an alternative source of patronage. In Byron's lifetime the Prince Regent for decades served this

function," but when he betrayed his allies, such interest "then gathered round the female members of the family," Princess Charlotte, and later, Queen Caroline (*Byron's Politics* 11–12).

18. Empson uses this phrase in the table of contents for *Seven Types of Ambiguity* (v) and studies this effect in Shakespeare's sonnets (62–63).

19. Although I admire Watkins's analysis of the poem's representation of social relations, I am more skeptical than he both about Byron's ultimate "challenge [to] accepted values" and the "undermining of conventional understanding" and, perforce, about his uncovering "new possibilities and directions for social life" (87–88). I think it is suggestive that even Piper can write of *The Corsair* that "although a romantic tale, [it] shows Byron's considerable responsiveness to the couplet's promptings toward order" (435).

20. The eighteenth-century "corsairs" were Mediterranean and African privateers, sea-going operators legally authorized "to carry out harassing operations against the ships of a hostile nation"; they thus "had many links with the economy of Western Europe" and a rationale for their activity going "back to the Christian-Moslem struggle" (Pat Rogers, 34–35; he cites Novak's *Economics* [104–5] for fuller discussion). Noting Byron's representation of the tale's social structure, Manning remarks that "even on the island" Conrad "does not live in solitude": he "participates in a community depicted as an alternative to the corrupt civilization on which it nonetheless parasitically preys for sustenance" (*Byron* 53). This dependency evokes the social coherence that Kelsall describes as the "paradox of Whig politics": "the language of opposition frequently has a republican ring because opposed to the Crown, and yet, in defending 'the Constitution' insists on the existence of the monarchy as part of the proper 'balance' of the state" (*Byron's Politics* 11).

21. For the most searching treatment of these economics, see Manning's "Hone-ing," a study of William Hone's involvement with pirated editions of Byron's works, including a cheap prose *Corsair* brought out in 1817. Byron fully expected *The Vision of Judgment* to "be *pirated* . . . & remedy refused according to law and lawyers" (*BLJ* 9: 125).

22. Geoffrey Shepherd reports that the terms "masculine rhyme" and "feminine rhyme," adapted from French prosody, were first used in English in Sidney's *Apology for Poetry* (235 n on p. 141, line 11). In closed-couplet history, Piper reports, although rhymes of one-syllable words are more common than those of two-syllable iambic words only the second syllables of which rhyme, both forms work to give "a strong emphasis on the end of the couplet" (14). There is another *driven / heaven* at 3.15–16. My tally of feminine rhymes omits the eight pairs using *bower, tower, shower, hour, power* (1.290–91, 305–6, 579–80; 2.366–67, 460–61; 3.159–60, 567–68, 678–79), which are at best faintly disyllabic; the lack of a medial consonant (the *w* is phonetically a vowel) makes them sound more nearly like stressed monosyllables. The other departures from masculine-rhyme couplets include some triplets, two dozen or so imperfect rhymings of stressed and unstressed syllables, and (allowing for judgment) about two dozen dissonant or slant rhymes.

23. Eliding the *v* retained in these disyllabic, feminine rhymings, Byron elsewhere contracts *never* to *ne'er* to rhyme with *share* (1.388–89), and *over* to *o'er* to rhyme with *corridore* (1.363–64), *wore* (2.57–58), *more* (2.247–48; 3.382–83), and *before* (2.332–33). *Beppo* explicitly coordinates feminine rhymes with laxity, passivity, the erosion of masculine vigor, and the near effacement of self:

> But I am but a nameless sort of person,
>   (A broken Dandy lately on my travels)
> And take for rhyme, to hook my rambling verse on,
>   The first that Walker's Lexicon unravels,
> And when I can't find that, I put a worse on,
>   Not caring as I ought for critics' cavils.... (52)

Christensen notes that the name of Byron's most easily mastered hero, *Juan*, is fated for feminine rhyming, as the famous declension in the poem's opening stanza, *new one / true one / Juan*, demonstrates (*Lord Byron's Strength* 96)—to which I would add the female embodied repetition of this feminine form: *Julia / truly a / newly a* (2.208). These feminizings draw on the Restoration and post-Miltonic prejudice against rhyme as a Frenchified effeminacy. To Dennis, for example, "soft and effeminate Rhyme" is "the very Reverse of . . . manly, and powerful, and noble Enthusiasm" (*Works* 2: 169); "Rime . . . has something effeminate it its jingling Nature, and emasculates our *English* Verse, and consequently is utterly unfit for the greater Poetry" (Preface to *Britannia Triumphans; Works* 1: 379); E. N. Hooker (1: 430 n. 4) cites a like opinion from Felton, *Dissertation on Reading the Classics* (1715).

24. Raymond Williams describes "keywords" as "significant, binding words in certain activities and their interpretation" and "significant, indicative words in certain forms of thought" (15), the significance involving both "ideas and values" (17). My attention to the latency of *fair* in *of air* is, again, indebted to Garrett Stewart's study of the poetic phonotext. It is telling that Byron uses the almost identical phrase to report a radical female interiority in the last stanza of *Lara*: Kaled (Lara's erstwhile cross-dressed page) is "left to waste" and talk "all idly unto shapes of air" (2.608–9).

25. Cheryl Giuliano offers an interesting discussion of Byron's representation of this Maid in relation to Kaled and Gulnare (799–802). George Ellis, in one of the first reviews, tartly remarks that Childe Harold surveys "her fairy form . . . but having no predilection for Amazon beauties, is anxious to exculpate this paragon of Spain, as well as her countrywomen, from any deficiency in the 'witching arts of love'" (*Quarterly* 7: 183).

26. This was the aspect of character codified by Byron's social circle. Mary Shelley remarks of Robert Finch, for instance, that he bore "the dear Corsair expression half savage half soft" (April 26, 1819; *Letters* 1: 94). G. Wilson Knight's essay focuses on the poem's repeated inscriptions of softness to define Conrad's androgyny.

27. *Byron* 47; Manning observes the epic analogue of Aeneas's departure from

Dido. Sensitive to the gendering of self-possession in this poem, Knight writes that Byron has cast his hero into a figure in whom "ruthless evil and cynical callousness enshrin[e] a strangely soft, almost feminine, devotion" (202).

28. Like "his mother's softness" (3.648), "woman's grief" has an ambiguous reference, naming both a personal attribute and a degrading identification. This doubleness is assisted by the double sense of *betray*: as Giuliano notes, "Conrad must not reveal his melting to grieving woman [Medora], nor must he betray himself or allow himself to be transformed into a woman grieving" (790). The double senses here gain effect from earlier counterpoints: the couplet-sharpened reports of Conrad's legendary skill in getting others to "betray / Some secret thought, than drag that chief's to day" (1.221–22) and Medora's opposite female helplessness: "Still must my song my thoughts, my soul betray" (1.368). The issue is recalled just as pointedly when Conrad, imprisoned and awaiting impalement, reminds himself, "Each hath some fear, and he who least betrays, / The only hypocrite deserving praise" (2.361–62).

29. Watkins discusses these reversals in relation to the internal social structures of the poem (83–86), as does Kelsall, who argues that *The Corsair* explores a "threat to the very essence of male sexuality and power as constructed upon the polarization of the roles of men and women" ("Byron and the Women of the Harem" 168).

30. For sonnet-like units in larger fields of verse, recall Wordsworth's pleasant discernment of such forms in *Paradise Lost* (Morley 2: 484). And for an example of an all-couplet sonnet, see Shakespeare's sonnet 126 (only 12 lines).

31. I study the politics of gender in these works in "'Their She Condition'" and "'A Problem Few Dare Imitate,'" where I also note relevant work by others. Even the *Monthly Review* wondered about Byron's (if not Conrad's) final attitude toward Gulnare's restoration: "we suspect that his Lordship felt the difficulty of the task, since he has abandoned it almost as soon as it was undertaken" (73: 189).

32. See the textual notes in *Poetical Works* 3: 204. Mark Rutherford, in his late Victorian assessment, shows a secure grasp of the allegory of gender: "When [Gulnare] has done the deed and [Conrad] sees the single spot of blood upon her, he, the Corsair is unmanned as he had never been in battle, prison, or by consciousness of guilt" ("Morality" 128).

33. If, as Caroline Franklin argues, Gulnare's passion is an image of revolutionary subversion made horrible by a transgression of codes of gender (82–83), I would argue that the heroic couplets are one way that Byron restores the aristocratic codes of order.

34. The English is Byron's terza-rima translation of this stanza in "Francesca of Rimini," a rendering of *Inferno* V.97–142 from March 1820. For the text and draft variants, see *Poetical Works* 4: 281, and for the first version, 4: 283.

35. In his letter to Byron about the sensational sales, Murray reports that William Gifford, the editor of the *Quarterly*, "did what I never knew him do before—he repeated several passages from memory, particularly the closing stanza—'His death yet dubious, deeds too widely known'" (Smiles 1: 223–24). In 1816, Byron's

former lover, Caroline Lamb, keyed the *roman à clef* of what Byron called her "kiss and tell" novel, *Glenarvon*, by using his closing couplet, by then famous, as its motto (*BLJ* 5: 85; she misquotes slightly, from memory).

Chapter 6

1. The gloss of "Negative Capability" is W. J. Bate's (*John Keats* 249); Paul de Man offers a similar assessment (*Keats* xxv).

2. Other than "To Fanny," the titles are editorial. Stillinger surmises that Charles Brown's copies of the four poems addressed to Fanny Brawne were based on now-lost holographs in her possession (*Poems* 673–74). Exact dates of composition are speculative: "To Fanny" was probably written early in 1820, after Keats's first major hemorrhage, and the others in late 1819 after he abandoned *The Fall of Hyperion*. As for "Bright Star": Brown's copy of the first draft is dated 1819, and according to Stillinger, more precision is not possible (although Bate [*John Keats* 618–19] and Allott [736–37] try); a later version in Keats's hand appears in the volume of Shakespeare that he took to Italy in autumn 1820; this is the text Milnes places at the close of *Life, Letters, and Literary Remains* (2: 306), where most of these poems were first published (2: 34–35, 284–86, 304–6); "The day is gone" and "Bright Star" had appeared earlier in obscure journals. "This living hand" was first published in 1898, in the 6th edition of H. B. Forman's *Poetical Works of John Keats*, and titled therein "Lines Supposed to Have Been Addressed to Fanny Brawne." For fuller accounts, see Stillinger's textual notes.

3. It is revealing that one critic, Ronald Primeau, tries to recuperate "What can I do?" as a late Great Ode: discerning an opposition between "visionary flight" and "the complexities of the real world," he traces the poet's "escapist flight to an ideal" to his "realization of [its] inadequacy" to his final "acceptance of the painful sweetness inherent in his existential situation" (111; cf. his explicit enlistment of the Odes on 117)—virtually retracing Stillinger's famous map for the Great Odes, one in which the poet indulges "a mental flight to visit the ideal, and then—for a variety of reasons, but most often because he finds something wanting in the imagined ideal, or because, being a native of the real world, he discovers that he does not or cannot belong permanently in the ideal—returns to the real" with "a better understanding" or "a change in attitude" ("Imagination and Reality" 101–2).

4. McGann helpfully distinguishes between the "personal" address of "To Fanny" and the utterly "private" text of "This living hand," which was "never deliberately communicated to anyone else" (ibid. 47). In the general polemic of *The Romantic Ideology*, he does allow "'purely' stylistic, rhetorical, formal" analysis on the condition "that such specialized studies . . . find their *raison d'être* in the socio-historical ground" (3).

5. I quote, as a representative and often cited text, Margaret Homans's statement at the opening of *Women Writers and Poetic Identity* (12). The case of Keats has given her some trouble, however, for his humble origins, limited education, and financial disadvantage participate in "certain aspects of women's experience as

outsiders relative to the major literary tradition . . . regardless of gender" (240 n. 25), and so thwart classification with poets of the dominant "masculine tradition." But later, in "Keats Reading Women, Women Reading Keats," she returns Keats to this tradition, emphasizing his "resentment of [women's] real and imagined power over him" and attending to the various ways "his compensatory wish to assert his own masculine authority" gets enacted in his writing (368). For another superb analysis of how women, in the Regency culture of literary production and consumption, challenged the male writer's fantasies of autonomous creativity, see Sonia Hofkosh's "The Writer's Ravishment."

6. The punning on *numbers* is more audible in the openings of two of the songs of spring: "O Goddess! hear these tuneless numbers, wrung / By sweet enforcement and remembrance dear," begs the poet of "Ode to Psyche," having seen or dreamt of a scene in which the goddess and her lover seemed "ready still past kisses to outnumber" (1–2, 19); "My heart aches, and a drowsy numbness pains / My sense," reports the poet of "Ode to a Nightingale," envying the nightingale's singing amid "shadows numberless" (stanza 1).

7. The aestheticizing is persistent. The poet of the early "Imitation of Spenser" yearns for a voice able to "beguile" Dido of "her grief . . . / Or rob from aged Lear his bitter teen" (21–22), and the wish endures as late as *The Fall of Hyperion* in Moneta's promise to the poet-dreamer that he may witness her agony "free from all pain, if wonder pain [him] not" (1.248). The deeper work of this unfinished poem is Keats's ironizing of this *if*: the dreamer will have to bear the suffering he witnesses, feeling it "Ponderous upon [his] senses" to the point of incorporation (1.388–92). For my fuller discussion of these ironies, see *Questioning Presence* 344–61.

8. Sidney Colvin, in one of the first full-scale biographies, quotes from several late lyrics to document Keats's "grotesque passion" (334–39, 377–78). In a chapter titled "Illness" (2: 353–464) Amy Lowell prints "The day is gone" to preface "the somewhat more tempered form" of the "same story" in the letter, printed in full, beginning, "—My sweet Girl, I am living to day in yesterday: I was in a complete fascination all day. I feel myself at your mercy" (*KL* 2: 222). The sonnet is "not among Keats's best," she concedes, but it is "certainly among the most pathetic that have ever been written." With similar sympathy, she cites "What can I do?" and "I cry your mercy" to show the "torture" of Keats's "growing jealousy"—the latter "all bitterness, and longing, agonizing, fevered love"—and she calls "This living hand" "one of the bitterest of all of Keats's personal expressions," a document in "agony" (2: 354–55; 375–76). "Hardly Keats at his best," Robert Gittings says more dryly; although these poems are "of intense moment to the poet and his immediate circle," they "look strangely in the company of his more considered work." He does devote a chapter of *The Mask of Keats* (from which I quote, 69) to "Bright Star" and another to the poems to Fanny Brawne, printing them all and attending to the "passionate self-identification" (78) in Keats's echoes of Troilus. While this attention is alert, its theme of "passionate hysteria" (77) ultimately gets him no further than Lowell, or for that matter, his

own earlier study, *The Living Year*, where the story was Keats "struck down by violent physical passion" (191).

9. Stuart M. Sperry (*Keats the Poet*) and Marjorie Levinson (*Keats's Life of Allegory*) say nothing at all, while Wolf Z. Hirst's story of the career as having "virtually" ended with "To Autumn" (154) cites the late poems without comment, despite his intent to give "a comprehensive and scholarly account of the poet's works" (9). John Barnard has an appendix on "The Poems to Fanny Brawne" (149–52) but notwithstanding his claim of "revaluation," he echoes everyone else, right down to the adjectives: a part of the biography, these texts chiefly sustain the letters' evidence "of Keats's loss of control over his conflicting emotions" in late 1819 and early 1820; aside from "Bright Star" ("in control of its emotions"), they are "unresolved in tone and subject, and marred by flaccid writing" (127); "To Fanny" is especially "callow" and "embarrassing" (149).

10. The standard study of Keats and sonnet tradition is Lawrence John Zillman's; see also Bate's *Stylistic Development*.

11. My reference to "imbalance" draws on Paul Fussell's description of this principle as the "structural identity" of the Petrarchan form (115). For a careful analysis of the separate decorums, tonalities, discourses, and social conventions that intersect in and are managed by the artistry of the Shakespearean form, see Rosalie Colie (esp. 70–96).

12. In a long journal-letter to his brother and sister-in-law of February–May 1819 (*KL* 2: 58–109), Keats included six sonnets as well as several other poems. Just after indenting "Here endethe yᵉ Ode to Psyche," he writes "Incipit altera Sonneta" below (108); *altera* thus signals an addition ("the other Sonnet" [109]), but I think it also puns on another way to write a sonnet.

13. In a wonderfully subtle reading of this sonnet, Hollander shows Keats's "original way of loosening the links of rhyming's chains without actually breaking them or having them slip off," a pattern in which the "distant rhyme words themselves tell intercalated tales in the sonnet's unfolding story" (*Melodious Guile* 94).

14. I emend Cook, who inexplicably (mis?)prints "his delight" (327); she claims the authority of Charles Brown's manuscript, but so do Stillinger and Allott, who both read the far richer "hid delight." Cf. Cook's obvious error in "I cry your mercy," where she has "withold" in line 10.

15. Jameson, *Prison-House* 140; "if the Symbolic Order is the source of all meaning, it is also and at the same time the source of all cliché" (ibid.). Keats's self-consciousness, of course, draws its energy from a self-critical strain in sonnet tradition. For recent discussions of this decentering effect, see Culler: "'I love you' is always something of a quotation" ("Meaning and Iterability" 120 n), and Eagleton (who cites Culler and tightens the noose): "Love is the ultimate self-definition," yet "in its very moment of absolute, original value, the self stumbles across nothing but other people's lines, finds itself handed a meticulously detailed script to which it must slavishly conform" (*William Shakespeare* 18–19).

16. Othello's sarcasm was also associated in Keats's mind with condescending abuse by the reviews, particularly the *Quarterly*, by force of Hazlitt's parody in

his flaming attack on Gifford's political agenda (*A Letter to William Gifford, Esq. from William Hazlitt, Esq.* [1819], part of which was republished in the *Examiner*, March 7 and 14). After a long list of charges, Hazlitt writes, "You, sir, do you not [do] all this? I cry your mercy then: I took you for the Editor of the Quarterly Review!" These sentences were included in the large portions of this *Letter* Keats transcribed for George and Georgiana (*KL* 2: 71–73).

17. I thank William Keach (who is brilliant about rhymes in *Shelley's Style*) for this observation about *all/thrall*. This same phonemic wit plays with a difference in the fateful stanza of "La Belle Dame sans Merci": "I saw pale kings and Princes too / Pale warriors death pale were they all / They cried La belle dame sans merci / Thee hath in thrall" (*KL* 2: 96). Whereas in "I cry your mercy," *all/thrall* polarizes conditions of plenitude and self-loss, its link in "La Belle Dame" multiplies the knight's individual plight into a visionary totality.

18. Keats's poetry displays several embedded sonnets (a form famous in *Romeo and Juliet*). *I stood tip-toe* opens with a double sonnet in couplets, a form to which its poet calls attention some lines on when he compares the pace of "nature's gentle doings" to the time it takes to "read two sonnets" (69); the opening tableau and first stanza of *Hyperion* is a blank-verse sonnet; and two wickedly apposite sonnet-stanzas occupy the couplets of *Lamia*: the first (1.171–84) parodies *ubi sunt* in an erotic vein ("Whither fled Lamia, now a lady bright?"); the second gives a satirical view of the wedding guests' intoxication (2.199–212). Keats also sets overt poetic forms into the couplets of *Endymion* ("Hymn to Pan" and "Sorrow Song").

19. Keats alludes to this complaint in explaining his rhyme of "sighed full sore" with "kisses four" in "La Belle Dame": "four because I wish to restrain the headlong impetuosity of my Muse—she would have fain said 'score' without hurting the rhyme—but we must temper the Imagination as the Critics say with Judgment" (*KL* 2: 97). Keats's *must* tweaks at what had become, by April 1819, a routine complaint about his style. Reviewing the 1817 *Poems*, Conder found him "a very facetious rhymer," too prone to the "pleasant rout" (Keats's own phrase) of surprise couplings (273); to Jeffrey, *Endymion* was patent self-indulgence: "It seems as if the author had . . . taken the first word that presented itself to make up a rhyme, and then made that word the germ of a new cluster of images—a hint for a new excursion of the fancy—and so wandered on . . . till he had covered his pages with an interminable arabesque of connected and incongruous figures, that multiplied as they extended" (204–5). Least forgivingly, Croker smirked in his notorious *Quarterly* review of *Endymion*, "At first it appeared to us, that Mr. Keats had been amusing himself and wearying his readers with an immeasurable game at *bouts-rimés*"—a French-origin parlor game whose object is to compose a poem using a pre-set, random list of words as reasonable end-rhymes; Lord and Lady Byron amused themselves thus (Marchand, *Biography* 2: 521). "It is an indispensable condition at this play," Croker cautions (with clear disdain of Keats's affectation of aristocratic pastimes) "that the rhymes when filled up shall have a meaning; and our author . . . has no meaning. He seems to us to write a line at random, and then he follows not the thought excited by this line, but that suggested by the

rhyme with which it concludes. There is hardly a complete couplet inclosing a complete idea in the whole book. He wanders from one subject to another, from the association, not of ideas but of sounds . . . the mere force of catchwords" (205–6).

About the only unqualified praise for Keats's rhymes came (in 1845) from *The Nation*: "DRYDEN confessed that the rhyme frequently helped him to an idea; but, with KEATS, it helps him to a hundred" (858). Leigh Hunt also recalled Dryden's remark in relation to Keats, yet even so loyal a defender as he rued the "willfulness" of rhyme in *Endymion*. While supporting Keats's "just contempt for the monotonous termination of every-day couplets" and the way "he broke up his lines," he found the effect "as artificial, and much more obtrusive than the one under the old system" (*Lord Byron* 218). Samuel Phillips admired the "originality and power" of *Endymion* but he, too, regretted that Keats, "instead of adapting rhymes to his subject, very frequently compelled his subject to bend obsequiously to his rhymes" (3). This metaphor of political power predicts recent attention to Keats's rhymes as a deliberate sociolinguistic practice. See especially: William Keach, who argues that "even at a level of performance where the specific political context of Keats's Cockney couplets ceases to be immediately instructive, the stylistic instincts encouraged and shaped by that context may produce writing with an important though momentarily suppressed political dimension" ("Cockney Couplets" 196); and Theresa Kelley, who sees the willful rhymes of "La Belle Dame" taking a "witty," "rebellious," and "aggressive stance toward neoclassical (and Tory) values implied and declared in negative reviews of *Endymion*" ("Poetics and the Politics of Reception" 352).

20. OED (1971), *Fit, fytte*, sense 1: "A part or section of a poem or song, a canto" (F: 262). Barbara Johnson comments on these oscillations of contradictory meaning (91–92).

21. Byron plays this pun more than once: at the end of *Hints from Horace*, he lampoons the "rhyming rage" of the bad poet's "versifying fit" (797–99); in *Don Juan*, he cartoons a baritone whose "passion" in "lovers' parts" is "scarce fit for ballads in the street" (4.89; perhaps an allusive dig at Wordsworth's ballad), and in describing young misses' "genius turned for fits" (12.52), he deftly poises the sense of the noun between the musical sense and behavioral one.

22. Hartman, *Wordsworth's Poetry* xix; Johnson 95. For my fuller discussion of this theoretical and poetically enacted tension, see "Romanticism and the Measures of Meter."

23. Fanny Brawne seemed fated to inhabit forms already well cultivated in Keats's psychology. Like the "witch" betrayers of his imagination—La Belle Dame, Circe, Lamia—she evokes "an overwhelming unconscious compulsion," argues Dorothy Van Ghent (133). Aileen Ward discusses the founding trauma of Keats's experience of his mother's erratic behavior (9–11); Leon Waldoff argues that Keats's recurrent imagining of "an enthrallment that reaches toward a death conceived as an incorporation of the self by an Other" (94) originates in his devotion to his mother and is renewed in his passionate dependency on Brawne. Of his

many marginalia in Mateo Alemán's *The Rogue: or, the Life of Guzmán de Alfarache*, Keats put a singularly suggestive exclamation next to this sentence: "My mother, young, faire, and full of wit, and knew so well how to provoke his appetite upon all occasions, that his disorder opened the doore to his death" (Lowell 2: 584). Gittings elaborates Keats's self-identification with Chaucer's Troilus (*Mask* 69–78), especially in his echoes of Troilus's "passionate hysteria" and his projection of Fanny both into Criseyde and Shakespeare's Cressida; see also Primeau's essay, cited in n. 3, above. Carol Cook's essay on masculine desire in *Troilus and Cressida*, though it does not comment on Keats, is very suggestive for his interest in the play.

24. Garrod's cranky note is an instance of the former: "What has the Bright Star got to do with any of it? The poet asks of the Star only steadfastness and unchangeability. But do they really matter to him? Does the Bright Star really stand for anything in which the sonnet culminates?" (*Poetical Works* 469). Showing the latter tendency, Ward writes as if the initial negatives were not there and Keats were identifying with the remote serenity of the star (298–300).

25. In *Life, Letters, and Literary Remains*, Milnes gives it the title "Keats's Last Sonnet" (2: 306), one repeated throughout the nineteenth century (e.g., *The Oxford Book of English Verse* 744).

26. These lines recast more than the verse to Tom; they evoke a career of hands figured as the expressive agent of poetic potency and the synecdoche of authorial presence. For my fuller discussion of this career, see "The Magic Hand of Chance" 214–17. Keats himself provides a poignant summary in his request for an epitaph that would withhold the name and the agent of its writing: "HERE LIES ONE WHOSE NAME WAS WRIT IN WATER" (reported by Severn and quoted in *London Magazine*'s obituary, and frequently thereafter; e.g., Hunt, *Lord Byron* 231, Milnes 2: 91). The epitaph intersects with the whole question of literary form: its medium of inscription is as solid as any Medusan legacy, but like all epitaphs, what it traces is the language of absence. And more: it is as if Keats, even in his last request, were still thinking meta-formally: the epigraph he authorizes does not even name "John Keats," but points to a prior inscription on a medium whose intractable properties of natural form instantaneously efface all evidence of the forms applied by human intention—anticipating the whole argument of de Man's "Intentional Structure": words, unlike "natural objects," originate in "a negation of permanence, the discontinuity of a death" (4).

27. Peter Manning remarked to me that Keats's violent contest between speaker and audience, or writer and reader, recalls other such moments of Romantic imagining: the Ancient Mariner infecting the Wedding Guest with the tale he resists hearing and then cannot forget; Shelley's hope that her "hideous progeny" of a ghost story, *Frankenstein*, will "frighten" readers as she had been frightened by its inspiring dream; even Wordsworth's aggressive and disruptive designs to claim his readers' imagination with unaccustomed intensities of feeling.

28. When he brings fuller and more theoretical focus to this subject in "Towards a Definition of Romantic Irony," Sperry reassesses his view of Keats's com-

mitment to perpetual indeterminacy, arguing instead that Keats entertained indeterminacy as a necessary phase in a dialectic ultimately "intent on achieving through poetry something more definite" (6–7), especially as he moved out of the contained forms of the odes into epic and allegory. Indeterminacy itself, especially when confronted in existential rather than aesthetic terms, becomes subject to ironic review.

29. With debts to Sperry's brilliant landmark reading (*Keats the Poet* 242–91), I examine the rhetoric of these poems in this perspective in *The Questioning Presence* (301–32).

Chapter 7

1. Unless otherwise indicated, quotations of Shelley's poetry and prose follow *SPP*, ed. Reiman and Powers. For an illuminating reading of how Shelley's "convictions about language fluctuate" as the polemic of *A Defence* "moves between the extravagance of the ideal and the frustrations of the actual," see William Keach's *Shelley's Style* (I quote from 3).

2. The probable contents would have included *The Mask of Anarchy*, "Lines Written During the Castlereagh Administration," "Song to the Men of England," "Similes for Two Poetical Characters," "What Men Gain Fairly," "A New National Anthem," "Sonnet: England in 1819," "Ballad of the Starving Mother," "Ode to Liberty" and "Ode to the West Wind." The last two were published in 1820 with *Prometheus Unbound* and all but the "Ballad" appeared in the 1830s. *Athenaeum* published "Lines" late in 1832 (267: 794), and even then introduced the poem with a caution: although "there is something fearful in the solemn grandeur of these lines," they may "be now published without the chance of exciting either personal or party feeling." A bolder Chartist press circulated them all. (For Shelley's reputation in the Chartist press, see Bouthaina Shaaban's essays, and for his status with the Owenites, see also M. Siddiq Kalim's study.) Yet not until 1990 was a unified publication achieved, when Paul Foot, noting "the enthusiasm of members of the S[ocialist] W[orkers] P[arty] for Shelley's revolutionary writings," packaged the poems with *A Philosophical View of Reform*, in a "marvellous, cheap volume" (£3.95 in 1990), which he exhorts socialists to use in "duty to their children to bribe or bully them to learn the poetry which carries revolutionary ideas through the centuries" (*Revolutionary Year* 9, 26).

3. Hunt published the "Hymn" in the *Examiner* 473 (January 19, 1817), where it shared a page with a report of a meeting on "economy, public order, and reform" whose "object was to take into consideration the present most alarming state of the country" and, specifically, to urge "a reduction in the present enormous and unconstitutional military establishment . . . and a constitutional Reform in the Commons House of Parliament" (41); a text of the keynote address followed on the next page (42). For assessments of reform politics in 1816–17, see Michael Scrivener 91–92 and E. P. Thompson 603–37.

4. Shelley's comments about *Epipsychidion* are from the "Advertisement" (*SPP*

373) and a letter to Charles Ollier (whose political sensitivity was being sharpened by his association with *Blackwood's*) indicating that he did not even care whether the poem would get published for sale or "merely one hundred copies" printed for coterie distribution (February 16, 1821; *PSL* 2: 263). Stephen C. Behrendt brings a detailed study to Shelley's wavering between a sense of poetry as a public address and his concentration on "a distinctly elite audience" toward the end of his career (230–31), and offers a brief but cogent discussion of the social function of the late lyrics as "very private *gifts* bestowed not upon a general and faceless public but upon intimate private friends . . . the purest sort of community" (244–45, his italics). Ronald Tetreault's study offers a more idealizing and less historically situated assessment of Shelley's poetics of audience and their consequences for poetic form, arguing that Shelley's growth "from oratory into art" involves a "search for forms of dissemination that foster community rather than alienation" (16).

5. The "Peterloo Massacre"—a name codified by the left press in sardonic parody of the celebrated English victory at Waterloo, and now the standard reference—was a savage, sabre-wielding attack by drunken local yeomanry (a militia of property-owners) on an orderly, non-violent demonstration of 80,000–100,000 men, women, and children in St. Peter's Fields, near Manchester, on August 16, 1819, gathered to hear Henry "Orator" Hunt urge parliamentary reform, specifically, greater representation for the Manchester working-class population. The militia killed about a dozen people and brutally wounded hundreds more (for detailed accounts, in addition to the several reports in the *Examiner* of August 22, 1819, see Thompson 681–89, and Richard Holmes 529–31). It is unclear whether the London Home Office collaborated in advance, in order to suppress the reform movement, or, with the Prince Regent, found it irresistibly convenient to "make themselves accomplices after the fact" with lavish congratulations (Thompson 684). The narrative to which Shelley reacted in early September was the one conveyed by the *Examiner* and other radical newspapers sent by Peacock; the *Examiner* featured its report on the front page of its August 22 issue (608: 529–31) and reprinted notices from the *Times* (539–41) and a set of seven "Letters from Manchester" (541–43), and continued for weeks after with a barrage of front-page reports, follow-ups, letters, and protest poetry (nos. 609–612; August 29–September 19). Shelley, in a torrent of indignation (*PSL* 2: 117–20, 136), wrote speedily in order to enter the debate, posting *The Mask of Anarchy* to Leigh Hunt on September 23 (*Journals of Mary Shelley* 298; cf. *Letters of M. W. Shelley* 1: 107), hoping for publication in the *Examiner*.

6. Most commentary on *The Mask of Anarchy* celebrates its political voice. Holmes calls it not only "the greatest poem of political protest ever written in English," but perhaps "the most powerfully conceived the most economically executed and the most perfectly sustained" of Shelley's poems (532), and to Foot, it is "one of the great political protest poems of all time" (*Revolutionary Year* 15; in *Red Shelley* [175], he endorses Holmes's praise). Even F. R. Leavis—who in general thinks that "the poetry in which Shelley's genius manifests itself characteristically, and for which he has his place in the English tradition, is much more closely re-

lated to his weakness"—admires *The Mask* for "its unusual purity and strength," its departure from "the usual Shelleyan emotionalism" (*Revaluation* 215).

7. Shelley detaches "Anarchy" from the standard sense of social chaos that Lord Chancellor Eldon meant in judging the Manchester meeting "an overt act of treason" posing a "shocking choice between military government and anarchy" (quoted in Thompson 684) and turns the term back on the Government itself to name its perversion by tyranny (Foot, *Revolutionary Year* 15); "anarchy will only be the last flash before despotism," Shelley wrote before he knew of the events at Manchester [August 24, 1819; *PSL* 2: 115]). Yet by spring of 1822, frustrated over the prospects for reform, he was resorting to the standard sense: "anarchy is better than despotism—for this reason, that the former is for a season & that the latter is eternal" (April 11; *PSL* 2: 412). For a succinct genealogy of anarchy from Milton to Shelley, see Keach, "Radical Shelley?"

8. Tetreault comments on the variety of oratorical devices (commendatory direct address; provocative question and answer; and impressive variations on the imperative mood) (205–6), and argues that this rich "aesthetic experience" is "a function of form and not just of content" (199). Behrendt (199–202) remarks on the several audiences variously addressed: the aristocracy (with warning and instruction), the oppressed workers (with encouragement, instruction, and inspiration), and the liberal, enlightened readers of the *Examiner* (with urgency). Stuart Curran considers the more precisely formalist poetics. Taking a lead from Hunt's note that Shelley purposely used "a lax and familiar measure" (Preface vii), Curran discerns a "considerable achievement in the low style, shrewdly coupling its radical politics to a balladlike meter and framing its exhortations within the iconography of chapbooks, penny pamphlets, and folk pageants" (*Annus Mirabilis* 186).

9. The introductory chapter of Michael McKeon's *Politics and Poetry* offers an analysis of the potential oxymoron of "political poetry" in ways that illuminate the ambiguous status of Shelley's *Mask*: McKeon defines "political poetry" as a "rhetorical" poetry involved in persuading its historical audience; this is the condition under which "poetry is also politics" (12–15, 42–3), one which Shelley's "popular songs" imagine but do not realize in 1819.

10. *The Mask*, a poem Shelley described as one of his "exoteric species" (*PSL* 2: 152), was written in a hiatus of *Prometheus Unbound*, a poem he projected "only for the elect" (2: 200). Roger Sales (196–97), Tetreault (199), and Goldsmith (243, 252–54) contrast the two works in terms of their designated audiences.

11. Although I'm impressed by Shelley's capacity to evoke such apologies, I'm not persuaded by the argument that his "physical and emotional distance from events in England, together with a certain characteristic naive rashness in all such matters, prevented him from understanding that Hunt would not publish the piece at the time" (Behrendt 202). That Shelley was aware of the hazards is clear in his long letter about the indictment of Richard Carlile for having published Paine's *Age of Reason*; the case was not tried until October 1819, but the "blasphemous libel" itself was published in 1818, with full alertness to the consequences, and Shelley's steady reading of *Galignani's Messenger* and the *Examiner* (as well

as Paine) could not have left him innocent of the challenge. Hunt, who was busy in the fall of 1819 with a series of papers for the *Examiner* defending Shelley's character from the *Quarterly*'s defamation in its review of *The Revolt of Islam* in April, may have felt that there was already enough hot Shelley to handle. It was clear, moreover, that the Hunts would reap a prosecution for publishing a poem denouncing the king in an address to the laboring poor (as opposed to aristocrats) and, as Scrivener notes (210), rooting liberty in an argument for their rights (an analysis that put Shelley more in company with Chartist socialism than with liberal reform); while Shelley remained in self-determined exile in Italy, the Hunts would be left to bear the legal and material penalties. Donald Reiman remarks that with the passage of the notorious Six Acts in late 1819 (including, among other measures, severe limitations on "the expression of antigovernment sentiments in the press"), publishing a poem "advocating mass nonviolent resistance to the government in an attempt to win over the army to the side of the people and thus to overthrow the government by popular demand would have risked fines, jail terms, or even transportation for fourteen years for everyone involved in the publication" (*Mask* xiv).

Hunt did publish *The Masque* in 1832, when the reformers gained control of Parliament and a mollifying Reform Bill was secured. By this time, the poem's hotter rhetoric could be read with historical distance, and its cooler rhetoric admired as a sensibly prophetic recommendation of passive resistance, the means by which (shallow) parliamentary reform had been brought about—and by which time, too, as Thompson notes, the notoriety of the event "as a *massacre* and as 'Peter-Loo'" was established, along with a national "moral consensus" about the right of peaceful assembly and the unlawful "riding down and sabreing of an unarmed crowd" (710). That *The Mask* was not publishable in 1819 (or in the repressive dispensation soon thereafter) is frankly conceded by Mary Shelley in her edition of 1839: Shelley "had an idea of publishing a series of poems adapted expressly to commemorate [the] circumstances and wrongs" of "the People," and "he wrote a few, but in those days of prosecution for libel they could not be printed" ("Note on Poems of 1819," *Poetical Works* 3: 205–7). For details on repression and prosecution "in those days," see Holmes 539–41 and Foot, *Red Shelley* 34–36; Foot, however, is hard on Hunt: although he realizes that "Shelley could not reasonably blame" him for his caution (221), he himself indicts Hunt as "the censor of some of the most powerful political writing in the English language" (219).

12. Even so sardonic a critic of the politics of Romantic poets as Sales endorses Holmes's praise of the poem (193) and generously grants Shelley the argument that "the poet's dream was more important than the politician's programme," although he concedes that the first stanza awkwardly raises a "contradiction between the dormant activist and the prophesying poet" (196). Aside from Sales, admirers of the poem's politics tend not to comment on Shelley's poetics of dormancy and the likelihood of non-publication. Scrivener decides that the issue of Shelley's self-imposed exile bears only on the poem's idiom of "symbolic refer-

ence," which he still wants to see as politically potent, a "proposal for massive nonviolent resistance" that would "push the reform movement leftwards" even at the risk of revolution (208, 198).

13. Raymond Williams comments on the eruption of this doubleness at the close of the *Defence*, another declaration unpublished in Shelley's lifetime: "The last pages . . . are painful to read. The bearers of a high imaginative skill become suddenly the 'legislators,' at the very moment when they were being forced into practical exile; their description as 'unacknowledged,' which, on the theory, ought only to be a fact to be accepted, carries with it also the felt helplessness of a generation" (*Culture and Society* 47).

14. Shelley sounds this phrase to Ollier on September 6, 1819 and to Peacock on the 21st (*PSL* 2: 117, 120). *The Cenci* was on his mind not only because it was just completed, but also because its drama of violent tyranny and redress by a woman whose voice was denied all authority had a pertinent revolutionary clarity: "I shall go mad. Aye, something must be done; / What, yet I know not . . . something which shall make / The thing that I have suffered but a shadow / In the dread lightning which avenges it; / Brief, rapid, irreversible, destroying / The consequence of what it cannot cure" (3.1.86–91). Although *The Cenci* was written a few months before the atrocity at St. Peter's Field, its publication in 1820 virtually guaranteed to its reception this contemporary reference.

15. Again, I use *keyword* in Raymond Williams's sense. Shelley's manuscript reads *Mask*, perhaps inspired by the report in the *Examiner* referring to the government and its henchmen as "Men in the Brazen Masks of power" (608 [August 22, 1819] 530), or more distantly by Keats's cry at the top of *Endymion* III, "Are then regalities all gilded masks?" (22), the last line of verses that *Blackwood's* "Z" cited as evidence of Keats's "sedition" (3: 524; August 1818). Shelley's pun on the literary-theatrical masque is obvious enough, however; he even refers to the poem as the "Masque of Anarchy" in his letter of November 1819 to Hunt (*PSL* 2: 152), and Hunt's edition uses this word. While Hunt defanged the poem by dropping its historically specifying subtitle and its namings of Eldon and Sidmouth, Shelley's generic designation of a "masque" is not an aesthetic evasion of the more politically demystifying metaphor, *Mask*. It is another version of it: the pun on *Masque* is amplified by the "ghastly masquerade" of government figures (27), a theatrical register that lets Shelley satirize the historical consolidation of the masque in the early seventeenth century as "the artistic property of the rich and powerful, performed as a ritual enactment of the received order of society and as a recommitment to its structures of authority" (Curran, *Annus Mirabilis* 188). Tetreault sees Shelley deploying masque conventions ironically "in order to condemn the values of the corrupt and anarchic court party"; "the dramatic ritual that would ordinarily confirm the monarch's power is turned against him" (201). Even Shelley's mixing of ballad and visionary poetry is a critique, for the dissonance contrasts how the mixture of forms in the Stuart masque (drama, song, dance, spectacle) is meant to reflect "a variety of social forms, each preserving its decorum within the ordered structure of the whole" (Curran ibid.).

16. Unaware of Edwards's work, Goldsmith offers a similar assessment: "the transformation from silence to speech, from death to life . . . ends oppression automatically, as if the dismantling of power on the terrain of political discourse were somehow a *generic* dismantling of domination itself"; "power appears to be insubstantial, a mere language effect that evaporates the moment one brings to an end its monopoly over representation" (256).

17. In "Ode to Liberty," by contrast, Shelley does not rhyme *sword* and *word* or claim their congruity, but exerts the former against the latter: "Ye the oracle have heard: / Lift the victory-flashing sword, / And cut the snaky knots of this foul gordian word" ("the impious name / Of KING"); "The sound has poison in it, 'tis the sperm / Of what makes life foul, cankerous, and abhorred" (216–23). The strong rhymes are *heard/word* and *sword/abhorred*. In both poems, I think, Shelley is recalling the famous stanza from *Childe Harold III* (1816), in which Byron puts *word* and *sword* into a meaningfully dissonant rhyme, attenuated, just as meaningfully, through an intermediary *unheard*: "Could I embody and unbosom now / That which is most within me . . . // . . . into *one* word, / And that one word were Lightning, I would speak; / But as it is, I live and die unheard, / With a most voiceless thought, sheathing it as a sword" (97, his italics). In this flamboyant advertisement of voiceless thoughts, Byron writes the rhymes so that the designator of the innermost self, the sheathed "sword," resists, in both voice and sense, an expressive link to one "word." In *Endymion*, Keats, too, gets semantic value out of the dissonance of *words* and *swords*, even as a couplet frames the rhyme; as in Shelley's "Ode" and *Childe Harold*, the heard melody is the stronger chime of the syllable heard (for him and Byron in the iamb, *unheard*): in the face of Endymion's melancholy silence, Peona feels that any "breathed words / Would all be lost, unheard, and vain as swords / Against the enchased crocodile" (*Endymion* 1.712–14).

18. See Scrivener for a sharp discussion of Shelley's evasion of the question of revolutionary action (209). For a fine analysis of how simile conveys Shelley's visionary imagination, see David Perkins, *Quest* 145. In this poetics of rapid transformation, David Simpson (thinking of *A Defence*'s "libertarian theory of history") discerns a political allegory: "The principle of creativity and liberation from habit is embodied in the unstable qualities of [Shelley's] metaphoric mode as it continues to create new metaphors in an ongoing displacement of figures already formed," and this is a dynamic "Shelley means to relate very directly to the nature of, and prospects for, historical change in society at large" (*Figurings* 117). I think this extension problematic, but what interests me is Shelley's capacity to charge his poetic forms with such appeal.

19. It was "the *discipline* of the sixty or a hundred thousand who assembled on St. Peter's Fields which aroused such alarm"; beyond the frightening size of the demonstration was the "profounder fear evoked by the evidence of the translation of the rabble into a disciplined *class*" (Thompson 681–82).

20. See British Library f. 12ᵛ in Reiman's edition (32); mindful of his caution that this "intermediary" holograph fair copy was "not intended as press copy" (1),

we can still note that Mary Shelley's later press-copy manuscript, which Shelley reviewed and corrected, also lacks a closing quotation mark, though it does have a period and "The End" (Library of Congress f. 3ᵛ [*Mask* 50]); so does Hunt's edition of 1832, perhaps under the added force of pumping up the last line of the Shelleys' manuscripts to climactic capitals: "Yᴇ ᴀʀᴇ ᴍᴀɴʏ —— ᴛʜᴇʏ ᴀʀᴇ ꜰᴇᴡ" (47).

21. My thinking about the ideological function of *The Mask*'s unclosed frame has been helped by Richard A. Burt's shrewd analysis of a similar structure in *The Taming of the Shrew*.

22. See the letter to Hunt in which he enclosed the sonnet (December 23, 1819; *PSL* 2: 167); "England in 1819" was published much later than *The Mask of Anarchy*, appearing for the first time, and with two decades of delay, in Mary Shelley's edition of 1839.

23. Paul de Man reads such syntaxes as a deconstructive contest between semiology and rhetoric: "the same grammatical pattern engenders two meanings that are mutually exclusive" ("Semiology" 9). Though Jerome McGann does not comment on poetic form, he reads a sad ambivalence in the grammatical mood: if Shelley's subjunctive *may* "hopes for a future promise, a glimpse of some far goal in time," it is also "deeply . . . allied to his sense of hopelessness"—"the consciousness out of which Shelley's greatest works were created" (*Romantic Ideology* 112–13).

24. I refer, of course, to the rival strains of Shelley's nineteenth-century cultural processing. For sharp assessments of the canon-culling, as well of the forces at work, see Foot's introduction to *Red Shelley* and Mark Kipperman's essay. *The Cenci* was published in Shelley's lifetime and was part of his notoriety.

25. To John Gisborne, Jan. 26 and March 2, 1822 (*PSL* 2: 388, 394). During his lifetime, Shelley was not widely purchased and even then, not widely appreciated. Of the two poems he regarded as his most aesthetically accomplished, he told Leigh Hunt that he did not expect *Prometheus Unbound* to "sell" (May 26, 1820; 2: 200), and he warned Ollier that *Adonais* "is little adapted to popularity" (June 11 1821; 2: 299). His prediction was accurate. Save radical-press piracies of *Queen Mab*, his poems appeared in small editions that moved slowly (see Ollier's report, *Letters of M. W. Shelley* 1: 401 n); other works (*The Mask, A Defence*) languished until posthumous publication. That only *The Cenci* had an authorized second edition in his lifetime (*SPP* 237) gives credit to Timothy Webb's surmise of some defensiveness in Shelley's rhetoric to publishers and friends (92).

26. To John Gisborne, Jan. 12, 1822 (*PSL* 2: 376). In varying elements and intensities, the tempests involved: Shelley's exasperation with Ollier for not promoting or, in the case of *Adonais* and *A Defence*, even publishing his work; his feeling of futility over the slender notice of works for which he had high expectation of appreciation by the right readers (in particular, *Adonais*, despite his hunch that it would not sell well); rumors circulated in Italy in the summer of 1821 about Claire Clairmont's having given birth to a child by Shelley; Claire's desperate petitions to Shelley in 1821–22 to "intercede" with Byron for access to her daughter by him, whom he had sequestered in a convent (and Allegra's death by typhus and

Claire's grief in the spring of 1822); Mary Shelley's ill health in the winter of 1821–22, her difficult pregnancy, her physical discomfort at Lerici, and her subsequent, nearly fatal miscarriage in June 1822; Shelley's own health problems and his painfully evolving alienation from Mary; his disappointment over Hunt's delayed sailing to Italy because of bad weather and his wife's ill health (he arrived about eight months later than planned, just before Shelley's death), coupled with irritation over Hunt's apparent expectation that Byron and Shelley would meet all his expenses; and his deep ambivalence about Byron (admiration, jealousy over his success, disapproval of his actions with Claire and Allegra, a growing sense of "detested intimacy" [*PSL* 2: 399]). Newman Ivey White, though with a bias against Mary Shelley's "occasional moodiness and self-absorption" (!) (2: 363), gives a good account of the last eight months of Shelley's life (2: 332–69). The best and brightest reading of these lyrics in this complicated social and ideological context is Keach's chapter in *Shelley's Style*, which assesses the historical and biographical pressures, including "sexual, domestic and personal literary perturbations" (234), on their composition. All references to Keach in this section are to this chapter, to which my discussion is indebted.

27. Hereafter, I refer to these poems by short titles: "The Invitation," "The Recollection," "With a Guitar," "The keen stars," "The Magnetic Lady," "The Serpent," and "Lines." Judith Chernaik details their dating (178–79 n. 1) as does White (2: 343–46, 364). Quotations of "The Magnetic Lady" (not in *SPP*) follow Chernaik 257–59.

28. Although some editions (Chernaik, Reiman and Powers) summarize or quote the inscriptions in footnotes, none that I know prints a composite text. Aside from Keach and Chernaik book-length studies tend to slight even the poems, or treat them briefly and only biographically. Curran's massive report in *The English Romantic Poets: A Review of Research and Criticism* (1985) lists very few items, and later studies do not compensate. Jerrold E. Hogle's *Shelley's Process* neglects these poems, as does Tetreault's study of "Shelley and Literary Form" (his last chapter is promisingly titled "'Last' Poems," but as his quotation marks indicate, these are not the very last, but the much-discussed *Hellas* and *The Triumph of Life*). Though with valuable attention to the manuscripts, Chernaik's attention is mostly thematic, reading the poems as expressions of Shelley's effort—failing his "apocalyptic hope, the ambition to change the world" (169)—to cherish intimate friendship and moments of happiness amidst "the deepening pessimism of his vision of life" (163). Seeing them less as successful retreats than refigurings of this pessimism, McGann ("Secrets") studies "the shift in the 1822 poetry away from the earlier Idealism," with some fine readings of the relevant moments in the late lyrics (31–34).

29. On the one hand, Derrida suggests, reading is scripted to recognize what is already complete and self-sufficient in writing: it is a supplement that "is a surplus, a plenitude enriching another plenitude. . . . It cumulates and accumulates presence"; on the other hand, its status as supplement emends an absence or

deficiency wherein the reading "adds only to replace." The two senses are "inseparable" (*Grammatology* 144–45).

30. "Magnetic" means "hypnotic"; not only Jane Williams but also Mary Shelley and Medwin experimented with hypnotizing Shelley to relieve his intense physical pain; for relevant anecdotes, see Medwin's "Memoir" (*Athenæum* 250 [August 11, 1832]: 522).

31. Mary Shelley's first edition of the 1839 *Poetical Works*, following Medwin's redactions for *Athenæum* in 1832, erases the name *Jane* from all these poems, most likely out of a sense of decorum (see n. 36 below), but also, I think, her own embarrassment. Line 42 of "The Magnetic Lady" replaces *Jane* with *pain*, to read: "'Twould kill me what would cure my pain" (4: 162; cf. *Athenæum* 250: 523), and the last line of "With a Guitar" becomes "For our beloved friend alone" (4: 164; cf. *Athenæum* 260: 680). When *Fraser's* printed the first stanza (1–42) as "TO A. B., WITH A GUITAR," it footnoted it thus: "A. B., the lady to whom these agreeable and melodious verses are addressed, is still alive. We therefore withhold her name" (7 [January 1833]: 79). Under this protocol, "The keen stars" (which Medwin retitled from "To Jane" to "An Ariette for Music. To a Lady Singing to her Accompaniment on the Guitar") was seriously marred by a cancellation of its first six, *Jane*-rhymed lines (*Poetical Works* 4: 165; cf. *Athenæum* 264: 746).

32. The "melancholy old song" was the poem beginning "Swifter far than summer's flight." Jane Williams must have given Mary Shelley this text for *Posthumous Poems*, where, titled "A Lament" (148), it appears just before "The Pine Forest" (the first, single-text version of "To Jane. The Invitation" and "To Jane. The Recollection"; see n. 36, below); cf. 1839 *Poetical Works* 4: 135.

33. Jones dates the note to Jane "*c.* 18 June 1822" (*Letters* 2: 437); I follow the text in Chernaik 260 and *SPP* 451. The apt description of the ideal reader is Gerald Prince's (9).

34. I'm indebted to Willard Spiegelman for calling my attention to this syntax (165); where he sees Shelley hedging with ambiguity, however, I see a motivated doubleness of meaning that amounts to a pun.

35. Trelawny reports Shelley's flirtation with drowning in the Arno late in 1821 (62), and recalls that by early 1822, the "careless, not to say impatient way in which the Poet bore his burden of life, caused a vague dread amongst his family and friends that he might lose or cast it away at any moment" (74). By mid June (a few weeks before his death), Shelley was asking him to procure a poison compound, adding, "I would give any price for this medicine . . . from the desire of avoiding needless suffering. I need not tell you I have no intention of suicide at present,—but I confess it would be a comfort to me to hold in my possession that golden key to the chamber of perpetual rest" (*PSL* 2: 433).

36. Not having seen "the exquisitely written out" fair copies of the two poems that Shelley inscribed and gave to Jane Williams (Chernaik 266), Mary Shelley based her slightly truncated single text (149–53), which she titled "The Pine Forest / of the Cascine, Near Pisa," on an earlier draft that blends seamlessly from

the invitation, "Dearest, best and brightest, / Come away," to the invocation to "Memory" to "trace / The epitaph of glory fled," to the recollection itself: "We wandered to the Pine Forest." For accounts of the manuscripts, see Chernaik, and Reiman and Powers, *SPP* 443. Mary Shelley retains the text of 1824 for the first edition of the 1839 *Poetical Works* (4: 174–78), and it is telling that even at this late date, her "Note on Poems of 1822" is silent about the details of the poem's historical origin, merely commenting that in 1822 "Spring sprang up early, and with extreme beauty" (227).

37. "――'s" is Chernaik's correct reading of the manuscript, not "S   's" or "S[helley]'s" as in *SPP*. In response to my query about the discrepancy between Chernaik and *SPP*, Donald Reiman admitted the error and indicated that the second edition, forthcoming and now coedited with Neil Fraistat, will correct it.

38. The excursion into the forest, near Pisa, with Mary and Jane on February 2, was first commemorated by Shelley in a single poem (the basis for the 1824 text), which he reworked during the spring, eventually breaking it into the two separately titled poems that he gave to Jane (Holmes 700–701). I follow Holmes (700) and Keach (208) in taking the date subtitled in "The Recollection," "Feb. 2, 1822," as the date of the walk; this is also the evidence of Mary Shelley's journal, where the entry for "Saturday [Feb.] 2nd" reads: "Go through the Pine Forest to the sea with Shelley and Jane" (393); there is no like entry elsewhere. Reiman and Powers (*SPP* 443 n. 7) and White (2: 343) date the walk a month earlier, without saying on what basis. Even with the February date, however, "The Invitation" remains an invitation after the fact.

39. Keach remarks that Wordsworthian elegy has replaced the Herrickian *carpe diem* of "The Invitation" as the dominant allusive mode (212).

40. My information about the manuscript situation draws on Reiman's variorum edition, *Shelley's "The Triumph of Life,"* 175 and 244–48, and his splendid edition of Shelley's holograph draft (whose plates contain "To Jane" and "Lines"); my parenthetical citations refer to the folio page in the Bodleian MS.

41. Keach gives subtle attention to these ambiguities: the verse allows the sense both that Rousseau's words "gave expression to sufferings he had actually lived through" and "that he, and others, eventually lived through sufferings brought about by, or first expressed theoretically and fictively in, his writing. Words can be 'seeds of misery' both because they are sown by and because they sow suffering" (201).

42. This is the Bodleian manuscript; its variants are given by Chernaik 260–61.

43. See Reiman's transcription (in *Shelley's "Triumph"* 245) of "the text as it appears in the draft" of the Bodleian manuscript (56r); this shows no punctuation other than commas until the stanza's final line: "Its own." (33v).

44. This value of a "sensual intensity" in words, "in contrast to their logical meaning," would be set forth by Henry Lanz in the 1930s: whereas in "ordinary speech, we entirely *forget* about the physical existence of words as signs or

sounds"—they "become transparent . . . fully resolved into what they mean"—
"Poetry is called upon to save the physical element of words and bring it to our
attention in the name of art. . . . Thus sound, the music of words, acquires an
independent artistic value which is largely indifferent to the meaning or sense of
it" (172). This is also Sigurd Burckhardt's theory: "the nature and primary function of the most important poetic devices—especially rhyme, meter, and metaphor—is to release words in some measure from their bondage to meaning, their
purely referential role"; to accomplish this "position of creative sovereignty over
matter," a poet must try to "drive a wedge between words and their meanings,
lessen as much as possible the designatory force and thereby inhibit our all too
ready flight from them to the things they point to" (24). Although I have been
arguing that poetic devices bear semantic value, and that Shelley (and other Romantics) are alert to this resource, Lanz and Burckhardt suggest how Shelley's
attraction to communication in which words are not the instruments points his art
toward a poetics of form that retreats from semantic and social referentiality. At
the same time, his retreat from such reference is also, potentially, a retreat from its
strictures into the kind of radical semiotics theorized by Julia Kristeva in *Revolution in Poetic Language*: "poetic language . . . attacks not only denotation (the positing of the object) but meaning (the positing of the enunciating subject) as well"
(58).

45. The latest stage of the manuscript, discerned by G. M. Matthews ("Shelley and Jane Williams" 40–43) and accepted by Reiman (Bodleian ed. 337, and
Shelley's "Triumph," the source of my textual information [175]), involves six lines
written into a space at the top of the page as a new beginning (1–6 in *SPP*: "Bright
wanderer, fair coquette of Heaven . . ."). Until Matthews, this sestet had been
printed as a separate fragment. See Keach's fine assessment of Shelley's revision
(229–30).

46. For a subtle analysis of the various elements of form that shape this emergence, and one to which I am indebted, see, again, Keach 231–32.

47. As his many remarks about *Hyperion* indicate, Shelley was reading Keats's
1820 volume in 1821–22 and apparently on the *Don Juan* just before the fatal
storm (Trelawny identified Shelley's corpse on the evidence of this volume in his
jacket pocket, doubled back, as if he had been reading it and then hastily thrust it
in [Trelawny 123]).

48. Chernaik's study of the manuscript convinces her that the last line was first
written as "Destroying life not peace," then "Seeking life alone," then "Seeking
life not peace" (or perhaps "Seeking life alone not peace," which does scan in the
dominant iambic tetrameter). She reports other editors' speculations (276 n. 58)
as do Reiman and Powers (*SPP* 453 n. 7); Reiman gives a full, and to me persua-
sive, analysis of the evidence in "The Biographical Problem" (*Romantic Texts* 296–
97). My sense from studying the photofacsimile and his transcription in *Bodleian
Shelley* (206–7) is that while Shelley crossed out "Destroy" from "Destroying,"
that he left "ing" indicates a desire for another (perhaps less absolute) verb.
Both the colon after "<u>peace</u>" (I follow Reiman's reading, rather than Cher-

naik's claim that the manuscript shows a period and "an unmistakable final quatrain" [276]) and the new line on which "Seeking" is written suggest to me, furthermore, that Shelley was not applying this verb in place of "Destroying" but
plotting a transition from whatever other verb would replace "Destroying" to a
continued "Seeking" (its object not yet indicated). I wonder, therefore, whether
the top of the next page, 37^r—

> The ~~days are flying fast away~~
> <u>Pleasure</u>

—may be a brief continuation. The first line retains the iambic tetrameter of the
previous "Lines," and if it does follow the colon at "<u>not peace,</u>" it may elaborate
thereby "the regret" that is associated with "pleasure." The similar scriptive emphasis given to "<u>Pleasure</u>" is a further link, even as the latter heads, and perhaps
demands, a new turn of verse: a set of rhyming dimeter lines that begin, "The
hours are flying / And joys are dying / And hope is sighing"—accelerating poetic
form itself into a sensation of rapid vanishing. Reiman is right that the fragmentary state of the manuscript makes all judgments speculative, but in a correspondence to me (September 10, 1993), he said he was fascinated by the possibility I
suggest here.

49. It is a poignancy of Mary Shelley's efforts to redraw the circuit of communication that her edition of Shelley's letters (in 1840) places this actual last
letter to Jane second-to-last and closes with the one that he wrote earlier the same
day to her—with the implication that his last written words were addressed to
his "Ever, dearest Mary"; see her edition, *Essays, Letters* 2: 246–48; cf. *PSL* 2:
443–45.

Afterword

1. In this scheme, Sprinker elaborates, the "material existence" of ideology
always encompasses aesthetic material, and even though aesthetic materiality "will
continue to exist within ideological practice," the formal structure of the latter
must "set aside the materiality of the work of art" as an object of primary critical
inquiry (272).

2. In the "Conclusion" of *Archaeology*, Foucault addresses a self-ventrilo-
quized question about the place of individual freedom and discursive practice:
"The positivities that I have tried to establish must not be understood as a set of
determinations imposed from the outside on the thought of individuals, or inhabiting it from the inside, in advance as it were; they constitute rather the set of
conditions in accordance with which a practice is exercised, in accordance with
which that practice gives rise to partially or totally new statements, and in accordance with which it can be modified. These positivities are not so much limitations
imposed on the initiative of subjects as the field in which that initiative is articulated (without, however, constituting its centre), rules that it puts into operation
(without it having invented or formulated them), relations that provide it with a

support (without it being either their final result or their point of convergence). It is an attempt to reveal discursive practices in their complexity and density" (208–9).

3. The uniqueness of any literary work, Attridge argues in behalf of this concept, is inseparable from its form, conceived not as a static, self-sufficient object, but "understood as its singular performance of linguistic and cultural norms"— a "performative response" called forth by such formal properties as "sound-patterns, rhythm, syntactic variation, metaphorical elaboration, narrative construction" (247). In this sense, Attridge contends *"form is always already meaning*; as an act of signification a literary work is meaning in motion, and there is no moment, not even a theoretical one, at which it is possible to isolate a purely formal property" (247, his emphasis).

✥ Works Cited

Abrams, M. H. "Coleridge, Baudelaire, and Modernist Poetics" (1966). In *Correspondent Breeze*, pp. 109–44.
——. *The Correspondent Breeze: Essays on English Romanticism*. New York: Norton, 1984.
——. *Natural Supernaturalism: Tradition and Revolution in Romantic Literature*. New York: Norton, 1971.
——. *The Mirror and the Lamp: Romantic Theory and the Critical Tradition*. 1953; New York: Norton, 1958.
——. "Structure and Style in the Greater Romantic Lyric" (1965). In *Correspondent Breeze*, pp. 76–108.
——. "Wordsworth and Coleridge on Diction and Figures" (1952). In *Correspondent Breeze*, pp. 3–24.
Adams, Hazard. "Revisiting Reynold's [sic] *Discourses* and Blake's Annotations." In Robert N. Essick and Donald Pearce, eds., *Blake in His Time*, pp. 128–44. Bloomington: Indiana University Press, 1978.
Addison, Catherine. "From Literal to Figurative: An Introduction to the Study of Simile." *College English* 55 (1993): 403–19.
Addison, Joseph. *The Works of Joseph Addison*. 3 vols. New York: Harper, 1845.
Allott, Miriam, ed. *The Poems of Keats*. London and New York: Longman, 1970.
Althusser, Louis. "Ideology and Ideological State Apparatuses" (1969). In *Lenin and Philosophy, and Other Essays*, pp. 121–73. London: New Left Books, 1971.
——. "A Letter on Art in Reply to André Daspre" (1966). In *Lenin*, pp. 203–8.
Andrews, Bruce. "Poetry as Explanation, Poetry as Praxis." In Charles Bernstein, ed., *The Politics of Poetic Form: Poetry and Public Policy*, pp. 23–43. New York: Roof, 1990.
Antijacobin Review 46 (March 1814): 209–37. Review of *The Bride of Abydos* and *The Corsair*.
Arac, Jonathan. "Wordsworth's Revisions and Wordsworthian Revisionism: Genetic Reflections." Paper presented at the MLA Convention, New York, 1981.

Aristotle. *The "Art" of Rhetoric.* Trans. John Henry Freese (1926). Cambridge, Mass.: Harvard University Press, 1959.

Arnold, Matthew. "Byron" (Preface to *Poetry of Byron,* 1881; *Essays in Criticism, Second Series,* 1895). In *Prose Works* 9 (1973): 217–37.

———. *The Complete Prose Works of Matthew Arnold.* Ed. R. H. Super. 11 vols. Ann Arbor: University of Michigan Press, 1973.

———. "The Function of Criticism at the Present Time" (1864; *Essays in Criticism,* 1865). In *Prose Works* 3 (1962): 258–85.

———. *The Letters of Matthew Arnold to Arthur Hugh Clough.* Ed. Henry Foster Lowry. London and New York: Oxford University Press / Henry Milford, 1932.

———. Preface, *Poems of Wordsworth,* pp. v–xxvi. London: Macmillan, 1879.

———. "The Study of Poetry" (1880; *Essays in Criticism, Second Series,* 1888). In *Prose Works* 9 (1973): 161–88.

The Athenæum: Journal of English and Foreign Literature, Science, and the Fine Arts 262 (November 3, 1832): 705–7. Review of *The Masque of Anarchy.*

———. 267 (December 8, 1832): 794. "Original Papers: Lines Written during the Castlereagh Administration. By the Late Percy Bysshe Shelley."

Attridge, Derek. "Literary Form and the Demands of Politics." In George Levine, ed., *Aesthetics and Ideology,* pp. 243–63.

———. *Peculiar Language: Literature as Difference from the Renaissance to James Joyce.* Ithaca: Cornell University Press, 1988.

———. *The Rhythms of English Poetry.* London and New York: Longman, 1982.

Auden, W. H. "*Don Juan.*" In *The Dyer's Hand and Other Essays,* pp. 386–406. 1948; New York: Random House, 1962.

Austen, Jane. *Jane Austen's Letters to her sister Cassandra and others.* Ed. R. W. Chapman. 2 vols. Oxford: Clarendon Press, 1932.

Averill, James H. *Wordsworth and the Poetry of Human Suffering.* Ithaca: Cornell University Press, 1980.

Bahti, Timothy. "Ambiguity and Indeterminacy: The Juncture." *Comparative Literature* 38 (1986): 209–23.

Baker, Jeffrey. "Pride and Prejudice." *The Wordsworth Circle* 13 (1982): 79–86.

Bakhtin, M. M. "Discourse in the Novel" (1934–35). Trans. Caryl Emerson and Michael Holquist. In Michael Holquist, ed., *The Dialogic Imagination: Four Essays by M. M. Bakhtin,* pp. 259–422. Austin: University of Texas Press, 1981.

[———] / Medvedev, P. N. *The Formal Method in Literary Scholarship: A Critical Introduction to Sociological Poetics* (1928). Trans. Albert J. Wehrle. Baltimore: Johns Hopkins University Press, 1978.

Balibar, Etienne, and Pierre Macherey. "On Literature as an Ideological Form: Some Marxist Propositions." Trans. Ian McLeod, John Whitehead, and Ann Wordsworth. *Oxford Literary Review* 3 (1978): 4–12.

Barnard, John. *John Keats.* Cambridge, Eng.: Cambridge University Press, 1987.

Barthes, Roland. "From Work to Text." In *Image-Music-Text,* pp. 155–64.

———. *Image-Music-Text*. London: Fontana / Glasgow: Collins, 1977.

———. "La mort de l'auteur" (1968). Trans. Stephen Heath as "The Death of the Author." In *Image-Music-Text*, pp. 142–48.

———. "Myth Today" (Paris, 1957). Trans. Annette Lavers. In *Mythologies*, pp. 109–59. New York: Hill and Wang, 1972.

———. *Roland Barthes by Roland Barthes*. Trans. Richard Howard. New York: Hill and Wang, 1977.

———. "Théorie du Texte" (Paris, 1968–75). Trans. Ian McLeod as "The Theory of the Text." In Robert Young, ed., *Untying the Text: A Post-Structuralist Reader*, pp. 31–45. Boston and London: Routledge and Kegan Paul, 1981.

Bate, Walter Jackson. *John Keats*. Cambridge, Mass.: Harvard University Press, 1963.

———. *The Stylistic Development of Keats*. New York: MLA, 1945.

Behrendt, Stephen C. *Shelley and His Audiences*. Lincoln: University of Nebraska Press, 1989.

Bell, Clive. *Art*. London: Chatto and Windus, 1914. New ed., 1915.

Belsey, Catherine. *Critical Practice*. London and New York: Methuen, 1980.

Bennett, Tony. *Formalism and Marxism*. London and New York: Methuen, 1979.

Bentley, G. E., Jr. *William Blake: The Critical Heritage*. London and Boston: Routledge and Kegan Paul, 1975.

Blackwood's Edinburgh Magazine 3 (August 1818): 519–24. "On the Cockney School of Poetry. No IV." Signed "Z."

Blair, Hugh. *Lectures on Rhetoric and Belles Lettres* (1783). Ed. Harold F. Harding. 2 vols. Carbondale: Southern Illinois University Press, 1965.

Blake, William. *The Complete Poetry and Prose of William Blake*. Ed. David V. Erdman. Garden City, N.Y.: Anchor / Doubleday, 1982.

———. *The Illuminated Blake*. Annotated by David V. Erdman. Garden City, N.Y.: Anchor / Doubleday, 1974.

B[lake], W[illiam]. *Poetical Sketches* (1783). Facsimile reprint. London: Noel Douglas Replicas, 1926.

Bloom, Harold. *The Anxiety of Influence: A Theory of Poetry*. New York: Oxford University Press, 1973.

———. *Blake's Apocalypse*. Garden City, N.Y.: Doubleday, 1963.

———. "The Breaking of Form." In *Deconstruction and Criticism*, pp. 1–37. New York: Seabury Press, 1979.

Bourdieu, Pierre. "Censorship and the Imposition of Form" (1975; 1988). In *Language and Symbolic Power*, pp. 137–59. Ed. John B. Thompson. Trans. Gino Raymond and Matthew Adamson. Cambridge, Eng.: Polity Press, 1991.

———. "The Production and Reproduction of Legitimate Language" (1980; 1982). In *Language and Symbolic Power*, pp. 43–65.

Bové, Paul A. *Destructive Poetics: Heidegger and Modern American Poetry*. New York: Columbia University Press, 1980.

———. "Variations on Authority: Some Deconstructive Transformations of the

New Criticism." In Jonathan Arac, Wlad Godzich, and Wallace Martin, eds., *The Yale Critics: Deconstruction in America*, pp. 3–19. Minneapolis: University of Minnesota Press, 1983.

Bowers, Fredson. "Current Theories of Copy-Text, with an Illustration from Dryden." *Modern Philology* 48 (1950): 12–20.

Bradley, A. C. "Poetry for Poetry's Sake" (1901). In *Oxford Lectures on Poetry*, pp. 3–27. London: Macmillan, 1920.

Breslin, James E. B. *From Modern to Contemporary: American Poetry, 1945–1965*. Chicago: University of Chicago Press, 1983.

Brinkley, Roberta Florence, ed. *Coleridge on the Seventeenth Century*. Durham: Duke University Press, 1955.

British Critic 14 (October 1799): 364–69. Review of *Lyrical Ballads* (1798).

British Review 5 (February 1814): 507–11. Review of *The Corsair*.

Brogan, Jacqueline Vaught. *Stevens and Simile: A Theory of Language*. Princeton: Princeton University Press, 1986.

Brooks, Cleanth. "The Artistry of Keats: A Modern Tribute." In Clarence D. Thorpe, Carlos Baker, and Bennett Weaver, eds., *The Major English Romantic Poets*, pp. 246–51.

———. "Coleridge as a Metaphysical Poet." In David Thorburn and Geoffrey Hartman, eds., *Romanticism: Vistas, Instances, Continuities*, pp. 134–54. Ithaca: Cornell University Press, 1973.

———. "Current Critical Theory and the Period Course." *CEA Critic* 7.7 (October 1950) 1, 5, and 6 (cols. 3–4).

———. "The Formalist Critic." *Kenyon Review* 13 (1951): 72–81.

———. "Implications of an Organic Theory of Poetry." In Meyer H. Abrams, ed., *Literature and Belief: English Institute Essays, 1957*, pp. 53–79. New York: Columbia University Press, 1958.

———. "Irony and 'Ironic' Poetry." *College English* 9 (February 1948): 231–37.

———. *Modern Poetry and The Tradition*. New York and Oxford: Oxford University Press, 1965.

———. *The Well Wrought Urn: Studies in the Structure of Poetry*. 1947; New York: Harcourt Brace Jovanovich, 1975.

Burckhardt, Sigurd. "The Poet as Fool and Priest" (1956). In *Shakespearean Meanings*, pp. 22–46. Princeton: Princeton University Press, 1968.

Burdett, Osbert. *William Blake*. London: Macmillan, 1926.

Burke, Edmund. *A Philosophical Enquiry into the Origin of Our Ideas of the Sublime and Beautiful*. 1757; 5th ed. London: J. Dodsley, 1767.

Burt, Richard A. "Charisma, Coercion, and Comic Form in *The Taming of the Shrew*." *Criticism* 26 (1984): 295–311.

Bush, Douglas, ed. *Selected Poems and Letters by John Keats*. Boston: Houghton Mifflin, 1959.

Byron, George Gordon, Lord. *Byron's Letters and Journals*. Ed. Leslie A. Marchand. 12 vols. Cambridge, Mass.: Harvard University Press, 1973–82.

———. *The Complete Poetical Works*. Ed. Jerome J. McGann. 7 vols. Oxford: Clarendon Press, 1980–91.

Chase, Cynthia. "The Accidents of Disfiguration: Limits to Literal and Figurative Reading of Wordsworth's 'Books'" (1979). In *Decomposing Figures: Rhetorical Readings in the Romantic Tradition*, pp. 13–31. Baltimore: Johns Hopkins University Press, 1986.

Chernaik, Judith. *The Lyrics of Shelley*. Cleveland: Case Western Reserve University Press, 1972.

Christensen, Jerome. *Coleridge's Blessed Machine of Language*. Ithaca: Cornell University Press, 1981.

———. *Lord Byron's Strength: Romantic Writing and Commercial Society*. Baltimore: Johns Hopkins University Press, 1993.

Christian Observer 13 (April 1814): 245–57. Review of *The Corsair*.

Cicero. *De Oratore*. Trans. H. Rackham. Cambridge, Mass.: Harvard University Press, 1947.

Coleridge, Samuel Taylor. *Aids to Reflection* (1825). Ed. John Beer. Princeton: Princeton University Press, 1993.

———. *Biographia Literaria* (1817). Ed. James Engell and W. Jackson Bate. 2 vols. Princeton: Princeton University Press, 1983.

———. *Coleridge's Miscellaneous Criticism*. Ed. Thomas Middleton Raysor. London: Constable, 1936.

———. *Collected Letters of Samuel Taylor Coleridge*. Ed. Earl Leslie Griggs. 6 vols. Oxford: Clarendon Press, 1956–71.

———. *The Friend*. Ed. Barbara E. Rooke. 2 vols. Princeton: Princeton University Press; London: Routledge and Kegan Paul, 1969.

———. *Lectures 1808–1819 On Literature*. Ed. R. A. Foakes. 2 vols. Princeton: Princeton University Press, 1987.

———. *The Notebooks of Samuel Taylor Coleridge*. Ed. Kathleen Coburn. 3 vols. Vols. 1 and 2, New York: Bollingen / Pantheon, 1957, 1961. Vol. 3, Princeton: Princeton / Bollingen, 1973.

———. *On the Constitution of the Church and State*. Ed. John Colmer. Princeton: Princeton University Press, 1976.

———. *The Poems of Samuel Taylor Coleridge*. Ed. E. H. Coleridge. 1912; London: Oxford University Press, 1960.

———. "On the Principles of Genial Criticism," Essay Third (1814). In J. Shawcross, ed. *"Biographia Literaria" by S. T. Coleridge, With his Aesthetical Essays*. 2 vols. London: Oxford University Press, 1907. 2: 228–43.

———. "On the Principles of Method," *The Friend* (1818). In *The Friend*, ed. Rooke 1: 448–57.

———. *The Statesman's Manual*. In *Lay Sermons*. Ed. R. J. White. Princeton: Princeton University Press, 1972.

———. *Table Talk (Recorded by Henry Nelson Coleridge and John Taylor Coleridge)*. Ed. Carl Woodring. 2 vols. Princeton: Princeton University Press, 1990.

Colie, Rosalie. "*Mel* and *Sal*: Some Problems in Sonnet-Theory." In *Shakespeare's Living Art*, pp. 68–134. Princeton: Princeton University Press, 1974.

Colvin, Sidney. *John Keats: His Life and Poetry, His Friends, Critics, and After-Fame.* New York: Charles Scribner's Sons, 1917.

[Conder, Josiah]. Review of Keats's *Poems* (1817). *Eclectic Review*, 2d ser. 8 (September 1817): 267–75. Attribution by Reiman, *Romantics Reviewed* C 1: 329.

Cook, Carol. "Unbodied Figures of Desire." *Theatre Journal* 38 (March 1986): 34–52.

Cook, Jon. "Paul de Man and Imaginative Consolation in *The Prelude*." In Nigel Wood, ed., *Theory in Practice: "The Prelude*," pp. 27–59.

Cox, Sidney. *A Swinger of Birches: A Portrait of Robert Frost.* New York: New York University Press, 1957.

Crane, R. S. *The Languages of Criticism and the Structure of Poetry.* Toronto: University of Toronto Press, 1953.

[Croker, John Wilson]. Review of *Endymion. Quarterly Review* 19 (April 1818): 204–8; pub. September. Attribution by Reiman, *Romantics Reviewed* C 2: 767.

Culler, Jonathan. "Apostrophe" (1977). In *Pursuit*, pp. 135–54.

———. "Jakobson's Poetic Analyses." In *Structuralist Poetics: Structuralism, Linguistics, and the Study of Literature*, pp. 55–74. Ithaca: Cornell University Press, 1975.

———. "Meaning and Iterability." In *On Deconstruction*, pp. 110–34.

———. "The Mirror Stage." In Lawrence Lipking, ed., *High Romantic Argument: Essays for M. H. Abrams*, pp. 149–63. Ithaca: Cornell University Press, 1981.

———. *On Deconstruction: Theory and Criticism after Structuralism.* Ithaca: Cornell University Press, 1982.

———. *The Pursuit of Signs: Semiotics, Literature, Deconstruction.* Ithaca: Cornell University Press, 1981.

———. "Story and Discourse in the Analysis of Narrative." In *Pursuit*, pp. 169–87.

Cunningham, J. V. "The Problem of Form." In *The Collected Essays of J. V. Cunningham*, pp. 247–50. Chicago: Swallow Press, 1976.

Curran, Stuart. "Percy Bysshe Shelley." In Frank Jordan, ed., *The English Romantic Poets: A Review of Research and Criticism*, 4th ed., pp. 593–663. New York: MLA, 1985.

———. *Poetic Form and British Romanticism.* New York: Oxford University Press, 1986.

———. *Shelley's Annus Mirabilis: The Maturing of an Epic Vision.* San Marino, Calif.: Huntington Library, 1975.

Damon, S. Foster. *A Blake Dictionary: The Ideas and Symbols of William Blake.* 1965; New York: E. P. Dutton, 1971.

Dante Alighieri. *Inferno.* Trans. John D. Sinclair (1939). New York: Oxford University Press, 1980.

Darbishire, Helen. *The Poet Wordsworth: The Clark Lectures, Trinity College, Cambridge, 1949.* Oxford: Clarendon Press, 1950.

Davis, Robert Con and Ronald Schleifer. *Contemporary Literary Criticism: Literary and Cultural Studies.* 2nd ed. New York: Longman, 1989.

De Luca, Vincent Arthur. *Words of Eternity: Blake and the Poetics of the Sublime.* Princeton: Princeton University Press, 1991.

de Man, Paul. "Aesthetic Formalization: Kleist's *Über das Marionettentheater.*" In *Rhetoric of Romanticism*, pp. 263–90.

————. *Allegories of Reading: Figural Language in Rousseau, Nietzsche, Rilke, and Proust.* New Haven: Yale University Press, 1979.

————. "Anthropomorphism and Trope in the Lyric." In *Rhetoric of Romanticism*, pp. 239–62.

————. "Autobiography As De-Facement" (1979). In *Rhetoric of Romanticism*, pp. 67–81.

————. *Blindness and Insight: Essays in the Rhetoric of Contemporary Criticism* (1971). 2nd ed. Minneapolis: University of Minnesota Press, 1983.

————. "The Dead-End of Formalist Criticism." In *Blindness*, pp. 229–45.

————. "Form and Intent in the American New Criticism." In *Blindness*, pp. 20–35.

————. "Intentional Structure of the Romantic Nature Image" (1960; trans. 1968). In *Rhetoric of Romanticism*, pp. 1–17.

————. "Literary History and Literary Modernity." In *Blindness*, pp. 142–65.

————. Preface to *Rhetoric of Romanticism* (1983), pp. vii–ix.

————. "The Resistance to Theory." *Yale French Studies* 63 (1982): 3–20.

————. *The Rhetoric of Romanticism.* New York: Columbia University Press, 1984.

————. "The Rhetoric of Temporality" (1969). In *Blindness*, 2nd ed., pp. 187–228.

————. "Semiology and Rhetoric." In *Allegories*, pp. 3–19.

————, ed. *John Keats: Selected Poetry.* New York: New American Library, 1966.

Demetrius. *On Style.* Ed. and trans. W. Rhys Roberts. Cambridge: University Press, 1902.

Dennis, John. *The Critical Works of John Dennis.* Ed. Edward Niles Hooker. 2 vols. Baltimore, Md.: Johns Hopkins University Press, 1939–43.

————. "Of Prosody" (1722). In *Critical Works* 2: 236–40.

————. "Preface to *Britannia Triumphans*" (1704). In *Critical Works* 1: 374–79.

————. "Preface to *The Monument*" (1702). In *Critical Works* 1: 296–98.

De Quincey, Thomas. "Samuel Taylor Coleridge." *Tait's Edinburgh Magazine* 1 (September 1834); rpt. *Recollections of the Lakes and the Lake Poets*, pp. 33–62. Ed. David Wright. Harmondsworth, Eng.: Penguin Books, 1970.

Derrida, Jacques. "Différance" (1968). Trans. David B. Allison. In *Speech and Phenomena and Other Essays on Husserl's Theory of Signs*, pp. 129–60. Evanston: Northwestern University Press, 1973.

————. *Of Grammatology* (1967). Trans. Gayatri Chakravorty Spivak. Baltimore: Johns Hopkins University Press, 1974.

————. "White Mythology: Metaphor in the Text of Philosophy" (1971). Trans. F. C. T. Moore. *NLH* 6 (1974): 5–74.

de Selincourt, Ernest. "Introduction" to Wordsworth's *Prelude* (1926). See Wordsworth, *"The Prelude or Growth of a Poet's Mind,"* ed. de Selincourt and Darbishire, pp. xix–lxxiv.

Dickens, Charles. *Great Expectations.* With a new preface by Bernard Shaw. Edinburgh: Limited Editions Club, 1937.

Dickstein, Morris. *Keats and His Poetry.* Chicago: University of Chicago Press, 1971.

Donne, John. *John Donne, The Complete English Poems.* Ed. A. J. Smith. Harmondsworth, Eng.: Penguin, 1971.

Dryden, John. *Of Dramatick Poesie. An Essay* (1668). In *Works* 17, ed. Samuel Holt Monk (1971), pp. 1–81.

———. "To the Right Honourable Roger Earl of Orrery" (Dedicatory epistle to *The Rival Ladies,* 1664). In *Works* 8, ed. John Harrington Smith and Dougald MacMillan (1967), pp. 95–102.

———. *The Works of John Dryden.* General ed. H. T. Swedenberg, Jr. 19 vols. Berkeley: University of California Press, 1961–79.

Eagleton, Terry. *Criticism and Ideology: A Study in Marxist Literary Theory.* 1976; London: Verso, 1978.

———. "The Idealism of American Criticism." *New Left Review* (1981); rpt. *Against the Grain: Essays, 1975–1985.* London: Verso, 1986, pp. 49–64.

———. "Ideology and Literary Form." In *Criticism and Ideology,* pp. 102–61.

———. *The Ideology of the Aesthetic.* London: Basil Blackwell, 1990.

———. *Literary Theory: An Introduction.* Minneapolis: University of Minnesota Press, 1983.

———. *Marxism and Literary Criticism.* Berkeley: University of California Press, 1976.

———. "Marxism and Aesthetic Value." In *Criticism and Ideology,* pp. 162–87.

———. *William Shakespeare.* Oxford: Basil Blackwell, 1986.

Easthope, Antony. *Poetry as Discourse.* London and New York: Methuen, 1983.

Eaves, Morris. *William Blake's Theory of Art.* Princeton: Princeton University Press, 1982.

Eclectic Review, 2d ser. 1 (April 1814): 416–26. Review of *The Corsair.*

Edwards, Thomas R. *Imagination and Power: A Study of Poetry on Public Themes.* New York: Oxford University Press, 1971.

Ehrstine, John W. *William Blake's "Poetical Sketches."* Washington: Washington State University Press, 1967.

Eichner, Hans. *Friedrich Schlegel.* New York: Twayne, 1970.

Eliot, T. S. "William Blake" (1920). In *Selected Essays,* pp. 275–80.

———. *The Complete Poems and Plays, 1909–1950.* New York: Harcourt, Brace and World, 1962.

———. Letter to the editor. *TLS,* September 27, 1928, p. 687.

———. *Selected Essays: 1917–1932.* New York: Harcourt Brace, 1932.

———. "Tradition and the Individual Talent" (1917). In *Selected Essays,* pp. 3–11.

[Ellis, George]. Review of *Childe Harold's Pilgrimage I–II. Quarterly Review* 7 (1812): 180–200. Attribution by Reiman, *Romantics Reviewed* B 5: 1984.

Empson, William. *Seven Types of Ambiguity*. Cleveland: Meridian Press, 1955.

————. *The Structure of Complex Words*. Ann Arbor: University of Michigan Press, 1967.

Engels, Friedrich. *The Condition of the Working Class in England* (1845). Trans. and ed. W. O. Henderson and W. H. Chaloner. Stanford: Stanford University Press, 1958.

Erdman, David V. *Blake: Prophet Against Empire*. Princeton: Princeton University Press, 1954.

————, ed. *A Concordance to the Writings of William Blake*. 2 vols. Ithaca: Cornell University Press, 1967.

Erlich, Victor. *Russian Formalism: History, Doctrine*. The Hague: Mouton, 1955.

Essick, Robert N. "How Blake's Body Means." In Nelson Hilton and Thomas A. Vogler, eds., *Unnam'd Forms: Blake and Textuality*, pp. 197–217. Berkeley: University of California Press, 1986.

Examiner 473 (January 19, 1817): 41. "Hymn to Intellectual Beauty" (Shelley).

————. 608 (August 22, 1819): "Disturbances at Manchester," 529–31; "Dispersal of the Reform Meeting at Manchester by a Military Force" (rpt. from the *Times*), 529–31; "Letters from Manchester," 541–43.

————. 609 (August 29, 1819): "Disturbances at Manchester and Matters Connected with them," 545–47; "Further Accounts from Manchester," 556–58.

————. 610 (September 5, 1819): "Liberation of Hunt—His Examination & c.," 561–62; "Arguments of the Reformers—How Met By the Corrupt," 562–64; [protest poetry] 567; "Further Accounts from Manchester," 571–74.

————. 611 (September 12, 1819): "Outrages at Manchester," 589–91.

Ferguson, Frances. "Coleridge and the Deluded Reader: *The Rime of the Ancient Mariner*." *Georgia Review* 31 (1977): 617–35.

Ferry, Anne. *Milton's Epic Voice: The Narrator in "Paradise Lost."* 1963; Chicago: University of Chicago Press, 1983.

Ferry, David. *The Limits of Mortality: An Essay on Wordsworth's Major Poems*. Middletown, Conn.: Wesleyan University Press, 1959.

Finney, Claude Lee. *The Evolution of Keats's Poetry*. Cambridge, Mass.: Harvard University Press, 1936.

Fogle, Aaron. "Pictures of Speech: On Blake's Poetic." *Studies in Romanticism* 21 (1982): 217–42.

Foot, Paul. *Red Shelley*. London: Sidgwick and Jackson, 1980.

————. *Shelley's Revolutionary Year: The Peterloo Writings of the Poet Shelley*. London: Redwords, 1990.

Forman, Harry Buxton, ed. *The Poetical Works and Other Writings of John Keats*. 6th ed. London: Reeves and Turner, 1898.

Foucault, Michel. *The Archaeology of Knowledge* (1969). Trans. A. M. Sheridan Smith, 1972; *The Discourse of Language* (*L'ordre du discours*, 1971). Trans. Rupert Swyer, 1971. New York: Pantheon, 1972.

————. *The Order of Things: An Archaeology of the Human Sciences* (*Les Mots et les choses*, 1966). Trans. Alan Sheridan. New York: Pantheon, 1970.

Franklin, Caroline. *Byron's Heroines*. Oxford: Clarendon Press, 1992.

Freud, Sigmund. *The Standard Edition of the Complete Psychological Works of Sigmund Freud*. Ed. James Strachey. 24 vols. London: Hogarth Press, 1953–68.

Friedman, Michael H. *The Making of a Tory Humanist: Wordsworth and the Idea of Community*. New York: Columbia University Press, 1979.

Frost, Robert. "The Craft of Poetry" (1959). In Edward Connery Lathem, ed., *Interviews with Robert Frost*, pp. 199–206. New York: Holt, Rinehart and Winston, 1966.

———. *The Poetry of Robert Frost*. Ed. Edward Connery Lathem. New York: Holt, 1969.

Fruman, Norman. *Coleridge, The Damaged Archangel*. New York: George Braziller, 1971.

Frye, Northrop. *Anatomy of Criticism: Four Essays*. 1957; New York: Atheneum, 1970.

———. *Fearful Symmetry: A Study of William Blake*. 1947; Princeton: Princeton University Press, 1969.

Fussell, Paul. *Poetic Meter and Poetic Form*. Rev. ed. New York: Random House, 1979.

Gallagher, Catherine. "Marxism and the New Historicism." In H. Aram Veeser, ed., *The New Historicism*, pp. 37–48.

Gallant, Christine, ed. *Coleridge's Theory of Imagination Today*. New York: AMS, 1989.

Galperin, William H. *Revision and Authority in Wordsworth: The Interpretation of a Career*. Philadelphia: University of Pennsylvania Press, 1989.

Garrod, H. W. *Keats*. Oxford: Clarendon Press, 1926.

———, ed. *Keats: Poetical Works*. 1956; London: Oxford University Press, 1970.

Gatta, John, Jr. "Coleridge and Allegory." *Modern Language Quarterly* 38 (1977): 62–77.

Gaull, Marilyn, ed. "'Waiting for the Palfreys': The Great *Prelude* Debate" (1984). *The Wordsworth Circle* 17 (1986): 2–38.

Gettmann, Royal A., ed. *"The Rime of the Ancient Mariner": A Handbook*. San Francisco: Wadsworth, 1961.

Gilchrist, Alexander. *The Life of William Blake, "Pictor Ignotus," With Selections from His Poems and Other Writings*. 2 vols. London: Macmillan, 1863. "Selections" in vol. 2, ed. Dante Gabriel Rossetti.

Gill, Stephen, ed. See Wordsworth, *"The Prelude or Growth of a Poet's Mind" (Text of 1805)*, ed. de Selincourt and Gill.

Gioia, Dana. "Notes on the New Formalism." *Hudson Review* 40 (1987): 395–408.

Gittings, Robert. *John Keats: The Living Year*. Cambridge, Mass.: Harvard University Press, 1954.

———. *The Mask of Keats*. Cambridge, Mass.: Harvard University Press, 1956.

Giuliano, Cheryl Fallon. "Gulnare / Kaled's 'Untold' Feminization of Byron's Oriental Tales." *Studies in English Literature* 23 (1993): 785–807.

Gleckner, Robert F. *Blake's Prelude: "Poetical Sketches."* Baltimore: Johns Hopkins University Press, 1982.

Glen, Heather. *Vision and Disenchantment: Blake's "Songs" and Wordsworth's "Lyrical Ballads."* Cambridge, Eng.: Cambridge University Press, 1983.

Goldsmith, Stephen. *Unbinding Jerusalem: Apocalypse and Romantic Imagination.* Ithaca: Cornell University Press, 1993.

Grant, John E. "The Apparition and Evanishment of Coleridgean Form in Recent Critical Discourse." In Christine Gallant, ed., *Coleridge's Theory of Imagination Today,* pp. 113–27.

Graves, Robert. *Contemporary Techniques of Poetry: A Political Analogy.* London: Leonard and Virginia Woolf at the Hogarth Press, 1925.

Greg, W. W. "The Rationale of Copy-Text." *Studies in Bibliography* 3 (1950–51): 19–36.

Hamlin, Cyrus. "The Hermeneutics of Form: Reading the Romantic Ode." *boundary 2* 7: 3 (Spring 1979): 1–30.

Hartley, David. *Observations on Man, His Frame, His Duty, And His Expectations* (1749). 2 vols. Gainesville, Fla.: Scholars' Facsimiles and Reprints, 1966.

Hartman, Geoffrey H. "Beyond Formalism" (1966). In *Beyond Formalism,* pp. 42–57.

———. *Beyond Formalism: Literary Essays 1958–1970.* New Haven: Yale University Press, 1970.

———. "Blake and the Progress of Poesy" (1969). In *Beyond Formalism,* pp. 193–204.

———. *Criticism in the Wilderness: The Study of Literature Today.* New Haven: Yale University Press, 1980.

———. "The Discourse of a Figure: Blake's 'Speak Silence' in Literary History." In Sanford Budick and Wolfgang Iser, eds., *Languages of the Unsayable: The Play of Negativity in Literature and Literary Theory,* pp. 225–40. New York: Columbia University Press, 1989.

———. *The Fate of Reading and Other Essays.* Chicago: University of Chicago Press, 1975.

———. "Retrospect 1971." In *Wordsworth's Poetry,* pp. xi–xx.

———. "The Voice of the Shuttle: Language from the Point of View of Literature" (1969). In *Beyond Formalism,* pp. 337–55.

———. "Wild, Fierce Yale" (1982). In *Easy Pieces,* pp. 188–95. New York: Columbia University Press, 1985.

———. *Wordsworth's Poetry, 1787–1814.* 1964; New Haven: Yale University Press, 1975.

Hazlitt, William. *The Complete Works of William Hazlitt,* ed. P. P. Howe. 21 vols. London and Toronto: J. M. Dent and Sons, 1930–1934.

———. "Lord Byron." (*The Spirit of the Age* [1825]). In *Complete Works* 11: 69–78.

———. "Observations on Mr. Wordsworth's Poem *The Excursion,* The Same Subject Continued." (*Examiner* [October 2, 1814]; *The Round Table* [1817]). In *Complete Works* 4: 120–25.

———. "On the Living Poets." (Lecture 8 in *Lectures on the English Poets* [1818]). In *Complete Works* 5: 143–68.

————. "On Milton's Versification." (*Examiner* [August 20, 1815]; *The Round Table* [1817]). In *Complete Works* 4: 36–41.

Hilton, Nelson. "Becoming Prolific Being Devoured." *Studies in Romanticism* 21 (1982): 417–24.

Hirst, Wolf Z. *John Keats*. Boston: Twayne, 1981.

Hodgson, John A. "'Was It for This . . . ?': Wordsworth's Virgilian Questionings." In Kurt Heinzelman, ed., *Romans and Romantics, Texas Studies in Literature and Language* 33 (1991): 125–36.

Hofkosh, Sonia. "The Writer's Ravishment: Women and the Romantic Author— The Example of Byron." In Anne K. Mellor, ed., *Romanticism and Feminism*, pp. 93–114. Bloomington: Indiana University Press, 1988.

Hogle, Jerrold E. *Shelley's Process: Radical Transference and the Development of His Major Works*. New York: Oxford University Press, 1988.

Holland, Henry Richard Vassall, 3rd Lord Holland. *Further Memoirs of the Whig Party, 1807–1821, with Some Miscellaneous Reminiscences*. Ed. Lord Stavordale. London: John Murray, 1905.

Hollander, John. *Melodious Guile: Fictive Pattern in Poetic Language*. New Haven: Yale University Press, 1988.

————. "Rhyme and the True Calling of Words." In *Vision and Resonance*, pp. 117–34.

————. "Romantic Verse Form and the Metrical Contract." In Harold Bloom, ed., *Romanticism and Consciousness: Essays in Criticism*, pp. 181–200. New York: Norton, 1970.

————. *Vision and Resonance: Two Senses of Poetic Form*. New York: Oxford University Press, 1975.

Holloway, John. *Blake: The Lyric Poetry*. London: Edward Arnold, 1968.

Holmes, Richard. *Shelley: The Pursuit*. 1974; New York: E. P. Dutton, 1975.

Homans, Margaret. "Keats Reading Women, Women Reading Keats." *Studies in Romanticism* 29 (1990): 341–70.

————. *Women Writers and Poetic Identity*. Princeton: Princeton University Press, 1980.

Hopkins, Gerard Manley. *A Hopkins Reader*. Ed. John Pick. New York: Oxford University Press, 1953.

House, Humphry. *Coleridge: The Clark Lectures 1951–52*. London: Rupert Hart-Davis, 1953.

Hunt, Leigh. "Mr. Keats, With a Criticism on His Writings." In *Lord Byron and Some of His Contemporaries; With Recollections of the Author's Life, and of His Visit to Italy*, pp. 213–35. London: Henry Colburn / Philadelphia: Carey, Lea & Carey, 1828.

————. Preface. *The Masque of Anarchy. A Poem. by Percy Bysshe Shelley*, pp. v–xxx. London: Edward Moxon, 1832.

[————]. "The *Quarterly Review*, and the *Revolt of Islam*." *Examiner* 613 (September 26, 1819): 620–21; 614 (October 3, 1819): 635–36; 615 (October 10, 1819): 653.

Iser, Wolfgang. *The Act of Reading: A Theory of Aesthetic Response* (1976). Baltimore: Johns Hopkins University Press, 1978.
———. "The Reading Process: A Phenomenological Approach." *NLH* 3 (1972): 278–99.
Jacobus, Mary. "Apostrophe and Lyric Voice in *The Prelude*." In Patricia Parker and Chaviva Hosek, eds., *Lyric Poetry Beyond New Criticism*, pp. 167–81.
———. *Tradition and Experiment in Wordsworth's "Lyrical Ballads" (1798)*. Oxford: Clarendon Press, 1976.
Jakobson, Roman. "Linguistics and Poetics" (1960). In Seymour Chatman and Samuel R. Levin, eds., *Essays on the Language of Literature*, pp. 296–322. Boston: Houghton Mifflin, 1967.
———. "On the Verbal Art of William Blake and Other Poet-Painters." *Lingusitic Inquiry* 1 (1970): 1–23.
Jameson, Fredric. *Marxism and Form: Twentieth-Century Dialectical Theories of Literature*. Princeton: Princeton University Press, 1971.
———. *The Political Unconscious: Narrative as a Socially Symbolic Act*. Ithaca: Cornell University Press, 1981.
———. *The Prison-House of Language: A Critical Account of Structuralism and Russian Formalism*. Princeton: Princeton University Press, 1972.
Jarvis, Robin. "The Five-Book *Prelude*: A Reconsideration." *JEGP* 80 (1981): 528–51.
Jauss, Hans Robert. *Question and Answer: Forms of Dialogic Understanding*. Ed. and trans. Michael Hays. Minneapolis: University of Minnesota Press, 1989.
Jay, Martin. *Force Fields: Between Intellectual History and Cultural Critique*. New York and London: Routledge, 1993.
———. "Modernism and the Retreat from Form." In *Force Fields*, pp. 147–57.
———. "What Does It Mean to Aestheticize Politics?" In *Force Fields*, pp. 71–83.
[Jeffrey, Francis]. Review of *The Corsair*. *Edinburgh Review, or Critical Journal* 23 (April 1814): 198–229. Attribution by Andrew Rutherford, *Byron: The Critical Heritage* 53.
———. Review of *Endymion* and the *Lamia* volume. *Edinburgh Review* 34 (August 1820): 203–13. Attribution by Reiman, *Romantics Reviewed* C 1: 385.
Johnson, Barbara. "Strange Fits: Poe and Wordsworth on the Nature of Poetic Language." In *A World of Difference*, pp. 89–99. Baltimore: Johns Hopkins University Press, 1989.
Johnson, Lee M. *Wordsworth and the Sonnet*. *Anglistica* 19 (Copenhagen, 1973).
Johnson, Samuel. "The dangers of imitation. The impropriety of imitating Spenser." *The Rambler* 121 (May 14, 1751). In *The Yale Edition of the Works of Samuel Johnson* vol. 4, ed. W. J. Bate and Albrecht B. Strauss, pp. 280–86. New Haven: Yale University Press, 1969.
———. *Lives of the English Poets* (1783). Ed. George Birkbeck Hill. 3 vols. Oxford: Clarendon Press, 1905. "Cowley" 1: 1–69; "Milton" 1: 84–200; "Pope" 3: 82–276; "Thomson" 3: 281–301; "Young" 3: 361–99; "Akenside" 3: 411–20.
Johnston, Kenneth R., Gilbert Chaitin, Karen Hanson, and Herbert Marks, eds.

Romantic Revolutions: Criticism and Theory. Bloomington: Indiana University Press, 1990.

Kalim, M. Siddiq. *The Social Orpheus: Shelley and the Owenites.* Lahore: Research Council, 1973.

Kames, Henry Home, Lord. *Elements of Criticism.* 3 vols. London: A. Millar / Edinburgh: A. Kincaid and Bell, 1762.

———. *Elements of Criticism by Henry Home, Lord Kames.* Ed. Abraham Mills. New York: Mason, 1857.

Kant, Immanuel. "Analytic of the Sublime" (1790). In *Critique of Aesthetic Judgement.* Trans. James Creed Meredith. Oxford, Clarendon Press, 1911.

Keach, William. "Blake, Violence, and Visionary Politics." In James A. W. Heffernan, ed., *Representing the French Revolution: Literature, Historiography, and Art,* pp. 24–40. Hanover, N.H.: University Press of New England, 1992.

———. "Cockney Couplets: Keats and the Politics of Style." *Studies in Romanticism* 24 (1986): 182–96.

———. "Radical Shelley?" *Raritan* 5: 2 (Fall 1985): 120–29.

———. *Shelley's Style.* London and New York: Methuen, 1984.

———. "'Words Are Things': Romantic Ideology and the Matter of Poetic Language." In George Levine, ed., *Aesthetics and Ideology,* pp. 219–39.

The Keats Circle. Ed. Hyder E. Rollins. 2nd ed. 2 vols. Cambridge, Mass.: Harvard University Press, 1965.

Keats, John. *John Keats.* Ed. Elizabeth Cook. New York and Oxford: Oxford University Press, 1990.

———. *The Letters of John Keats, 1814–1821.* Ed. Hyder E. Rollins. 2 vols. Cambridge, Mass.: Harvard University Press, 1958.

———. *The Poems of John Keats.* Ed. Jack Stillinger. Cambridge, Mass.: Harvard University Press, 1978.

Kelley, Theresa M. "The Economics of the Heart: Wordsworth's Sublime and Beautiful." *Romanticism, Past and Present* 5 (1981): 15–32.

———. "Poetics and the Politics of Reception: Keats's 'La Belle Dame sans Merci.'" *ELH* 54 (1987): 333–62.

———. "Wordsworth's Figural Interventions and the Drowned Man." Paper presented at the MLA Convention, New York, 1981.

———. *Wordsworth's Revisionary Aesthetics.* Cambridge, Eng.: Cambridge University Press, 1988.

Kelsall, Malcolm. "Byron and the Women of the Harem." In Alice Levine and Robert N. Keane, eds., *Rereading Byron: Essays Selected from Hofstra University's Byron Bicentennial Conference,* pp. 165–73. Hamden, Conn. and London: Garland Press, 1992.

———. *Byron's Politics.* Totowa, N.J.: Barnes and Noble / Sussex, Eng.: Harvester, 1987.

[Kingsley, Charles]. "Alexander Smith and Alexander Pope." *Fraser's Magazine* 48 (October 1853): 452–66.

Kipperman, Mark. "Absorbing a Revolution: Shelley Becomes a Romantic, 1889–1903." *Nineteenth-Century Literature* (1992): 187–212.

Knight, G. Wilson. "The Two Eternities: An Essay on Byron." In *The Burning Oracle: Studies In the Poetry of Action*, pp. 197–288. London: Oxford University Press, 1939.

Knights, L. C. "Early Blake." *Sewanee Review* 79 (1971): 377–92.

Kristeva, Julia. *Revolution in Poetic Language* (*La révolution du language poétique*, 1974). Trans. Margaret Waller. New York: Columbia University Press, 1984.

Kuzniar, Alice A. *Delayed Endings: Nonclosure in Novalis and Hölderlin*. Athens: University of Georgia Press, 1987.

Lake, Paul. "Toward a Liberal Poetics." In Frederick Feirstein, ed., *Expansive Poetry: Essays on the New Narrative and The New Formalism*, pp. 113–23. Santa Cruz, Calif.: Story Line Press, 1989.

Lanz, Henry. *The Physical Basis of Rime: An Essay on the Aesthetics of Sound*. Stanford: Stanford University Press, 1931.

Leader, Zachary. "Wordsworth, Revision, and Personal Identity." *ELH* 60 (1993): 651–83.

Leavis, F. R. "Justifying One's Valuation of Blake." In Morton D. Paley and Michael Phillips, eds. *William Blake*, pp. 66–85.

———. "Shelley." In *Revaluation: Tradition and Development In English Poetry*. pp. 191–224. 1936; Harmondsworth, Eng.: Penguin, 1972.

Lentricchia, Frank. *After the New Criticism*. Chicago: University of Chicago Press, 1980.

Lerner, L. D. "The Miltonic Simile." *Essays in Criticism* 4 (1954): 297–308.

Levine, George. "Introduction: Reclaiming the Aesthetic." In George Levine, ed., *Aesthetics and Ideology*, pp. 1–28.

———, ed. *Aesthetics and Ideology*. New Brunswick, N.J.: Rutgers University Press, 1994.

Levinson, Marjorie. *Keats's Life of Allegory: The Origins of Style*. New York: Basil Blackwell, 1988.

———. *The Romantic Fragment Poem: A Critique of a Form*. Chapel Hill: University of North Carolina Press, 1986.

———. *Wordsworth's Great Period Poems: Four Essays*. Cambridge, Eng.: Cambridge University Press, 1986.

Lindenberger, Herbert. *On Wordsworth's "Prelude."* Princeton: Princeton University Press, 1963.

Lindsay, Jack. "The Metric of William Blake." In *"Poetical Sketches" By William Blake*, pp. 1–20. London: Scholartis Press, 1927.

Lipking, Lawrence. *The Life of the Poet: Beginning and Ending Poetic Careers*. Chicago: University of Chicago Press, 1981.

Liu, Alan. "The Power of Formalism: The New Historicism." *ELH* 56 (1989): 721–71.

———. *Wordsworth: The Sense of History*. Stanford: Stanford University Press, 1989.

Locke, John. *Essay Concerning Human Understanding* (1690). 3 vols. London: Allen and West, 1795.

Lockhart, John Gibson. *Memoirs of the Life of Sir Walter Scott, Bart.* 2d ed. 10 vols. Edinburgh: Robert Cadell, 1839.

London Magazine (Baldwin's) 3 (April 1821): 426–27. "Town Conversation. No. IV." Obituary of Keats, by "L" [Barry Cornwall]. Attribution by G. M. Matthews, ed., *Keats: The Critical Heritage* 241.

Lowell, Amy. *John Keats.* 2 vols. Boston and New York: Houghton Mifflin, 1925.

Lowery, Margaret Ruth. *Windows of the Morning: A Critical Study of William Blake's "Poetical Sketches," 1783.* New Haven: Yale University Press, 1940.

Lyotard, Jean-François. *The Postmodern Condition: A Report on Knowledge* (1979). Trans. Geoff Bennington and Brian Massumi. Foreword by Fredric Jameson. Minneapolis: University of Minnesota Press, 1984.

Macdonald, D. L., and Kathleen Scherf, eds. See Shelley, Mary Wollstonecraft.

MacGillivray, J. R. "The Three Forms of *The Prelude,* 1798–1805." In Millar MacLure and F. W. Watt, eds., *Essays in English Literature from the Renaissance to the Victorian Age Presented to A. S. P. Woodhouse,* pp. 229–44. Toronto: University of Toronto Press, 1964.

Macherey, Pierre. *A Theory of Literary Production* (1966). Trans. Geoffrey Wall. London: Routledge and Kegan Paul, 1978.

MacLean, Kenneth. *Agrarian Age: A Background for Wordsworth.* 1950; Hamden, Conn.: Archon, 1970.

Magnuson, Paul. "'The Eolian Harp' in Context." *Studies in Romanticism* 24 (1985): 3–20.

Manning, Peter J. *Byron and His Fictions.* Detroit: Wayne State University Press, 1978.

———. "Childe Harold in the Marketplace: From Romaunt to Handbook." *Modern Language Quarterly* 52 (1991): 170–90.

———. "The Hone-ing of Byron's *Corsair*" (1985). In *Reading Romantics,* pp. 216–37.

———. "Placing Poor Susan: Wordsworth and the New Historicism" (1987). In *Reading Romantics,* pp. 300–20.

———. *Reading Romantics: Texts and Contexts.* New York and London: Oxford University Press, 1990.

———. "Reading Wordsworth's Revisions: Othello and the Drowned Man" (1983). In *Reading Romantics,* pp. 87–114.

———. "Tales and Politics: *The Corsair, Lara,* and *The White Doe of Rylstone*" (1981). In *Reading Romantics,* pp. 195–215.

———. "Wordsworth, Margaret, and the Pedlar" (1976). In *Reading Romantics,* pp. 9–34.

Marchand, Leslie A. *Byron: A Biography.* 3 vols. New York: Knopf, 1957.

———. *Byron: A Portrait.* Chicago: University of Chicago Press, 1970.

Marx, Karl, and Friedrich Engels. *Selected Works.* 2 vols. London: Lawrence and Wishart, 1950.

Matthews, G. M. "Shelley and Jane Williams." *Review of English Studies* NS 12 (February 1961): 40–48.

———, ed. *Keats: The Critical Heritage.* New York: Barnes and Noble, 1971.

Maxwell, J. C., ed. See William Wordsworth, *"The Prelude": A Parallel Text.*

McCall, Marsh H., Jr. *Ancient Rhetorical Theories of Simile and Comparison.* Cambridge, Mass.: Harvard University Press, 1969.

McGann, Jerome J. "The Book of Byron and the Book of a World." In *The Beauty of Inflections: Literary Investigations in Historical Method and Theory,* pp. 256–93. 1985; Oxford: Clarendon Press, 1988.

———. *Historical Studies and Literary Criticism.* Madison: University of Wisconsin Press, 1985.

———. "Keats and the Historical Method in Literary Criticism" (1979). In *Beauty,* pp. 9–65.

———. *The Romantic Ideology: A Critical Investigation.* Chicago: University of Chicago Press, 1983.

———. "The Secrets of an Elder Day: Shelley After *Hellas.*" *Keats-Shelley Journal* 15 (1966): 25–41.

McGowan, James. "The Integrity of Blake's *Poetical Sketches*: A New Approach to Blake's Earliest Poems." *Blake Studies* 8 (1979): 121–44.

McKeon, Michael. *Politics and Poetry in Restoration England: The Case of Dryden's "Annus Mirabilis."* Cambridge, Mass.: Harvard University Press, 1975.

McLuhan, Herbert Marshall. "Aesthetic Pattern in Keats's Odes." *University of Toronto Quarterly* 12 (1943): 167–79.

McPhillips, Robert. "Reading the New Formalists." *Sewanee Review* 97: 1 (1989): 73–96.

Medwin, Thomas. *Conversations of Lord Byron: Noted During a Residence with His Lordship at Pisa, in the Years 1821 and 1822.* London: Henry Colburn, 1824.

[Medwin, Thomas.] "Memoir of Shelley." *Athenæum* 250 (August 11, 1832): 522–24.

[———]. "Continuation of the Shelley Papers: *With a Guitar.*" *Athenæum* 260 (October 20, 1832): 680.

[———], ed. "An Ariette for Music. To a Lady Singing to Her Accompaniment on the Guitar." *Athenæum* 264 (November 17, 1832): 747.

Mellor, Anne K. *Blake's Human Form Divine.* Berkeley: University of California Press, 1974.

———. "Choosing a Text of *Frankenstein* to Teach." In Stephen C. Behrendt, ed., *Approaches to Teaching Shelley's "Frankenstein,"* pp. 31–37. New York: MLA, 1990.

———. *English Romantic Irony.* Cambridge, Mass.: Harvard University Press, 1980.

———. *Mary Shelley: Her Life, Her Fiction, Her Monsters.* New York and London: Methuen, 1988.

Mileur, Jean-Pierre. *Vision and Revision: Coleridge's Art of Immanence.* Berkeley: University of California Press, 1982.

Miller, J. Hillis. "The Still Heart: Poetic Form in Wordsworth." *NLH* 2 (1971): 295–310.

———. "The Stone and the Shell: The Problem of Poetic Form in Wordsworth's Dream of the Arab." In *Mouvements premiers: Études critiques offertes à Georges Poulet*, pp. 125–47. Paris: José Corti, 1972.

Milnes, Richard Monckton. *Life, Letters, and Literary Remains, of John Keats*. 2 vols. London: Edward Moxon, 1848.

Milton, John. *Complete Poems and Major Prose*. Ed. Merritt Y. Hughes. New York: Odyssey, 1957.

Mitchell, W. J. T. *Blake's Composite Art: A Study of the Illuminated Poetry*. Princeton: Princeton University Press, 1978.

———. "Visible Language: Blake's Wond'rous Art of Writing." In Morris Eaves and Michael Fischer, eds., *Romanticism and Contemporary Criticism*, pp. 46–86. Ithaca: Cornell University Press, 1986.

Modiano, Raimonda. *Coleridge and the Concept of Nature*. Tallahassee: Florida State University Press, 1985.

———. "Words and 'Languageless' Meanings: Limits of Expression in *The Rime of The Ancient Mariner*." *Modern Language Quarterly* 38 (1977): 40–61.

Monboddo, Lord [James Burnet]. *Of the Origin and Progress of Language*. 6 vols. Edinburgh: J. Balfour / London: T. Cadell, 1774–92.

Monthly Magazine 2 (July 1796): 453–56. "The Enquirer. No. VI. Question: *Is Verse essential to Poetry?*"

Monthly Review; or Literary Journal 2d ser. 73 (February 1814): 189–200. Review of *The Corsair*.

Morley, Edith J., ed. *Henry Crabb Robinson on Books and Their Writers*. 3 vols. London: J. M. Dent, 1938.

Mukařovský, Jan. *Aesthetic Function, Norm and Value as Social Facts* (1936). Trans. Mark E. Suino. Ann Arbor: University of Michigan Press, 1970.

———. "On Poetic Language" (1940). In *The Word and Verbal Art: Selected Essays by Jan Mukařovský*, pp. 1–64. Trans. and ed. John Burbank and Peter Steiner. New Haven: Yale University Press, 1977.

———. "Poetic Designation and the Aesthetic Function of Language" (1938). In *Word*, pp. 65–73.

The Nation (October 11, 1845): 858–59. "Recent English Poets. No. IV.—John Keats."

Nitchie, Elizabeth. "Form in Romantic Poetry." In Clarence D. Thorpe, Carlos Baker, and Bennett Weaver, eds., *The Major English Romantic Poets*, pp. 3–16.

Norris, Christopher. *Deconstruction: Theory & Practice*. New York and London: Methuen, 1982.

———. *Paul de Man: Deconstruction and the Critique of Aesthetic Ideology*. New York and London: Routledge, 1988.

Norton Anthology of English Literature. Vol. 2. General ed. Meyer H. Abrams. New York: Norton. 3rd ed., 1974; 4th ed., 1979; 5th ed., 1986.

Novak, M. E. *Economics and the Fiction of Daniel Defoe*. 1962; University of California Press, 1976.

O'Donnell, Brennan. *The Passion of Meter: A Study of Wordsworth's Metrical Art.* Kent, Ohio: Kent State University Press, 1995.

Onorato, Richard. *The Character of the Poet: Wordsworth in "The Prelude."* Princeton: Princeton University Press, 1971.

Orgel, Stephen. "What Is a Text?" *Research Opportunities in Renaissance Drama* 24 (1981): 3–6.

Ostriker, Alicia. *Vision and Verse in William Blake.* Madison: University of Wisconsin Press, 1965.

Owen, W. J. B., ed. See William Wordsworth, *The Fourteen-Book "Prelude."*

Oxford Book of English Verse, 1250–1900. Ed. Arthur Quiller-Couch. Oxford: Clarendon Press, 1906.

Paine, Thomas. *The Rights of Man.* In *Two Classics of the French Revolution*, pp. 267–515. New York: Anchor / Doubleday, 1973.

Paley, Morton D., and Michael Phillips, eds. *William Blake: Essays in Honour of Sir Geoffrey Keynes.* Oxford: Clarendon Press, 1973.

Parker, Patricia, and Chaviva Hosek, eds. *Lyric Poetry Beyond New Criticism.* Ithaca: Cornell University Press, 1985.

Parker, Reeve. *Coleridge's Meditative Art.* Ithaca: Cornell University Press, 1975.

Parrish, Stephen M. "The Whig Interpretation of Literature." *TEXT* 4 (1988): 343–50.

———, ed. See William Wordsworth, *"The Prelude" 1798–1799.*

Partridge, Eric. "Introduction." In *"Poetical Sketches" by William Blake*, pp. ix–xxiv. London: Scholartis Press, 1927.

Pearce, Zachary. *A Review of the Text of the Twelve Books of Milton's "Paradise Lost": In which the Chief of Dr. Bentley's Emendations Are Consider'd; And several other Emendations and Observations are offer'd to the Public.* London: John Shuckburgh, 1733.

Pecora, Vincent P. "The Limits of Local Knowledge." In H. Aram Veeser, ed., *The New Historicism*, pp. 243–76.

Perkins, David. "How the Romantics Recited Poetry." *Studies in English Literature* 31 (1991): 655–71.

———. *The Quest for Permanence: The Symbolism of Wordsworth, Shelley, and Keats.* Cambridge, Mass.: Harvard University Press, 1959.

Pettet, E. C. *On the Poetry of Keats.* Oxford: Clarendon Press, 1957.

Phillips, Michael. "Blake's Corrections in *Poetical Sketches*." *Blake Newsletter* 4 (1970): 40–47.

———. "Blake's Early Poetry." In Morton D. Paley and Michael Phillips, eds., *William Blake*, pp. 1–28.

———. "The Reputation of Blake's *Poetical Sketches*." *Review of English Studies* 26 (1975): 19–33.

———. "William Blake and the 'Unincreasable Club': The Printing of *Poetical Sketches*." *Bulletin of the New York Public Library* 80 (1976): 6–18.

[Phillips, Samuel]. "The Life of John Keats." *The Times* (September 19, 1848): 3. Attribution by G. M. Matthews, *Keats: The Critical Heritage* 320.

Piper, William Bowman. *The Heroic Couplet*. Cleveland: Press of Case Western Reserve University, 1969.

Poirier, Richard. "Prologue: The Deed of Writing." In *The Renewal of Literature: Emersonian Reflections*, pp. 3–66. New Haven: Yale University Press, 1988.

Pomorska, Krystyna. *Russian Formalist Theory and Its Poetic Ambience*. The Hague: Mouton, 1968.

Pope, Alexander. *Poems of Alexander Pope*. General ed. John Butt. 11 vols. London: Methuen, 1961–69. *An Essay on Criticism*, vol. 1, ed. E. Audra and Aubrey Williams; *An Essay on Man*, vol. 3, ed. Maynard Mack; *Translations of Homer*, vol. 7, ed. Maynard Mack.

Pöschl, Viktor. *The Art of Vergil: Image and Symbol in "The Aeneid"* (1950). Trans. Gerda Seligson, 1962. Ann Arbor: University of Michigan Press, 1970.

Priestley, Joseph. *A Course of Lectures on Oratory and Criticism*. London: J. Johnson, 1777.

Primeau, Ronald. "Chaucer's *Troilus and Criseyde* and the Rhythm of Experience in Keats's 'What can I do to drive away.'" *Keats-Shelley Journal* 23 (1974): 106–18.

Prince, Gerald. "Introduction to the Study of the Narratee" (1973). Trans. Francis Mariner. In Jane P. Tompkins, ed., *Reader-Response Criticism*, pp. 7–25.

Punter, David. "Shelley: Poetry and Politics." In David Aers, Jonathan Cook, and David Punter, *Romanticism and Ideology: Studies in English Writing 1765–1830*, pp. 155–72. London and Boston: Routledge and Kegan Paul, 1981.

Quintilian. *Institutio Oratoria*. 4 vols. Trans. H. E. Butler (1921). Cambridge, Mass.: Harvard University Press, 1966.

Rajan, Tilottama. "Coleridge, Wordsworth, and the Textual Abject." *The Wordsworth Circle* 24: 2 (Spring 1993): 61–68.

———. *Dark Interpreter: The Discourse of Romanticism*. Ithaca: Cornell University Press, 1980.

———. "Displacing Post-Structuralism: Romantic Studies After Paul de Man." *Studies in Romanticism* 24 (1985): 451–74.

———. "Romanticism and the Death of Lyric Consciousness." In Patricia Parker and Chaviva Hosek, eds., *Lyric Poetry Beyond New Criticism*, pp. 194–207.

———. "The Web of Human Things: Narrative and Identity in *Alastor*." In G. Kim Blank, ed., *The New Shelley: Later Twentieth-Century Views*, pp. 85–107. Houndsmill, Eng.: Macmillan, 1991.

Ransom, John Crowe. *The New Criticism*. Norfolk, Conn.: New Directions, 1941.

Raysor, T. M. "Unpublished Fragments in Aesthetics by S. T. Coleridge." *Studies in Philology* 22 (1925): 529–37.

Reed, Arden. *Romantic Weather: The Climates of Coleridge and Baudelaire*. Hanover, N.H.: University Press of New England, 1983.

Reed, Mark L., ed. See William Wordsworth, *The Thirteen-Book "Prelude."*

Reiman, Donald H. *Intervals of Inspiration: The Skeptical Tradition and the Psychology of Romanticism*. Fla.: Penkevill Press, 1988.

———. Review of Norton Critical Edition of *The Prelude* (1982). In *Romantic Texts*, pp. 151–55.

———. *Romantic Texts and Contexts*. Columbia: University of Missouri Press, 1988.

———. "Shelley's 'The Triumph of Life': The Biographical Problem" (1963). In *Romantic Texts*, pp. 292–320.

———. *Shelley's "The Triumph of Life": A Critical Study, Based on a Text Newly Edited from the Bodleian Manuscript*. 1965; New York: Octagon, 1979.

———. "'Versioning': The Presentation of Multiple Texts." In *Romantic Texts*, pp. 167–80.

———, ed. *The Bodleian Shelley Manuscripts. A Facsimile Edition, with Full Transcriptions and Scholarly Apparatus*. Vol. 1 (*Peter Bell the Third* and *The Triumph of Life*). New York and London: Garland Press, 1986.

———, ed. *"The Mask of Anarchy": A Facsimile Edition, with Scholarly Introductions, Bibliographical Descriptions, and Annotations*. Vol. 2 of *Percy Bysshe Shelley* in *The Manuscripts of the Younger Romantics*. New York and London: Garland Press, 1985.

———, ed. *The Romantics Reviewed: Contemporary Reviews of British Romantic Writers*. Part B: *Byron and Regency Society Poets*; Part C: *Shelley, Keats, and London Radical Writers*. New York and London: Garland Press, 1972.

Reiman, Donald H., and Sharon B. Powers, eds. *Shelley's Poetry and Prose*. See Shelley, Percy Bysshe.

Reynolds, Joshua. *The Works of Sir Joshua Reynolds*. Ed. Edmond Malone. 2nd ed. 3 vols. London: Cadell and Davies, 1798.

Ricks, Christopher. *Milton's Grand Style*. 1963; London, Oxford, New York: Oxford University Press, 1967.

———. "William Wordsworth: 'A pure organic pleasure from the lines'" (1971). In *The Force of Poetry*, pp. 89–116. Oxford and New York: Oxford University Press, 1987.

Ricoeur, Paul. *The Rule of Metaphor: Multi-disciplinary studies of the creation of meaning in language* (1975). Trans. Robert Czerny, with Kathleen McLaughlin and John Costello. Toronto: University of Toronto Press, 1977.

Rieger, James, ed. See Shelley, Mary Wollstonecraft.

Riffaterre, Michael. *Semiotics of Poetry*. Bloomington: Indiana University Press, 1978.

Roe, Richard. *The Elements of English Metre, Both in Prose and Verse*. London: Walker, 1801.

Rogers, Pat. *Robinson Crusoe*. London: George Allen and Unwin, 1979.

Rossetti, Dante Gabriel, ed. See Gilchrist.

Rossetti, William Michael, ed. *The Poetical Works of William Blake, Lyrical and Miscellaneous*. Aldine Edition. London: Bell, 1875.

Rowe, John Carlos. "Structure." In Frank Lentricchia and Thomas McLaughlin, eds., *Critical Terms for Literary Study*, pp. 23–38. Chicago: University of Chicago Press, 1990.

Rutherford, Andrew, ed. *Byron: The Critical Heritage*. New York: Barnes and Noble, 1970.

Rutherford, Mark [William Hale White]. "The Morality of Byron's Poetry. 'The

Corsair.'" In *Pages from a Journal with Other Papers*, pp. 125–32. London: T. Fisher Unwin, 1900.

Saintsbury, George. *A History of English Prosody*. 3 vols. London: Macmillan, 1910.

Sales, Roger. *English Literature in History 1780–1830: Pastoral and Politics*. New York: St. Martin's Press, 1983.

Santa Cruz Blake Study Group. "What Type of Blake?" In Nelson Hilton, ed., *Essential Articles for the Study of William Blake, 1970–1984*, pp. 301–33. Hamden, Conn.: Archon, 1986.

Schlegel, Friedrich. *"Dialogue on Poetry" and "Literary Aphorisms."* Trans. Ernst Behler and Roman Struc. University Park: Pennsylvania State University Press, 1968.

Schorer, Mark. *William Blake: The Politics of Vision*. 1946; New York: Random House, 1959.

[Scott, Walter]. Review of *Childe Harold's Pilgrimage, Canto III* and *The Prisoner of Chillon*. *Quarterly Review* 16 (October 1816; pub. February 11, 1817): 172–208. Attribution by Reiman, *Romantics Reviewed* B 3: 2028.

Scrivener, Michael Henry. *Radical Shelley: The Philosophical Anarchism and Utopian Thought of Percy Bysshe Shelley*. Princeton: Princeton University Press, 1982.

Shaaban, Bouthaina. "The Romantics in the Chartist Press." *Keats-Shelley Journal* 38 (1989): 25–46.

———. "Shelley in the Chartist Press." *Keats-Shelley Memorial Bulletin* 34 (1983): 41–60.

Shakespeare, William. *Othello*. Arden Edition. Ed. M. R. Ridley (1958). London: Methuen, 1977.

———. *Titus Andronicus*. Arden Edition. Ed. J. C. Maxwell (1953). London and New York: Methuen, 1987.

———. *The Two Gentlemen of Verona*. Arden Edition. Ed. Clifford Leech. London: Methuen, 1972.

Shapiro, Alan. "The New Formalism." *Critical Inquiry* 14: 1 (1987): 200–13.

Sharp, William. *The Life and Letters of Joseph Severn*. London: Sampson Low, Marston, 1892.

Shawcross, John. "Coleridge's Marginalia." *Notes and Queries* 10th ser.: 4 (October 28, 1905): 341–42.

Sheats, Paul D. *The Making of Wordsworth's Poetry, 1785–1798*. Cambridge, Mass.: Harvard University Press, 1973.

Shelley, Mary Wollstonecraft. *"Frankenstein; or, The Modern Prometheus," The 1818 version*. Ed. D. L. Macdonald and Kathleen Scherf. Ontario: Broadview Press, 1994.

———. *"Frankenstein; or, The Modern Prometheus" (The 1818 Text)*. Ed. James Rieger. 1974; Chicago: University of Chicago Press, 1982.

———. *The Journals of Mary Shelley, 1814–1844*. Ed. Paula R. Feldman and Diana Scott-Kilvert. 1987; Baltimore: Johns Hopkins University Press, 1995.

———. *The Letters of Mary Wollstonecraft Shelley*. Ed. Betty T. Bennett. 3 vols. Baltimore: Johns Hopkins University Press, 1980–88.

————, ed. *Essays, Letters from Abroad, Translations and Fragments by Percy Bysshe Shelley*. 2 vols. London: Edward Moxon, 1840 [1839].

————, ed. *The Poetical Works of Percy Bysshe Shelley*. 4 vols. London: Edward Moxon, 1839.

————, ed. *The Poetical Works of Percy Bysshe Shelley*. Rev. 1-vol. edn. London: Edward Moxon, 1840 [1839]. Rpt. *The Complete Works of Percy Bysshe Shelley* in *The Complete Poems of Keats and Shelley with Mrs. Shelley's Notes*. New York: Random House, n.d.

[————], ed. *Posthumous Poems of Percy Bysshe Shelley*. London: John and Henry L. Hunt, 1824.

Shelley, Percy Bysshe. *A Defence of Poetry*. In *Shelley's Poetry and Prose*, pp. 480–508.

————. *Letters of Percy Bysshe Shelley*. Ed. Frederick L. Jones. 2 vols. Oxford: Clarendon Press, 1964.

————. Manuscripts. See Donald Reiman, ed; and Judith Chernaik.

————. *The Masque of Anarchy. A Poem*. Preface by Leigh Hunt. 1832. Facsimile rpt. with introduction by Jonathan Wordsworth. Oxford and New York: Woodstock Books, 1990.

————. *Shelley's Poetry and Prose*. Ed. Donald H. Reiman and Sharon B. Powers. New York: Norton, 1977.

————. "To A. B., With a Guitar." *Fraser's Magazine for Town and Country* 7 (January 1833): 79.

Shepherd, Geoffrey, ed. *An Apology for Poetry, or the The Defence of Poesy. By Sir Philip Sidney*. Manchester: Manchester University Press, 1973.

Shepherd, Richard Herne, ed. *The Poems of William Blake, Comprising "Songs of Innocence and Experience" Together with "Poetical Sketches" and Some Copyright Poems not in any other collection*. London: Basil Montagu Pickering, 1874.

————. "Preface." In *"Poetical Sketches" By William Blake. Now first reprinted from the Original edition of 1783*, pp. vii–xiv. London: Basil Montagu Pickering, 1868.

Sheridan, Thomas. "Of the Recitation of Poetic Numbers." In *A Complete Dictionary of the English Language, Both with regard to Sound and Meaning*, pp. xlvii–li. 2nd ed., revised, corrected, and enlarged. London: Charles Dilly, 1789.

Shetley, Vernon. *After the Death of Poetry: Poetry and Audience in Contemporary America*. Durham: Duke University Press, 1993.

Shklovsky, Viktor. "Art as Technique" (1917). Trans. Lee T. Lemon and Marion J. Reis. In *Russian Formalist Criticism: Four Essays*, pp. 3–24. Lincoln: University of Nebraska Press, 1965.

————. *Mayakovsky and His Circle*. Ed. and trans. Lily Feiler. New York: Dodd, Mead, 1972.

————. "Sterne's *Tristram Shandy*" (1921). Trans. Lee T. Lemon and Marion J. Reis. In *Russian Formalist Criticsm*, pp. 25–57.

Sidney, Philip. *The Poems of Sir Philip Sidney*. Ed. William A. Ringler, Jr. Oxford: Clarendon Press, 1962.

Simpson, David. "Coleridge on Wordsworth and the Form of Poetry." In Christine Gallant, ed., *Coleridge's Theory of Imagination Today*, pp. 211–25.

———. *Irony and Authority in Romantic Poetry*. London: Macmillan, 1979.

———. *Wordsworth and the Figurings of the Real*. Atlantic Highlands, N.J.: Humanities Press, 1982.

———. *Wordsworth's Historical Imagination: The Poetry of Displacement*. London and New York: Methuen, 1987.

Siskin, Clifford. *The Historicity of Romantic Discourse*. New York and Oxford: Oxford University Press, 1988.

Smiles, Samuel. *A Publisher and His Friends: Memoir and Correspondence of the Late John Murray with an Account of the Origin and Progress of the House, 1768–1843*. 2 vols. London: John Murray / New York: Charles Scribner's Sons, 1891.

Spenser, Edmund. *The Faerie Queene*. Ed. Thomas P. Roche, Jr. Middlesex, Eng.: Penguin, 1978.

———. *The Shepheardes Calender*. "August." In *Complete Poetical Works of Edmund Spenser*. Ed. R. E. Neil Dodge. Boston: Houghton, Mifflin, 1908.

Sperry, Stuart M. *Keats the Poet*. Princeton: Princeton University Press, 1973.

———. "Towards a Definition of Romantic Irony." In George Bornstein, ed., *Romantic and Modern: Revaluations of Literary Tradition*, pp. 3–28. Pittsburgh: University of Pittsburgh Press, 1977.

Sperry, Willard L. *Wordsworth's Anti-Climax*. Cambridge, Mass.: Harvard University Press, 1935.

Spiegelman, Willard. *Majestic Indolence: English Romantic Poetry and the Work of Art*. New York and Oxford: Oxford University Press, 1995.

Sprinker, Michael. *Imaginary Relations: Aesthetics and Ideology in the Theory of Historical Materialism*. London: Verso, 1987.

Stevens, Wallace. *The Collected Poems of Wallace Stevens*. New York: Vintage, 1990.

———. "Three Academic Pieces" (1947). In *The Necessary Angel: Essays on Reality and the Imagination*, pp. 71–89. New York: Vintage, 1951.

Stewart, Garrett. *Reading Voices: Literature and the Phonotext*. Berkeley: University of California Press, 1990.

Stillinger, Jack. *Coleridge and Textual Instability: The Multiple Versions of the Major Poems*. New York: Oxford University Press, 1994.

———. "Imagination and Reality in the Odes" (1968). In *"The Hoodwinking of Madeline" and Other Essays on Keats's Poems*, pp. 99–119. Urbana: University of Illinois Press, 1971.

———. *Multiple Authorship and the Myth of Solitary Genius*. New York: Oxford University Press, 1991.

———. "The Multiple Versions of Coleridge's Poems: How Many Mariners Did Coleridge Write?" *Studies in Romanticism* 31 (1992): 127–46.

———, ed. *John Keats: Poetry Manuscripts at Harvard: A Facsimile Edition*. Cambridge, Mass.: Harvard University Press, 1990.

———, ed. *Wordsworth's Selected Poems and Prefaces*. Boston: Houghton Mifflin, 1969.

Swann, Karen. "Harassing the Muse." In Anne K. Mellor, ed., *Romanticism and Feminism*, pp. 81–92. Bloomington: Indiana University Press, 1988.

———. " Public Transport: Adventuring on Wordsworth's Salisbury Plain." *ELH* 55 (1988): 811–34.

Swinburne, Algernon Charles. *William Blake: A Critical Essay* (1866). 2nd ed. London: John Camden Hotten, 1868.

Symons, Arthur. *The Romantic Movement in English Poetry.* New York: Dutton, 1909.

Tate, Allen. "Poetry Modern and Unmodern: A Personal Recollection." In *Essays in Four Decades*, pp. 222–36. Chicago: Swallow Press, 1968.

———. *Reason in Madness: Critical Essays.* New York: G. P. Putnam's Sons, 1935.

Tatham, Frederick. "Life of Blake" (?1832). Selections in G. E. Bentley Jr., ed., *William Blake: The Critical Heritage*, pp. 213–19.

Tetreault, Ronald. *The Poetry of Life: Shelley and Literary Form.* Toronto: University of Toronto Press, 1987.

Theatrical Inquisitor and Monthly Mirror 4 (February 1814): 105–8. Review of *The Corsair.*

Thompson, E. P. *The Making of the English Working Class.* London: Victor Gollancz, 1964.

Thompson, Ewa M. *Russian Formalism and Anglo-American New Criticism: A Comparative Study.* The Hague: Mouton, 1971.

Thomson, James. "Autumn." In *The Seasons.* Boston: Phillips and Sampson, 1846.

Thorpe, Clarence D., Carlos Baker, and Bennett Weaver, eds. *The Major English Romantic Poets: A Symposium in Reappraisal.* Carbondale. Southern Illinois University Press, 1957.

Thorpe, James. *Principles of Textual Criticism.* San Marino, Calif.: Huntington Library, 1972.

Tomachevski, B[oris]. "Sur le vers" (1927). In Tzvetan Todorov, ed. and trans., *Théorie de la littérature, textes des Formalistes Russes*, pp. 154–69. Paris: Seuil, 1965.

Tompkins, Jane P., ed. *Reader-Response Criticism: From Formalism to Post-Structuralism.* Baltimore: Johns Hopkins University Press, 1980.

Trapp, Joseph. *Lectures on Poetry Read in the Schools of Natural Philosophy at Oxford* (1715). Trans. London: C. Hitch and C. Davis, 1742.

Trelawny, E. J. *Recollections of the Last Days of Shelley and Byron.* Boston: Ticknor and Fields, 1858.

Urkowitz, Steven. *Shakespeare's Revision of "King Lear."* Princeton: Princeton University Press, 1980.

Vaihinger, Hans. *The Philosophy of "As if": A System of the Theoretical, Practical and Religious Fictions of Mankind* (1911). Trans. C. K. Ogden (1924). London: Routledge and Kegan Paul, 1949.

Van Ghent, Dorothy. *Keats: The Myth of the Hero.* Rev. and ed. Jeffrey Cane Robinson. Princeton: Princeton University Press, 1983.

Veeser, H. Aram, ed. *The New Historicism.* New York: Routledge, 1989.

Vendler, Helen. *The Odes of John Keats*. Cambridge, Mass.: Harvard University Press, 1983.

——. *On Extended Wings: Wallace Stevens' Longer Poems*. Cambridge, Mass.: Harvard University Press, 1969.

Vickers, Nancy. "Diana Described: Scattered Woman and Scattered Rhyme." In Elizabeth Abel, ed., *Writing and Sexual Difference*, pp. 95–109. Chicago: University of Chicago Press, 1982.

Vitale, Marina. "The Domesticated Heroine in Byron's *Corsair* and William Hone's Prose Adaptation." *Literature and History* 10 (1984): 72–94.

Vogler, Thomas A. *Preludes to Vision: The Epic Venture in Blake, Keats, Wordsworth, and Hart Crane*. Berkeley: University of California Press, 1971.

Wakoski, Diane. "The New Conservatism in American Poetry." *American Book Review* 8: 4 (1986): 3.

——. "The New Conservatism In American Poetry In Spite of the 'Expanding Canon.'" *New Letters* (Fall 1989): 17–38.

Waldoff, Leon. *Keats and the Silent Work of Imagination*. Urbana and Chicago: University of Illinois Press, 1985.

Walker, J[ohn]. *Elements of Elocution, Being the Substance of a Course of Lectures on the Art of Reading*. 2 vols. London: Walker, 1781.

——. *A Rhetorical Grammar: In Which the Common Improprieties in Reading and Speaking are Detected, and the True Sources of Elegant Pronunciation are Pointed Out*. 3rd ed. London: Walker, 1801.

Wallen, Martin. "Return and Representation: The Revisions of 'The Ancient Mariner.'" *The Wordsworth Circle* 17 (1986): 148–55.

Ward, Aileen. *John Keats: The Making of a Poet*. New York: Viking, 1963.

Ward, Patricia. "Coleridge's Critical Theory of the Symbol." *Texas Studies in Literature and Language* 8 (1966): 15–32.

Warminski, Andrzej. "Facing Language: Wordsworth's First Poetic Spirits." In Kenneth R. Johnston, Gilbert Chaitin, Karen Hanson, and Herbert Marks, eds., *Romantic Revolutions*, pp. 26–49.

Wasserman, Earl R. "The English Romantics: The Grounds of Knowledge." *Studies in Romanticism* 4 (1964): 17–34.

——. *The Finer Tone: Keats' Major Poems*. 1953; Baltimore: Johns Hopkins University Press, 1967.

——. *Shelley: A Critical Reading*. Baltimore: Johns Hopkins Press, 1971.

Watkins, Daniel P. *Social Relations in Byron's Eastern Tales*. New Jersey: Fairleigh Dickinson University Press, 1987.

Watts-Dunton, Theodore. *Old Familiar Faces*. 1916; Freeport, N.Y.; Books for Libraries Press, 1970.

Webb, Timothy. *Shelley: A Voice Not Understood*. Atlantic Highlands, N.J.: Humanities Press International, 1977.

Weber, Samuel. "Criticism Underway: Walter Benjamin's *Romantic Concept of Criticism*." In Kenneth R. Johnston, Gilbert Chaitin, Karen Hanson, and Herbert Marks, eds., *Romantic Revolutions*, pp. 302–19.

Wellek, René. "Concepts of Form and Structure in Twentieth-Century Criticism" (1958). In *Concepts of Criticism*, ed. Stephen G. Nichols, Jr., pp. 54–68. New Haven: Yale University Press, 1963.

———. "The New Criticism: Pro and Contra." *Critical Inquiry* 4 (1978): 611–24.

Wellek, René, and Austin Warren. *Theory of Literature*. 1942; rev. ed. New York: Harcourt Brace, 1956.

Weller, Barry. "Shakespeare, Shelley and the Binding of the Lyric." *MLN* 93 (1978): 912–37.

Wesling, Donald. *The Chances of Rhyme: Device and Modernity*. Berkeley: University of California Press, 1980.

———. *The New Poetries: Poetic Form Since Coleridge and Wordsworth*. Lewisburg, Pa.: Bucknell University Press, 1985.

Whaler, James. "The Miltonic Simile." *PMLA* 46 (1931): 1034–74.

W[halley], G[eorge]. "Simile." In *Princeton Encyclopedia of Poetry and Poetics*. Ed. Alex Preminger, with Frank B. Warnke and O. B. Hardison, Jr. Princeton: Princeton University Press, 1974.

White, Newman Ivey. *Shelley*. 2 vols. New York: Alfred A. Knopf, 1940.

Williams, Raymond. *Culture and Society, 1780–1950*. 1958; New York: Harper and Row, 1966.

———. *Keywords: A Vocabulary of Culture and Society*. Rev. ed. New York: Oxford University Press, 1983.

———. *Marxism and Literature*. Oxford: Oxford University Press, 1977.

Williams, William Carlos. "Choral: the Pink Church." *The Collected Later Poems of William Carlos Williams*, pp. 159–62. New York: New Directions, 1963.

[Wilson, John]. Review of *Childe Harold's Pilgrimage, Canto IV*. *Edinburgh Review* 30 (June 1818): 87–120. Attribution by Donald Reiman, ed. *The Romantics Reviewed* B 2: 893.

Wimsatt, W. K., Jr. "The Domain of Criticism" (1950). In *Verbal Icon*, pp. 218–32.

———. "One Relation of Rhyme to Reason" (1944). In *Verbal Icon*, pp. 153–66.

———. "The Structure of Romantic Nature Imagery" (1949). In *Verbal Icon*, pp. 103–16.

———. *The Verbal Icon: Studies in the Meaning of Poetry*. Lexington: University of Kentucky Press, 1954.

———. "What to Say about a Poem" (1963). In *Hateful Contraries: Studies in Literature and Criticism*, pp. 215–44. Lexington: University of Kentucky Press, 1966.

Wimsatt, W. K., Jr., and Monroe C. Beardsley. "The Intentional Fallacy" (1956). In *Verbal Icon*, pp. 3–18.

Wimsatt, W. K., Jr., and Cleanth Brooks. *Literary Criticism: A Short History*. New York: Vintage, 1957.

Wolfson, Susan J. "Answering Questions and Questioning Answers: The Interrogative Project of *The Prelude*." In Nigel Wood, ed., *Theory in Practice: "The Prelude*," pp. 124–65.

———. "*The Fourteen-Book 'Prelude,'* ed. W. J. B. Owen." *The Wordsworth Circle* 17 (1986): 209–213.

———. "The Illusion of Mastery: Wordsworth's Revisions of 'The Drowned Man of Esthwaite,' 1799, 1805, 1850." *PMLA* 99 (1984): 917–35.

———. "The Language of Interpretation in Romantic Poetry: 'A Strong Working of the Mind.'" In Arden Reed, ed., *Romanticism and Language*, pp. 22–49. Ithaca: Cornell University Press, 1984.

———. "The Magic Hand of Chance: Keats's Poetry in Facsimile." *Review* 14 (1992): 213–24.

———. "More *Prelude* to Ponder; Or, Getting Your Words-worth." *Review* 16 (1994): 1–20.

———. "'A Problem Few Dare Imitate': *Sardanapalus* and 'Effeminate Character.'" *ELH* 58 (1991): 867–902.

———. *The Questioning Presence: Wordsworth, Keats, and the Interrogative Mode in Romantic Poetry.* Ithaca: Cornell University Press, 1986.

———. "Questioning 'The Romantic Ideology.'" *Revue Internationale de Philosophie* 44 (1990): 429–47.

———. "Romanticism and the Measures of Meter." *Eighteenth Century Life* (1992): 162–80.

———. "'Their She Condition': Cross-dressing and the Politics of Gender in *Don Juan.*" *ELH* 54 (1987): 585–617.

Wood, Nigel. Introduction. *Theory in Practice: "The Prelude,"* pp. 1–26. Buckingham, UK and Philadelphia: Open University Press, 1993.

Wordsworth, Christopher. *Memoirs of William Wordsworth.* Ed. Henry Reed. 2 vols. Boston: Ticknor, Reed, and Fields, 1851.

Wordsworth, Dorothy. *Journals of Dorothy Wordsworth.* Ed. Mary Moorman. 2d ed. Oxford, London, and New York: Oxford University Press, 1973.

Wordsworth, Jonathan. *William Wordsworth: The Borders of Vision.* Oxford: Clarendon Press, 1982.

———. "The Five-Book *Prelude* of Early Spring 1804." *JEGP* 76 (1977): 1–25.

———. "The Two-Part *Prelude* of 1799" (1970). In *"The Prelude," 1799, 1805, 1850* (Norton Critical Edition), pp. 567–85.

Wordsworth, Jonathan, and Stephen Gill. "The Two-Part *Prelude* of 1798–99." *JEGP* 72 (1973): 503–25.

Wordsworth, William. "Essay, Supplementary to the Preface" [of 1815]. In *Prose* 3: 62–84.

———. *The Excursion.* In *William Wordsworth: The Poems.* Ed. John O. Hayden. 2 vols. Middlesex: Penguin, 1977.

———. *"Lyrical Ballads" and Other Poems, 1797–1800, by William Wordsworth.* Ed. James Butler and Karen Green. Ithaca: Cornell University Press, 1992.

———. *"Poems, In Two Volumes," and Other Poems, 1800–1807.* Ed. Jared Curtis. Ithaca: Cornell University Press, 1983.

———. "Preface to the Edition of 1815." In *Prose* 3: 26–39.

———. *"The Prelude": 1798–1799.* Ed. Stephen Parrish. Ithaca: Cornell University Press, 1977.

———. *"The Prelude": A Parallel Text.* Ed. J. C. Maxwell (1971–72). Middlesex, Eng.: Penguin, 1976.

———. *William Wordsworth: "The Prelude or Growth of a Poet's Mind."* Ed., with Introduction, Textual and Critical Notes, by Ernest de Selincourt; 2d ed. rev. Helen Darbishire. Oxford: Clarendon, 1959.

———. *Wordsworth: "The Prelude or Growth of a Poet's Mind" (Text of 1805).* Ed. Ernest de Selincourt (1926). New ed. corrected by Stephen Gill. London: Oxford University Press, 1970.

———. *"The Prelude": 1799, 1805, 1850.* Norton Critical Edition. Ed. Jonathan Wordsworth, M. H. Abrams, and Stephen Gill. New York: Norton, 1979.

———. *The Fourteen-Book "Prelude."* Ed. W. J. B. Owen. Ithaca: Cornell University Press, 1985.

———. *The Thirteen-Book "Prelude."* Ed. Mark L. Reed. 2 vols. Ithaca: Cornell University Press, 1991.

———. *The Prose Works of William Wordsworth.* Ed. W. J. B. Owen and Jane Worthington Smyser. 3 vols. Oxford: Clarendon Press, 1974.

———. *"The Ruined Cottage" and "The Pedlar",* ed. James Butler. Ithaca: Cornell University Press, 1979.

———. [The Sublime and the Beautiful]. Appendix 3. *A Guide through the District of the Lakes.* In *Prose* 2: 349–60.

———. [An Unpublished Tour]. Appendix 2, *A Guide through the District of the Lakes.* In *Prose* 2: 287–348.

Wordsworth, William, and Dorothy Wordsworth. *The Letters of William and Dorothy Wordsworth.* Ed. Ernest de Selincourt. *The Early Years, 1787–1805,* 2d ed. rev. Chester L. Shaver. Oxford: Clarendon Press, 1967.

———. *The Middle Years, 1806–1820. Part I, 1806–1811,* 2d ed. rev. Mary Moorman. Oxford; Clarendon Press, 1969. *Part 2, 1812–1820,* 2d ed. rev. Mary Moorman and Alan G. Hill. Oxford: Clarendon Press, 1970.

———. *The Later Years, 1821–1853,* 2d ed. rev. and arranged Alan G. Hill. 4 Parts. Oxford: Oxford University Press, 1978–88.

Yeats, William Butler. "A General Introduction for my Work" (1937). In *Essays and Introductions,* pp. 509–26. London: Macmillan, 1961.

———, ed. *Poetical Works of William Blake.* London: George Routledge and Sons, 1910.

Young, Robert. "A Reply to 'Prelude and Prejudice,' by Jeffrey Baker." *The Wordsworth Circle* 13 (1982): 87–88.

Z. See *Blackwood's.*

Zillman, Lawrence John. *John Keats and the Sonnet Tradition: A Critical and Comparative Study.* Los Angeles: Lymanhouse, 1939.

❧ Index

In this index an "f" after a number indicates a separate reference on the next page, and an "ff" indicates separate references on the next two pages. A continuous discussion over two or more pages is indicated by a span of page numbers, e.g., "57–59." *Passim* is used for a cluster of references in close but not consecutive sequence.

Abrams, M. H., 64f; and New Criticism, 11; on poetic structure, 14, 103, 255n1, 259n20
Adams, Hazard, 249n1
Addison, Catherine, 256n9
Addison, Joseph, 257n15
Allegory, 64, 110–11, 260n27; and analogy, 93; and didacticism, 199, 210; and simile/similitude, 69, 255n5; vs. symbol, 69, 92. *See also* Coleridge; de Man
Allott, Miriam, 178, 246n55
Althusser, Louis: and formalism, 243n35; on imaginary form, 229; "Letter on Art," 18, 229, 243n35; on "literary effect," 242n32. *See also* Distantiation and aesthetic agency
Ambiguity, and poetic form, 9, 16, 191–92
Anagrams, and poetic form: in Coleridge, 74; in Shakespeare, 170
Analogy, 260n25; Barthes on, 86; in Bowles, 64, 66; and Brooks, 16, 241n25, 261n30; Coleridge and, 64–70 *passim*, 79–87, 258n17; de Man on, 259nn20, 24; in Hartley, 80, 258n17; in Wordsworth, 124–25, 269n38. *See also* Allegory; Simile; Symbol

Anaphora: in Blake, 41, 44, 47; in Keats, 171, 173; in Shelley, 223
Andromeda, and poetic form, 170–72
Anti-formalism: in criticism, 5–10, 235nn1–2, 256n7; in Romanticism, 20, 62
Apostrophe: and Blake, 37–43, 251n13; and Keats, 177, 180; in Shelley, 214–16; and Wordsworth, 84, 110–16 *passim*, 267n21. *See also* Culler
Arac, Jonathan, 263n5
Aristotelian form, 4, 22, 238n10
Aristotle, 64; on simile, 71, 256n9
Arnold, Matthew, 237n7; on Byron, 133–34; on Keats, 167; on laws of poetry, 5–6; on Romanticism, 236n6; on Wordsworth, 6
As if / As though: in Byron, 158; in Coleridge, 68ff, 75–82 *passim*, 86–99 *passim*; in Keats, 75; in Shelley, 197–98, 223; in Stevens, 256n6; Vaihinger on, 94, 256n6; in Wordsworth, 88–89, 126–27. *See also* Baudelaire
Attridge, Derek, 1–2, 3, 227, 232, 297n3
Auden, W. H., 133
Austen, Jane, on Byron, 161
Averill, James H., 269n35, 270n40

Blank verse, 27, 43, 55–56, 119–20, 138–39, 250n10, 253nn28–29, 272n2; and eighteenth-century poetic theory, 24, 27, 247n61; as music, 273n8; as natural, 27; as political trope, 20, 27, 56–58, 120, 139; and prose, 27, 247nn60–61; amid rhymes, 52, 171–72, 177f. *See also* Blair; Blank spaces; Enjambment; Line endings; Morris; Prose form; Sheridan; Suspension; *see also under* Blake; Byron; Dennis; Dryden; Easthope; Johnson, Dr. Samuel; Kames; Milton; Saintsbury; Thomson; Walker; Wordsworth, W.

Bloom, Harold, 240n20; on Blake, 48, 253n27; on poetic form and formalism, 12–13, 227

Bourdieu, Pierre, 228–30, 231

Bové, Paul, 15, 239n13, 241n27

Bowers, Fredson, 263n7

Bowles, William Lisle, 64, 66f, 81f

Bradley, A. C., 236n7; "Poetry for Poetry's Sake," 6

Breslin, James, 1, 235n1

Brogan, Jacqueline, 256n6, 260n27

Brooks, Cleanth, 64, 235n2, 239n14; on analogy, 261n30; on Blake, 48–49; on Coleridge, 15f, 92; on form as meaning, 6, 11, 168, 236n7; 240n19; on Keats, 192; on poetic structure and form, 11, 164, 168, 255n1; *The Well Wrought Urn*, 8, 15–17

Brun, Sophie Christiane Friederika, 67, 255n4

Burckhardt, Sigurd, 295n44

Burdett, Osbert, 36, 250n7

Burke, Edmund, 254n30; on Miltonic sublime, 90; politicized aesthetics, 142, 240n23

Burt, Richard, 291n21

Bush, Douglas, 168, 265n12

Byron, George Gordon, Lord, 29, 133–63, 267n20; and "Anti-Byron," 144–45; on blank verse, 27, 247n60; "Byronism" and "Byronic hero," 144–45, 149, 163–63, 274n15, 275n16, 277nn23, 26; as "the Corsair," 143; and Dante's Francesca (*Inferno* V), 161, 278n34; double grammar in, 146, 152–53, 278n28; "Eastern tales," 138, 247n60, 274n15; enjambment in, 145–49 *passim*, 154–

55; and gender, 134–35, 140, 149–62, 276n22, 277nn23, 27, 278nn28–29, 31–33; and heroic couplets, 133–63; laws, political and poetic, 133–41, 146; meter, 26; Parliamentary speeches, 141–42, 274n12; poetry as "lava of the imagination," 134; Regency politics, 141–45 *passim*, 162, 274n14, 275n17, 276n20; on "self," 143–44, 162–63; *Sardanapalus*, 159; similes, 82, 259n20; and sonnet form, 158–60, 247n60; speed in, 134, 154–55; on verse forms, 247n60. *See also As if / As though*; Closure; Erotic desire; *Form*; Grammar; Hazlitt; Hunt; Jeffrey; Line endings; Madness; Performance; Puns; Simile
—and rhyme: as bondage/obligation, 133–41 *passim*, 147f, 274n11; *bouts-rimés*, 282n19; dissonant, 155, 157; *Don Juan* and, 26, 140–41, 273n10, 277n23, 283n21; embedded, 147, 151, 290n17; facility with, 247n60; feminine, 149–50, 276n22, 277n23; latent, 151; and madness, 182; masculine, 150, 155–57, 277n23; medial, 147ff, 155, 157; and reason, 140–41, 273n10; rhyme field, 150–58 *passim*, 278n28; semantics of, 147–58, 273n10; Spenserian stanza, 247n60; triple, 161; weak, 148–49, 155, 157, 276n22
—*Childe Harold's Pilgrimage*, 145, 151, 182, 274n15, 277n25; popularity of, 144, 275nn16–17, 290n17
—*The Corsair*, 29, 133–63; dedicatory preface, 135ff, 141, 143, 274n14; elitism, 143f; epigraphs, 143, 162; popularity, 144, 275nn16–17; reviews of, 137–38, 144, 153f, 278n31; summary, 271n1. *Key episodes and passages:* Byronic hero, 147–48; closing lines, 152, 162–63, 278n35; Conrad departs from Medora, 154–55, 156, 277n27, 278n28; Gulnare's murder of Seyd, 147, 158–61 *passim*, 278n32; hero's debut, 145; liberation of Conrad, 157–61; pirates' anthem, 137; in prison, 148–50, 155–58 *passim*. *Key rhymes:* fair/Gulnare/Corsair, 150–52, 160–61, 277n24; *manned*, 155–61 *passim*; *reveal/conceal*, 147–48

Cook, Carol, 284n23
Cook, Jon, 270n43
Couplet: enjambment and rhyme, 146, 179, 204–5, 247n61, 272n3; of pairing, 215; as trope of order, 146–47, 278n33. *See also* Rhyme
—"Cockney," 136, 272nn2–3, 282n19. *See also under* Keats
—heroic, 29, 143; Coleridge on, 135; Dryden on, 143, 247n61; feminine rhymed, 276n22; as trope of social class / order, 136, 138, 143; Wordsworth on, 179. *See also under* Byron; Neoclassical theory
—and sonnet closure, 61, 160, 170f, 178, 204–5, 248n63. *See also under* Sonnet
Crane, R. S., on poetic form, 3–4, 235n2, 240n19
Culler, Jonathan: on apostrophe, 38, 110–11, 177, 180, 251n13; on Donne's *Canonization*, 241n29; on iteration, 281n29; on Keats's refusal of apostrophe, 189; on narrative, 110; and New Criticism, 11f, 238n13; and structuralism, 12
Cultural forms and formation, 9–10, 14, 19f, 24–25, 30, 227–32
Cunningham, J. V., on formal variation, 133
Curran, Stuart, 28, 177, 204–5, 249n66, 287n8, 289n15, 292n28

Damon, S. Foster, 57, 253n27
Dante Alighieri, 125; Francesca (*Inferno* V), 162
Darbishire, Helen, 264n9
Davis, Robert Con, and Ronald Schleifer, 239n14
Deconstruction: critique of, 17, 214n26; and New Criticism, 9–13 *passim*, 241n28; and New Historicism, 17–18; and poststructuralism, 248n65. *See also* de Man
Defamiliarization: and Futurism, 238n10; in Russian Formalism, 7, 19, 237nn9–10, 245nn43–44; Shelley and Coleridge on, 21; Shklovsky on, 7, 19
De Luca, Vincent Arthur, on Blake, 32–33, 55
de Man, Paul, 37, 131, 291n23; on analogy, 259nn20, 24; on autobiography, 110,

267n19; on Barthes' formalism, 18; on Blake, 31, 249n1; on Coleridge, 65, 70–71, 92; on formalist criticism and New Criticism, 9–10, 71, 191–92, 239n16, 241n28; on "intentional structure," 271n45, 284n26; on Keats, 169, 178, 185, 279n1; on political critique, 239n17, 240n18, 243n36; on "rhetoric of temporality," 16, 65, 91f, 187; on Romantic theory, 11, 13
Demetrius, on simile, 86
Dennis, John, on rhyme: and blank verse, 139, 273n8; as effeminate, 277n23; as similitude, 257n12, 272n5
De Quincey, Thomas, on Coleridge's "plagiarism," 255n4
Derrida, Jacques: on chain of signifiers, 92; on "différance," 35, 98; on metaphor and simile, 72, 256n9; on supplement, 70, 207, 292n29
de Selincourt, Ernest, on *The Prelude*, 102, 265n9
Dickstein, Morris, on Keats, 169
Distantiation and aesthetic agency, 229, 243n35. *See also* Althusser
Donne, John: *The Canonization* and New Criticism, 17; "The Sun-Rising," 216; "The Triple Fool," 181; "A Valediction Forbidding Mourning," 73. *See also under* Coleridge; Puns
Dryden, John: Arnold on, 6; on blank verse, 27, 47, 55–56, 137, 247nn59–61, 253n28; couplets, 146; on heroic couplet, 136, 143; on rhyme, 47, 140, 143, 283n19; on verse form, 20, 244n40

Eagleton, Terry: on "Culler's structuralism," 12; on de Man, 240n18; on formalist criticism, 243n38; on ideology and literary form, 3, 18f, 238n12, 242nn32–33, 243nn34–35; on language as "event," 236n3; as prescription, 281n15; on New Criticism, 238n12; on Romantic formalism, 13–14; on Russian Formalism, 238n10; on Wordsworth, 27
Easthope, Antony: on blank verse, 27, 246n48, 248n61, 254n29; on Romantic poetic theory, 23

Library of Congress Cataloging-in-Publication Data

Wolfson, Susan J.
Formal charges : the shaping of poetry in British romanticism /
Susan J. Wolfson.
    p. cm.
   Includes bibliographical references and index.
   ISBN 0-8047-2657-4
    1. English poetry—19th century—History and criticism.
2. Romanticism—Great Britain. 3. Poetics. I. Title.
PR590.W55 1997
821'.709145—dc20
96-7340 CIP

⊗ This book is printed on acid-free,
recycled paper.

Original printing 1997
Last figure below indicates year of this printing:
06 05 04 03 02 01 00 99 98 97